Mary Astell

Theorist of Freedom from Domination

Philosopher, theologian, educational theorist, feminist and political pamphleteer, Mary Astell was an important figure in the history of ideas of the early modern period. She contributed to the British debate over toleration and dissent from the 1690s, which inaugurated the modern secular state. Among the first systematic critics of John Locke's entire corpus, she is best known for the famous question that prefaces her *Reflections on Marriage*: 'If all men are born free, how is it that all women are born slaves?' She is claimed by modern Republican theorists and feminists alike, but as she is a High Church Tory, the peculiar constellation of her views sits uneasily with modern commentators. Patricia Springborg's study addresses these apparent paradoxes and recovers the historical and philosophical contexts for her thought. She shows that Astell was not alone in her views; rather, she belonged to a cohort of early modern female philosophers who were important for the reception of Locke and Descartes and who grappled with the existential problems of a new age.

Patricia Springborg is Professor of Political Theory at the University of Sydney and Adjunct Professor in the School of Economics at the Free University of Bozen-Bolzano.

Mary Astell

Theorist of Freedom from Domination

PATRICIA SPRINGBORG

University of Sydney
Free University of Bozen-Bolzano

CAMBRIDGE UNIVERSITY PRESS
Cambridge, New York, Melbourne, Madrid, Cape Town, Singapore, São Paulo

Cambridge University Press
40 West 20th Street, New York, NY 10011-4211, USA

www.cambridge.org
Information on this title: www.cambridge.org/9780521841047

First published 2005

Printed in the United States of America

A catalog record for this publication is available from the British Library.

Library of Congress Cataloging in Publication Data

Springborg, Patricia.
Mary Astell: theorist of freedom from domination / Patricia Springborg.
p. cm.
Includes bibliographical references and index.
ISBN 0-521-84104-6 (hardback)
1. Astell, Mary, 1668–1731 – Political and social views. 2. Women's rights –
Great Britain – History – 18th century. 3. Feminism – Great Britain –
History – 18th century. I. Title.
JC176.A88S67 2005
305.42′092 – dc22 2004027523

ISBN-13 978-0-521-84104-7 hardback
ISBN-10 0-521-84104-6 hardback

This book is dedicated to the memory of the missing, to early modern women, in general, and, in particular, to those peculiarly modern souls whose lives I mourn: Christine Main Ambrose, who died so young while the book was in progress, and without whose excellent research assistance it would not have been possible; my editor at Cambridge University Press, who had great enthusiasm for this project, the late Terence Moore; the late Dick Ashcraft, an exemplary Locke scholar with whom I was privileged to be acquainted; the late Bruce Cochrane, a literary scholar who was so generous in answering my queries on specialist points; and my dear friend and fellow New Zealander, Susan Moller Okin, a pioneering feminist political theorist who made a prestigious career at Brandeis and Stanford and of whose early death I learned as I finished the revisions for the book.

May they rest in peace and in the knowledge that their labours were not in vain.

Contents

Acknowledgements

This book grew out of my project to publish scholarly editions of Astell's works, and in the course of it I have incurred many debts. The Vice-Chancellor's Publication Fund of the University of Sydney and the Research Council of Australia, through ARC Small Grant F10.26994 93/94/95, covered research expenses specific to this project, particularly the salaries of my excellent research assistants, Christine Main Ambrose and Kathy Dempsey, to whom I am greatly indebted. To the Librarian of Fisher Library, University of Sydney; the State Library of New South Wales, in particular Sue Thomas; the State Library of Victoria; the Rare Book Librarian of the Library of Congress; Georgiana Ziegler, Betsy Walsh and the unfailingly helpful staff of the Folger Shakespeare Library, many thanks for assistance.

   I am enormously thankful to those institutions that provided support for full-time research for this and other projects in the years 1993–5: the University of Sydney and the Folger Institute (1993); the Woodrow Wilson International Center for Scholars (1993–4); the Brookings Institution, Washington, D.C., and the John D. and Catherine T. MacArthur Foundation for a Research and Writing Grant that the Brookings Institution administered (1994–5). To my program directors at these institutions, Lena Orlin at the Folger Institute; Jim Morris, Michael Lacey and Ann Sheffield at the Woodrow Wilson Center; John Steinbruner at Brookings; and Kate Early at the MacArthur Foundation, I am truly thankful for support and kind understanding as I juggled my projects. I owe the Wissenschaftskolleg zu Berlin a great debt of gratitude for a fellowship in 2000–1, which provided the ideal conditions and library facilities for the completion of this work. I owe important insights on republicanism and freedom from domination to Zhiyuan Cui in discussions at the Wissenschaftskolleg zu Berlin, January 12–16, 2004, for which I truly thank him and the Kolleg. And some of the revisions were done during the tenure of my fellowship at the Swedish Collegium for Advanced Study in the Social Sciences (SCASSS), in Uppsala, 2002–3, and I wish to thank the Collegium's directors Björn Wittrock, Barbro Klein and Göran Therborn – and their magnificent staff – for their support.

To those I must thank for offering assistance on points of information and reading drafts of my material on Astell, I must single out Quentin Skinner, Regius Professor of Modern History at the University of Cambridge; Mark Goldie, Vice-Master at Churchill College, Cambridge; John Pocock, Professor Emeritus at the Johns Hopkins University; Professors Carole Pateman of the University of California, Los Angeles; Johann Sommerville, at the University of Wisconsin-Madison; Margaret Sommerville, Lois Schwoerer and Philip Hamburger at George Washington University; Ann Kelly at Howard University; Steven Zwicker at Washington University–St. Louis; Kathleen Lesko, Scholar-in-Residence at the Folger Shakespeare Library; Patricia Stablein, Scholar-in-Residence at La Trobe University, Australia; the late Dick Ashcraft of the University of California, Los Angeles; the late Bruce Cochrane of the University of Canterbury, New Zealand; and the late Christine Main Ambrose, my research assistant at the University of Sydney. To Joseph Brinley at the Woodrow Wilson Press, who so graciously gave up his prebendary right to publish the book, to his readers including Ruth Perry, and to Eileen O'Neill and Sarah Hutton, readers for Cambridge University Press, I am truly grateful for knowledgeable and careful comments. It is with great sadness that I include my editor at Cambridge University Press, the late Terence Moore among the dedicatees; grateful thanks also to Shari Chappell, the Production Editing Supervisor, Louise Calabro, my production editor, and Christa Tappeiner of the Free University of Bolzano, who helped me with the index. Last, but not least, I thank my sons, Ziyad Latif and George Daniel Springborg, who have shown such support for their mother's writing projects.

Grateful thanks are due to my publishers for permission to reuse material from the following essays: 'Mary Astell (1666–1731), Critic of Locke', *American Political Science Review*, 89, 3 (September 1995): 621–33; 'Astell, Masham and Locke', in Hilda L. Smith, ed., *Women Writers and the Early Modern British Political Tradition* (Cambridge: Cambridge University Press, 1998), 105–25; 'Mary Astell and John Locke', in Steven Zwicker, ed., *The Cambridge Companion to English Literature, 1650 to 1750* (Cambridge:

Cambridge University Press, 1998), 276–306; 'Republicanism, Freedom from Domination and the Cambridge Contextual Historians', *Political Studies*, 49, 5 (2001): 851–76; and 'Mary Astell (1666–1731), Critic of the Marriage Contract/Social Contract Analogue', in Anita Pacheco, ed., *A Companion to Early Modern Women's Writing* (Oxford: Blackwell, 2002), 216–28; as well as from the introductions to my three editions of Astell's works: *Mary Astell (1666–1731): Political Writings* (Cambridge: Cambridge University Press, 1996); *Mary Astell: 'A Serious Proposal to the Ladies'* (London: Pickering & Chatto, 1997); and *Mary Astell's A Serious Proposal to the Ladies, Parts I (1694) and II (1697)* (Peterborough, Ont., Canada: Broadview Press, 2002).

A Note on Editions of Astell's Works Cited

Page numbers of Astell's works are to the original editions, where they lack a modern edition, as in the case of *Moderation Truly Stated* (1704), *The Christian Religion* (1705) and *Bart'lemy Fair* (1709). Citations to *Reflections upon Marriage* of 1700 are to the third (1706) edition, which includes Astell's famous 1706 preface; citations from *A Fair Way with the Dissenters* (1704) and *An Impartial Enquiry* (1704) are to the original editions. In the case of the three latter works, page numbers are also given, followed by a forward slash to my 1996 Cambridge edition. Citations from Astell's *A Serious Proposal to the Ladies, Parts I* (1694) and *II* (1697) are to the original editions and to my 2002 edition for Broadview Press.

A Note on the Structure of the Book

The Introduction, which begins with 'A Reply to My Critics', addresses the central issue upon which this study turns: Astell and early modern feminism. Astell, as a High Church Tory, presents, or appears to present, a paradox for modern feminist thought. My purpose here is to try to show that this paradox has its source in our own presuppositions and a Whiggish progressivism that imputes to historical actors assumptions that could only be the product of the historical processes in which they participated. This is particularly ironic in the case of Astell, who lived through the birth pangs of Whiggism as Whig and Tory positions consolidated in political parties. The issue of Astell and classical republicanism turns, in my view, on just such false presuppositions. I address associated misconceptions: women and 'myth of the state' and the social gendering of knowledge, and I try to establish a context for her thought among women philosophers, dramatists, novelists and political pamphleteers of her day.

Chapter 1, 'Mary Astell, Philosopher, Theologian and Polemicist', is devoted to establishing briefly the context for the work of a woman intellectual, who was considerably influential in her day but who subsequently dropped out of the canon, and about whose personal life we know very little. As well as introducing Astell's political and philosophical milieus, it includes an overview of her corpus and sketches of the major figures with whom she interacts. It includes an account of the bitter debates between Norris and Locke, and between Astell and Masham, over the Cartesian mind–body problem. Astell's own vacillation between Malebranchean occasionalism and a more Lockean solution in the form of a 'sensible congruity' between mind and body represent the horns of this dilemma.

Chapter 2, 'Astell, Drake, Education, Epistemology and the *Serious Proposal*', sets Astell's most famous work in her day in the context of other works on female education. More importantly, since Part II of *A Serious Proposal* is a disquisition on the Port Royal logic and a critique of Locke's epistemology, this aspect of her work is also treated. Among contemporary advocates of female education, Judith Drake, whose *Essay* was until recently credited to Astell and catalogued in Locke's library along with Astell's *A Serious Proposal*, is closest to her thought and is also discussed here.

Chapter 3, 'Astell on Marriage, Patriarchalism and Contractarianism', establishes the social context for Astell's important critique of marriage mores and the more general principle to which they appeal, customary right, addressing her principal argument against the proto-liberal positions of Milton and Locke. Astell argued that, by defending the public–private distinction, these proto-Whigs created a public zone of political participation, from which women were excluded, and a private realm of domesticity, where women were 'enslaved' as legal minors, dependent on their husbands and sons for any form of social standing. Ultimately renowned for her 1706 preface to *Reflections upon Marriage*, Astell, as a High Church Tory, argues a position more complicated than at first appears.

Chapter 4, 'Mary Astell and the Settlement of 1689', addresses the specific context for Astell's three Tory political pamphlets of 1704, *Moderation Truly Stated*, *A Fair Way with the Dissenters*, and *An Impartial Enquiry into the Causes of Rebellion and Civil War*, the first two analyzed in more detail in Chapter 5. *An Impartial Enquiry*, Astell's history of the English Civil War, is a cautionary tale that takes 1649 as an analogue for the possible return of civil unrest due to the settlement of 1689. It became a classic work in the Tory canon but has remained relatively unexamined.

Chapter 5, 'A Fair Way with the Dissenters and Their Patrons', recounts Astell's bitter debates with Daniel Defoe and James Owen. *Moderation Truly Stated*, the first of Astell's three political pamphlets of 1704, possibly commissioned by her printer and written in the heat of the occasional conformity debate against the dissenters, is a reply to Owen's *Moderation a Virtue* of 1703, while *A Fair Way with the Dissenters* is a response to Defoe's *More Short-Ways with the Dissenters* of 1704.

Chapter 6, 'Astell, Locke and the Highway Man: A Test Case', is what it claims to be: a test case for my proposition that Astell is indeed, so far as one can establish, the first systematic critic of John Locke's entire corpus, an honour usually credited to Charles Leslie. Astell's arguments, made in the main body of her *Reflections upon Marriage* of 1700, and later amplified in her 1706 preface to that work, can be shown to have predated Leslie's by three years. Moreover, they are arguments characteristic of Astell's entire philosophical critique of Locke and his incipient liberalism, based on the distinction between the public and private realms. Astell's bitter protests in her pamphlets of 1704 that her arguments are unfairly credited to the High Flyers, High Church and Tory *men*, particularly Leslie, are evidence enough, if more were needed, that it was an occupational hazard of women, whose works were by convention published anonymously, to be plagiarized. Astell's challenge to Locke, repeated by Leslie, was quite simply to apply in the private realm of the family the standards of accountability and fairness that, as a democrat, he demanded of political institutions in the public sphere.

The final chapter, Chapter 7: 'Astell, Drake and the Historical Legacy of Freedom', takes a new look at Astell's legacy and that of her contemporary, Judith Drake. Perhaps due to the recent upsurge of scholarly work, Astell has been enlisted by Philip Pettit in his recent book as a republican, on the strength of her arguments for freedom from domination. This not only flies in the face of her avowed royalism and High Church Tory politics, but it also reduces her to the author of the famous rhetorical question about freedom. It is important to see why the question was rhetorical, and how in this regard her position contrasts with that of Judith Drake, who argues quite literally that women are enslaved. Astell does not, precisely because she does not accept Locke's argument that human beings have property in their own selves and cannot therefore consistently argue that the self can be alienated by slavery. Her arguments for freedom from domination surely rest on different grounds, namely, the integrity of the person as body and soul in Christian doctrine. Indeed, as I shall try to show, seventeenth-century arguments for freedom from domination in general tended to be an exercise in rhetorical forensics that cashed out in terms of specific justiciable rights. But Astell was not a rights theorist, and it is ironic that, in the long haul, she should be seen to join her bitter adversary, Locke, as a defender of natural rights, and in particular the right to freedom, in the legacy they bequeathed to future feminists and civil libertarians.

The Appendix comprises a Glossary and Selective Biographical Notes containing additional material that would have unduly encumbered the text. Asterisks preceding the names of persons and events mentioned in the chapters indicate entries there. Where I have not had access to specialist treatments, I have resorted to the usual range of encyclopedias and biographical dictionaries: the *Dictionary of National Biography* (*DNB*), the *Dictionary of British and American Writers 1660–1800* and the *New Encyclopaedia Britannica*, as well as the 1911 *Encyclopaedia Britannica*, the *Encyclopedia of Philosophy*, the *Encyclopedia of Feminist Theories*, the *Routledge Encyclopedia of Philosophy* and online databases and sources such as *European Writers, 1000–1900*. Unless otherwise acknowledged, the reader can assume that the biographical information I give is from some combination of these sources.

Mary Astell, A Brief Chronology

1666 November 12, Mary Astell is born to Mary Errington and Peter
      Astell and is baptized at St. John's Church in Newcastle-on-Tyne.
1672 Charles II's Declaration of Indulgence for Protestant Dissenters.
1673 Declaration of Indulgence revoked and the Test Act banning
      Catholics from holding office passed.
1678 Sancroft becomes Archbishop of Canterbury. Astell's father,
      Peter Astell, dies.
1679 Exclusion Bill to ban James II from the throne debated.
1681 Oxford Parliament meets.
      Oxford Parliament dissolved.
1683 Rye House Plot.
1684 October 16, Mary Errington, Astell's mother, dies.
1685 Charles II dies and is succeeded by James II.
      James II's Parliament.
1686 Astell moves to London, living mainly in Chelsea.
1687 James II's Declaration of Indulgence for liberty of conscience.
1688 James dissolves Parliament.
      Birth of James's son and possible heir.
      Invasion of Prince William of Orange and his wife, Mary, James's
      own daughter.
      James flees to France.
1689 Convention Parliament meets and offers the crown to William
      and Mary jointly.
      Coronation of King William III and Queen Mary II.

Nine Years' War against France begins. Bill of Rights, regulating the English succession, nominates Mary's sister Anne and her children as next in line to the throne.

Toleration Act passed, allowing freedom of worship for Protestant dissenters.

1690   Secession of nonjurors from the Church of England.

1693   Astell begins her correspondence with John Norris of Bemerton.

1694   Queen Mary II dies childless.

Astell's *A Serious Proposal to the Ladies* is first published anonymously.

1695   The Astell–Norris correspondence is published as *Letters Concerning the Love of God*.

Second corrected edition of Astell's *A Serious Proposal to the Ladies* is published.

1696   The Fenwick Conspiracy, a plan by James II and King Louis XIV of France to assassinate King William, is uncovered.

Third corrected edition of Astell's *A Serious Proposal to the Ladies* is published.

1697   Astell's *A Serious Proposal to the Ladies*, Part II, is published, dedicated to Princess Anne of Denmark, who later became Queen Anne.

1700   Anne's only child, William, dies.

Astell's *Reflections upon Marriage* is published anonymously.

1701   The Act of Settlement establishes the Dowager Electress Sophia of Hanover, a granddaughter of James I, as next in line to the throne.

James II dies in exile.

Louis XIV of France nominates the son of James II, James III, known as the Old Pretender, as heir to the English throne.

1702   King William III dies in an accident.

Queen Anne, daughter of James II and the last of the Stuarts, succeeds to the throne.

1704   Astell's *An Impartial Enquiry* is published.

Astell's *Moderation Truly Stated* is published.

Astell's *A Fair Way with the Dissenters* is published.

1705   An octavo volume of Astell's *The Christian Religion* is published anonymously.

Second corrected edition of Astell's *Reflections upon Marriage* is published.

1706   Astell engaged in controversy with Bishop Atterbury.
        Third edition of Astell's *Reflections upon Marriage* is published, to
        which is added a preface.
1707   The first Parliament of Great Britain meets.
1709   Astell's *Bart'lemy Fair* is published anonymously.
1711   Occasional Conformity Act is passed.
1712   Tax records indicate that Astell is now living in her own
        residence on the street called By the Swan.
        At some indeterminate date between 1712 and 1720, Mary
        refocused her energy on creating a charity school for girls rather
        than a women's college. Her friends, Lady Catherine Jones,
        Lady Elizabeth Hastings and Lady Ann Coventry, along with
        others, establish a charity school for girls. The school remained
        active until the latter part of the nineteenth century.
1714   The Electress Sophia of Hanover dies.
        Queen Anne dies and is succeeded by the Lutheran King
        George I, Sophia's next descendant in line.
1715   First Parliament of George I meets.
1719   Occasional Conformity Act is repealed.
1722   Atterbury's plot to launch an armed invasion of Britain in favour
        of the Old Pretender is discovered.
        Atterbury is exiled, and Robert Walpole seals his position as the
        King's first minister, a position he holds for twenty years.
        Astell's *An Enquiry after Wit* is published as the second edition of
        Bart'lemy Fair.
1727   George I dies and is succeeded by George II.
1730   Fourth edition of Astell's *Reflections upon Marriage* is published
        'with additions' in London.
        Fifth edition of Astell's *Reflections upon Marriage* is published in
        Dublin.
        Third edition of Astell's *Letters Concerning the Love of God* is
        published.
        Third edition of Astell's *The Christian Religion* is published.
1731   May 9, Astell dies of breast cancer and is buried in Chelsea
        Churchyard.

Introduction

Astell and Early Modern Feminism

1. A Reply to My Critics: Astell, Locke and Feminism

Mary Astell (1666–1731) is now best known for her famous rhetorical question in the 1706 Preface to *Reflections upon Marriage*: 'If all men are born free, how is it that all women are born slaves?'.[1] These well-chosen words have earned her a place not only in the feminist but also in the republican canon as a theorist of 'freedom from domination'.[2] Prior to her recent resurrection she was best known as the author of *A Serious Proposal*, which advocated a Platonist academy for women, a project that seems briefly to have attracted the support of Queen Anne, to whom it was dedicated, until the ridicule to which it was subjected made it too politically risky. As the promoter of women's causes, and particularly women's education, Astell is said to have been the model for Richardson's *Clarissa;*[3] and, as late as 1847, Lilia, heroine of Alfred Lord Tennyson's *The Princess*, dreams of a women's college cut off from male society. Astell's female academy was later famously lampooned in Gilbert and Sullivan's *Princess Ida*, but this time at one remove, through Tennyson.[4] Over its gates the inscription would read, 'Let no man enter on pain of death', a deliberately truncated version of the famous inscription that adorned the doors of Plato's Academy, 'Let No Man Enter Here Unless He Study Geometry'.

It is noteworthy that Astell, who has been deemed 'England's First Feminist',[5] has only recently been republished and reinstated as a significant late-seventeenth-century political commentator. For reasons that we cannot gauge, although her High Church Toryism might be suspected, she appears to have already disappeared from feminist social and political discussion in the eighteenth and nineteenth centuries.[6] Mary Hays, a friend of Mary Wollstonecraft, mentions her in a *Female Biography*, but there is no direct evidence that either Wollstonecraft or Catharine Macaulay had in fact read her.[7] Revived in the twentieth century, her works have so far attracted two biographies,[8] two anthologies,[9] three diplomatic editions[10] and a growing collection of articles.[11] Astell's twentieth-century reception focuses primarily on her 'proto-feminist' critique of the condition of women, flagged by her famous rhetorical question. But her feminism is seen to sit uneasily with her Anglican High Church and Tory views, and the critical literature rarely does justice to the extraordinary range of her thought or treats in sufficient detail her substantive arguments to resolve this *prima facie* problem. This book tries to remedy this deficit, at the same time attempting to recover the contexts for Astell's thought at the turn of the seventeenth and eighteenth centuries.

I make no apology for the fact that much of the material this book contains has already appeared in articles and book chapters. I have a particular reason for wishing to collect the material between two covers, as an attempt at a coherent overall assessment of Astell, a thinker of great range who adopted complex positions on questions philosophical and political, not least the problem of women. My reason is that the struggle for the appropriation of Astell as a thinker seems, ironically, to mirror in emotional intensity and the degree of personalism the very struggles in which she was engaged. My work on Astell has attracted a fair degree of comment, and while some commentators endorse and, indeed, expand on my line or argument, I find that I have been strangely misread and misrepresented by others. I do not take this personally, although, perhaps because feminism is such a contentious issue, the language is sometimes unduly personal. In many respects this mini-debate over Astell is symptomatic of the Academy in general, ours – which lives off the creation and destruction of straw men – as well as hers, for Astell was no stranger to polemic.

Those who take issue with me do so on two counts: first, the role of Locke in Astell's thought, and second, her feminism. Let me say at the outset that Astell, like other early modern feminists, has been largely the monopoly of literary scholars and early modern historians, and only in exceptional cases treated by political theorists – Carole Pateman is the outstanding exception. For the historians, 'Saint Locke', who so greatly influenced the Founding Fathers of America, seems to stand in the way of a serious consideration of Locke as Astell or contemporaries saw him – a

more unflattering picture of the party man. For literary scholars the problem is a different one: how to reconcile Astell's feminism with her High
Church Tory politics. As I shall argue at some length, this is a problem
falsely posed – and bespeaks progressivist assumptions about a 'proper'
feminism that are anachronistic when applied to seventeenth-century
women.

Of my two central claims about Astell, that she is indeed a feminist,
albeit a High Church Tory, and that her work belongs in an important way
to the reception of John Locke, representing one of the most important
early critiques of his entire corpus, the second seems to be the more contentious. While taken for granted by some writers and further expanded
upon by others, it has been summarily dismissed by yet others again.
My most critical reader, who deems my claim to be 'hugely inflated and
unsustainable', supports his/her argument in the following way: 'In part,
the problem is that Springborg does not have a sufficient sense of practical politics. Astell was writing party propaganda against politicians and
other propagandists; her target was not an abstracted [*sic*] philosopher
like Locke and [Springborg's claim that] the tract *Moderation* "traces the
contours of Locke's career" is fantasy. *Moderation* is chiefly an attack on
religious Dissenters, and Locke was never a Dissenter'.[12] But this is a point
that I have been very careful to make. It was not that Locke was in fact a
dissenter, but that he was taken to be one by Astell, either in ignorance
or, more likely, in willful misrepresentation. The question of whether or
not Locke was principally an 'abstracted philosopher' is a bit more tricky.
Personally I believe, and I try to make the case, that Astell was probably
right and that the man who today might look like an abstracted philosopher, in her day looked like a thorough-going Whig and party man. The
more critical modern reception of his works, including that of Ashcraft,
finds not only that Locke's *pièces d'occasion*, the *Two Treatises of Government*
of 1689, the Letters on Toleration of 1667 and 1690 and the Minute
to Edward Clarke of 1690, were overtly political, but also that Locke's
apparently academic treatises like the *Essay Concerning Human Understanding* of 1690, his 'Remarks upon Some of Mr. Norris' Books, wherein he
asserts P. Malebranche's Opinion of seeing all Things in God' of 1693,
and *The Reasonableness of Christianity* of 1695, have strongly polemical
targets.

But Astell's feminism is not uncontentious either. In my various pieces
I have tried to emphasize that no simple view of her as a proto-feminist
does justice to the complexity of her thought, or the importance of the
substantive issues with which she was preoccupied, through which her

feminism was mediated. A brief perusal of her titles is enough to tell us that this was a woman politically and philosophically engaged in substantive debates, which could not be simply reduced to feminist issues. The subjects she treated ranged, in chronological order, from, first, philosophical questions concerning human agency and the capacity for personal salvation that belong to the reception of Descartes and concern the standing of the Malebranchistes, Port Royal Jansenists and Cambridge Platonists; second, to practical questions of women's education and the possibility of establishing a female academy along the lines of the Port Royal School; third, to the political question of a Tory, as opposed to Whig, version of the English Civil War, as establishing precedents for the regime change that took place in 1688–9; and fourth, to the constitutional issues of religious toleration and occasional conformity for dissenters. No one perusing such a list could sensibly claim that Astell was a feminist *tout court*. Indeed, what is of particular interest in her *corpus* is how comprehensively it ranges across the issues that divided the polity in her day. From the English Civil War in mid-century, to the Glorious Revolution of 1688, and through two dynastic changes, seventeenth-century Britain suffered great fissures in church–state relations that were the consequence of old political polarities and brought new ones into being. Roundhead and royalist gave way to Whig and Tory, but there was a persistent tendency to keep the old alignments alive by seeing the newly emerging political parties as their surrogates. How to heal these fissures and bring about an accommodation between conflicting poles of opinion took the form of an intense debate around the issue of toleration. For religious and political polarities were to some extent overlapping and, if Toryism was associated with High Church Anglicanism, Whiggism was associated with non-conformity and dissent. A number of Astell's most important works are specific contributions to the debates surrounding these critical political and constitutional issues.

If Astell is not simply a feminist, she is not simply a political pamphleteer either. She brings to the political stage a peculiar constellation of philosophical and theological views, expounded in works crucially important for the study of early modern conceptions of human agency. To reduce these philosophical questions to politics would be profoundly mistaken. Astell's own agonizing over mind–body problems and the nature of freedom, which bring her at some moments within the Cartesian orbit as a Malebranchean, then closer to Locke in her search for a 'sensible congruity' in the unity of personhood, and finally to a distancing once again from this figure whom she associates with toleration and dissent, is evidence enough of the seriousness with which such fundamental questions engaged her. It is not at all surprising that, having canvassed such a wide philosophical spectrum, Astell should be the subject of very different interpretations of her views. The intelligent essays of E. Derek Taylor and Sarah Ellenzweig work through the possibilities to reach quite different but, I suggest, not entirely incompatible conclusions.[13]

The claim for Astell as a theorist of freedom from domination, and therefore a republican, is much more difficult to accommodate, as we shall see. Not only was Astell not a republican but an out-and-out royalist, but she was not a rights theorist either. She explicitly argued against the Hobbesian and Filmerian notion of freedom as the power 'to do as one lists', and in favour of the classical notion of freedom as the power to erect a principle of action and follow it. In this respect she followed Aristotle, the Stoics and, curiously, John Locke, foreshadowing also the position on freedom of that neo-Stoic Rousseau. For this reason, perhaps, exponents of republicanism and rights theory have claimed her as their own, but mistakenly, I believe. It is true that in her satire of the morals and mores of marriage, on the issue of women's education, and even in her religiosity, Astell appeals to civic values that have been identified as peculiarly Roman or neo-Roman. Those who look for the origins in England of civil society and the state tend to ascribe these values to classical republicanism, but mistakenly, in my view. These values, which became enshrined in Protestant thought from the time of Luther on, represent rather the diffusion of Renaissance classical humanism, with its discernible Roman roots, but which was not necessarily republican, if it bespoke political institutions at all. Its very diffuseness, and the capacity of humanism to meld seamlessly with vernacular culture, militates against such a simple identification.

Nevertheless, despite the complexity of the intellectual landscape in which Astell was operating, it is hard to overestimate the power of certain issues to polarize opinion and to create predictable alignments. This makes it possible to map certain constellations of opinion. For the polarities of the political theatre of action were seen by contemporaries to have their analogue in philosophy and theology. Nor were the relations between political polarities and fundamental philosophical and theological divisions simply analogical. They clustered together. If one were to summarize them, one could say that Hobbesian materialism and Lockean physical realism characterized one of the poles, while Cartesian dualism and its various modifications by the Malebrancheans and the Port Royal School, along with the Cambridge Platonists, characterized the other. And while the late Hobbes and Locke tended to be associated with Whiggism, the Cartesians and Platonists tended to be identified with a conservative or Tory mindset. Although altogether too crude a schematization to account for the complex alignments that in fact obtained, such a characterization is not wide of the mark in terms of the way in which the opposing parties depicted one another. These alignments were sometimes worked through in surprising contexts. One of the most unexpected, for instance, is the battle between the ancients and moderns. Here, as in the reception of Descartes, women philosophers tended to take a predictable position – on the side of the moderns – in part because they saw a classical education and the veneration of the Greeks and Romans as a barrier erected by men against them, as that half of the human race denied the right to formal schooling at all. It was on the issue of education that they tended to be most outspokenly feminist, and no one more famously than Astell.

The issue of Astell's feminism requires an admission on my part. Having myself referred to Astell mostly as a proto-feminist, I realize now that I was wrong to do so. The refusal to apply the term 'feminist' to those women who early engaged in the struggle to be recognized as minds and bodies with the autonomy and rights granted to men involves a kind of reverse anachronism.[14] It assumes that we moderns, or postmoderns, have a monopoly on the claim to feminism, and that to pass the test earlier thinkers would have to exhibit the sort of Whiggish political progressivism that could only be the outcome of the process in which they were engaged. Although equivocating over application of the label in my earlier writing on Astell, I nevertheless took care to stress that her Toryism could not be seen to stand in the way of her feminism. Living under a constitutional monarchy and an established church, these Tory women, Mary Manley and Aphra Behn as well as Astell, could not be sure, in advance of the French Revolution, that progressivism – let alone republicanism – would win out, and they were far too pragmatic to tie their programme to such high-stakes politics.

This is to state the problem from the point of view of an external observer in terms of a counterfactual proposition, which is not, of course, how they saw it. For them it did not need explaining because, as Anglicans under the Crown, Toryism was orthodoxy, whereas republicans, seen to resist the monarchy, and dissenters, seen to resist the church, were believed to be deviants, if not indeed heretics. It was convenient for Tories to associate republicanism and dissent with the Whigs. One cannot sufficiently stress that fears about political instability that prevailed under the late Stuarts – fears dating from the Exclusion Crisis to the death of Queen Anne – were as much fears for the church as for the state. The fact of an established state church meant that religion and politics were inextricably intertwined and, if the fact of a Catholic Duke of York posed a peculiar kind of threat to the Crown, the fact of widespread religious non-conformity and dissent posed a peculiar threat to the church. These issues were of such a pressing nature that they served to polarize most political thought, as I have suggested, and it is not surprising that this is the period in which party politics characterized as Whig and Tory emerged. They also led to the conflation of positions by adversaries, not just for polemical purposes but because, in the struggle to understand these emerging political alignments, stereotyping had a role to play. So, for Astell and Aphra Behn, for instance, it was axiomatic that dissenters and Whigs were one and the same,[15] whereas, for the Whigs, it was easy to conflate Toryism with Catholicism and Caesaropapism.

2. Early Modern Women and 'Myth of the State'

The relative absence of texts in the history of political thought on and by early modern women, which is often remarked, reflects not their political or literary incapacity but rather the separate spheres that the social construction of gender imposed. The public and private worlds into which social life was divided, and which it was the intention of the theoreticians of the early modern state to entrench, were founded on homologous contracts. One, the social contract, constituted the political world of men; the other, the marriage contract, governed the private world of women. Female, let alone feminist, texts in political thought were an anomaly, given that women until the twentieth century were officially not political creatures – and yet in rare cases, like that of Astell, we have them. The status of married women as legal minors in Western Europe and North America until enactment of married women's property acts of the 1880s barred their participation in states in which political rights were tied to the capacity to own property. Astell's percipient critique of the marriage contract–social contract analogue, her critique of John Locke, perhaps the first to encompass his entire *corpus,* and her exposure of the theories of Locke and Hobbes as fathers of a liberalism that did not extend to women anticipated modern feminist critiques of a liberal democratic state as yet unborn.

How do we explain this? It does little justice to the capacity of women to fabricate an existence amid the legal and structural constraints within which they found themselves, to harp too much on their absence from the official record, if it were even true.[16] To some extent the problem is definitional. But that we so readily acquiesce in a definition of the public realm that restricts it to the nation-state and its forms is a story in itself. It belongs to the much larger phenomenon of myth of the state, which has allowed public life and its manifold forms to be co-opted by the nation-state as the privileged bearer of community, the authoritative promulgator of rules, and the sovereign source of law, exercising a monopoly of coercive force within its territorial borders. It is a corollary of the civil society and the state, or public–private distinction, to sideline those engaged in endeavours that do not serve state purposes – and here we have a possible explanation of the social gendering of 'winners' and 'losers' as 'masculine' and 'feminine', sanctioned by the belief that the masculine was definitively public, the feminine characterizing the quintessentially private sphere.[17]

This crude conception of male as winner, female as loser, traces a straight line from state-of-nature arguments, where power falls to the stronger, presumed to be male – at least by Hobbes and Locke – a notion against which Plato was among the first to campaign in his rebuttal of Thrasymachus in the *Republic*.[18] But to little avail; the sophist notion that Thrasymachus represents, of politics as structured by a struggle for power in which it falls to the strongest to rule in their own interests, prevailed, only to be reinstated by Hobbes – and later by Marx – and to this day, notions like 'soft power' and 'strong democracy' seem to appeal to brute strength as the test of social power.[19] Even in the academy, the social gendering of knowledge continues apace, arts and humanities being thought of as feminine and 'soft' subjects, the 'hard' sciences as masculine, with important consequences for the wider social division and specialization of labour. Myth of the state describes a body of theory not much in vogue any longer, but in the hands of Ernst Cassirer and Friedrich Meinecke, it represented an early critique of the totalizing power of the state in which 'clubs are trumps' – to use Hobbes's memorable phrase.[20] I note with interest that the very theorists whom Cassirer and Meinecke credit with pioneering *étatism* are the same theorists – particularly Machiavelli – now being repackaged as 'classical republicans'.

Perhaps this is not surprising, given that classical republicanism belongs also to myth of the state as one of its subtler forms. Under the classical republican aegis, early modern nation-states of the West succeeded in laying claim to the mantle of the Athenian *polis* and the Roman Republic, at the same time distancing themselves from the East as 'oriental', 'despotic' and 'other', as I have argued in various pieces.[21] Ironically, the dynamics of legitimacy described by one of the greatest *étatists*, Thomas Hobbes, provide us with the most promising approach to the phenomenon of cultural distancing – but at one remove, through Carl Schmitt, architect of the juridical system of the most demonic expression of myth of the state, that great Leviathan, the Third Reich. Hobbes, in describing the relentless anarchy of the war of all against all as the perpetual threat to peace and security outside state boundaries, provided Schmitt with a model for the logic of anarchy within. Extrapolating from Hobbes's characterization of the state of nature as a condition in which men were wolves to their fellows, his own reflection on the ancient phrase *homo homini lupus* employed by Hobbes, Schmitt arrived at a theory of generalized hostility to the Other.[22] The ubiquitous human tendency to create social distance in terms of the stereotypes 'Freund und Feind' – 'friend and foe', 'insider and outsider' – that Schmitt describes provides an explanatory vehicle for the social gendering of knowledge and forms of social stereotyping congruent with the masculinization of winners and feminization of losers, to which Eileen O'Neill refers. The human genius for creating out of the known the unknown, out of sameness otherness, out of the familiar the foreign that Schmitt describes is the same phenomenon that Sigmund Freud described as 'the narcissism of minor differences', the dynamic behind racism and ethnic conflict. Where the distance between individuals in terms of gender, race or ethnicity is small, the search for markers to create social distance between insider and outsider requires the amplification of minor differences.[23]

The ubiquitous prejudice that accompanies myth of the state and its restrictive public–private binary distinctions – whether expressed as strong–weak or masculine–feminine – has led in turn to a narrowness in the definition of public life that excludes not only women. So, for instance, Elizabethan and early Stuart England, which saw the richest flowering of commentary on the changing forms of public life in all their social and political dimensions, has been virtually expunged from the history of political thought. This is due to exclusions on the basis of genre rather than gender. The works of Marlowe, Kyd, Jonson, Spenser and Shakespeare, intensely political in the broad sense, were cast for the stage or in verse, for a complex of reasons that included forms of lyric expression favoured by Renaissance writers; a preference for 'veiled allegory' due to religious, Hermetic and magical beliefs; involvement in foreign and sometimes treasonable causes; and, not least, the activities of secret police particularly draconian under Elizabeth's secretary of state, Walsingham. New Historicists are now seeking to rectify the loss for which the old historians are guilty, but political theorists have yet to leap into the fray.[24]

Commentators have noted the capacity of seventeenth-century women to live in the interstices of social institutions as novelists, dramatists and political pamphleteers.[25] Astell is a curious case. On the one hand, she undertook a self-conscious critique of the very institutions at the root of female oppression: contemporary education and marriage practices. On the other, she was a High Church Tory pamphleteer, and probably a commissioned one, who in essential aspects defended the existing social order, church and queen. This gives some commentators pause in applying to her the epithet 'feminist'.[26] But while caution against anachronism is prudent, the belief that Toryism disqualifies women as feminists is anachronism of a different kind. It makes Whiggish assumptions about progressivism as a qualification for feminism that could only be made with post-Enlightenment hindsight. In a curious way this refusal to see Astell, along with Manley, Judith Drake and Aphra Behn, all of them Tories, as fully fledged feminists is the same category mistake of which Carole Pateman so cleverly convicts post-modern, post-colonial theorists who see feminism as an extension of the white male, one-dimensional Enlightenment culture of rights[27] – but in reverse. Such consequentialism is fallacious; if these women could not be expected to anticipate Enlightenment progressivism, they were not responsible for its ill effects either. Feminism does not come as a neatly tailored political package, nor is it even a political persuasion, far less primarily a social movement. What counts as feminist is the long struggle against misogyny and for a woman's voice, dating from the Middle Ages on in Europe – and probably manifested in different forms at different times in most cultures – that by exerting relentless pressure eventually, in the English case, made the conjunction of Whig progressivism and feminism possible. Those post-modern and post-colonial theorists who see feminism as an attenuated consequence of the European Enlightenment, could therefore be accused of the same sort of myopia and Eurocentrism of which they convict others!

In many instances the apparent absence of European women from the public sphere is due to genre rather than gender. In so-called less developed countries women have often been more visible as farmers, shopkeepers, piece workers, and sometimes the owners of small domestic businesses, than in Europe, which suffered from 'housewifization' much earlier.[28] But at critical political junctures women burst onto the European political stage also, as pamphleteers and petitioners, sometimes in surprising contexts. The celebrated 'warming pan scandal' in which the Catholic James II and his wife, Mary, were believed to have smuggled in a baby imposter Prince of Wales in a warming pan in order to forestall the monarchy's passing to the Protestant Prince and Princess of Orange, is a case in Astell's time.[29] The dramatist Aphra Behn and the midwife Elizabeth Cellier both leapt into print with the rumour of the false pregnancy, hazarding a guess, like Princess Anne, that the outcome would be a boy![30] The role of female pamphleteers among Astell's contemporaries was in rare cases, like that of the celebrated Mary Manley, critical to the rise and fall of ministries, as we shall see.

In some genres women were consistently present, as novelists, poets and letter writers. Feminist interventions in the history of philosophy, more often than not anonymous, were typically in an epistolary mode, which suggests private rather than public circulation, contributing to their anonymity. The relationships of Elizabeth of Bohemia (1618–60) to René Descartes, Anna Maria van Schurman (1607–78) to Pierre Gassendi and Marin Mersenne, Margaret Cavendish (1623–73) to Thomas Hobbes, Anne Conway (1631–79) to Henry More, Mary Astell to John Norris (1657–1711) and Damaris Masham (1658–1708) to John Locke are among the most philosophically important epistolary relationships of the early modern period. Not only did seventeenth-century women philosophers – Elizabeth of Bohemia, Margaret Cavendish, Anne Conway, Mary Astell and Damaris Masham – represent an important contribution to the reception of Descartes, but they also mounted a serious, and to some extent consistent, critique of Cartesian dualism with reference to the *Cambridge Platonists, and particularly Henry More.[31] In the same way, Astell, Masham and Catharine Cockburn (1679–1749) made important, and in Astell's case critical, contributions to the reception of Locke. Astell, like so many women who contributed to the reception of new philosophical ideas, presented her most serious theological works, her *Letters Concerning the Love of God* and *The Christian Religion*, in the epistolary mode. A comprehensive treatment of Astell's philosophy or theology is beyond the scope of this book. We still lack modern editions of the *Letters Concerning the Love of God* and *The Christian Religion*, as we do of *Bart'lemy Fair* and *Moderation Truly Stated*.

The fact of Astell's being both a Tory and a feminist poses no paradox that a full understanding of her intellectual and political context cannot explain – as it takes only a little reflection to see. In Astell, Mary Manley and Aphra Behn we have three outstanding examples of just how possible it was to be a High Church Tory and a feminist. It was not a problem for them, and it is only because of our progressivist assumptions that it could be a problem for us. The scholar who has perhaps done most to analyze Whig and Tory rhetorical strategies in the age of Anne, Rachel Weil, concludes that both parties had 'multiple ideologies of gender', but that in terms of the benefit to women there was not much to choose between them.[32] The new wave of Astell scholars who demur at applying the term 'feminist' to Astell as too narrowly contextualizing her work, and who rightly believe that only a full appraisal of her work across the many genres in which she wrote will produce an appropriate understanding of her contribution, err, it seems to me, if they consider her feminism in any way incidental.

Astell was not alone in the constellation of views that she expressed, and if they characterized contemporary female publicists as significant as Manley and Behn, they were also shared by some males, including John Norris – who promoted both Astell and Masham – and Richard Allestree, who both anticipated Astell's critique of seventeenth-century marriage mores as demeaning to females – even using the term 'female slavery'[33] – and urged on women a Christian dignity and spiritual independence. These were coherent views, given the constraints their religious and political commitments placed on possible solutions to the problem of human agency for these thinkers and the social hierarchies that constituted for them the nexus of agency. Tory feminism, it seems to me, is an interesting candidate for *Begriffsgeschichte*, and we have to be able to get past the modern *Gestalt* of feminism in order to retrieve the phenomenon in its infancy – as we must for all concepts if we are properly to understand the past.[34]

3. Astell, Seventeenth-Century Women Philosophers and the Reception of Descartes

Astell is no longer the monopoly of Stuart historians, and literary scholars and historians of philosophy have recently also made their mark. Work important to a critical assessment of Astell the philosopher-theologian has already been completed by Jacqueline Broad, Kathleen Squadrito, Eileen O'Neill and Sarah Hutton,[35] but a full analysis of her arguments has yet to be made. Sometimes insensitivity to context flaws their interpretations as well. This is true of the widely cited essay by Kathleen Squadrito, 'Mary Astell's Critique of Locke's View of Thinking Matter',[36] which has been shown by E. Derek Taylor to simply misread Astell on Lockean sensationalist psychology and to miss, therefore, the main point of her critique.[37] Both Taylor and Sarah Ellenzweig have produced finely nuanced accounts, emphasizing the degree to which Astell's philosophical and religious works were attentive to political agendas, steering a path between the Charybdis of Malebranchean 'occasionalism' and the Scylla of Lockean sensationalist psychology.[38] Taylor not only accepts my claim that the critique of Locke was among Astell's primary targets, but refines it with respect to Astell's most weighty work, *The Christian Religion*. And Ellenzweig may well be right that Astell's temporary departure from Malebranchean occasionalism in the last of her *Letters Concerning the Love of God* could have been motivated by worries that this doctrine of Norris and Malebranche, which made it impossible to distinguish ontologically between the divine and profane, could be construed as a species of Spinozism or pantheism and therefore heretical. Astell's return to occasionalism in *The Christian Religion*, as Taylor points out, is probably due to the fact that her antipathy to Locke had now reached battle pitch and finally outweighed her fears of being tarred with the Spinozist brush.

Recent work by Jacqueline Broad, Eileen O'Neill and Sarah Hutton has contributed to our understanding of Astell's Platonist theology and laid the groundwork for a full assessment of her philosophy and theology.[39] But no book-length treatment of Astell has been produced in any of these fields, and Ruth Perry's excellent biography still stands as the most substantial work on Astell that we have – a gap this book tries to fill. Eileen O'Neill's recent writing is among a growing body of work suggesting the reception of Descartes as the common philosophical ground that unites seventeenth-century women philosophers, most of whom were conservative and anti-materialist.[40] The divide between Cartesians and materialists was as profound in philosophy as the divide between Tories and Whigs in politics, creating similar and sometimes overlapping polarizations. So, for instance, if English materialists from the late Hobbes on tended to be Whiggish, the Cartesians tended to be Tory. Women philosophers in the seventeenth century, given the nature of church–state relations, strongly tended towards Cartesianism and, in England, the High Church Tory Party. This is not to claim that to be devoutly Christian necessarily entailed conservatism – witness Astell's contemporary, the 'pro-Locke dualist' Judith Drake, and the later pro-Locke and republican Catharine Macaulay – but that socio-political contingencies encouraged Anglicanism and monarchism. But Whig and even revolutionary women could also be devoutly Christian, as in the case of Gilbert Burnet's wife, Elizabeth, and Mary Wollstonecraft.[41]

Their characterization as Cartesian and conservative conveys no sense at all of the energy and ingenuity with which early modern women interrogated Cartesian dualism for solutions to the peculiar problems that they faced. And it does not even begin to suggest the intellectual fluidity that allowed them to inhabit and vacate Platonist, and specifically Malebranchean, positions in the struggle to reconcile mind–body questions with the demands of their religious beliefs. Not least was the problem of standing. In this respect, Cartesian mind–body duality created space. As long as women had souls, however they might be disqualified as bodies, they had the same right to self-improvement and the same duty to salvation as men. It was on this precise argument that Astell based her claim for women's right to education in *A Serious Proposal, Part I*: 'Let such as therefore deny us the improvement of our Intellectuals, either take up *his* Paradox, who said, *That Women have no souls*; which at this time a day, when they are allow'd to Brutes, wou'd be as unphilosophical as it is unmannerly; or else let them permit us to cultivate and improve them.'[42] Astell in this short statement signals not only that in her campaign for women's education she is on the side of Descartes, but also that she is speaking principally to his critics, those who opposed the Cartesian 'beast-machine' as according undue dignity to the intelligence of animals, and yet treated women, in the scope they afforded them for the exercise of their capacities, as less than human.[43]

But Cartesians did not monopolize this position. Judith Drake, the pro-Lockean dualist, as Eileen O'Neill characterizes her, took the same stand as Astell on women's capacity for self-improvement while treating the Cartesian beast-machine with withering contempt. Addressing Princess Anne of Denmark, later Queen Anne, the royal dedicatee of her *Essay in Defence of the Female Sex* of 1696, Drake bases her argument for female equality on a highly satirical parody of the Hobbesian state of nature, which she submits to a *reductio ad absurdum*, characterizing it in terms, not of perpetual warfare between men, but of the sex relations between beasts:[44]

I shall only once more take notice that in Brutes and other Animals there is no difference betwixt Male and Female in point of Sagacity, notwithstanding there is the same distinction of Sexes, that is between Man and Woman. I have read, that some Philosophers have held Brutes to be no more than meer Machines, a sort of Divine Clock-work, that Act only by the force of nice unseen Springs without Sensation, and cry out without feeling Pain, Eat without Hunger, Drink without Thurst, fawn upon their Keepers without seeing 'em, hunt Hares without Smelling, *etc.* Here Madam is cover for our Antagonists against the last Argument so thick, that there is no beatin 'em out. For my part I shall not envy 'em their refuge, let 'em lie like the wild *Irish* secure within their Boggs; the field is at least ours, so long as they keep to their Fastnesses. But to quit this Topick, I shall only add that if the learnedest He of 'em all can convince me of the truth of this Opinion, He will very much stagger my Faith; for hitherto I have been able to observe no difference between our Knowledge and theirs, but a gradual one; and depend upon Revelation alone, that our Souls are immortal and theirs are not.

In point of fact Drake, in attacking misogynists who conflate Descartes' peculiar views about animals with their own beliefs about the inferiority of women, comes very close to Hobbes's own attack on the Cartesian beast-machine in the opening lines of the Preface to *Leviathan*, but to very different ends.[45] Far from condoning the argument of last resort to which Hobbes and Locke appeal to justify the power of men over women – that it falls to them as the stronger to extract obedience in exchange for protection – Drake turns the argument on its head. If in the distribution of talents men have the brawn, women have the brains, and therefore, in the corresponding division of labour they are the ones best fitted to intellectual pursuits and better leave the labouring to the men:[46]

I have yet another Argument from Nature, which is, that the very Make and Temper of our Remedies shew that we were never design'd for Fatigue; and the Vivacity of our Wits, and the Readiness of our Invention (which are confess'd even by our Adversaries) demonstrate that we were chiefly intended for Thought and the Exercise of the Mind. Whereas on the contrary it is apparent from the strength and size of their Limbs, the Vigour and Hardiness of their Constitutions, that Men were purposely fram'd and contriv'd for Action and Labour. And herein the Wisdom and Contrivance of Providence is abundantly manifested; for as the one Sex is fortified with Courage and Ability to undergo the necessary Drudgery of providing Materials for the sustenance of Life in both; so the other is furnish'd with Ingenuity and Prudence for the orderly management and distribution of it, for the Relief and Comfort of a Family; and is over and above enrich'd with a peculiar Tenderness and Care requisite to the Cherishing their poor helpless offspring.

Noting that 'our Opposers usually miscall our quickness of Thought, Fancy and Flash, and christen their own heaviness by the specious Names of Judgment and Solidity', Drake nevertheless goes on to argue that if the nature of non-gendered souls admits women across the threshold of sex equality, and the nature of their biological differences peculiarly suits women for intellectual pursuits, then in fact neither mind nor body gives ground for gender differentiation that would discriminate against women:[47]

For a Man ought no more to value himself upon being Wiser than a Woman, if he owe his Advantage to a better Education, and greater means of Information, then he ought to boast of his Courage, for beating a Man, when his Hands were bound. Nay it would be so far from Honourable to contend for preference upon this Score that they would thereby at once argue themselves guilty both of Tyranny and of Fear.

Drake's case of the 'fettered fighter' is an argument equivalent in structure to that of the contemporary 'shackled runner' – an argument to which defenders of affirmative action have typically appealed.[48] The deprivation of women, she goes on to conclude, could only be a product of custom and convention, pride, prejudice and fear:[49]

For nothing makes one Party slavishly depress another, but their fear that they may at one time or other become Strong or Couragious enough to make themselves equal to, if not superiour to their Masters. This is our Case; for Men being sensible as well of the Abilities of Mind in our Sex, as of the strength of Body in their own, began to grow Jealous, that we, who in the Infancy of the World were their Equals and Partners in Dominion, might in process of Time, by Subtlety and Stratagem, become their Superiours; and therefore began in good time to make use of Force (the Origine of Power) to compell us to a Subjection, Nature never meant; and made use of Natures liberality to them to take the benefit of her kindness from us. From that time they have endeavour'd to train us up altogether to Ease and Ignorance; as Conquerors use to do to those, they reduce by Force, that so they may disarm 'em, both of Courage and Wit; and consequently make them tamely give up their Liberty, and abjectly submit their Necks to a slavish Yoke. As the world grew more Populous, and mens Necessities, whetted their Inventions, so it increas'd their Jealousie and sharpen'd their Tyranny over us, till by degrees, it came to that height of Severity, I may say Cruelty, it is now at in all the Eastern parts of the World, where the Women, like our Negroes in our Western Plantations, are born slaves, and live Prisoners all their Lives. Nay, so far has this barbarous Humour prevail'd, and spread it self, that in some parts of Europe, which pretend to be most refin'd and civiliz'd, in spite of Christianity and the Zeal for Religion that which they so much affect, our condition is not very much better.

This is a clearly feminist argument that reworks Machiavellian and Hobbesian arguments about the origins of *imperium* in coercion while replicating Hobbes's argument that mothers in the state of nature have *dominion* over their children because only they have the power to name the father.[50] It was an argument repeated by Rousseau – with acknowledgement to Hobbes – in the Second Discourse, *On the Origins of Inequality*, a work that, in its distinction between '*bourgeois*' and '*citoyen*',

may be read as anticipating Marx, in *On the Jewish Question*, on the excluding power of bourgeois rights, as well as Marxist feminist applications
of these arguments in the works of Catherine MacKinnon and others.[51]
Imperium and the systematic subordination of women as an exercise in
power politics – of which both Astell and Drake were aware – is a consideration to which we will return in the final chapter of this book. There I
urge that due weight be given to the concept of *imperium*, as belonging
to the constellation of juridical concepts, including *ius* and *lex*, in terms
of which civil rights were debated, at least from the time of the codifi-
cation of Roman law, and in the many waves of its reception, including
seventeenth-century rights debates. If such an argument on my part is
deemed anachronistic, I hasten to add that I am not for one moment
assuming that Drake could have foreseen the resonance of her argument
for the future. Indeed it is important to point out the precise context for
her work, which belongs, like Astell's, to the counterattack against a considerable misogynist and anti-marriage pamphlet literature (addressed
in Chapter 1, Section 5) that had seen an upsurge at the time at which
they wrote. This, at the onset of the eighteenth century, was the age of
the gallant and the fop, charming but fickle, tricked out for his role as
seducer and romancer of women by the new affluence that grew on the
back of international commerce – a topic discussed at great length by
Astell in *Reflections upon Marriage* and, more scientifically, in her long
Preface on Charles Davenant's *Essays on War and Peace* that she attached
to her *Moderation truly Stated*,[52] and addressed anecdotally by Drake in
her caricatures of the various male types of her day in her *Essay in Defence
of the Female Sex.*[53]

4. Astell, Women Philosophers and the *Querelle des Femmes*

Astell's *Serious Proposal* and *Reflections upon Marriage* belong to a rather
well-established Continental tradition of proto-feminist writing that
focuses on education as the root and branch of female inequality and
customary right as the conventional strategy to entrench it. Dating at
least from Christine de Pizan's *Book of the City of Ladies* of 1405, this genre
of early feminist political writing includes, notably, two feminist tracts by
Marie de Gournay (1565–1645), *The Equality of Men and Women* (1622)
and *The Ladies' Grievance* (1626).[54] While there is no direct evidence
that Astell had read either Pizan or Gournay, and we know that she did
not read French,[55] similarities of genre between these thinkers are striking. These include catalogues of exemplary women from antiquity to the

present, especially powerful female biblical figures; critical exegesis focusing on scriptural passages that affirm or deny female equality; and arguments from Christian theology that postulate ungendered souls. These are marked traits of Astell's 1706 Preface to *Reflections upon Marriage*, as they were of Judith Drake's earlier *Essay in Defence of the Female Sex*. In *The Equality of Men and Women*, de Gournay had added to the roster of authorities on female equality a number of ancient and modern philosophers, perhaps after the example of her Dutch acquaintance, the very erudite Anne Marie Von Schurman (1607–78),[56] who is reputed to have studied Seneca at age eleven. They included Plutarch, Seneca, Erasmus, Politian and Castiglione, as well as the Church Fathers. Judith Drake, although like Astell unlearned in classical languages, also added a roster of proto-feminist philosophers, ancient and modern, to her account. Astell and Drake, like de Gournay, attributed women's apparent mental inferiority to lack of education, believing that men and women are inherently alike except in the matter of reproduction. Women, like men, were made in the image of God, and Saint Paul had excluded women from active participation in the church only because he feared that their charms would distract men from their devotion to God. Astell hints at such an argument when, in her famous 1706 Preface to *Reflections upon Marriage*, she reproduces passages from Paul stipulating that women cover their heads in church, dress modestly and generally ensure that they are seen and not heard.[57]

To what degree these early generations of feminist thinkers in fact knew of one another is still often difficult to ascertain. We know, for instance, that Bathsua Makin, Anna Maria van Schurman and Marie de Gournay corresponded together.[58] Margaret Cavendish, Duchess of Newcastle, although a Hobbesian materialist, and Anne Finch Conway, Viscountess Conway, a vitalist and a strong influence on Leibniz, were not as philosophically distant as they may seem.[59] We know, moreover, that Conway was acquainted with Cavendish's writings through her correspondence with More, who encouraged her to respond to the duchess's *Philosophical Letters*.[60] But we have no real evidence for connections between Astell and Drake, or even between Astell and contemporary aristocratic women philosophers as prominent as Cavendish and Conway. Conway's only surviving work, *The Principles of the Most Ancient and Modern Philosophy*, first published in Latin in Amsterdam in 1690 as part of a three-part collection, *Opuscula philosophica*, and most likely prepared for publication by More, would have been inaccessible to Astell in that language, but was available in English translation in 1692, although anonymously.[61] Given that More had dedicated his *Antidote against Atheism* to Conway, it is likely, however, that Astell, who was certainly familiar with some of More's works, would have known of her views at least at second hand. Margaret Cavendish, who had followed the court of Charles I into exile in France as the maid of honour to his queen, Henrietta Maria, in 1643, was a prolific writer and a royalist.[62] To the extent that Astell knew of her, she would probably have associated her with Hobbes, through his Cavendish patrons, as a materialist and, therefore, the member of a hostile camp. Sometimes Astell's attributions are surprising, however. In *A Serious Proposal*, for instance, she cites *Ann Dacier,[63] the gifted antiquarian scholar, so important in the French debate between the ancients and moderns, along with Katherine Philips (1631–64), author of *Orinda* (1661),[64] and the author Madeleine de Scudéry (1607–1701).[65] She names all three, to set them apart from the general run of authors of 'idle *Novels* and *Romances*' whom she scorns as occupying the time of too many English gentlewomen.[66]

There is a further context for Astell's work that is important but difficult to establish, and that is her relation to the late-seventeenth-century resurgence of what is referred to as the *querelle des femmes* in the form of Restoration satires on women and marriage.[67] Prominent among these is Robert Gould's *Love Given O're: Or, A Satyr against the Pride, Lust and Inconstancy etc. of Women*, first published in 1682, which went through five editions up to 1690 and, according to Felicity Nussbaum, 'incited two decades of lively attacks and counterattacks'.[68] An upsurge of such publications from 1691 on, perhaps in response to the fifth printing of Gould's work, culminated in the anonymous *Satire against Marriage* of 1700 and Edward Ward's *Pleasures of a Single Life, or the Miseries of Matrimony: occasionally writ upon the many divorces lately granted by Parliament* of 1701, which also went through many printings.[69] The timing of Astell's *Reflections upon Marriage* of 1700 may be an important piece of *external* evidence for her relation to this genre, in which 'women's boundless lust' is a commonplace, and the satirists dreamed either of a life without marriage or a life without women. Richard Ames's satire *The Folly of Love*, reprinted in 1701, dreams of the latter. For while Restoration satires were ostensibly moral, designed to reform behaviour, their aggressively misogynist tone is hardly distinguishable from outright invective, marriage being viewed as an institution that suited the needs of women but not of men.

There is also considerable *internal* evidence to suggest, although Astell does not name names, that the *Reflections upon Marriage*, as well as being a contribution to the defense of an unfairly maligned woman, Hortense Mancini, Duchess of Mazarin, who was her neighbour, was also Astell's response to this genre. So, for instance, she states that 'marriage, notwithstanding all the loose talk of the Town, the Satyrs of Ancient or Modern pretenders to Wit, will never lose its due praise from judicious persons'.[70] She asks, 'Upon what are the Satyrs against Marriage grounded? Not upon the state itself, if they are just, but upon the ill choice or foolish conduct of whose who are in it. . . . '[71] She defends the married state against those who complain that it benefits only women: 'Certainly Men may be very happy in a Married State; 'tis their own fault if they are at any time otherwise'.[72] And again, she admits that 'there may indeed be Inconveniencies in a Married Life; but is there any Condition without them? And he who lives single that he may indulge Licentiousness and give up himself to the conduct of wild and ungovern'd Desires . . . may rail as he pleases against Matrimony, but can never justifie his own Conduct, nor clear it from the imputation of Wickedness and Folly'.[73] In the fourth edition of the *Reflections* of 1730, perhaps as an indication of the degree to which the debate had heated up, Astell added new material: 'Whoever scoffs at this, and by odious Representation would possess the married Pair with a frightful Idea of each other, as if a Wife is nothing better than a Domstick Devil, an Evil he must tolerate for his own Conveniency; and an Husband must of necessity be a Tyrant or Dupe, has ill Designes on both, and is himself a dangerous Enemy to the Publick, as well as to private Families'.[74] Even more explicitly in the fourth edition Astell claims that she is 'far from designing a Satire upon Marriage, as some pretend, either unkindly or ignorantly, through want of Reflection in that sense wherein I use the Word'.[75] In her own attack on the scorning 'Wits', Astell appeals to her female audience: 'as to the Female Reader, I hope she will allow I've endeavour'd to do her Justice, not betray'd her Cause as her Advocates usually do under Pretence of defending it. . . . To plead for the Oppress'd and to defend the Weak seem'd to me a generous Undertaking'.[76] By comparison:[77]

Your whissling Wits may scoff at [women], and what then? It matters not, for they Rally everything tho' ever so Sacred, and rail at the Women commonly in very good Company. . . . But that your grave Dons, your Learned Men, and which is more, your Men of Sense, as they wou'd be thought, should stoop so low as to make Invectives against the Women, forget themselves so much as to jest with their Slaves, who have neither the Liberty nor Ingenuity to make Reprizals! that they shou'd waste their Time, and debase their good Sense which fits them for the most weighty Affairs, such as are suitable to their profound Wisdoms and exalted Understandings! To render those poor Wretches more ridiculous and odious who are already in their Opinion sufficiently contemptible, and find no better exercise of their Wit and Satyr than such as are not worth their Pains, tho' it were possible to Reform them, this indeed may justly be wondered at!

It is not clear whom among the Dons and Men of Sense Astell is singling out, or even whom among the Wits, but it does seem to be the case that she is explicitly indicating the misogynist anti-marital satire as her target. In *Reflections upon Marriage* she makes a case for non-marriage as an alternative for women, as it is for men, although in the case of women a virtuous alternative, predicated upon informed choice, women's education and the possibility of a community of women without men, which was her own choice and the project of her *Serious Proposal.*

5. Astell, Women Dramatists, Publicists and Pamphleteers

Astell earned her credentials as beneficiary of a patronage system that admitted noblewomen and gentlewomen of talent to limited participation in the political sphere from which they were, however, officially excluded. But this is to accept the now orthodox account of the rise of the state in terms of the creation of a public sphere.[78] In fact the public–private divide was one that significant numbers of women, and by no means always aristocrats, crossed, among them dramatists, publicists and pamphleteers. Astell and those women like her, Aphra Behn (1640–89) and *Mary de la Riviere Manley (c. 1663–1724), politically active and, indeed, Tory publicists, gave the lie to the very spatial distinctions Locke and the Whigs were concerned to instate, as women nibbling at the margins of politics had done for centuries. Behn, for instance, of whose personal life we know too little, is acknowledged to be the foremost Restoration dramatist, an important translator, a critic of Britain's colonial policy and reputed to be a spy.[79] As 'the most various and exploratory of Restoration dramatists', unequalled in terms of the number of her plays actually staged,[80] Behn addressed topics that find an echo in Astell's commentary on social mores and particularly those of marriage. So, for instance, Behn's sex comedies of the 1670s, including *The Town-Fop* (1676), deemed 'quintessential for the genre', and *The City-Heiress* (1682), regarded as 'one of the masterpieces of Restoration comedy',[81] establish a milieu for Astell's *Reflections upon Marriage*. The Restoration stage, like the Elizabethan, was a forum for social debate, and one in which women participated in surprising numbers.[82] Mary Manley, court wit and royal favourite, produced plays and novellas sufficiently powerful to assist in the demise of the Duke of Marlborough and the ministers surrounding him. And Astell, whose rhetoric in many respects belied her considered commitments as a true daughter of the Church of England, High Church Tory pamphleteer and supporter of the institutions of monarchy and marriage, was almost as notorious a pamphleteer as the scurrilous Manley.

Sarah Ellenzweig, in situating Astell as primarily a Radical Enlightenment figure, downplays her role as a political pamphleteer, claiming that 'in her own lifetime, at least, Astell was seen as most subversive where she has been least discussed, in her writings on religion and philosophy'.[83] But Ellenzweig's claim depends on our accepting, first, that Astell is properly situated 'in unexpected proximity to Spinoza, a figure condemned by contemporaries as the most abominable heretic of the seventeenth century'[84] and, second, that Spinoza is the most central figure on whom the Radical Enlightenment turned, the thesis of Jonathan Israel's recent book of that title.[85] Third, it depends on our accepting that Astell was 'radical'. But this argument of guilt by association is fallacious, in my view. Ellenzweig, like Israel, by assuming that the Radical Enlightenment is a movement to which only radicals could contribute, is faced with the choice of either relabeling significant thinkers as radical or excluding them from consideration. So, for instance, Israel concludes that Hobbes was not radical, overlooking numerous important attributions to him by Enlightenment thinkers, as well ignoring the more diffuse ways in which his ideas were propagated, in particular, by his enemies. Ellenzweig takes the opposite tack, deeming Astell radical and thereby accommodating her to the Enlightenment tradition by the stroke of a pen and with an appellation that, at the time, was meaningless. But there are appropriate empirical benchmarks for the appraisal of an author's reception. One of the best tests we have for the popular reception of Astell's work is the rate at which it was reprinted. *Reflections upon Marriage,* first published in 1700, went through four editions in England, each with a probable print run of at least 2,500 copies, and one in Ireland.[86] Her *Serious Proposal to the Ladies* (1694) ran to four editions. By comparison, Astell's strictly philosophical works, *The Letters Concerning the Love of God* and *The Christian Religion,* were reprinted three times, while her tracts, *Moderation truly Stated* and *A Fair Way with the Dissenters,* like *An Impartial Enquiry* – for all that it is reputed to have been a standard item in the Tory canon – remained at one edition.

6. Astell, Drake and the Social Gendering of Knowledge

This is not to suggest that labeling is not important, so long as it respects historical appropriateness and is attentive to the idiom of the day. This leads me to consider the clever argument on the peculiar ramifications of misogynist philosophical labeling made by Eileen O'Neill, who, in her essay 'Women Cartesians, "Feminine Philosophy" and Historical Exclusion', asks two questions: 'First, who were the women Cartesians of the seventeenth and eighteenth centuries? Second, why have women Cartesians been omitted from the standard histories of early modern philosophy?'.[87] In answering these questions, O'Neill develops a compelling argument about the exclusion of women that both satisfies the demand for specificity and recognizes historical contingency – this exclusion was not foreordained, although it appears to have been over-determined. Appealing to Foucault's concept of the 'episteme of similitude', to which she argues seventeenth-century Neoplatonism and the philosophy of the salons belonged, O'Neill argues that, as the experimental sciences founded on the Aristotelian hypothetico-deductive method gradually won the day, philosophies on the losing side came to be characterized as feminine.[88] So, for instance, Thomas Sprat, in his *History of the Royal-Society of London* of 1667, provided a mission statement for that institution that was devoted above all to the propagation of the New Science while castigating the insinuation of French salon culture into the English Republic of Letters in the following gendered terms:[89]

As the *Feminine* Arts of *Pleasure*, and Gallantry have spread some of our Neighbouring Languages [e.g., French], to such a vast extent: so the *English Tongue* may also in time be more enlarg'd, by being the Instrument of conveying to the World, the *Masculine* arts of *Knowledge*.

There is a certain prescience to this remark. It is true that English-language philosophy, for instance, tends to be analytic, as opposed to the more *Verstehende* modes of Continental philosophy, phenomenology and existentialism, and that the modern experimental sciences were initially pioneered in Britain. But to show that this instance of gendering is not merely a case of Francophobia in disguise, it is worth noting that the nineteenth-century French progressive Pierre-Joseph Proudhon (1809–65), who in answer to his own question posed in the pamphlet *What is Property?* (1840), answered 'All Property is theft', could in a period in which the hard natural sciences were hegemonic, and the emerging social sciences emulated them, sanguinely declare: 'The woman author does not exist; she is a contradiction. . . . [A] woman's book . . . is . . . philosophy on nothing'.[90]

Not only were women Cartesians excluded from the philosophical canon, but an entire generation of male Platonists also more or less disappeared from view as philosophers on the losing side. Eileen O'Neill, having noted, first, that anonymous publication did not help women Cartesians to promote themselves and, second, that the sidelining of religious concerns on which women philosophers were focused, as 'of purely anthropological interest', by German historians influenced by Kantianism, contributed to keeping women Cartesians out of the canon, further notes:[91]

Third, with respect to the women's views that were considered 'solidly philosophical' even from a post-eighteenth century vantage point, some utilized a style, employed a method, or expressed an underlying episteme that simply did not 'win out'. For example, the writings of Suchon, because of their scholastic exposition, or of Scudéry and Conway, with their underlying Neoplatonic episteme, may seem too removed from our present philosophical concerns to be of any but marginal historical interest. But an odd feature of 'philosophical views that do not win out' is that they frequently have been characterized as feminine. As we have just seen, the episteme of salonists such as Scudéry, and of Platonists such as More and Vaughn, came to be regarded at the end of the seventeenth century as feminine. The point was not that it was the philosophy of women, but that it was a degenerate philosophy of both men and women that was on its way out.

The equation feminine = degenerate was not innocent of misogynist prejudice, and O'Neill notes:[92]

But as I have discussed elsewhere, there was a good deal of slippage between feminine (i.e. outdated) philosophy that perhaps 'deserves' to be left out of the canon, and philosophy written by women. For example, when Rousseau attacks the scholarly style issuing from the French salons, it is not feminine style *per se* that he attacks, but the influence of real women on style. Similarly, when Kant describes the masculine character of the profundity of philosophy, he refers not to gendered systems or styles but to sexual difference.

O'Neill's observation suggests to me that we would do well to investigate so-called Kuhnian paradigm shifts for their normative and gendered dimensions.[93] By this I mean that we cannot simply assume that new paradigms are representative of the practices of a community of scientists and leave it at that. The scientific episteme by its very nature represents a structure of values that may stand in a more or less contingent relation to the practice of scientists – at least we cannot assume out of hand that one determines the other – and it seems highly likely that these values include a gendered element. Moreover, the triumph of materialism and the doctrine of progress have meant that far too little effort has been made to reconstruct the alternative pathways to modernity that were lost – even O'Neill's throwaway remark about outdated philosophy that ' "deserves" to be left out of the canon' leaves me wondering if she too has not been infected! In the account of modernity as an unfinished project, Tory women and Platonist men are among the missing.[94] This book is a small contribution to a growing literature on both that represents a project of retrieval.

Not least among the topics this book is intended to address is the percipience of Astell and Drake in attacking the Achilles heel of the marriage contract–social contract analogue as first made by Hobbes and Locke, which is the resort to customary right to explain how those who enter the contract as free and equal beings exit it as radically unequal. The prospective critique of the foundations of the liberal democratic state that Astell and Drake undertake kicks away the chocks from customary right and historicist appeals that put precedent above reason, process above principle, as well as undermining the social anthropology in which contractarianism was embedded. Drake is especially effective in this manoeuvre, attacking social contract both as an analytic construct – as in Hobbes – and as a primitive event in the social anthropology of progress – towards which Locke and Rousseau tend. The notion of a primitive contract in pre-antiquity from which authority devolved makes specious assumptions about the nature of civilization. More grievous still, it endorses authorization by genetic title, a specious form of historicism whereby, merely by having taken place, an event is deemed to have set a precedent – in this case the exercise of paternal power that gives rise to 'father right'. In this respect it matters little whether the original contract was between God and Abraham – according to Filmer – or between a secular people and their fearless leader – as in the case of Hobbes and Locke. It takes only a little reflection to see that the Hobbesian exchange of obedience for protection upon which the marriage contract–social contract analogue trades is only a more elaborate version of the Filmerian father right against which it was directed.

The ramifications of this feminist critique of contractarianism are profound, for it attacks the very foundations of modern rights theory based on the project of Hobbes and Locke to historicize the transition from *ius naturale*, as the law of nature, to *ius gentium*, the laws of particular nations. Reformulated as the transition from the state of nature to civil society, this transition, once postulated as a primitive event, was a further exercise in historicist argument, as creating a non-revocable order brought into force by the transition. The logic was simple: the state of nature, once abandoned, was only re-entered by a crisis of authority such as civil war, a perpetual reminder of the anarchy that lay beyond the boundaries of states and an important sanction for their coercive force. One of the *quid pro quos* of the transition from the state of nature to civil society was that natural law, which provided the motive to contract, was superseded by the positive law of states, and was no longer available as a court of appeal in the form of canon law or ecclesiastical law, as it had been hitherto. The net result of the historicization of the old Roman and canon law natural law–positive law distinction, to which Grotius, Hobbes, Pufendorf and Locke contributed, was the denaturalization of natural law, so to speak, and its eclipse by the law of nations, which yielded the now legendary realist picture of the international system as a jungle of anarchic states. Only with the pressure exerted by critics of liberalism over at least two centuries was the *status quo ante* restored in which natural law once again represented residual norms to which the laws of nations were accountable. For this project, achieved under the pressure of Kantian theories of subjective right, and eventually implemented with the institutional support of the United Nations, feminist critics of the foundations of liberal democratic state can be given some credit, a claim further discussed in the final chapter of this book.

1

Mary Astell, Philosopher, Theologian and Polemicist

1. Astell's Life and Works

Mary Astell was born in a century in which Great Britain had experienced a civil war, a regicide, the (successful) attempt to exclude an heir to the throne on religious grounds, a constitutional revolution and two changes of dynasty. By her day it was already a landscape politically divided between the Whigs, generally pro-Parliament and pro-religious toleration, and the Tories, generally pro-king and anti-religious toleration, respectively. It was a century that saw the passing of a Bill of Rights,[1] a Toleration Act and the consolidation of a constitutional monarchy that recognized specified civil rights in a path-breaking way. The Bill of Rights Act of 1689, together with the Toleration Act of the same year, promoting limited religious toleration, and the Triennial Act of 1694, which ensured regular elections and prevented the king from dissolving Parliament at will, represented major constitutional reforms that were the enduring achievement of the Glorious Revolution of 1688. These developments took place in an environment of strong politicking, personal intrigue, pamphlet warfare and an ideological climate that embraced a relatively wide spectrum of society. It was an environment in which, like the Restoration, women writers were to find a niche as novelists, dramatists and, in Astell's case, political pamphleteers. The seventeenth century had seen the flourishing of important philosophical schools that also claimed female adherents, both in England and on the Continent. Empiricists and materialists in England and France, including Thomas Hobbes, members of the circle around Marin Mersenne, Pierre Gassendi and the Great Tew and Cavendish circles, in England, had pioneered an atomistic physics, mechanistic psychology[2] and religious views about the mortality of the soul, heaven and hell, that were considered unorthodox.[3] These views were met by philosophical schools that maintained the integrity of the spiritual realm, were anti-materialist, although pro-science, and religiously orthodox, such as the followers of Descartes, Malebranche and the Cambridge Platonists. It is to these anti-materialist movements that most of the female seventeenth-century philosophers, including Astell, belonged.

Astell was a complex figure. About her private life we know very little, and not even a likeness remains of her – strange, given that as a High Church Tory pamphleteer, interlocutor with Cambridge Platonists, and critic of the dissenters, the Whigs and Locke, she was equally revered and reviled by prominent men and women in her day. A North Country gentlewoman whose royalist family through death and debt had fallen upon hard times, she had departed her native Newcastle-upon-Tyne for London at around the age of twenty. She immediately introduced herself to Anglican circles by presenting a book of juvenile religious poems to the former Archbishop of Canterbury and subsequent nonjuror William Sancroft, who may have provided her financial support. She entered a circle of like-minded intellectual women, high church prelates and their wives, eventually settling in the house of Lady Catherine Jones,[4] to whom two of her works were dedicated. She lived in Chelsea, where she eventually owned a house, dying in 1731 of breast cancer. A *Rawlinson Manuscript* of her poems, dated 1689, survives, along with a small archive of her letters to her friends, including John Norris, Henry Dodwell, Lady Ann Coventry and her publisher, Richard Wilkin.[5]

How is it that a little-known North Country English gentlewoman, who in fact barely qualified for this rank, could have challenged the basis of early modern liberal democratic state almost at the moment of its birth? These were years in which illiteracy for North Country women, as measured by their ability to sign court documents (admittedly a class-weighted measure) ran at 83 percent in the 1660s and 1670s and 72 percent in the 1680s and 1690s.[6] Born into a declining Northern gentry family in 1666, Catholic on her mother's side, Astell gave the lie to most received wisdom about the prospects of an academic career for girls in her era. Although there is no record of her childhood or education, it is generally believed that she was educated by her clergyman uncle Ralph Astell (1617–88), who belonged to the group of Platonists associated with Emmanuel and later Christ's College, Cambridge, and this would in part account for her philosophical orientation.[7] Once in London, Astell had access to intellectual circles and a fine library to equip herself. The Duchess of Mazarine, subject of a scandalous divorce case that occasioned Astell's *Reflections upon Marriage*, Elizabeth Elstob, Anglo-Saxon scholar and correspondent of George Ballard,[8] and the learned Bishop *Francis Atterbury were among her Chelsea neighbours. Both Ballard and Atterbury have left accounts of her, the former an important source for the contemporary reception of her work more generally, the latter an eminent cleric under both William and Anne, who gave a very particular report of her.

Atterbury gave some indication of Astell's audaciousness. Writing to George Smalridge, Bishop of Bristol, in a letter dated 1706, he referred to Astell's comments on a sermon he had written in response to Bishop Benjamin Hoadly's contentious *The Measures of Submission to the Civil Magistrate* of 1705, first preached as a sermon at St. Paul's on the occasion of the election of the Lord Mayor of London in September 1705 and published in an expanded version in the same year. Addressing the famous Chapter 13 of Paul's Epistle to the Romans, 'Let every soul be subject to the higher powers', Hoadly, a Whig, had confronted the Tory doctrine of passive obedience by arguing that it was more contrary to the will of God than outright rebellion. This sermon and its aftermath were of no small significance in the debates of the day – and that Atterbury allowed Astell to comment on his response with a view to printing it is in itself telling. Astell was apparently an 'artful' critic and, clearly offended by her remarks, Atterbury reported:[9]

I happen'd about a fortnight agoe to dine with Mrs Astell. She spoke to me of my Sermon & desired me to Print it: & after I had given her the proper answers, hinted to me that she should be glad of perusing it. I comply'd with her & sent her the Sermon the next day. Yesterday she return'd it with this sheet of Remarks, which I cannot forbear communicating to you because I take 'em to be of an extraordinary Nature, considering that they came from the Pen of a Woman. Indeed one would not imagine that a Woman had written 'em. There is not an expression that carries the least Air of her Sex from the Beginning to the End of it. She attacks me very home you see, & Artfully enough, under a Pretence of taking my Part against other Divines, who are in Hoadley's measure. Had she as much good Breeding as good sense, she would be perfect: but she had not the most decent manner of insinuating what she means, but is now or then a little offensive & shocking in her expressions; which I wonder at because a Civil Turn of Words (even where the matter is not pleasing) is what her Sex is always Mistress of. She, I think, is wanting in it. But her Sensible & rational Way of Writing makes amends for that defect, if indeed any Thing can make amends for it. I dread to engage her; so I wrote a general civil Answer to her & leave the rest to an oral conference with her. Her way of solving the Difficulty about swearing to the Queen is somewhat singular.

Ballard, reporting on the event some forty years later, astutely observed that, given Atterbury's habit of condescending to women, Astell 'might probably sharpen her Style designedly when she had that lucky opportunity of conversing with him', and went on to defend her character based on reports of those who knew her:[10]

If she was deficient in the little niceties & punctilios in the Arts of Address it's not at all to be wonder'd at by those who are acquainted with her retired & studious way of Life, for she was so wholly wrapt up in Philosophical, Metaphysical & Theological & indeed all kinds of Divine Speculations, that she had but small opportunities of making her self acquainted with the Worlds Theatre or any of it's Appendages: So that a Thinking Person, or one that had had but a small share of candour or good nature wou'd readily and easily have made allowances upon this Score, & not have troubled the World with such uncharitable Exclamations, for so small a Transgression.

Having introduced herself to High Church circles by presenting her religious poems *Dedicated to the most Reverend Father in God William by Divine Providence Lord Archbishop of Canterbury* to the man himself, William Sancroft, Astell had gone on to establish her theological credentials in a correspondence with John Norris, rector of Bemerton. The correspondence, instigated by Astell, was published under the title *Letters concerning the Love of God* (1695) by Norris, a well-known Platonist, although in this case an Oxford rather than a Cambridge graduate, and a figure central to the reception of Locke.[11] A man opposed to both Whigs and nonconformists, Norris had criticized Locke's *Essay Concerning Human Understanding* (1689) in what is believed to be the first public response to the *Essay*, his '*Cursory Reflections upon a book called, An Essay Concerning Human Understanding*', appended to his *Christian Blessedness, or Discourses upon the Beatitudes*, of 1690 – a work that was to run to fifteen editions by 1728.[12] There Norris had expounded Malebranche's doctrine of 'occasionalism' in order to refute Locke, from whom it prompted a written response in his 'Remarks upon Some of Mr. Norris' Books, wherein he asserts P. Malebranche's Opinion of seeing all Things in God' of 1693. Norris' comments had deeply disturbed Locke, but he withheld publication of the reply in his lifetime, noting that he thought the fad of Neoplatonism would pass.

Norris' magnum opus, the *Essay towards the Theory of an Ideal and Intelligible World*, was published in two volumes in 1701 and 1704, and although he has never enjoyed the posthumous career of a Hobbes or a Locke, he was considered to be a formidable philosopher in his day, principally as a transmitter of Malebranchean ideas. So, for instance, a contemporary, the publisher John Dunton, in the Preface 'to the Impartial Readers' appended to his biography of 1705, had remarked: 'PHILOSOPHY it self had never been improv'd, had it not been for *New Opinions*, which afterwards were rectified by abler Men (such as *Noris* and *Lock*)'.[13] In the long run Norris was eclipsed by Locke in the competition for notice, as being on the losing side in what was, in this case, a personal confrontation. For Locke's hostility towards Norris may not have been for strictly philosophical reasons, in fact. The *Cursory Reflections* had been published in 1690, but in 1692 Locke had personally interceded with the Earl of Pembroke to confer on Norris the living at Bemerton, suggesting that the *Reflections* were not the cause of the bitter animosity that inspired his response. Rather, it is said to lie in Locke's mistaken belief that Norris had broken the seal of a personal letter to Lady Damaris Masham that Locke had requested Norris deliver for him – an incident that would have to have taken place between 1692 and 1693.[14] If this is indeed the case, it is one more piece in the puzzle of these entangled personal relations. For Norris had also corresponded with Masham, Locke's companion, previous to his correspondence with Astell. Perhaps to his amazement, certainly to Astell's, the Astell–Norris correspondence, published in 1695, immediately attracted a hostile response – as Astell believed from Locke, but in fact from Masham – in her anonymous *A Discourse Concerning the Love of God* (1696).

It is not difficult to see Norris's influence on the subsequent development of Astell's thought and her animus against Locke, in particular his theory of the association of ideas. Descartes, the philosopher who most profoundly influenced Astell, and whose Platonist idealism Locke followed Hobbes in rejecting, was also perhaps mediated through Norris.[15] Astell drew from the Cartesian *cogito* the following conclusion: if the great truths of existence were affirmed by the solitary thinking subject, and if the mental processes of the thinking subject facilitate reason, the claims of men to rule women are baseless and the equality of all believers that Christianity preaches had better include women or its very foundations are breached. Astell's defense of Cartesianism and critique of Locke on 'thinking matter' in *The Christian Religion as Profess'd by a Daughter of the Church of England* (1705) lie at the heart of her refutation of Locke's *The Reasonableness of Christianity* in particular and his epistemology in general.[16] Too frequently modern commentators have missed this, tracing her feminist reformism, like that of Mary Wollstonecraft and Harriet Taylor, whose views are otherwise so different, to an epistemology founded in Lockean sensationalist psychology.[17] Astell's assault on the marriage contract–social contract homology, a legacy of Hobbes and Locke and a paradigm for the future, was as percipient in *Reflections upon Marriage* as her assault on the Whig view of history in *An Impartial Enquiry*. She thus attacked the program of Locke and the circle surrounding the first Earl of Shaftesbury on all fronts.

The Astell–Norris correspondence, begun in 1693 although published only in 1695, had introduced a considerable female philosopher and theologian – as Norris himself acknowledged – but anonymously. If it was as a religious writer that Astell made her debut, it was as a theologian that she returned with her magnum opus, *The Christian Religion*. But she was equally famous as a political pamphleteer in her lifetime. Among the first to provide a published critique of Locke's *Two Treatises of Government*, in her *Reflections upon Marriage* of 1700, Astell undertook a critique of the Whig version of the history of the English Civil War in *An Impartial Inquiry into the Causes of Rebellion and Civil War in this Kingdom in an Examination of Dr. Kennett's Sermon, 31 Jan. 1703/4 and Vindication of the Royal Martyr* of 1704. From 1703 to 1709, as an already established writer known for her support of women's causes, she had been engaged – probably by her publisher and correspondent, Richard Wilkin – as a High Church Tory pamphleteer, and in this capacity she produced two important pamphlets in the debate on the occasional conformity of dissenters, the issue on which religious toleration in fact turned, *A Fair Way with the Dissenters and their Patrons* and *Moderation truly Stated: or A Review of a Late Pamphlet, Entitul'd, Moderation a Vertue*. . . . In 1709 in a work entitled *Bart'lemy Fair, or an Enquiry after Wit in which due Respect is had to a Letter Concerning Enthusiasm*, Astell closed her career as a writer with an elegant philosophical response to Anthony Ashley Cooper, the third Earl of Shaftesbury and grandson of Locke's mentor, the first earl, whose *Letter Concerning Enthusiasm*[18] it targets.

Astell presents to the public a consistent High Church Tory profile and yet, as a champion of women's causes, this seems anomalous to modern readers. For instance, Philip Pettit, in his now renowned work on republicanism, alights on Astell's famous rhetorical question, '*If all Men are born free*, how is it that all Women are born slaves?' to claim her as an advocate for freedom as non-domination and the republican cause.[19] Astell's question has a peculiarly modern ring, it is true, but in fact the point had already been made less controversially by Richard Allestree (1619–81), author of *The Ladies Calling* (1673), a homiletic work, where he claimed that marriage is 'a Bargain and Compact, a Tyranny perhaps on the Man's part and a Slavery on the Woman's'.[20] If such a claim did not render Allestree a republican, it did not render Astell, an out-and-out royalist, one either. Indeed, Astell, like her contemporary, Judith Drake, purposefully addressed her works to Princess, later Queen, Anne, a known supporter of women's causes. Drake is noteworthy for the way in which she too makes the comparison between marriage and slavery, her work until recently attributed to Astell perhaps for this reason, and listed in Locke's library along with *Reflections upon Marriage* as Astell's work.[21] As constitutional monarchists, Astell and Drake were typical of early modern feminists, who were too pragmatic to connect the freedom they so ardently desired with a republicanism they could not imagine.

To what degree can we credit the environment for their success to a woman on the throne? Anne, princess of Denmark (1665–1714), the second daughter of James, Duke of York, who became King James II in 1685, became queen of Great Britain in 1702. Despite her father's Catholicism, and at the insistence of her uncle, King Charles II, she had been raised a Protestant and, in 1683, married the Lutheran Prince George of Denmark. Her favourite, Sarah Churchill, proved influential in persuading Anne to support the Protestant William III of Orange, married to Anne's elder sister Mary, when William overthrew their own father in 1688. When in 1700 the death of Anne's only child exhausted the supply of Protestant successors to the Stuart line, Anne agreed to the 1701 Act of Settlement, which designated the Hanoverian descendants of King James I as her successors, rather than her own exiled Catholic brother James, the Old Pretender. The constitutional issues raised by the royal succession provoked the political crises of Astell's era, and their resolution in terms of limitations on the monarchy and civil rights legislation set the path for the Westminster system of government.

It was in her capacity as the dedicatee of various works by women, both as Princess Anne of Denmark and as Queen Anne, that Astell applied to her for support for the education of women in her *Serious Proposal* (1696–7), the work that made Astell so notorious. It is worth reflecting on the reasons her publisher might have had for signing on as a Tory propagandist a woman already renowned for her insistence on women's need for education and her very critical reflections on marriage. Did Richard Wilkin appreciate perhaps the peculiar vulnerability of the Whigs to Astell's assaults? The extension of Hobbesian and Lockean contractarianism to family relations, always the bedrock of state institutions, produced anomalies that cast doubt on the whole argument for the social contract. Did Astell intentionally choose the marriage contract as a vehicle to mock the Whigs? Perhaps Wilkin understood what so many of her critics failed to appreciate: that Astell was as provocative as a Tory spokesperson as she was seditious as a champion of justice for women. In the 1706 Preface to her *Reflections upon Marriage*, Astell presents both faces. Alluding to the hostile reception earlier editions of the work had received, Astell restates her thesis with characteristic irony. Accused of 'stir[ring] up Sedition', 'undermin[ing] the Masculine Empire' and 'blow[ing] the Trumpet of Rebellion to the Moiety of Mankind', Astell turns to the culprits. Whiggish defenders of the right of resistance against the state and dissent against the church had better reflect on their treatment of women, she insists, noting that it is far from the intention of the author of the *Reflections* to exhort women to demand in the home the kind of freedom these liberals demand of the state. Has she been heard to exhort women 'to Resist, or to Abdicate' their spouses? Rather the contrary; she has insisted that they had better submit to the yoke that by the marriage contract they have bound themselves, even though 'the Laws of GOD and the Land make special Provision' for their release from a brutal and tyrannical 'Lord and Master'. Referring in the third person to the author of the *Reflections*, she declares:[22]

Far be it from her to stir up Sedition of any sort, none can abhor it more; and she heartily wishes that our Masters wou'd pay their Civil and Ecclesiastical Governors the same Submission, which they themselves extract from their Domestic Subjects. Nor can she imagine how she any way undermines the Masculine Empire, or blows the Trumpet of Rebellion to the Moiety of Mankind. Is it by exhorting Women, not to expect to have their own Will in any thing, but to be entirely Submissive, when once they have made choice of a Lord and Master, tho' he happen not to be so Wise, so Kind, or even so Just a Governor as was expected? She did not indeed advise them to think his Folly Wisdom, nor his Brutality that Love and Worship he promised in his Matrimonial Oath, for this required a Flight of Wit and Sense much above her poor Ability, and proper only to Masculine Understandings. However she did not in any manner prompt them to Resist, or to Abdicate the Perjur'd Spouse, tho, the Laws of GOD and the Land make special Provision for it, in a case wherein, as is to be fear'd, few Men can truly plead Not Guilty.

2. Astell's High Church Tory Milieu

It is important to try to recover the contours of Astell's political and philosophical milieu, and prominent political and ecclesiastical figures of her day who are now less well known, better to understand the anomaly of proto-feminist writers who nevertheless supported Tory, and in Astell's case, High Church Anglican causes. Hobbes, Descartes, Locke, and Shaftesbury, Malebranche and the Platonists, although well known indeed, are encountered by Astell perspectivally, and it behoves us to be open to seeing them through her eyes.[23] Likewise, because they are still terms in circulation, it is also important to try to recapture the meaning of Whig and Tory, High Church and dissenter in their freshness, tuning our ear to the peculiar style of late-seventeenth-century political debate. Astell, who could ascend to the heights of ecstatic Platonism, was, as her political pamphlets prove, quite capable of competing in the Grub Street gutter press, which put no limits on the level of vitriol beyond what the laws of seditious libel stipulated.[24] Precisely because of the libel laws, however, political writers sought surrogates in their analysis of contemporary events. So it was common to discuss the politics of 1689, and constitutional limits on the Crown stipulated in the Bill of Rights that William III was forced to sign as a condition of his accession, in terms of the abuse of the royal prerogative that led to the regicide of Charles I in 1649. This constant doubling is particularly marked in Astell's account of the English Civil War in *An Impartial Enquiry*, but is notable in political debate in general. It is as if participants kept the entire century before them, moving back and forth between the Elizabethan age and the last of the Stuarts, in their search for precedents at a time of unparalleled constitutional change. For this reason, we have to reach back to philosophers and ecclesiastics from the early Stuart period to recapture the milieu in which Astell was operating.

To set the political scene first, Whig and Tory politics were consolidated in the period 1679–81 during the heated struggle over the Exclusion Bill intended to exclude James, Duke of York, from the throne on the grounds of his conversion to Roman Catholicism in 1669. Initially terms of abuse, 'Whig', referring to horse thieves and later Scottish Presbyterians, was applied to those who claimed the exclusion power, while 'Tory', once designating Irish cattle rustlers and later papal outlaws, was applied to those who supported the hereditary right of James despite his Catholic faith. In 1679 *Anthony Ashley Cooper, the first Earl of Shaftesbury (1621–83) and patron of John Locke, had put together a party later known as the 'first Whigs', and a list of members of the House of Commons survives in which he had rated with the letters W for worthy and H for honest those whose views coincided with his own and on whom he could count.[25] In the course of the work of the 1689 Convention, summoned to resolve the political crisis centering on the 'abdication' of James II, the terms 'Tory' and 'Whig' gained greater definition, not yet referring to structured political parties but rather to predictable political alignments. Thirteen of the Whigs who worked on the committee to draft the Declaration of Rights that set the constitutional terms for the accession of William of Orange and Mary, daughter of James II, had been marked with a W or an H on Shaftesbury's list.[26] These 'radical Whigs' were distinguished from the first Whigs, not only because they were deemed worthy and honest, and had been active in the exclusion of James, but by other significant marks. Some had also been involved in the *Rye House Plot of 1683, some were members of the *Green Ribbon Club, and most, if not themselves dissenters, were associated with non-conformity to the established Church of England and its episcopacy.[27] No one better exemplifies the profile of a typical Whig, and at the same time the fluidity of politics in this period, than the first Earl of Shaftesbury.

Compared with the Whigs, the Tories in this period did not enjoy the same degree of identity or level of organization.[28] Under the leadership of Thomas Osborne, Earl of Danby, they were firmly supportive of the monarchy and implicated in its policies from 1681 to 1685. But the Settlement of 1689 had been a joint achievement and thus modified the division between the two factions. Most Tories came to accept Whig doctrines of limited constitutional monarchy rather than divine-right absolutism, and it was only in the course of the eighteenth century that the terms connoted structured political parties. Under Queen Anne, the Tories represented the resistance, mainly from the country gentry, to religious toleration and foreign entanglements, and Toryism became identified with Anglicanism and the squirearchy, where as Whiggism was increasingly associated with the aristocratic landowning families and the financial interests of the wealthy middle classes. John Pocock gives a witty characterization of this tendency and its consequences for political stereotyping when he notes that, when in the eighteenth century the faction out of power attacked the government,[29]

[t]hey attacked the alliance between high politics and high finance, which usually dominated both London and national politics through the structure of public credit that kept governments solvent and the government's creditors powerful. These governments were usually Whig, conducted by the great families of the Whig aristocracy, and when we call [their] politics . . . 'radical Whig', we are simply appealing to usages of the term like 'Old Whig', 'True Whig', 'Real Whig', 'Honest Whig', which indicated that there was a faction of purists according to whom the Whig aristocracy had deserted the principles of their ancestors.

If the Tories did not exhibit such a finely calibrated array of factions in the eighteenth century, it may have been because they represented the aristocratic fragment on their way out, shunted aside by the 'sure-to-rise' grand bourgeoisie, represented in England by the Whigs. But in the post-Restoration seventeenth century, when this tendency was not yet apparent and the Tories were still hegemonic, no one better typified Tory politics than *Edward Hyde, first Earl of Clarendon (1609–74), eminent statesman, author of the *History of the Rebellion*, much quoted by Astell in *An Impartial Enquiry* and an authoritative source for Tory historians of the eighteenth century.

Astell was a High Church Tory, the term 'High Church' referring to that group within the Church of England that stressed its historical continuity with the Catholic Church, placing great importance on the authority of the church, the claims of the episcopate and the nature of the Sacraments. To understand the significance of these affiliations, it is necessary to reach back deeper into the seventeenth century. Some of the earliest of the High Churchmen had resisted the attacks of Puritan reformers during the time of Elizabeth I, although the term did not come into general use until the late seventeenth century when *Archbishop William Laud and others argued the doctrine of the divine right of kings. Laud (1573–1645), archbishop of Canterbury, cast a long shadow over the seventeenth century, as both a churchman and a politician who contributed to setting High Church politics on their course, but was executed as a 'Romanist'. If the execution of an archbishop of Canterbury, although not the first, was an enormous shock to the established church, the 'martyrdom' of the king of the realm, who was also head of the church, had created an even greater dilemma. *Charles I, king of Great Britain (1600–49), was executed 30 January 1649. As the last regicide in the history of the realm, this requires some explaining. Charles I is glorified in the church calendar as the 'royal martyr'. The date of his execution was commemorated down the centuries by anniversary ceremonies, to which White Kennett's sermon preached on that day, Astell's subject in *An Impartial Enquiry*, belongs.

The Glorious Revolution of 1688 opened a new chapter for High Churchmen who had prospered under the reigns of Charles I and under his Stuart successors but now found their position compromised by the crowning of William III, the former William of Orange, known as the 'Dutch Imposter', which broke the line of succession to which their oaths committed them. Those who remained within the established church were excluded from ecclesiastical preferment as tainted with Jacobitism and largely fell into obscurity. But a significant number became 'nonjurors', a term referring to those churchmen who refused to take the oaths of allegiance to William and Mary after the Revolution of 1688, because they had previously taken similar oaths to James II. Even the death of James in 1701 was not seen to release them from their obligation, for they had sworn to be faithful not just to him, but also to 'his heirs and lawful successors', and the Pretender still lived. An Act of Settlement passed soon after William's accession had required the nonjurors 'to abjure the pretended Prince of Wales', whom they believed was the lawful heir of James II, and to acknowledge William III and each of his successors. The oath of allegiance had been altered, with the words 'rightful and lawful' being omitted, so that those who were not willing to recognize the new sovereigns as *de jure* rulers could at least acknowledge them as *de facto* sovereigns, and anyone who refused to take this altered oath was deprived of his post, whether lay or clerical. Only Archbishop Sancroft, 5 bishops and around 400 clergy chose to do so. Nonjurors insisted on the independence of the church from the monarchy and/or state in matters of spiritual authority. By excluding nonjuring bishops from practicing and replacing them with bishops appointed by the civil power, the monarchy was seen to have overstepped its prerogative, creating a schism within the Church of England. But by denying the monarch's divine and indefeasible right, the nonjurors for their part made themselves susceptible to the (unfair) claim that they supported the pope. Of the nonjuring bishops, *William Sancroft, (1617–93), Archbishop of Canterbury, to whom Astell first appealed for support with the presentation of her religious poetry, was the most important, and his career is illustrative of the troubled times for senior clergy. Thomas Tenison (1636–1715), Archbishop of Canterbury from 1694 to 1714, when Astell was publicly active, was also a significant figure, although of a very different ilk.

As we have noted, as much as the crisis of 1688–9 centered on the exclusion of a Catholic heir, just as much did it concern the political inclusion of Protestant dissenters. The term 'dissenter', used to designate those English Protestants who did not conform to the doctrines or practices of the established Church of England, was generally applied in England and Wales to Baptists, Congregationalists, Presbyterians and Unitarians, but also to independent groups such as the Quakers. Constitutional issues were at stake, for the very role of the monarch as head of the established church was liable to make all forms of religious dissent not only heretical but even treasonable, a view with which Astell concurred. The constitutional ramifications did not stop there, for religious dissent had important consequences for citizenship. As a technical disqualification from holding public office, nonconformity led to the practice of 'occasional conformity', whereby dissenters who attended an Anglican service once a year received a certificate of attendance from the vicar to qualify them for public service. Astell was not alone in campaigning against the perceived hypocrisy of this practice, and in the Parliament of 1702–5 three occasional conformity bills were introduced by the Tories to ban it. All were defeated, and it was not until the Tories gained power in 1711 that the Occasional Conformity Act, which forbade the practice, was finally passed, only to be repealed by the Whig-dominated Parliament in 1719.

For Astell, as a committed Anglican and no tolerationist, dissenters were an important target of her polemic. Consistently hostile to the notions of freedom of speech and freedom of the press, she argued that the nature of the established church stipulated strict adherence to its doctrines and that non-conformity was tantamount to treason. Astell, who contributed importantly in the pamphlet skirmishing on the occasional conformity debate, chose *Daniel Defoe (1661?–1731), a leading dissenter, as her target. Defoe was not quite the foe we might suspect from the invective Astell directed against him. He wrote a chapter on 'An Academy of Women' in *An Essay upon Projects* (1697) in response to Astell's *A Serious Proposal* and joined her in defending education for women, even if he took a cheap shot in characterizing her female academy as a Protestant nunnery. The pamphlet warfare in which Astell and Defoe engaged from 1703 to 1704 is the subject of Chapter 6.

3. The Philosophical Milieu, Hobbes, Descartes, Locke and Shaftesbury

Turning now to the philosophical milieu, *Hobbes, *Descartes, *Locke and Antony Ashley Cooper, the third Earl of Shaftesbury, represent for Astell important if different strands of thought. Thomas Hobbes (1588–1679),[30] although as far as I can establish never named by Astell, typifies the materialist philosophy that she rejects,[31] embracing rather the metaphysics of Descartes and the Cambridge Platonists against which Hobbes so vigorously campaigned.[32] René Descartes (1596–1650), French philosopher and mathematician, who disputed with Hobbes, rather won the day and is now regarded as the father of modern philosophy, having formulated basic philosophical positions on the relationship between mind and matter and between mathematical ideas and reality that were to shape philosophical debate for the future. Without doubt Descartes is the single most important philosophical figure Astell encountered, and it is largely in Cartesian terms that she responded to Hobbes, Locke and Malebranche.

That the work of Descartes should, in the seventeenth century, have been associated with manuals for self-improvement is not inappropriate. If Descartes's work, like that of Antoine Arnauld and Pierre Nicole, was aimed at the Jesuit stranglehold on theology, it was equally aimed at Calvinist casuists, who imported scholastic arguments to challenge the Catholic Church and even to question the very possibility of truth. Descartes's earliest work, his unfinished *Regulae ad Directionem Ingenium,* or *Rules for the Direction of the Mind,* written around 1628 but unpublished until 1701, represented a method for the arrival at certain knowledge in response to the sceptic Chandoux, who believed that science was at best founded on probabilities.[33] Descartes's *Discourse on Method* (1637), prefacing three treatises on mathematics and physics, had been followed by his *Meditations on First Philosophy* (1641), published together with six sets of *Objections,* among them those of Thomas Hobbes, Antoine Arnauld and Pierre Gassendi.

John Locke (1632–1704), philosopher and political secretary, was Astell's lifelong nemesis. From his 'Essay on the Roman Republic', written around 1666, and his 'Essay on Toleration', written in 1667 but published only in 1690, we know that Locke was almost as anti-clerical as Hobbes, admiring the civic religion of Rome and advocating religious toleration.[34] As a democrat he was even accused of republicanism, a slur tantamount to heresy and treason, as we have remarked. In 1666 Locke took up residence with his Oxford acquaintance, Ashley Cooper (1621–83), later first Earl of Shaftesbury, whom we have already profiled, acting as Cooper's physician as well as managing his affairs. Cooper, on being made Earl of Shaftesbury in 1672 and Lord Chancellor later in the same year, made Locke Secretary of Presentations, responsible for church affairs under the chancellor's care and required to appear with him on state occasions. It was in this capacity that he assisted Shaftesbury on the occasion of his famous speech 'Delenda est Cathargo', reported by Astell.[35] In 1673, Locke became secretary to the reconstructed Council of Trade until it was dissolved in 1674–5, whereupon he went to France, returning to Shaftesbury's service only in 1679.

Locke's *Two Treatises of Government,* written between 1679 and 1681, constantly revised and secretly guarded until their release was safe after 1689, belong to this period.[36] With Shaftesbury's dismissal in 1680 and his escape to Holland in 1682, Locke found himself implicated in Shaftesbury's plotting, and he was expelled from England in 1683.

Living quietly in Holland under the threat of extradition, Locke became associated with Philipp van Limborch, the Amsterdam theologian, and Jean Le Clerc, later his biographer. He returned to England after the 1688 Revolution and accepted William III's offer to become Commissioner of Appeals, a post he held until his death. His work *An Essay Concerning Humane Understanding* was published in 1690 and the *Two Treatises of Government* followed in the same year, canonizing Whig political theory for the next century. In 1691 Locke went to live in the household of Sir Francis and Damaris Masham in Essex. His *Reasonableness of Christianity*, which addressed the Cambridge Platonists, was published in 1695 and immediately attacked by John Edwards and John Norris, to whom Locke replied, the first at length in 'A Vindication of the Reasonableness of Christianity, etc., from Mr. Edwards Reflections' (1695); the second in 'Remarks upon Some of Mr. Norris' Books', written in 1693, but published only posthumously. In 1696 Locke was appointed member of a new Council of Trade, at which he worked conscientiously until his poor health forced his retirement in 1700, writing little before his death in 1704.[37] One may fairly say that Locke's religious writings occasioned Astell's *Serious Proposal, Part II* of 1697 and her *Christian Religion* of 1705, while his political writings animated her entire corpus.

Anthony Ashley Cooper (1671–1713), third Earl of Shaftesbury, moral philosopher and grandson of the first Earl of Shaftesbury, Locke's patron, is also worthy of brief notice. His *Characteristics of Men, Manners, Opinions and Times*, which first appeared in 1711 and was reprinted four times by 1773, indicates his religious scepticism, which may cast some light on Locke, who had superintended his education.[38] His most systematic work, *Inquiry Concerning Virtue*, which was first published surreptitiously by the deist John Toland, shows affinities to Cambridge Platonism, the work of Ralph Cudworth (1617–88) and *Richard Cumberland and became the inspiration for the 'moral sense theories' of Francis Hutcheson, his follower. It attracted the criticism of *John Leland, *William Warburton, *Bishop Berkeley and Astell, whose *Bart'lemy Fair* (1709) is a virulent attack on Shaftesbury's *Letter Concerning Enthusiasm* (1708).

The sceptical response to the Cartesian project of the English philosophers, Hobbes, Locke, Shaftesbury and later Hume, was of great significance in the history of philosophy. Among those anxious to refine the Cartesian method for certain knowledge, *Nicholas Malebranche (1638–1715) and Antoine Arnauld were important friendly critics. Some of Arnauld's criticisms still stand, in particular his charge that the proof of the *cogito* involves circularity – by affirming the truth of God's existence in terms of a prior certainty that 'whatever we clearly and evidently perceive is true'.[39] If Descartes distinguishes between our ideas and ideas in the mind of God, Arnauld asked, on what grounds do our ideas conclusively demonstrate mind to be incorporeal? Arnauld questioned the basis on which Descartes arrived at a categorical distinction between mind and body, and here Locke followed him. But Arnauld was a constructive critic, and it was in the spirit of Descartes's *Regulae* that he and Nicole set out in *The Art of Thinking* (1662) or *The Port Royal Logic*, as it is known, to improve on the Cartesian method for establishing certain truth.

Having countered Descartes on one side of the mind–body problem, the more sceptical English philosophers faced Malebranche on the other. For if Descartes's solution involved crediting human thinking with the power of certitude *a priori*, Malebranche subsumed all human cognition in the mind of God. Arnauld, in *True and False Ideas* (1683), published his rebuttal to the famous thesis of Malebranche's *Search after Truth* (1674), that 'we see all things in God', reclaiming relative cognitive autonomy for individuals. Arnauld showed Cartesian sensitivity in accounting for the element of representation in human cognition – something that Malebranche, in subsuming all ideas under the perfect (Platonist) ideas of God, denied. At the same time, he was unwilling to determine the ontological level of those representations, whether as emanations of divine ideas or as a reflection of the power of material objects and processes. Arnauld rejected Malebranche's Platonism as redundant – representations obviated the necessity for ideas – something that not even Locke was prepared to concede. To this Malebranche issued the countercharge that Arnauld was in grave danger of the Pyrrhonic scepticism he was devoted to refuting: the problem of knowing that our perceptions are true. For although we can perceive external objects, ideas of truth and falsity involve more than perceptions – they require ideas and the ability to compare ideas by means of criteria. The debate turned to a discussion over 'mental substance' in which Malebranche stalwartly maintained a distinction between mind and body that ruled out perceptions as containing ideas, and in which Arnauld charged Malebranche with redundancy for endowing Descartes's 'triangle in the mind' with ontological integrity. These are issues that were to engage Locke, Norris, Stillingfleet and Astell, as we shall see.

4. The Theological Climate: Arminianism and Neoplatonism

Mary Astell grew up in the Restoration Church and was a creature of some of its most symptomatic currents.[40] Her High Church Tory affiliations were firmly grounded in the epistemology and metaphysics of Platonism, as we have noted, a movement that, like its counterpart, Dutch *Arminianism, challenged Calvinism with a liberal theology of grace. Arminian soteriology, emphasizing love of God as the saving response to divine grace, had made two important departures from Calvinism and the soteriology of Foxe's *Book of Martyrs*, which represented Anglican orthodoxy under Queen Elizabeth and James I. It had powerful representatives in Archbishop Laud, Charles I's appointee, and the Dutch jurist Hugo Grotius (1583–1645), who visited England in 1613, thinkers who minimized the distance between the Catholic tradition of the Church Fathers, whom they rehabilitated, and Protestant soteriology. Arminianism emphasized good works as an omen of faith, and it rejected Aristotelian psychology for the Stoic unitary psyche that reconciled will and the passions in the belief that every act of desire involved assent. Its presupposition that to know and love God was within human reach had brought about the reintroduction of the doctrine of innate ideas, accepted by Grotius and Tilenus but debated by Descartes, Hobbes and Locke. It also involved theologians in the reconceptualization of perceptual, appetitive and cognitive processes, questions in the discussion of which the resources of Greek philosophy and the Church Fathers were martialed. These debates traversed the Greek schools, Platonism, Aristotelianism, Stoicism and Epicureanism, the metaphysics of the Church Fathers, the ecclesiology of the Conciliar movement and the polemics of the Counter-Reformation in what represented a great reaching back into the past to resolve schisms of the present. Puritan soteriology and Neoplatonist metaphysics, which began with a specific mandate to redefine the way of salvation in a newly constituted national church, ended with a general redescription of religious phenomena. The route traversed by Puritan divines and Cambridge Platonists was discursive – it took in early Christian mysticism, a reversion to the Church Fathers, and the Platonist tradition of Pythagoras, Chrysippus, Plato, Boethius, Clement of Alexandria and St. Augustine. It was countered on the Latitudinarian side by the pagan philosophies of the Stoics, Epicurus, Cicero and the modern Epicurean Gassendi.

If the philosophy of Descartes was an intervention catalyzing modern philosophy of mind in the reflective understanding of the *cogito*, the Platonists, undertaking to reinvestigate Christian fundamentals, made their own contribution to the reception of Descartes arrived by way of a redescription of the soul. For Cambridge Platonism, although like Arminianism concerned with theology of grace, targeted certain prevalent technical doctrines concerning the nature of spiritual entities, doctrines that were the outcome of philosophical investigations undertaken

by Hobbes, Descartes, Locke and their followers, to which Nicolas Malebranche, Antoine Arnauld, Ralph Cudworth, Henry More and less well-
known Platonists responded. Specifically under attack were Hobbesian
materialism, 'mortalism' (or the belief that the soul could not subsist
without the body) and Descartes's denial of extension to spirit.[41]

Neoplatonism came in different varieties, the ecstatic Platonism of
John Norris and Malebranche distinguishable from the 'rational' Platonism of the Cambridge Platonists, who eschewed 'rhapsody' and
'enthusiasm' in the belief that man came closest to God through reason.[42]
Malebranche, whose philosophy engaged Astell in the *Letters*, also
belongs to the reception of Descartes, but his solution to the metaphysical problem posed by mind–body dualism is a different one. Charles
McCracken in his excellent study of the British reception of Malebranche
concludes:[43]

Among British readers of his books, some, like [John] Sergeant, [Henry] Bolingbroke, and [James] Beattie, saw only the inconsistency or bizarreness of his
ideas; others like Norris, [Thomas] Taylor and [Arthur] Collier, seemed oblivious
to his defects and embraced large parts of his doctrine. But the most interesting
and fruitful response to his ideas came from those, notably [George] Berkeley,
[David] Hume and [Thomas] Reid, who recognized the inadequacy of his views
but who also perceived their subtlety and found in the *Search after Truth* a rich
vein of ideas that they could tap to their own philosophical profit.

Astell numbers among the latter and, despite doubts expressed in the
final letter appended to her *Letters Concerning the Love of God*, in her most
authoritative philosophical treatise, *The Christian Religion*, she returns to
Malebranchean occasionalism. The reasons she may have had for doing
so have been the subject of recent interesting speculation.[44] But, as we
shall see, Malebranche had views on biological differences between the
sexes that called into question women's capacity for reason that Astell
most certainly could not accept.

The Cambridge Platonists were a type of Platonist with whom, as
a Cartesian, Astell had much in common and for whom Archbishop
Sancroft may well have been the conduit. The current of Platonism fos-
tered at Cambridge produced a spiritual metaphysics that owed a great
deal to Cartesianism as a response to the 'materialism' of Hobbes, Sir
Robert Boyle (1627–61), William Cavendish (1592–1676), and those
who posited corporeal substance but denied immaterial substance. The
Cambridge Platonists were attracted to Cartesianism as a means of proving the existence of the incorporeal soul, arguing that the concept of
body proposed by the mechanists, particularly Hobbes, invited some

non-mechanical explanation of its movement, which they ascribed to spiritual substance. For if bodies consist of inert extended substance differentiated only by the size, shape and position of their constituent particles, they are incapable of self-motion. Accordingly, a motor of some kind must be posited and that, More claimed, was spirit, which drives, so to speak, the body in motion. More's theology, like that of Cudworth, was in many respects defensive, a reaction to materialism that saw Platonism and Cartesianism as the best redoubt against atheism. As he put it at the close of *An Antidote against Atheisme* (1653), 'That Saying is not less true in Politicks, *No Bishop, no King*, than this in Metaphysics, *No spirit, no God*'.

If Ralph Cudworth and Henry More reconceptualized the Neoplatonist soul as a spiritual, self-active, incorporeal substance and consciousness as a redoubling of the soul to produce a focussed centre,[45] the Cambridge Platonist John Smith (1618–52) held the movement of ideas to be analogical to the movement of sensations, transforming the latter from spiritual to physical entities.[46] He subscribed to the notion of spirit as an ecstatic union of the soul and divine substance.[47] The search for spiritual entities, vehicles of the soul, took the Cambridge Platonists in the direction of Neoplatonist pneumatology. The newly introduced doctrine of innate ideas and Cambridge Platonist Plotinian *nous* coalesced in a view of the world in which the ideas in the mind of God that lay at the foundation of the world were held to be both present in germ in the soul and out there to be 'seen' in the world. As a consequence, Cambridge Platonists described the processes of perception in a number of characteristic metaphors in which the individual is a spectator on the cosmic stage; by appealing to Platonist images of light and shadows to explain the principles of intelligibility and their surrogates; and by reference to music, harmony, numbers and specifically geometry as the fabric out of which the foundations of the world were built. Smith exhorted his followers, 'the Soul itself hath its sense, as well as the Body', declaring that 'to know the Divine Goodness, calls not for *Speculation* but Sensation, *taste and see* how good the Lord is'.[48]

Cambridge Platonists' preoccupation with optic metaphors led them to seek a medium of translation between the soul and God, most simply expressed in the notion of the mind as the mirror of God, from which they inferred the 'deification of man'.[49] True to the master, Cambridge Platonists held open the possibility of error in perceiving the 'Efflux from the Divine Light', calling for a '*Deification* as is not transacted merely upon the Stage of *Fancy* by Arrogance and Presumption, but in the highest Powers of the Soul by a living and quickening spirit of true Religion'.[50] Smith

Platonized the ancient *theatrum mundi* image of man as spectator and spectacle, locating it in the theatre of the Imagination: 'and there all those things which God would have revealed unto him were acted over *Symbolicallie*, as in a *Masque*'.[51] The role of memory and its rehearsal of sense-event sequences in the formation of consciousness was a notion of Hobbes, who extended it to account for history as a function of collective memory.[52] In this sense the Cambridge Platonist attempt to explain the soul by means of structures parallel to those of sense perception constituted an important contribution to the scientific discussion of philosophy of mind. Then as now, the crucial question was the status of such entities and the nature of proof. Here the Cambridge Platonists produced a heterogeneous array. Moving back and forth between analysis and metaphor, they were caught between the dispassionate requirements of philosophy and a commitment to prophecy as the contingent source of revealed truth. The upshot was the substitution of a physical for a metaphysical notion of the soul.[53] It was a small step from Cambridge Platonist belief in the visibility of the mind of God, through its projections in the world and in the mind, to Latitudinarian belief in the world as externalization of spirit accessible to discursive reason.[54] Reason, which became the test of Christianity, represented the deification of man.

Latitudinarianism characterized a tendency that grew up one generation after Cambridge Platonism. The notion of a Latitudinarian movement is tendentious, but the term is convenient to isolate certain characterstics that might be roughly labeled Latitudinarian, while allowing that this term is shorthand for a disparate group of thinkers who do not necessarily constitute a religious movement as such. Among these characteristics is a tendency to natural theology, to rational Christianity and to 'toleration' – the last a less consistent tendency. 'Latitude men' were believed to substitute reason and moderation for the 'airy Faith' of Puritanism and its Calvinist soteriology. [55] Convicted of being 'time servers' or 'trimmers', and accused by *Richard Baxter of being Arminians and followers of Descartes, 'reason, reason, reason' was believed to be 'their only Trinity'.[56] Defended in turn by the Cambridge Platonist Henry More, and with some claim to being the Cambridge Platonists' legitimate successors, the Latitude men recommended Christian piety and 'the inner life' as a salve for doctrinal dissension. Such a pietism characterized a heterogeneous array of devotional works, in fact, including those of thinkers as diverse as Richard Allestree, Simon Patrick and John Tillotson, who saw 'a perswasive to frequent communion' as an inducement to inner piety, as compared with the noisy preaching and praying of the Puritans.[57] This diversity once again casts doubt on this tendency's constituting a religious movement as such. Robert South, in the same vein, had compared the new soteriology, in which faith stands 'by metonym' for 'the obedience of an holy life performed in the strength or virtue of such a persuasion', with Puritan 'solafidianism', a 'naked inoperative faith', which the Puritans would characterize as a 'Recumbency and rowling upon a naked Christ'.[58]

The Latitude men, otherwise disparate, could be said to be united only in their rejection of the Arminian label and of the whole 'controversy about those matters', seeking instead a 'middle [way] betwixt the *Calvinists* and *Remonstrants*', between the Manicheism of the Puritans and the Pelagianism of the Cambridge Platonists.[59] This did not prevent them from using the language of the ecstatic Platonists. Simon Patrick had conceived the love of God as a medium between the soul and God, inflamed passions having the power to close the distance between them, representing the heat generated by the soul's motion.[60] Both Joseph Glanvil and Patrick spoke of human affections giving form to the spirit as reason. In this way, love of God represented a stream of affectivity flowing between the soul and God as well as the high road to salvation, conforming both to the requirments of Arminian soteriology, as the 'spirit of Elijah', and to the Latitudinarian requirement that reason be externalized in socially verifiable phenomena subject to the ministerial guidance of the church.[61] To a degree that has remained largely unrecognised, John Locke, whose *Essay Concerning Human Understanding* pioneered the propositional logic of modern analytic philosophy, was responding to doctrinal and ecclesiological imperatives that placed him in the forefront of the Latitude men.

Historical hindsight has served to obscure the degree to which these questions arose in the context of specific religious and ecclesiological disputes in which the very survival of the early modern national church was at stake. Calvinist predestinarian philosophy, which had infused both orthodox Protestantism and the Puritan sects, gave rise to serious ambiguity on questions of membership in the community of the elect, the role of the church in salvation and the role of government in the church. To some extent, but not always, theological debates were politically driven. To an almost corresponding degree, political treatises were theologically driven, and in between, a great number of works reflected genuine piety and a concern to understand the truth of Scripture. Church–state relations dominated the debates not only up to and including the Civil War, but through the Restoration as well, reflected in the preponderance of attention given to them in political treatises as well. So, for instance, Elizabeth I, demonstrating her customary acuity, had early recognized the political dynamism of Puritanism, standardizing sermons with the introduction of the *Book of Homilies*, forbidding 'prophesying' and exhibiting a general distrust of the clergy. It was this general climate of anti-clericalism that pervaded the works of Erastians and Latitudinarians like Locke, to whom the term was often applied. Standing over against them were those who tried to renew Anglican metaphysics and ecclesiology in Platonist explorations of the nature of the soul, as the foundation for Protestant soteriology, and an intellectual elite that might translate into an ecclesiastical hierarchy. On the other side stood those unrelenting Presbyterians and Independents whom the national Catholic Church, try as it would in this period, could not accommodate. The possibility that the original Protestant–Catholic schism might remain an open wound into which increasing numbers of sectarians would fall was considered both politically and ecclesiastically terrifying. Non-conformity, a matter of high treason to some, Astell among them, was the occasion on which theories of toleration were pioneered in the Latitudinarian camp, especially by Locke. Of all the debates on the life of faith and salvation, the debate over toleration and occasional conformity was to be the most heated.

Such a description is already too intentionally schematic and programmatic to account for the contingent and dialogic nature of the debates as they unfolded. It serves, however, as a summary with the advantage of providing historical hindsight on what the debates served to accomplish. To this very important task of redefining not only the nature of the church and its mission in the new Protestant dispensation, but also the life of faith and devotion, its epistemological and ontological foundations in the nature of mind, Mary Astell contributed along with John Norris, John Locke and Damaris Masham, and by implication Masham's father, Ralph Cudworth, conforming Whigs like White Kennett, and dissenters like James Owen and Daniel Defoe, Astell's interlocutors. Out of these technical discussions of the nature of the soul, the language and concepts of modern philosophy of mind were developed. Astell was a contributor on the losing side.

5. Locke and the Neoplatonists: Norris and Malebranche

Locke's *Essay Concerning Human Understanding* had been written to investigate philosophy of mind in light of the new corpuscular science of *Boyle, Harvey and Newton. Locke's reflections on the philosophy of Descartes had caused him to conclude that thinking was not the sole activity of mind, arguing that the doctrine of innate ideas led to dogmatism, discouraging critical thought. However, it would be a mistake to see Locke as either a nominalist or a materialist of the Hobbesian sort. A physical realist, he focused on the primary and secondary qualities of the objects of sensation. Primary qualities are powers inhering in the objects of which we form an impression in the mind – extension, mass, solidity, fluidity and so on. Secondary qualities are resemblances in the mind that primary qualities have the power to effect – such notions as bulk, colour, smell, sound and temperature. Locke thus maintained a role for ideas as intermediaries between the mind and its objects, although challenged by Stillingfleet to abandon it.

Locke, whose longest chapter in the *Essay Concerning Human Understanding* is on 'powers', generated a theory of perception whose startling originality was to influence philosophers as diverse as the sensationalist psychologists and 'man-machine' theorists, Condorcet, Helvetius and d'Holbach, on the one hand, and Hegel, on the other. It may come as a surprise, then, to learn to what extent Nicolas Malebranche had preceded him in these conclusions. Malebranche undertook to investigate the same range of problems in Cartesian philosophy: matter as extension; the autonomy of physical bodies and explanation of their behaviour in terms of the internal movement of their parts; and the understanding of forms, qualities, powers and faculties as secondary qualities, mental constructs generated in the process of explanation. Malebranche thus subscribed to Cartesian dualism, positing the existence of the soul as distinct from the body and the awareness of mental states as qualitatively different from sense perception. Like Locke he insisted on 'ideas' as necessary entities mediating between the mental and physical realms. In his desire to dislodge the Platonist concept of innate ideas, he developed the notion of 'seeing all things in God'. Innate ideas involve the impossible regress of a possible infinity of ideas exactly replicated over and over in the mind of each individual and yet of a universally common structure – so geometry is the same in France and China. Malebranche applied Occam's razor, arguing rather that we are given ideas along with sense experiences, both informing them but logically separable from them. Arnauld in *True and False Ideas* took Malebranche to task for a fallacy analogous to that of which he accused Descartes, which was to believe that the perception of external objects could only take place through surrogate representations. Malebranche's explanation of the moon illusion, for instance, posited a series of misrepresentations of the distance between the horizon and the meridian that made it seem smaller. His account of dreams and hallucinations was consistent with the view that ideas as mental constructs mediating sense perception could be mistaken but, at the same time, that where they were true, they conformed to a divine pattern in the thing, and were not simply an innate capacity of the soul to generate true ideas.

Locke scholars have long pondered what unmentioned subject it was, as he tells us in the 'Epistle to the Reader', that had perplexed him and friends meeting in his chamber and caused him to begin writing the *Essay Concerning Human Understanding*. At the very least, we can see that Locke was deeply implicated in the revisions of Cartesianism undertaken by Malebranche and Arnauld and that these set the range of problems he wished to investigate. Nevertheless, certain aspects of his thought remained relatively undeveloped, in particular experience and its modes. His emphasis on knowledge as the process of thinking, rather than knowledge as an object of the mind, suggested the importance of different modes of experience: feeling, enjoying, suffering, reflecting, remembering, deliberating, reasoning, judging and willing. Given important definition in the philosophy of Aristotle, these modes had received extensive treatment by the scholastics to whom Locke was otherwise indebted. But although emphasizing the relational quality of ideas, he devoted relatively little attention to differentiating modes of knowing, or even the phenomena of pleasure and pain, on which the motivational structure of his theory depended. He similarly neglected to distinguish between reasons and causes, avoiding a systematic investigation of the physical structure of mind as the bearer of cognitive experience. In this way he circumvented some of the most difficult issues with which the Cambridge Platonists, and Astell after them, had attempted to grapple.

John Norris, in his *Cursory Reflections upon a book called, an Essay Concerning Human Understanding*, appended to his *Christian Blessedness, or Discourses upon the Beatitudes of our Lord and Saviour Jesus Christ*,[62] convicted Locke of not having 'given an account of the nature of ideas'. This Locke himself tells us in his response, 'Remarks upon Some of Mr. Norris' Books, Wherein he asserts P. Malebranche's Opinion of our seeing all things in God',[63] signed by him and dated at Oates, the Masham home, in 1693. Locke had made his own critical notes on Malebranche's philosophy, recorded in his journal in 1684–5, at about the time that Astell and Norris began their correspondence, and had considered adding a new chapter to the revised edition of his *Essay* to 'shew the weakness of [Malebranches' hypothesis] very clearly', an emendation that did not come to pass, however. Locke in his comments had charged

Malebranche and Norris with egregious heterodoxy but, foreseeing that it served him poorly to put them in print, only days before his death he advised his executor to refrain from publishing his *Examination of Malebranche*, noting, 'it is an opinion that spreads not and is like to die of itself or at least to do no great harm'.[64]

Locke's thirty-five numbered remarks deal summarily with the arguments of Malebranche as expressed by Norris in his *Cursory Reflections* and in *Reason and Religion; or the Grounds and Measures of Devotion Parts I and II*.[65] They are a useful guide to his own difficulty with the problem of ideas and the reasons for his reluctance to develop further explanation of perception and its modes. He begins by quoting Norris's *Cursory Reflections*:[66]

There are some, who think they have given an account of the nature of ideas, by telling us, 'we see them in God', as if we understood, what ideas in the understanding of God are, better than when they are in our own understandings; or their nature were better known, when it is said, that 'the immediate object of our understandings are the divine ideas, the omniform esssence of God, partially represented or exhibited'.

Locke notes sardonically that this seems to settle the matter: 'the divine essence is more familiar, and level to our knowledge than any thing we think of'.[67] Leaving aside refutation of such an incongruous hypothesis, Locke turns to Norris's specific complaint – that Locke gives an inadequate account of the nature of our ideas – and what could be meant by it. He points out that Norris could not be complaining that he, Locke, 'should make known to men their ideas; for I think nobody can imagine that any articulate sounds of mine, or any body else, can make known to another what his ideas, that is, what his perceptions are, better than what he himself knows and perceives them to be; which is enough for affirmations or negations, about them'.[68] He quite rightly judges that Norris's complaint is that he fails to account for 'their causes and manner of production in the mind, *i.e.* in what alteration of the mind this perception consists'. 'As to that', he says:

I answer, no man can tell; for which I not only appeal to experience, which were enough, but shall add this reason, viz. because no man can give any account of any alteration made in any simple substance whatsoever; all the alteration we can conceive being only of the alteration of compounded substances; and that only by a transposition of parts. Our ideas, say these men, are the 'divine ideas, or omniform essence of God,' which the mind sometimes sees, and sometimes not. Now I ask these men, what alteration is made in the mind upon seeing? For there lies the difficulty, which occasions the inquiry.

Locke elaborates with his example of the man seeing or not seeing a marigold, which is not in itself problematic. The problem is rather at the level of explanation: 'what alteration is made in his mind; what changes that has in itself, when it sees what it did not see before, either the divine idea in the understanding of God, or, as the ignorant think, the marygold in the garden'. He challenges Norris and the Malebranchistes: 'I desire them to explain to me, what the alteration in the mind is, besides saying, as we vulgar do, it is having a perception, which it had not the moment before'.[69] Locke does not pretend to be able to give an account himself of the physiological or mental processes of perception. But he seizes on the arguments provided by the Malebranchistes to buttress their claim to be able to do so. The first is economy, which Locke summarizes in Remark 3:[70]

P. Malebranche says, 'God does all things by the simplest and shortest ways,' *i.e.* as it is interpreted in Mr. Norris's Reason and Religion [1689, Part II. Contemplation II. §17, p. 195], 'God never does any thing in vain'.

Locke located a number of difficulties with this argument. He launched a serious attack on occasionalism, which allowed Malebranche and his followers to account for physical causation as contingent rather than necessary, making superfluous the machinery of sense perception. The Malebranchistes held firm to the notion that God was the only efficient cause of all our sensations, which left it unclear how other bodies impinge on the processes of perception; they maintained that other bodies enter the causal chain 'occasionally', not as necessary but as contingent agents. Locke argued that if making present to the mind the idea of God were God's only purpose in allowing the perception of objects to be the occasional cause of this idea, as the Malebranchistes maintained, God could certainly have arrived at more economical means to achieve the given effect. For the blind are as capable of such an idea as the seeing, the deaf as the hearing, and so on. Locke puts it rather nicely:[71]

For if the perception of colours and sounds depended on nothing but the presence of the object affording an occasional cause to God Almighty to exhibit to the mind the idea of figures, colours, and sounds; all that nice and curious structure of those organs is wholly in vain: since the sun by day, and the stars by night, and the visible objects that surround us, and the beating of a drum, the talk of people, and the change made in the air by thunder; are as much present to a blind and deaf man, as to those who have their eyes and ears in the greatest perfection. He that understands optics ever so little, must needs admire the wonderful make of the eye, not only for the variety and neatness of its parts; but as suited to the nature of refraction, so as to paint the image of the object in the retina; which these men must confess to be all lost labour, if it contributes nothing at all, in the ordinary way of causes and effects, to the producing that idea in the mind. But that only the presence of the object gave occasion to God to show to the mind that idea in himself, which certainly is as present to one that has a gutta serena, as to the quicksightedest man living.

Locke throws back the argument that Norris had thrown at him: 'we do not know how, by a natural operation, this can produce an idea in the mind'. This time it is he who makes the charge of hubris – against the Malebranchistes: 'and therefore (a good conclusion!) God, the author of nature, cannot this way produce it. As if it were impossible for the Almighty to produce any thing, but by ways we must conceive, and are able to comprehend'.[72] In fact Locke's charge is unfair, for Malebranche was not satisfied to presume knowledge of the nature of God as a sufficient explanation of physical causation. He never ceased to inquire into the causal mechanisms of natural phenomena, following contemporary developments in physics and chemistry and arriving, for instance, at an explanation of colour differences in terms of frequencies of vibrations.[73]

In his fourth remark Locke accurately locates the central thrust of the proposition 'seeing all things in God' as an attempt to resolve the problem of universals: 'The perception of universals also proves that all beings are present to our minds; and that can only be by the presence of God, because all "created things are individuals"'.[74] But once again Locke finds ways of accounting for the role of ideas in perception – in the form of mental processes of representation and abstraction – more economical than by the invocation of 'universals' or God as a *deus ex machina*. He refers to 'circles', to 'bigness', to 'equidistance' and other abstractions from particulars that had been the subject of the *Essay Concerning Human Understanding*, Book 4, Chapter 3, §29.[75] But to the question 'wherein universality consists', he answers, 'only in representation, abstracting from particulars', without, however, specifying further. Locke goes on to demolish a series of deductive arguments made by Norris as to why 'seeing all things in God' is an answer to the problem of universals. We may 'have a distinct idea of God', he says in Remark 5, but whether it is an adequate idea of God is another matter. In Remark 6, he considers Norris's argument that 'we have an idea of infinite before the idea of finite, because we conceive infinite being, barely by conceiving being, without considering, whether it be finite or infinite', declaring it a possible case of mistaking 'priority of nature, for priority of conception'.[76] He points to the obvious fallaciousness of Norris' argument that because 'God made all things for himself', therefore we 'see all things in him', which Norris takes to be proof that God could not permit us to perceive things immediately, apart from perceiving God in them, without violating his own purposes. But it is an empirical matter whether people can perceive things without at the same time perceiving God, Locke points out, and experience affirms that they can. Moreover, number, extension and essences do not exhaust the contents of the mind, as Norris suggests, since they 'are not half the ideas that take up men's minds', demonstrating that we are only half made for God if they demonstrate anything at all.[77] In what the other half consists, however, is the area in which Locke is weakest, as we have noted.

Locke levels the charge against the Malebranchistes that they anthropomorphize God, presuming to know his essence from the contents of the human mind. They have moved from Platonist preoccupations with spiritual bodies as real intermediaries between the divine and human realms to the notion of the mind as a mirror of God. Perhaps their metaphysics are even pantheist.[78] He quotes Norris:[79] ' "The simple essences of things are nothing else but the divine essence itself considered with his connotation, as variously representative, or exhibitive of things, and as variously imitable or participable by them" [*Reason and Religion*. Part I, Contempl. V. §19, p. 82]; and this he tells us are ideas [*ibid.*, §20]'. Because 'God knew, from eternity, he could produce a pebble, a mushroom, and a man', these 'ideas' are deemed to belong to his essence and, once realized, represent his extension! At this rate, as Locke remarks, 'we will allow ourselves to be ignorant of nothing; but will know even the knowledge of God, and the way of his understanding!'[80]

Locke has his own way out. The very consideration that led the Malebranchistes to see ideas as an extension of God, his infinite powers externalized in physical objects, allows us to see intervening physical mechanisms as divinely sanctioned instrumentalities. If 'God has always a power to produce any thing that involves not a contradiction',[81] he also 'can give that power to another; or, to express it otherwise, make any idea the effect of any operation on our bodies'[82] – a notion that does not violate the principle of non-contradiction, as he notes. Indeed, without such a notion of intervening mechanisms, Locke argues, we are brought back 'to the religion of Hobbes and Spinosa', requiring the direct intervention of God in each act-event sequence, and 'resolving all, even the thoughts and will of men into an irresistible fatal necessity'.[83] As we shall see, to associate occasionalism with 'the religion of Hobbes and Spinoza' was not as innocent a suggestion as it may seem. It was a charge of pantheism that in the theological climate of the day was tantamount to heresy. Locke's explicit purpose in *The Reasonableness of Christianity* had been to show that Platonism was a form of pantheism that served to undermine Christian piety rather than promoting it.

The superiority of Locke's explanation, which involves the refutation of the notion of occasional causes as a spurious addendum to the Male-branchiste argument that all beings exhibit the mind of God, lies in its success in explaining the following phenomena systematically:[84]

Outward objects are not, when present, always occasional causes. He that has long continued in a room perfumed with sweet odours, ceases to smell though the room be filled with those flowers; though, as often as after a little absence he returns again, he smells them afresh. He that comes out of bright sun-shine into a room where the curtains are drawn, at first sees nothing in the room; though those who have been there some time, see him and every thing plainly. It is hard to account for either of these phenomena, by God's producing these ideas upon the account of occasional causes. But by the production of ideas in the mind, by the operation of the object on the organs of sense, this difference is easy to be explained.

Locke appeals to the appropriateness of his account as meeting the requirements of what is required to be explained. Compare it, he suggests, to occasionalism and its ramifications:[85]

No machine of God's making can go of itself. Why? Because the creatures have no power; can neither move themselves, nor any thing else. How then comes about all that we see? Do they do nothing? Yes, they are the occasional causes to God, why he should produce certain thoughts and motions in them. The creatures cannot produce any idea, any thought in man. How then comes he to perceive or think? God upon the occasion of the motion in the optic nerve, exhibits the colour of a marygold or a rose to his mind. How came that motion in his optic nerve? On occasion of some particles of light striking on the retina, God producing it, and so on. And so whatever a man thinks, God produces the thought; let it be infidelity, murmuring, or blasphemy. the mind doth nothing; his mind is only the mirror that receives the ideas that God exhibits to it, and just as God exhibits them; the man is altogether passive in the whole business of thinking.

It is noteworthy how Cartesian Locke's solution to the problem of occasionalism really is. Pointing to Norris's unwarranted inference from the principle that God is the cause of all things, the conclusion that he admits no intermediate causes, Locke asks, 'But, because all being was from him, can there be nothing but God himself? or, because all power was originally in him, can there be nothing of it communicated to his creatures?'.[86] His answer alludes to the famous Cartesian dualism of the clockmaker:[87]

For which (I beseech you, as we can comprehend) is the perfectest power; to make a machine, a watch, for example, that when the watch-maker has withdrawn his hands, shall go and strike by the fit contrivance of the parts; or else requires that whenever the hand, by pointing to the hours, minds him of it, he should strike twelve upon the bell?

Locke concludes his 'Remarks upon Some of Mr. Norris' Books' by confessing to his inability to get much further in his account of ideas beyond arguing for their logical necessity – never a sufficient answer to him – and their confirmation by experience:[88]

Ideas may be real things, though not substances; as motion is a real being, though not a substance; and it seems probable that, in us, ideas depend on, and are some way or other the effect of motion; since they are so fleeting; it being, as I have elsewhere observed, so hard, and almost impossible, to keep in our minds the same unvaried idea, long together, unless when the object that produces it is present to the senses; from which the same motion that first produced it being continued, the idea itself may continue.

In Remark 17,[89] Locke expresses humility in discussing the inadequacy of his account of ideas that does not prepare us for the momentous departure in his theory of propositional truth that follows from it. Precisely because we have no direct access to things in themselves, or to ideas in themselves, truth can lie only in the relation between ideas, he declares. With direct reference to Norris's *Reason and Religion*,[90] Locke then embarks on one of the most succinct accounts of what is to become the canon of modern analytic philosophy:[91]

Truth lies only in propositions. The foundation of this truth is the relation that is between our ideas. The knowledge of truth is that perception of the relation between our ideas to be as it is expressed.

In one of the simplest formulations of the conventional theory of language, Locke goes on profoundly to observe:[92] 'The immutability of essence lies in the same sounds, supposed to stand for the same ideas. These things considered, would have saved this learned discourse'. Remarks 21 through 23 assert important ontological axioms: that 'whatever exists, whether in God, or out of God, is singular'; that 'if no proposition should be made, there would be no truth or falsehood; though the same relations still subsisting between the same ideas, is a foundation of the immutability of truth in the same propositions, whenever made'. The constant signification of words is a function of human conventions – which Locke illustrates with reference to Descartes's triangle.[93]

He broaches the question of different ways of feeling but, once again implying the inadequacy of the mind to approach the mechanisms accounting for such differences directly, he restricts himself to their semantic manifestations. Referring to Norris's *Reason and Religion*,[94] he notes:[95]

He that considers the force of such ways of speaking as these, 'I desire it, pray give it me, she was afraid of the snake, and ran away trembling;' will easily conceive how the meaning of the words 'desire' and 'fear,' and so all those which stand for intellectual notions, may be taught by words of sensible significations.

Little attention has been paid to Locke's refutation of Norris, but in the course of it he succinctly develops basic tenets of analytic philosophy on propositional truth, signs, signification and a theory of learning that reach back to Hobbes and even further back to Saint Augustine and forward to twentieth-century analytic philosophers.

It is worth noting that in the more than 120 pages Damaris Masham devotes to refutation of Norris's *Practical Discourses*, she reproduces none of Locke's arguments verbatim, although in some important instances alluding to and developing his ideas, testimony to her independence of mind, if such were needed. Masham may have been an important source for the influence of Malebranche and the Cambridge Platonists on Locke. From his correspondence of January 1682, we learn that Locke discussed with her John Smith's Discourse 'Concerning the True Way or Method of Attaining Divine Knowledge'[96] and that Masham was not inclined to dismiss Smith's Platonist taxonomy of knowledge. She even conceded with him that there may be a 'Higher Principle', named by Henry More 'Divine Sagacitie': 'a Degree of Perfection to be attain'd to in this Life to which the Powers of meere Unassisted Reason will never Conduct a Man', quickly reassuring Locke, 'not that I think more meanly of Reason I beleeve then you do, much less would lay aside the use of it as many do'.[97] Locke, whose epistemological system does not admit differentiation of modes, had quickly rejected Smith's specification of 'four types of knowledge', preferring to call them 'several degrees of the love of God and practise of vertue', which may assist knowledge but do not constitute different types of knowledge. Reason is a natural faculty; analysis cannot dissolve it into parts but, like eyesight, it can be assisted. Use of the eye metaphor, with which the *Essay Concerning Human Understanding* begins, suggests that for Locke too, the image of 'seeing all things in God' was powerful, if controversial: 'The Understanding, like the Eye, whilst it makes us see, and perceive all other Things, takes no notice of it self: And it requires Art and Pains to set it at a distance and make it its own Object'.[98]

Locke's *Correspondence* gives several instances of Masham's efforts to explain the Platonists to Locke – and one of her despair at being asked by him to further explain Smith's book, where she begs Locke:[99]

let me know what those things that you dislike in it, without applying your self (I beseech you) any more to mee to make you understand any thing which you did not before. What you Comprehend not I am not very likely to make you, and you may be still ignorant if the Author have not sufficiently explain'd himself.

Hutton takes this statement by Masham to express an early lack of confidence compared with her mature self-assurance as a follower of Locke.[100] But it may equally be interpreted as expressing the view that Locke is never going to commit himself on such matters because of epistemological doubts. Masham's letter of 1688 further suggests that she does not harbour Lockean scepticism on such matters just because the mechanical details of perception cannot be supplied:[101]

Besides, that being my self Cur'd of some sort of Scepticisme by arguments However Solid in themselves have beene to me effectual, I think that I may much more Advantageously employ my Houres in Pursuing the end of these Speculations then in indeavouring to Extricate those Difficulties that the Witts of Men have Intangled them with.

6. Astell's *Letters Concerning the Love of God*

It is to the Malebranchean thesis of seeing all things in God that Astell responds in the *Letters Concerning the Love of God*. Norris, like Malebranche, drew from the Cartesian mind–body dualism the radical conclusion that minds and bodies do not interact: 'And therefore since Spirits make no resistance against Bodies, it is not possible that Bodies should have any Action, or make any Impression upon Spirits'.[102] Sensation and cognition require divine intervention, and physical objects are only the 'occasion' for that intervention: 'Tis not the most delicate Fruit, or the richest Perfume, that delights either our Tast or our Smell', he says, 'but 'tis God alone that raises Plesure in us by the Occasion of these bodies'.[103] Norris drew his position to Astell's attention in his letter of November 13, 1693:[104]

though according to the Law of this State Pain be always occasioned by some Motion or Change in the Parts of the Body, yet since 'tis the Soul that truly feels it, and GOD that truly raises it, I can easily conceive, that God can, if he pleases, raise the Sensation of Pain in her though no Change be made in the Body, nay though she had no body at all. That GOD for instance can raise the Sensation of Burning in the soul without any Impression of Fire upon her Body.

Such a position entailed the absurd corollary that, in the first place, we can never in fact know that we have these sensations or what their causes are; and second, that even if the material world did not exist, we could still have them. To Norris's conclusion that God, as the only causally efficacious being, must be the only object of our love, Astell countered that God, if he is the only cause of our pleasure, must correspondingly be the only cause of our pain. She softens the barb with the observation that 'that which Causes Pain does us Good as well as that which Causes Pleasure',[105] to which Norris, in his letter of 13 October 1693, concedes, adding rather arbitrarily that 'the pain comes from God only indirectly and by Accident'.[106]

Malebranche's doctrine of seeing all things in God is the focus of this set of issues. But in a letter to Norris dated 14 August 1694, after the correspondence was completed, Astell revisits Norris's argument, putting the case *against* Malebranchean occasionalism on two scores: 'First, That this Theory renders a great Part of GOD's Workmanship Vain and Useless', and 'Secondly, That it does not comport well with his Majesty'.[107] Astell posed the following question with direct reference to More's doctrine of 'the spirit of nature' and implicit reference to Cudworth's theory of 'Plastic Nature':[108]

Why therefore may there not be a *sensible Congruity* between those Powers of the Soul that are employ'd in Sensation, and those Objects which occasion it? Analogous to that vital Congruity which your Friend Dr. *More* (*Immor. of the Soul, B. II. Chap.* 14. S. 8) will have to be between some certain Modifications of Matter, and the plastick Part of the Soul, which Notion he illustrates by that Pleasure which the perceptive Part of the soul (as he calls it) is affect with by good Musick or delicious Viands, as I do this of Sensible by his of vital Congruity, and methinks they are so symbolical that if the one may be admitted the other may.

Norris responded to Astell's disagreement in the *Letters*, arguing: 'The Bodies that are about us are not the true Causes of those Sensations which we feel at their Presence, but . . . GOD only is the Cause of them, who being the Author of our Beings has the sole Power to act upon our Spirits, and to give them new Modifications. I say *Modifications*, for that well expresses the general Nature of Sensation'.[109] Taylor concludes, and here he disagrees with both Ruth Perry and Jacqueline Broad: 'Astell, it seems clear, did not conceive of her final contribution to *Letters* as the last word on the subject of "occasionalism"; by the time she wrote *Christian Religion*, at least, she had carefully considered and accepted Norris's reply'.[110]

Astell's solution to the mind–body problem and challenge to Male-branchean occasionalism in terms of a notion of 'sensible congruity', a revision of More's concept of 'vital congruity', was a move both bold and plausible. But, as we shall see, it brought her perilously close to the position of Locke. The Malebranchean notion that a personal God would be required to exercise his powers in every instance of human sensation credits the divinity with little economy and 'render[s] a great Part of GOD's Workmanship vain and useless', Astell notes. But she is able to salvage divine purpose with respect to the organs of sense, arguing: 'it seems more agreeable to the Majesty of GOD, and that Order he has established in the World, to say that he produces our Sensations medi-ately by his Servant Nature, than to affirm that he does it immediately by his own Almighty Power'.[111] Astell's appeal to divine majesty is con-sonant with arguments about divine design throughout her works, but she nevertheless fails to develop the notion of sensible congruity as a solution to the mind–body problem that she foreshadows. So in *A Serious Proposal, Part II* she expresses her doubts: 'We know and feel the Union between our Soul and Body, but who amongst us sees so clearly, as to find out with Certitude and Exactness, the secret ties which unite two such different Substances, or how they are Able to act upon each other?'.[112] It is a reservation that she repeats in *The Christian Religion*, where she remarks: 'neither do I comprehend the Vital Union between my Soul or Body...though I am sure that it is so'.[113] In that work Astell seems to revert to an explicit defence of occasionalism:[114]

Without controversy, it is for very good Reasons that [God] has *so* united a Corruptible Body to an Immortal Mind, that the impressions which are made on the former, shall be perceiv'd and attended with certain Sensations in the other. And this by ways altogether mysterious and incomprehensible, and only to be resolv'd into the Efficacy of the Divine Will.

As Taylor notes, what Astell offers here is simply a paraphrase of Norris's response to her renunciation of occasionalism in the *Letters*, where he had argued:[115]

GOD has united my Soul to a certain Portion of organized Matter [which] I call my Body....Other Bodies according to the Laws of Motion established in the World...make different Impressions upon it [and] since as far as they respect the Preservation of the Machine, and the good of the Bodily Life ... it is fit they should be attended with sensations essentially different, such as Pleasure and

Pain, which therefore GOD raises in the soul in Consequence of those general Laws of Union which he has established between it and the Body.

As Taylor further notes, Astell's 'second invocation of occasionalism, in which she describes the pleasures of eating as "the Powers of GOD giving you divers modifications,"' virtually repeats Norris's response to her dissent in *Letters*, where he had argued that 'GOD only [as] the Author of our Beings has the sole Power to act upon our Spirits, and to give them new Modifications' – where for *Modifications* we should read sensations.[116]

Was this simply a capitulation on Astell's part, or is there another explanation? While commentators have tended to treat Astell's arguments for and against occasionalism as incongruous, E. Derek Taylor and Sarah Ellenzweig have given important, if different, explanations in terms of the contemporary philosophico-political context for her work. Taylor gives an account of why Astell failed to develop the notion of sensible congruity foreshadowed in the last of her *Letters* and at the same time an explanation of why Astell prevaricates in *A Serious Proposal, Part II*, returning to the Malebranchean fold only in *The Christian Religion*. His answer is in terms of Astell's relation to Locke. As Ruth Perry has already noted, Astell's employment of 'More's [Cudworth's] "plastick part of the soul" to explain the congruence between object and sensation' in the form of a 'sensible Congruity . . . wanting in the Case of Blindness, Deafness of the Palsie Etc. [where] the Soul has no Sensation of Colours, Sound, Heat and the like' comes strikingly close to Locke's posthumously published 'Remarks upon Some of Mr. Norris' Books'.[117] There, by a remarkable coincidence, Locke had made precisely the argument Astell made, and also with regard to what appears to be a 'lawful' relation between sounds, colours and the organs of sense: 'if the perception of colours and sounds depended on nothing but the presence of the object affording an occasional cause of the God Almighty to exhibit to the mind the idea of figures, colours, and sounds; all that nice and curious structure of those organs is wholly in vain.'

It seems to be the case that Astell and Locke arrived independently at this line of argument, given that Astell's remarks were published in 1695 and Locke's, although written in 1693, were not published until 1704. It is possible, however, that Norris knew about them earlier. Whatever the case, Astell seems ambivalent about Locke in *A Serious Proposal, Part II*, and therefore less reluctant to run a Lockean line on occasionalism, while in *The Christian Religion*, as Taylor puts it, 'she makes no mention of the "Lockean" compromise she had proposed in the Letters, that is, a

"*sensible congruity*" to explain the effects of "delicious Viands"'.[118] Taylor
speculates as to the reason: 'Astell may silently have laid the groundwork in *A Serious Proposal, Part II* for her open attack on Locke in *The
Christian Religion* – but she has not yet begun to fight',[119] crediting her
change of heart to a 'changing understanding of Locke's political, theological, and philosophical principles' and specifically to her realization,
some time around 1700, the date of *Reflections upon Marriage*, that Locke
was the author of 'that great defense of Whig principles, *Two Treatises
of Government* (1689)'. Furthermore, Taylor notes, 'in his *Reasonableness
of Christianity* (1695) and in his well publicized Trinitarian debate with
Bishop Edward Stillingfleet (1635–99) Locke had aligned himself, in the
eyes of devoutly conservative Anglicans like Astell, with Deism, Socinianism, and Dissent'.[120] Taylor argues that Astell's animus against Locke
was given particular focus due to her (mistaken) belief that he, and not
Masham, had written the *Discourse Concerning the Love of God*.[121]

Sarah Ellenzweig's account of Astell's apparent inconstancy takes a different tack. Noting, with reference to Taylor, that Astell's sudden renunciation of occasionalism shortly before the printing of the *Letters* requires
explanation, Ellenzweig focuses on the reasons Astell might have had for
inserting the sensations as cognitive mechanisms, albeit as instruments
of divine will. After all, Astell's primary attraction to Norris and Malebranche, who understood that 'this world is a mere shew, a shadow, an
emptiness', was precisely as opponents to the 'mechanism' of Hobbes
and Locke. 'Our pretenders to Wit', she declared – that is, both of the
latter – might 'discredit every thing that is not the Object of Sense', but 'in
[the] right estimate Spirits are the only Realities, and nothing does truly
and properly occasion good or evil to us but as it respects our Minds'.[122]
So far, so good. 'Why then', Ellenzweig asks, 'would Astell suddenly ally
herself with a sensation-based theory that she had previously censured as
profanely materialist?'[123]

Ellenzweig believes that Astell came to equate Spinozism with occasionalism as a form of pantheism, along lines foreshadowed by Leibniz
and Richard Burthogge. In a letter to Arnauld of January 1688, Leibniz
had noted that occasionalism, by depriving nature of causal efficacy, was
tantamount to Spinozism. To 'refuse all force and all power to things', he
observed, is 'to change them from the substances they are into modes.
That is what Spinoza does; he thinks that only God is a substance and that
all other things are only modifications'. Occasionalism, like Spinozism,
made it impossible to differentiate ontologically between God and nature,
the creator and the created, and was therefore, he concluded, guilty of

pantheism of a gross kind.[124] In England, Richard Burthogge, whose *Essay upon Reason* appeared in April 1694, early enough for Astell to have read him prior to the publication of her *Letters*, had equated Malebranche and Spinoza even more forcefully, complaining that 'their Ambitious Researches in that higher way have [not] edified the World...to any great degree'. To the contrary, a false notion of God's infinity led Spinoza and 'others' to the misguided conception 'that [God] is the Ingredient, Immanent Cause of all Things', an idea that 'shocks' the 'distinction and singularity' of God's Being'.[125] As Ellenzweig suggests, when Astell delicately noted that occasionalism 'does not well comport with [God's] Majesty', she might well have been trying to distance herself from charges of Spinozism.[126]

This is a vexed question. Occasionalism had a theologically respectable pedigree, and Descartes himself had subscribed to occasionalism without in any way compromising his theism.[127] Cambridge Platonists, to whom she was close, had, moreover, set out to create just such philosophical distance. There were additional reasons to do so. Pantheism was associated with radical elements among the Civil War sects, the Levellers, for instance, and their leader, Gerard Winstanley, whose belief that God is 'in every place and every creature' was seen to shore up democratic politics.[128] William Warburton in *The Divine Legation of Moses Demonstrated* deemed pantheism a heresy that could be traced back to the Greeks but noted that it had been revived by Spinoza, accused of 'catch[ing] this epidemical contagion from antiquity'.[129] Warburton did not fail to notice the corollary, that pantheism served to occlude not only the Christian dualism of secular and sacred realms, but also the legitimacy of social, political and religious hierarchies that it shored up. The issue had become so hot by 1694, the year in which two rival editions of Malebranche's *Search after Truth* were published in England, and possibly a turning point for Astell, that one of them, the Oxford edition published by Thomas Taylor, planned to include an abridged version of the twenty-year correspondence between Arnauld and Malebranche, where the matter was aired. For various reasons the Taylor edition went ahead without including the correspondence but, as Ellenzweig speculates, Astell probably knew about it, particularly as the rival edition translated by Richard Sault had been printed by John Dunton and Samuel Manship, both of whom were close to Norris.

Locke himself had been charged with pantheism, one of the many heterodoxies of which he was deemed guilty. But he had also been charged with Spinozism, the allegation against Malebranche that he circled around so delicately in his *Examination of Malebranche* to 'avoid controversy' and because 'he had a personal kindness for the author'.[130] He nevertheless ventured the opinion that the Malebranchean principle of 'seeing all things in God . . . seems to me to come very near saying not only that there is variety in God . . . but that material things are God, or a part of him; which, though I do not think to be what our author designs, yet thus I fear he must be forced to talk, who thinks he knows God's understanding so much better than his own'.[131] He finds unacceptable the corollary of Malebranche's principle that 'an infinite simple being, in whom there is no variety, should represent a finite thing', concluding, 'To make things thus visible in [God], is to make the material world a part of him'.[132] Against Norris, as Ellenzweig notes, Locke was blunter. In his 'Remarks upon Some of Mr. Norris' Books' he openly charges him with a pantheism peculiarly Spinozist, declaring of Norris's belief that the essence of God contains all the creatures that will issue forth by his power: 'what is this better than what those say, who make God to be nothing but the universe; though it be covered under unintelligible expressions of simplicity and variety, at the same time, in the essence of God'.[133]

But Locke was not alone in these charges, and the High Church divine Robert South, to whom Locke had sent a copy of his *Examination of Père Malebranche*, praised it in his letter of 1699 as a 'Clear and Excellent Confutation of a very Senseless Hypothesis', declaring:[134]

The Drift and Tendency of the Philosophy here Confuted by You . . . is to make the Universe god and god the Universe; albeit the Assertion be too Black to be owned in Terminis: But where Principles are once laid, the Abettors of them Know well enough, That their Consequences will Work out them selves, though Vulgar shortsighted minds may not be aware of them.

It is in this spirit that Locke in *The Reasonableness of Christianity* addresses both Malebranchistes and Deists, whom he conflates as undermining Christian piety with their pantheistic notions, an attack that would have resonated with Astell, particularly as he seemed to include women among them. With surprising superciliousness he remarks:[135]

Where the hand is used to the Plough, and the Spade, the head is seldom elevated to sublime Notions, or exercised in mysterious reasoning. 'Tis well if Men of that rank (to say nothing of the other Sex) can comprehend plain propositions, and a short reasoning about things familiar to their Minds, and nearly allied to their daily experience. Go beyond this and you amaze the greatest part of mankind.

Masham in the *Discourse Concerning the Love of God* had been even blunter, for her attack included the accusation that the Platonists – and specifically the Malebranchistes – denied the first premise of Christian humanism, human sociability:[136]

And those seem more than a little to indanger Christianity . . . who lay the great stress of their proof upon the Hypothesis of seeing all things in God. . . . And I doubt not, but if it were generally receiv'd and Preach'd by our Divines, that this Opinion of Seeing all things in God was the Basis upon which Christianity was built, Scepticism would be so far from finding thereby a Cure, that it would spread it self much farther amongst us than it has yet done. And . . . many who find Christianity a very Reasonable Religion in the Scriptures, would think it a very unaccountable one in a System that . . . adds also further, That the Desire we have to the Creature, is the Punishment of Sin, not the Institution of Nature: For this Concupiscence is transmitted to us from our first Parent.

It is worth mentioning that Astell on at least one important issue had good reason for putting distance between herself and Malebranche, and that concerned his treatment of sex differences. In Part 2 of *The Search for Truth*, 'Concerning the Imagination', 1.1, 'Of the Imagination of Women', Malebranche went so far as to postulate different structures of mind between the sexes, a position that Astell vehemently rejected on Cartesian grounds.[137] Discussing the purportedly greater excitability of women than men, Malebranche had claimed:[138]

But though it be certain, that this Delicacy of the Fibres of the Brain is the principal Cause of all these Effects; yet it is not equally certain, that it is universally to be found in all Women. Or if it be to be found, yet their Animal Spirits are sometimes so exactly proportion'd to the Fibres of their Brain, that there are Women to be met with, who have a greater solidity of Mind than some Men. 'Tis in a certain Temperature of the Largeness and Agitation of the Animal Spirits, and Conformity with the Fibres of the Brain, that the strength of parts consists: And Women have sometimes that just Temperature. There are Women Strong and constant, and there are Men that are Weak and Fickle. There are Women that are Learned, Couragious, and capable of every thing. And on the contrary, there are Men that are Soft Effeminate, incapable of any Penetration, or dispatch of any Business. In Fine, when we attribute any Failures to a certain Sex, Age, or Condition, they are only to be understood of the generality; it being ever suppos'd, there is no general Rule without Exception.

Taylor and Ellenzweig are right to focus on the philosophico-political context for Astell's change of heart. Already displaying well-developed philosophical interests and mature opinions on political matters, Astell had roved widely in the *Letters*, broaching topics she would later address in detail in subsequent works. We 'put on our Religion as we do our Cloaths in Conformity to the Fashion', she says,[139] complaining against 'the sottishness of those dull *Epicureans*, who make it their Business to hunt after

Pleasures as vain and unsatisfactory as their admirers are Childish and Unwise'.[140] Later she pillories those 'pretenders to piety' whose language of utility, interest, advantage and pleasure betrays their intentions.[141] By her lights Locke would qualify. She displays familiarity with the language of passive obedience and resistance, a debate in which Locke was so heavily implicated, noting in a throwaway remark:[142] 'I cannot discern wherein the Virtue of a bare Submission consists, such a passive Obedience to GOD is like the new Notion some have got of passive Obedience to their Governors'. She also betrays some acquaintance with the demarcations made by Aristotle between the familial, political and economic realms, to which Locke subscribed, observing: 'I cannot forbear to reckon it an irregular Affection, and an Effect of Vitious Self-love, to love any Person merely on account of his Relation to us'. She concludes, 'I should therefore chuse to derive the Reasons why we are in the first place to regard our Relations, rather from Justice, and the Rules of Oeconomy [Aristotle's household management], than from Love'.[143]

The Malebranchean thesis that God is the only efficient cause of all our sensations and therefore the only worthy object of our love had as its corollary the antithesis that to love our neighbour as ourselves was therefore a species of benevolence and not of love. On this point Astell joins Malebranche, taking strong exception to sociability as the basis for civil society, on which Locke's political philosophy is founded. In the idiom of Platonism she disclaims: 'He that has discovered the Fountain will not seek for troubled and failing Streams to quench his Thirst'; and again: 'He can never be content to step aside to catch at the Shadow who is in Pursuit and View of the Substance'.[144] Drawing on the metaphor of the love of God as a stream of affectivity whereby like attracts like, she declares: 'The Soul that loves GOD has no occasion to love other things, because it needs nor expects Felicity from them; whenever it moves towards the Creature it must necessarily forsake the Creator'.[145] Wondering whether 'this may be thought a skrewing up things to too great Height, a winding up our Nature to a Pitch it is not able to reach',[146] she does not hesitate boldly to declaim:[147]

And therefore an ardent Lover of GOD will consider how incongruous it is to present him with a mean and narrow Soul, a Heart grovling on the Earth, cleaving to little dirty Creatures.

We see in what follows the faint outlines of a critique of Hobbes and Locke. We have no obligation to persons, she seems to be saying, except as they derive from our obligation to God. Addressing herself 'to the World, to persons not sensible of their Obligations', she interrogates them:[148]

then let me ask them if they do not feel the Rays of his Goodness sweetly insinuating into every Part, clearing up the Darkness of their Understanding, warming
their benummed Affections, regulating their oblique Motions, and melting down
their obstinate, ingrateful, disingenuous Wills? Do they not feel these Cords of a
Man as himself is pleased to call them, these silken Bands of Love, these odorif-
erous Perfumes drawing them after him, uniting them to him by the most potent
Charms?

It is noteworthy that Astell's strictly religious works both took epistolary form. It is a commonplace that eighteenth-century women were
often confined to this mode, and Astell's *Letters Concerning the Love of God*
are epistolary in this sense. This did not stand in the way of their being
taken seriously as a theological essay, and it is noteworthy that the *Letters*
are her work first mentioned in Astell's obituary published on 29 May
1731 in *The Daily Journal*, which noted that her 'Correspondence with
the famous Mr. Norris of Bemerton, on the celebrated subject of the *Love
of God*, gain'ed her no small Applause'.[149] The *Letters* were read and highly
praised by public figures like Leibniz and Thomas Burnet, as well as by
private women like Sara Chapone, who considered them Astell's most
'sublime work'.[150] Mary Evelyn, wife of the famous diarist, commended
them to her son, explaining, 'not that I recommend them from my owne
judgment or liking', but because 'the witts and those of the clergy think
them worth reading', and going on to remark: 'I confess the Notions
in the letters are so refined I dare not give my opinion that the woman
has a good Character for virtue and is very little above twenty which adds
to her praise, to be so early good and knowing'.[151] Astell's most systematic theological work, *The Christian Religion as Profess'd by a Daughter of the
Church of England*, is epistolary in a different mode, in imitation of the correspondence between the bishop of Worcester, Edward Stillingfleet, and
John Locke, a philosophical debate over Locke's *Essay Concerning Human
Understanding*, of which, among other things, it represents a continuation.
Astell's career closes where it began on questions of the life of faith, the
epistemology and metaphysics on which it is founded, the structures of
church and government required to promote it, political machinations
and the conspiracy of manners and mores designed to subvert it.

7. Masham's *Discourse Concerning the Love of God*

The Astell–Norris exchange published as *Letters Concerning the Love of God*
named Norris on the title page but referred to Astell only as the author
of the *Serious Proposal* of 1694. This means that we cannot be sure that
Masham's *Discourse Concerning the Love of God*, published anonymously a

year later, and believed by Astell to be written by Locke, was intended as a rebuttal.[152] There is, however, circumstantial evidence to suggest that it may have been. Masham seems to mimic the title of the *Letters* in her own title, as well as making at least one explicit reference to them.[153] In any event, what is important for our purposes is that Astell believed the work to be an attack on her – although by Locke rather than Masham – and cast *A Serious Proposal, Part II,* as a reply. In my essay 'Astell, Masham and Locke', I equivocated as to whether Astell was Masham's intended target, pointing out that I could find no direct reference to the Astell–Norris correspondence in the *Discourse* – a remark that I would revise to claim rather that there is no direct reference to Astell in the *Discourse* – there are references to *Letters Philosophical and Divine,* but from Norris's contribution to the correspondence rather than Astell's. Taylor takes me roundly to task for equivocating about Hutton's claim that 'The Book which occasioned [Masham's] attack was a collection of letters by Norris and Mary Astell published as *Letters Concerning the Love of God'*, arguing: 'But as Hutton and Astell well knew, Masham makes several explicit references to "*Letters Philosophical and Divine*"'.[154]

Buickerwood has persuasively argued, however, that Masham seems to indicate Norris as her target and makes no mention of Astell at all, presenting as evidence the fact that Masham cites as her principal target a sermon by Norris, 'lately brought into our Pulpits', which she singles out for her attention because of the force Norris gives to the imperative that we love only God.[155] Norris's sermon in question is a reflection upon Matthew 22:37, entitled 'A Discourse concerning *The measure of Divine Love, with the Natural and Moral Grounds upon which it stands'*, which Masham reads as an illustration of Norris's Malebranchiste claim as set out in his *Practical Discourses*: '1. *That God is the only Cause of our Love'* and '2. *That he is also the only proper Object of it'*.[156] In the Preface to the Discourse, Masham declared her task in short: '*to show the weakness and extravagance of such of Mr. N's late Practical Discourses as are built upon the Principles of Pere Malebranche'*.[157] She affirms at greater length:[158]

The ensuing Discourse is publish'd with this View: It being intended to show the unserviceableness of an Hypothesis lately recommended to the World for a Ground of Christianity, and Morality; As likewise, the farther injuriousness of that Hypothesis to True Religion, and Piety; Which, I think, I may securely affirm, neither ever have suffer'd, or ever can suffer so much, from the Arguments of any Opposers, as from theirs, who induced by Weakness, Vanity, or any other Motive, have undertaken, or pretended to Support them, upon false Grounds and wrong Reasonings.

Masham, this author sensibly argues, rather than being a Platonist, after her father, Ralph Cudworth, and despite the Cambridge Platonists she numbers among her friends – without necessarily subscribing to their views – may quite simply have been a doctrinal minimalist opposed to the fractiousness induced by rival Christian camps. If so, she would have come close to the positions of Hobbes and Locke, the former of whom believed Christian Platonism to be the best example of the 'Greekification' of Christianity by unemployed or underemployed philosophers who jumped on the church's bandwagon to their own profit. Masham expressed the view, later taken to be quintessentially Latitudinarian, that 'the chief Aim of Christianity [is] a good life. For whatsoever else its Professors, divided into Parties, may contend about; this they must all Agree in, That we ought to be a People zealous of Good Works'.[159] In such a view she echoed not only Locke but also Stillingfleet, whom she quoted, on the dangerousness of 'an unintelligible way of practical *Religion*', for 'no men of sense and reason will ever set themselves about' such a standard of devotion but instead will 'leave it to be understood by *madmen* and *practised by Fools*'.[160] A reflection, Masham goes on to observe,[161]

it were to be wish'd all would make, who may be tempted by Affectation of Novelty, Fondness of an Hypothesis, or any other better Reason, to build their Practical and Devotional Discourses upon Principles which not only will not bear the Test, but which oblige them to lay down such Assertions in Morality, as sober and well disposed Christians cannot understand to be practicable: Than which, I think there never was any more evidently so, than that Mankind are obliged strictly, as their Duty, to love with Desire, nothing but God only; Every Degree of Desire of any Creature whatsoever, being Sin. This Assertion, though not altogether new, yet has been but lately brought into our Pulpits, and been pretended to be set on Foot upon a Philosophical or Natural Ground, *viz. That God, not the Creature, is the* immediate, *efficient Cause of our Sensations: For whatever gives us Pleasure* (say they who hold this Hypothesis) *has a right to our Love; but God only give us Pleasure, therefore he only has a right to our Love.*

Masham, who does not name Astell once, Buickerood claims, 'expressly quotes, alludes or refers to Norris' sermon at least twenty-six times in the course of her criticism; she deliberately quotes, alludes or refers to Malebranche's work ten times; and she *explicitly* quotes, alludes or refers to the Norris–Astell Letters a total of three times', but quoting only Norris's letters, '*never*–Astell's'.[162] I think that this author is right, that Masham's philosophical concerns relate more to Norris than to Astell – and specifically to Norris's Malebranchiste assumptions – while adding that they are concerns shared by Locke, who in his response to Norris's

Cursory Reflections built the case, as we have seen, that Platonism, far from advancing Christian piety, served to undermine it. Buickerood argues, persuasively, I think, that her attack on Platonist quietism leading to monastic seclusion should be read in light of opinion at the time about the Malebranchean version of Catholic Augustinianism and its tendency to quietism and monastic withdrawal from the world.[163] The author reads in this light Masham's express intent in the opening pages of her Discourse against those who 'carry their Zeal for the Doctrinal part of Religion so far, that they seem to lay little Stress on the Performance of those Vertues recommended by our Saviour Christ, as the Way to Eternal Life', and instead strain the duties of morality to 'an impractical Pitch; or pretend to ascend by it to something beyond it'.[164] The 'strain of Augustinian Roman Catholicism that tended to mystical vision and the recommendation of humans' withdrawal from the world of sense and society to a retreat to religious houses, of which Malebranche is qualifiedly representative', is the context in which we should read Masham's indictment of monasticism, Buickerood recommends.[165] Indeed, 'this is the direction toward which Malebranche's hypothesis itself points, as the Oratorian himself unabashedly advertises in the closing dialogue of *Conversations chrétiennes*, the work on which Masham concentrates her critical attention in the concluding fifth of her own book'.[166] It is in this context, then, rather than with reference to the Astell–Norris exchange in the *Letters*, that we should read Masham's indictment of Norris.

I am not persuaded that the connection between Masham's attack on the Malebranchean advocacy of monasticism and Astell's reputation for wishing to found a female monastic academy in a *Serious Proposal* was entirely fortuitous. It could not have been too difficult for Masham to establish Astell's authorship of the *Letters*, given that she is acknowledged on the title page as the author of the *Serious Proposal* of 1694; and it was probably known in Masham's circle that Queen Anne's original interest in funding the women's academy Astell had in mind had been cooled by precisely the charge by Bishop Burnet that it smacked too much of Anglican monasticism. Moreover, Buickerood introduces a piece of evidence that suggests that Masham, on her own admission, knew Astell's authorship when, discussing occasionalism, she observed[167]

how unserviceable or injurious soever it really is to Piety, it has yet been Seriously and Zealously pretended to be of great Use to Religion; And that not only by a young Writer, whose Judgment may, perhaps be thought Byassed by the Affectation of Novelty; But also it is made the very Ground of Christianity, by a Man of establish'd Character in the World for Philosophical Science.

Arguing that this was a reference to Astell, on the grounds that Norris's coauthor of the *Letters* 'is identified in the preface to the book as a "young gentlewoman"', Buickerood goes on to assert that it was 'arguably benignly intended' and 'hardly the stuff of intellectual antagonism and vituperative exchange, however much Astell may have read insults into Masham's text'.[168] It is worth noting that an 'Affectation of Novelty' is the mark by which Masham first identified her target, Stillingfleet's '*madmen* and . . . *Fools*', in the passage quoted previously,[169] and Astell – and the rest of us – might be forgiven for thinking it included her.

As being among those, including Ruth Perry, Sarah Hutton and E. Derek Taylor, singled out as leaping too quickly to the conclusion that there was a 'Masham–Astell dispute', I am prepared to revise my view.[170] It is interesting that no sources other than Ballard make mention of a dispute between them,[171] and I am ready to stand corrected, believing that caution is in order in interpreting the vitriolic and apparently vituperative language in which seventeenth- and eighteenth-century polemicists indulged. For my purposes, it does not matter whether this language referred to a real dispute; the salient fact is that Astell, who tended to be paranoid about the reception of her works (see the way in which she handled Daniel Defoe and James Owen in the Postscript to *A Fair Way with the Disssenters* and her reading of the allegations of Swift/Steele in the *Tatler*, discussed later), believed there was one, reading Masham's *Discourse* as a personal attack. There are some grounds for her reading, as I say. Not only could Masham's insistence that Malebranche's thesis tended ineluctably to support monasticism be read as an indictment of Astell's *Serious Proposal*, but Astell read Masham's attack on Norris's Malebranchean occasionalism as an attack upon herself as well.

Compared with Locke's attack on Cambridge Platonism in *The Reasonableness of Christianity*, for instance, Masham's attack has a much sharper focus – although not compared with Locke's response to Norris's *Cursory Reflections*, his 'Remarks upon Some of Mr. Norris' Books' of 1693, which preceded Masham's work by three years, it should be noted. Launching a second line of attack on the heterodoxy of Malebranche, Masham emphasizes the inherently solipsistic nature of his notion of the love of God, the exclusivity of which represents a denial of Christian sociability, argued in such a way that it could certainly be read as targeting Astell as well. By making love of God the medium of perception in general and by deeming love of creatures other than as images of the divinity idolatrous, Malebranche, Norris – and by implication Astell – as Platonists, oriented individuals towards the otherworldly and away from society, Masham claimed. Such a denial of inherent human sociability, vouchsafed by the second commandment, made 'it impossible to live in the daily Commerce and Conversation of the World, and love God as we ought to do'.[172] Masham connects Norris's quietism to Malebranche's love of retirement, arguing once again that far from promoting religion and piety, their positions serve to undermine it:[173]

These Opinions of Mr. *N.* seem also to indanger the introducing, especially amongst those whose Imaginations are stronger than their Reason, a Devout way of talking; which having no sober, and intelligible sense under it, will either inevitably by degrees beget an Insensibility to Religion, in those themselves who use it, as well as others; By thus accustoming them to handle Holy things without Fear; or else will turn to as wild an Enthusiasm as any that has been yet seen; and which can End in nothing but Monasteries, and Hermitages; with all those sottish and Wicked Superstitions which have accompanied them where-ever they have been in use.

Masham accuses Malebranche, author of the *Christian Conversations*, of foreseeing this consequence and perhaps even intending it: 'This in a Papist, and one of a Religious Order amongst them, cannot seem strange'.[174] In an Anglican divine it was much less excusable, and Masham echoes Stillingfleet in declaring:[175]

But there can certainly be no greater Disparagement to Christian Religion, than to say; That it unfits Men for Society; That we must not only literally become Fools for Christ's sake; but also cease to be Men. Can any Rational Man, not bred up in the Bigottry of Popery, ever perswade himself that such a Religion can be from God?

Masham's indictment of Norris, once held by her in regard, is surprising, coming from the daughter of Ralph Cudworth and dedicatee of an earlier work by Norris, *Reflections upon the Conduct of Human Life: with reference to the Study of Learning and Knowledge. In a Letter to the Excellent Lady, the Lady Masham* (1690). This was the second of two books Norris had dedicated to her, in fact, the first having been his book of 1688, *The Theory and Regulation of Love. A Moral Essay*, while the second, the *Reflections*, are addressed to her as someone who had admired his previous work.[176] Buickerood rightly points out that probably Masham collected a number of Platonist acquaintances in the years she spent in her father's household at Christ's College, Cambridge, and subsequently, so that we should not take her mention of them as an endorsement of their views. Much less should we take the opinions of George Ballard as fact, given that his *Memoirs* are strongly biased in Astell's favour and were written at the prompting of Elizabeth Elstob, an acquaintance at least, if not 'a one-time associate', of Astell's. Among the commentators who have speculated on likely causes for Masham's animus against Norris, Ballard's explanation is given in no uncertain terms:[177]

Soon after [Damaris Cudworth] was married, the fame of her learning, piety and ingenuity induced the celebrated Mr. Norris to address and inscribe to her by way of letter his *Reflections upon the conduct of human life with reference to the study of learning and knowledge*, London, 1689, duodecimo. This began a friendship between them, a friendship which having its foundation in religion, seemed very likely to be firm and lasting. But it seems to have been in great measure dissolved before it had been of any long continuance, occasioned by this lady's contracting an indissoluble friendship with Mr. Locke, whose divinity and philosophy is well known to differ very much from Mr. Norris's.

Masham's indictment of a man who had once dedicated two books to her seems to indicate a change of heart, at the very least, and does require some explanation. She may have been offended, as Hutton suggests, by his misinformation that her poor eyesight had already resulted in blindness and his subsequent advice to her that the pursuit of learning could only divert a mind that should be directed to spirituality.[178] Or she may have known of his apparent betrayal of trust in opening a sealed letter sent to her by Locke – this sequence of events, if it is true, smacking of *opera buffa* and better suited to the stage. Whatever the case, her well-reasoned response is devastating and by no means suggests a mere acolyte of Locke.

Masham begins by observing that from Norris's central proposition '1. *That god is the only Cause of our Love*', his conclusion, '2. *That he is also the proper object of it*', does not follow.[179] His proof for the first proposition rests on 'what (plainly express'd) cannot be contested; *viz.* That we receive the Power which we have of Desiring, from God'. Proof of the second, 'That God is the only proper Object of our Love, as being the only Cause of all our pleasing Sensations', is lacking. Instead Norris offers 'his Opinion, that God (who doubtless made all things for himself) because his own Glory was his primary End in creating all things, had not therefore Secondary, and intermediate Ends for which he made the Creatures to operate one upon another: Which is but a tacit Way to beg the Question'.[180] '*Upon this Hinge*', says he, '*the whole Weight of the Theory turns*, viz. That God is the only proper Object of our Love as being the only Cause of all our pleasing Sensations'.[181] It is interesting that Masham does not accept the necessary revision that Astell pointed out:[182] that if God is the only cause of our pleasure, he is equally the only cause of our pain. This introduces a Manichean principle forcing Norris to conclude that if God is therefore the only object of our love, he is equally the object of our fear. Astell had a way out of the theodicy problem, which makes God the author of good and evil: if not only pleasure but also pain can be said to contribute to our Good, then God as the only author of our Good is the only worthy object of our love.

It is a solution to which Masham only later alludes, addressing instead the corollary of Norris's argument, Malebranchean occasionalism, to the refutation of which her work is devoted. Masham defines occasionalism as the principle of God's 'Creatures having no Efficiency at all to operate upon us; they being only occasional Causes of those Sentiments which God produces in us', and further, that 'every Act that carries our Desires towards the Creature is sinful'. Masham immediately declares: 'Which Opinion if receiv'd and follow'd, must necessarily bring in the like unintelligible Way of Practical Reason, which the Bishop of *Worcester* has justly censured in the Church of *Rome*'.[183] Her remark, published in 1696, is prescient. The Bishop of Worcester, Edward Stillingfleet, was to be Locke's respondent in an important epistolary debate, from 1697 to 1699, over the doctrinal implications of Locke's epistemology, as we shall see.

If other creatures are occasional causes of our sensations, only God can be the object of desire, Norris had argued, taking desire clearly to be a motivational force consistent with Epicurean attraction to pleasure and resistance to pain. Masham rejects the corollary, that we 'desire God' but experience only 'benevolent love' for our fellows.[184] She follows Locke in declaring love to be a disposition towards that which pleases us, denying Norris's differentiation of love into modes, which she attributes to a confusion between love and its consequents determined by its different, and equally legitimate, objects.[185] Masham insists that love is a simple, focused act of mind.[186] That we receive all good from God does not entail that God is the author of our pleasing sensations, a precarious hypothesis that pays no tribute to God[187] – and here Masham may indeed be addressing Astell's revision. For she dismisses as paying equally scant honour to God: '[p]ompous Rhapsodies of the soul debasing herself, when she descends to set the least part of her Affections upon any thing but her Creator, [which] (however well they may possibly be intended) are plainly but a complementing God with the contempt of his Works, by which we are the most effectually led to Know, Love and Adore him'.[188]

Masham deals a cruel blow to the Platonists, of whose 'Extravagance' 'perhaps some of the Mystical Divines are an Example', claiming that their revolt against the passions has led them 'to dress out in an intire

System intelligible only by Sentiment, not to Reason'.[189] Norris has abandoned any claim to credibility as a professional philosopher by breaking the rule that, 'whenever any one pretends to prescribe Measures of Duty, not suited to a Popular Audience, but such as shall challenge the strictest Attention and Scrutiny of Reason, he ought to exclude all Metaphor and Hyperbole'.[190] The outcome is devastating for his own theory. For, 'Notions...which are usher'd in, or attended with Flights, not only out of the reach of common Sense, but which oppose the Experience of Mankind',[191] can only be accepted on the basis of dogma and not of reason. 'Seeing all things in God' cannot advance us 'one jot further in the Knowledge of our Ideas, and Perceptions; which is the thing it was Primarily pretended to be design'd for'.[192] 'They who advance this Notion, do only fetch a Circuit',[193] at the same time rendering the Malebranchiste formulation of efficient and occasional causes irrelevant.

Masham demonstrates considerable philosophical agility in her technical discussion, employing a Lockean conception of strict entailment to demolish Malebranche's and Norris's distinction between 'efficient' and 'occasional' causes:[194]

The Creatures they say are occasional Causes of our pleasing Sensations. Then, however, they are Causes of them. They deny not also, That they are such Causes as are always accompanied with the Effect, and without which the Effect is not produced. And are they not then consider'd as Goods to us, just the same as if they were efficient Causes?

Masham's employment of Locke's strict definition of cause as 'that which produces any simple or complex idea' and of effect as 'that which is produced'[195] earned her work its reputation as a work by Locke. Her demonstration of the argument against Malebranche and Norris is strikingly Lockean. Taking the example of a flower, reminiscent of Locke's image of the 'marygold', Masham, using Lockean language of powers, argues that we cannot know how colour, one of Locke's secondary qualities, mediates between God's intention and the excitation of enjoyable sensations:[196]

Or must we think a beautiful Flower has not the same Appearance, whether it be believ'd that God has lodg'd a power in the Flower to excite the Idea of its Colour in us, or that he himself exhibits the Idea of its Colour at the presence of that Object? If the Flower is either way equally pleasing (as certainly it is) then it is also equally desireable.

Masham delivers her master stroke when she points out that Malebranchiste distinctions are not only irrelevant but also irreverent. Here she uses an argument straight from Locke's refutation of Norris[197] to accuse him of rendering God's creations pointless and superfluous:[198]

But the Wisdom of God cannot herein be equally admired, because it is not equally conspicuous. For if God immediately exhibits to me all my Idea's [*sic.*], and that I do not truly see with my Eyes and hear with my Ears; then all that wonderful Exactness and curious Workmanship in framing the Organs of Sense, seems superfluous and vain; Which is no small Reflection upon infinite Wisdom.

It is an argument that Masham extends into territory into which Locke, in his response to Norris, does not venture. Just as seeing all things in God renders perceptual apparatus of sensation irrelevant, occasional-ism renders the instrumentalities God has chosen willfully perverse. If creatures cannot excite pleasure (love), due only to God, then God has willfully obscured our purposes here on earth.[199] Masham develops a powerful argument about the presumptuousness of Norris's theory by pointing out that by accepting it we posit the period up to the enlight-enment provided by 'Heads cast in *Metaphysical Moulds*', like Norris's, as millennia-long, dark ages of ignorance concerning God's purposes.[200] But Norris's thesis is patently false, the result of misapplied 'Logick and Grammar' to Scripture the understanding of which is accommodated to ordinary language, and not 'the Opinion of Divines'.[201] Masham discusses at length the second commandment to Moses, 'love thy neighbour', cit-ing in defence a jingle by Henry More, 'no Religious Rant' but a principle made good by experience.[202] God 'has laid no traps and snares, to ren-der us Miserable',[203] from which she draws some surprising conclusions. Far from our senses misleading us, they affirm divine purposes in the construction of nature.

Developing ideas that were the mainstay of Stoic and Epicurean thought in the injunction to lead 'a life according to Nature' (*kata phusin*), Masham goes on to discuss 'Wants of Nature' compared with 'Wants of our own making'.[204] These are ideas that in early modern thought awaited full discussion until Rousseau in his *First* and *Second Discourses*, indebted, as he acknowledges, to Locke. Masham's discussion, noting the legacy of Chrysippus,[205] may be evidence of familiarity with the arguments of Jensenists Nicole and Arnauld, who broached the topic in terms of a dis-tinction between *amour de soi* and *amour propre*.[206] Whatever the case, the proposition that 'the gratification of Appetites which are not properly Natural, but which we have receiv'd from Custom, and Education, is not always sinful', and the admission that 'Custom . . . is oftentimes as strong as Nature in us',[207] are in stark contrast to Norris's claim that no creature can be loved without idolatry and that we may desire only God. Even more challenging is her argument that 'God is an invisible Being' and 'the Loveliness of his Works' is what causes us to love him, and specifically the Loveliness of his creatures.[208]

Aware that she has in fact reversed the thesis of Norris (this time accepting Astell's revision), Masham notes that the Malebranchistes would counterclaim 'That we have Pleasing Sensations ('tis true) as soon as Perception; But that we have them not from the Beings which surround us, but from God'.[209] To this she responds with observations from the behaviour of infants that knowledge of God does not accompany the first 'cry for the Fire, or the Sucking-Bottle', but 'is a Proposition containing many complex Ideas in it; and which we are not capable of framing, till we have been long acquainted with pleasing Sensations'.[210] It is an idea certainly beyond the capacity of the child in the cradle to frame, who in the meantime necessarily learns to love that which appears to be the cause of its pleasure.[211]

This passage in Masham reads as a direct refutation of Letter IX of Astell's correspondence with Norris, in which she expresses the Malebranchiste notion that 'we suck in false Principles and Tendencies betimes, and are taught, not to thirst after GOD as our only good' apparently from an early age:

'tis our Misfortune that we live an animal before we live a rational Life; the good we enjoy is mostly transmitted to us through Bodily Mediums, and contracts such a Tincture of the Conveyance through which it passes, that forgetting the true Cause and Sourse of all our good, we take up with those occasional goods that are more visible, and present to our animal Nature.

This is a tendency reinforced by education, Astell maintains, in a surprising concession to the principles of Lockean sensationalist psychology.[212] But it is an argument Masham simply denies. Distinguishing between reality and appearances, she argues that while the passions and appearances move us first, we learn to sift appearances through the filter of ideas:[213]

So soon as we do begin to leave off judging by appearances, and are Capable of being convinc'd that the Diameter of the Sun exceeds that of a Bushel; We are capable also of understanding that there is a Superior Invisible Being, the Author of those things which afford us pleasing Sensations, who is therefore supreamly to be loved.

Her example of the appearance of the sun probably draws on the moon illusion discussed by Malebranche, whose *Conversations chrétiennes* she quotes on concupiscence at length in French, along with Norris' translation in the *Unintelligible Way of Practical Religion*.[214] She refutes as ridiculous Malebranche's notion of the transmission of ideas – a revision of the Platonist theory of innate ideas – that the baby in the mother's womb feels like her and thinks like her, desires bodies, and is born a sinner.[215] She expends considerable effort in refuting Malebranche's belief that love of creatures, based on an error of deduction, is a punishment of the Fall, as a proposition not only false, but pernicious to piety and morals.[216] And she simply rejects as 'utterly false' Norris's claim that love of God and love of creatures are mutually exclusive, because '*our Capacities are too narrow and scanty to be employ'd upon two such vastly different Objects*'.[217] Experience tells us, she insists, that there is no more reason 'That Love of the Creature should exclude the Love of God; any more than that the Love of Cherries should exclude the love of our Friend that gives them us'.[218]

Norris had entered the dangerous waters of distinguishing between 'our good' and 'our true good', where Masham easily catches him: 'But certainly whatever is a Good to us, is a *True Good*, since whatever pleases us, pleases us':[219] 'the word *True* (otherwise very impertinent here) is Subtily to insinuate that which should be prov'd, *viz. That the Creatures are not the Efficient Causes* of our Pleasing Sensations'.[220] She notes the incongruousness of the Malebranchiste position that cannot admit creatures as the proper object of our love and sees them only as a derogation from the duty to love God, and yet can admit God as the author of sinful as well as innocent feelings of pleasure:[221]

But the Author of this Hypothesis tells us, That this is that indeed which makes Sin to be so exceeding sinful, *viz.* That we oblige God in Virtue of that first immutable Law or Order, which he has establish'd (that is, of exciting Sentiments of Pleasure in us upon some operation of Bodies upon us) to Reward our Transgressions against him with Pleasure, and Delight. It is strange that we cannot seem sinful enough, without having a Power of forcing God to be a Partner in our Wickedness!

This is a formidable argument for rejecting Malebranche and Norris' position. But without doubt Masham considers yet more telling the argument to which she returns. It is the Aristotelian argument of appropriateness, matched to the Ciceronian argument for man's natural sociability. The Malebranchiste thesis does no justice to man's nature as a social and worldly creature. It is no more appropriate to wish for men the nature of 'Angels, and Arch-Angels . . . (at least whilst upon Earth) then it would be for the Fishes (if they were capable of it) to propose, or pray to God, that they might fly in the Air like Birds; or Ride Pose-Horses as Men do'. She points to the *hubris* of those 'who will venture to ask God for their sakes, to change the Order of Nature, which he has establish'd'. Furthermore, 'It is certain, that if we had no Desires but after God, the several Societies of Mankind could not long hold together, nor the very Species be continued'.[222] It is an argument, made after a curious discussion of the possibility of other worlds, to which Masham finally returns,[223] insisting that the greatest condemnation of the Malebranchiste thesis is its injuriousness to social life, making it 'absolutely necessary to renounce the World, and betake ourselves to Woods and Desarts', and 'impossible to live in the daily Commerce and Conversation of the World, and love God as we ought to do'.[224] Masham comes perilously close to the Deists and Arminians in her Ciceronian eulogy to human sociability:[225]

There is nothing more evident than that Mankind is design'd for a Sociable Life. To say that Religion unfits us for it, is to reproach the Wisdom of God as highly as is possible; And to represent Religion as the most mischievous thing in the World, dissolving Societies. And there could not be a greater Artifice of the Devil, or Wicked Men to bring Christianity into contempt than this.

Masham beautifully crafts an image that Astell had already presaged: women, whom men cast in the role of observers, were the true practitioners of *theoria*: observation as the basis of philosophy and science. It is an argument that Judith Drake made in the same year, with pointed reference to the state-of-nature arguments of Hobbes and Locke, that if it is true that it customarily falls to men, as the physically stronger, to have power over women, then it is also true that women, as more cerebral and less physical, are better suited to philosophy. For Masham, they may know not only other minds, but possibly other worlds:[226]

Yet were our Views larger than to comprehend only the compass of our little Globe, they would probably afford us still further Matter for our Admiration. For 'tis a thought too limitted [*sic*] and narrow for Women and Children now to be kept in, that this Spot of ours is all the Habitable part of the Creation. But without understanding the System of the World, or considering what Mathematicians and Naturalists offer to convince us, that so many Regions fit for Inhabitants are not empty Desarts, and such numberless Orbs of Light more insignificant than so many Farthing Candles; We read, in the Scripture, of other Ranks of Intelligent Beings besides our selves; Of whom, tho' it would be Presumption to affirm any thing beyond what is reveal'd, yet we know not what Relation may possibly be between them and us.

Masham's paean to the possibility of other worlds is curious. Is it a concession to Locke on 'thinking matter'? Or is it a venture into the New Science, for which Astell herself was to claim that women as reflective persons were exceptionally well suited?[227]

And since it is allow'd on all hands, that the Mens Business is without Doors, and theirs is an Active Life; Women who ought to be Retir'd, are for this reason design'd by Providence for Speculation: Providence, which allots every one an Employment, and never intended that any one shou'd give themselves up to Idleness and Unprofitable Amusements. And I make no question but great Improvements might be made in the Sciences, where not women enviously excluded from this their proper Business.

2

Astell, Drake, Education, Epistemology
and the *Serious Proposal*

1. *A Serious Proposal*, Text and Context

Astell's educational work, a *Serious Proposal to the Ladies for the Advancement of their True and Greatest Interest*, brought her to greater public notice. Published in 1694, it is one of the most important and neglected in a long series of works advocating the establishment of educational academies for women. Republished in 1695, its reception was sufficiently controversial to cause Astell to respond with a lengthy sequel, *A Serious Proposal, Part II* (1697). Her project, set out in the first part of the *Proposal*, was to establish a religious community for 'Ladies of Quality' funded by the dowries they brought with them and monies earned by founding a school.[1] Of all of Astell's works, this one has the most complicated textual history. For when in 1694 Astell had completed the first part of *A Serious Proposal*, the work, ironically, was taken for that of Damaris Masham, Locke's companion, as typical of what might be expected of the daughter of the Cambridge Platonist Ralph Cudworth. In fact, Astell's *Proposal*, together with the Astell–Norris correspondence, attracted a fierce response from Lady Masham in *Discourse Concerning the Love of God* (1695), to which Astell in turn responded without mentioning Masham by name – if she was even aware of her authorship – in *A Serious Proposal, Part II*.[2] This was followed in 1700 with *Reflections upon Marriage*, which ran through five editions, to the third edition (1706) to which Astell added a controversial Preface, expanding her argument to include one of the earliest critiques of Locke's political arguments.

Certainly there were earlier proposals for women's education in England. Juan Luis Vives of Valencia (1492–1540), author of *De*

Institutione Christianae Feminae (1523), translated as *Instruction of a Christian Maid*, during a five-year stay in England, had promoted the education of women, writing a specific course of studies for Princess Mary, later Queen Mary I, entitled *Satellitium*. Vives's translator, Richard Hyde, had written a preface in praise of Margaret Roper's English translation of Erasmus's *Treatise upon the Pater Noster*.[3] The exiled Thomas Becon (1512–67) had demanded in his *Catechism* that 'schools for women and children be erected and set up in every Christian Commonwealth' by public authority, in imitation of the 'monasteries of solitary women whom we heretofore call nuns'.[4] More immediately, George Hickes (1642–1715), former chaplain to Charles II, a High Churchman who refused to swear allegiance to William and Mary, and suffragan to the nonjuring Archbishop Sancroft of Astell's acquaintance, had in a 1684 sermon called for the endowment of 'colleges for the Education of young Women, much like unto those in the Universities for the Education of young Men'.[5] Hickes, the rather free translator of Fénelon's *De l'Education des Filles*,[6] knew and possibly influenced Astell.[7] We have no direct evidence that Astell had read Fénelon, despite similarities of opinion, but the renown of the Maison de Saint Louis at Saint-Cyr, a school for noblewomen founded in 1686 by Louis XIV's mistress and later wife, with which Fénelon was closely associated, suggests a possible model for *A Serious Proposal*.[8]

Closer to home, the irrepressible Bathsua Makin, author of *An Essay to Revive the Antient Education of Gentlewomen* of 1673, had also provided a model in tune with Astell's proposal. Makin, who was tutor to Princess Elizabeth, daughter of Charles I, around 1641 established the Tottenham Cross girls' school, a boarding school that would turn out women properly equipped to perform their roles as wife and mother. Her work followed closely the program of her correspondent, the famous scholar from the University of Utrecht, Anna Marie van Schurman, whose *De Ingenii Muliebris* was translated into English as *The Learned Maid* in 1659.[9] Makin also espoused the educational theories of John Amos Comenius, whose *Great Didactic* of 1632 had argued for the education of girls and modernization of the curriculum to make this possible. Astell shares with Makin a desire to abandon the tyrannies of custom and William Lily's *Grammar*. Indeed, Makin's opening remarks on custom anticipate the remarks by William Wotton, later repeated by Astell in the first part of *A Serious Proposal* (1694) and elaborated at length by Judith Drake in her *Essay*.[10]

Custom, when it is inveterate, hath a mighty influence: it hath the force of Nature it self. The Barbarous custom to breed Women low, is grown general amongst us, and hath prevailed so far, that it is verily believed (especially among a sort of debauched Sots) that Women are not endued with such Reason, as Men; nor capable of improvement by Education, as they are. It is lookt upon as a monstrous thing, to pretend to the contrary. A Learned Woman is thought to be a Comet, that does Mischief, when ever it appears.

Makin's language has a direct echo in Astell's injunctions to 'reform these Exorbitancies', to abandon 'Toyes and Trifles', and to see the men who denied women's intellectual potential for what they were, 'debauched Sots' who care only for their 'Lusts and Pleasure'.[11] Like Astell, Makin supported traditional authority, warning her readers that 'God hath made Man the Head' and that 'To ask too much is the way to be denied all'.[12] Astell does not mention her predecessor by name, perhaps due to the earlier woman's Puritanism and political sympathies on the Parliament side. Worse yet, Makin had addressed her *Essay* to Lady Mary, Duchess of York, daughter of James II, who in 1689 was to become Queen Mary II, as wife of William of Orange, while Astell's friends numbered among the Jacobites and nonjurors who refused to swear allegiance to this perceived imposter.

Astell's *Proposal* made her famous and eventually ran to five editions, attracting the momentary support of Queen Anne for her proposed women's academy. It earned her praise from Daniel Defoe, the leading pamphleteer and dissenter, who used it as a model for his own version of a women's academy, as well as the unsigned criticisms of either Jonathan Swift (1667–1745)[13] or, more probably, Richard Steele (1672–1729) in *Tatler* nos. 32 and 63. But for every George Wheler, who gave unqualified acknowledgement to Astell's influence in *A Protestant Monastery* of 1698, there were ten who stole her ideas without acknowledgement and then satirized her to cover their tracks.[14] So Gilbert Burnet (1643–1715), Bishop of Salisbury, while persuading against support of Astell's project as being too monastic, himself proposed for women 'something like Monasteries without Vows which would be a glorious design'.[15] Daniel Defoe, although expressing admiration for Astell's proposal, argued against it on account of women's incorrigible levity, substituting his own proposal in an 'Academy for Women' (1697) that differed in no significant aspects from hers.[16] Richard Steele (1672–1729), Irish essayist, dramatist and politician, lampooned Astell in the *Tatler* as the founder of an 'order of Platonick Ladies . . . who . . . gave out, that their Virginity was to be their State of Life during their Mortal condition, and therefore resolv'd to join their Fortunes and erect a Nunnery'. Astell, in her Foreword to the second edition of *Bart'lemy Fair* of 1722, suggests that Swift put Steele up to the satire of her *A Serious Proposal* of 1694 in *Tatler* no. 32, from White's Chocolate-house, June 22, 1709, 'a little after the *Enquiry* [*Bart'lemy Fair*] appear'd':[17]

But tho' the *Enquirer* had offended the *Tatler*, and his great Friends, on whom he so liberally bestows his Panegyrics, by turning their Ridicule very justly upon themselves; what had any of her Acquaintances done to provoke him? Who does he point at? For she knows of none who ever attempted to *erect a Nunnery*, or declar'd *That Virginity was to be their State of Life.* . . .

Despite Astell's protests, even the stage did not spare her. Susanna Centlivre (c. 1667–1723), in her play *The Basset Table* (1706), has Valeria, 'that little She-Philosopher' doubtless modelled on Astell, 'founding a College for the Study of Philosophy where none but Women should be admitted'.[18] And as late as 1847, as we have noted, Tennyson's *The Princess* and Gilbert and Sullivan's *Princess Ida* lampooned Astell's *Proposal.*[19] As we have seen, however, Astell's project did not lack powerful advocates, and in 1752, at the end of her life, Lady Mary Wortley Montagu, an early travel writer whose *Letters from the East* are prefaced by Astell, confessed to her daughter a lifelong attraction to the proposal to found an 'English monastery' for ladies, to which she would have elected herself 'Lady abbess'.[20] Lady Montagu's letter to her daughter chiefly concerned criticisms of Samuel Richardson's novel *Sir Charles Grandison*, whose only redeeming feature, in her estimate, was his proposal to found Protestant nunneries 'in which single women, of small or no fortunes might live with all manner of freedom' in every English county.[21] Lady Montagu was not the only one to deal rather roughly with Richardson,[22] whose friend, and admirer of Astell, Sarah Chapone, may have advised him to read the author of *A Serious Proposal*[23] and whose *Clarissa* some claim to have been modelled on Astell.

2. Drake, Swift, Wotton and the Battle between the Ancients and Moderns

Judith Drake's anonymous *Essay*, falsely attributed to Astell, as we have noted, was also a tract on education addressed to Princess Anne of Denmark that focused on the tyranny of custom. It warrants attention here not only because for so long it was folded into the Astell corpus, but also because Drake's literal claim that 'Women, like our Negroes in our Western Plantations, are born slaves, and live Prisoners all their Lives',[24] casts important light on the rhetorical status of Astell's own claim regarding women and slavery.

Drake, like Astell, is a royalist, and participates in the debate over the ancients and moderns critical to a curriculum for women's education. She opens her royal dedicatory Preface with reference to a conversation she and the princess had had "tother day' upon which, apparently, the princess had commanded her to draft an essay for her royal instruction. 'The strength of Judgment, sprightly Fancy, and admirable Address, you shew'd upon that Occasion, speak you so perfect a Mistress of that Argument', Drake demurs, 'Yet to let you see how absolutely you command me, I had rather be your Eccho, than be silent when You bid me speak'.[25] Drake's essay, like Astell's earlier *Serious Proposal* (1694),[26] is a plea for women's education, but one with an important immediate context. Her inspiration, Drake tells us, is a work she had apparently discussed with the princess, 'made three or four years since by one' fellow,' A *Don Quixot* of the Quill left to succour the distressed Damsels'.[27] The work, further identified as 'Mr. W's. Common Place Book', she threatens to leave to 'Pedants and School-Boys to rake and tumble the Rubbish of Antiquity, and muster all the *Heroes* and *Heroins* they can find to furnish matter for some wretched Harangue, or stuff a miserable Declamation with instead of Sense or Argument'. It is almost certainly William Wotton's *Reflections upon Ancient and Modern Learning* of 1694.

Wotton's work was an important intervention in the controversy between the ancients and moderns, begun in France by Fontenelle and transported to England by the statesman Sir William Temple with his essay *The Gardens of Epicurus* of 1692. There the Englishmen Charles Boyle, Richard Bentley and Wotton and the Irishman Jonathan Swift joined in the fray. Swift, Temple's adopted son, took the side of the ancients; Wotton, although a formidable classical scholar, took the side of the moderns. As a member of the Royal Society and an ardent promoter of its causes, the latter argued for the superiority of the new science and the sophistication of modern philology that could marshal the wisdom of antiquity and adapt ancient learning to modern causes. It is perhaps for this reason that Astell used Wotton's name as a pseudonym in *Bart'lemy Fair, or an Enquiry after Wit in which due Respect is had to a Letter Concerning Enthusiasm. To my Lord XXX by Mr. Wotton [pseud.]*, the first edition of which was published in London in 1709. The 1722 edition appeared under a different title, *An Enquiry after Wit, wherein the Trifling Arguing and Impious Raillery of the Late Earl of Shaftesbury in his letter concerning Enthusiasm and other Profane Writers are fully answered and justly exposed*, and in the Preface to that edition Astell explained that it was only after her work appeared under this new title that the *Tatler* undertook its lampoon:[28]

The first edition of the Enquiry, which 'appear'd at first under a borrow'd Name' – that of Wotton, whom Swift in *Tale of a Tub* parodied – 'drew upon her indeed the Resentment of that sort of Men of Wit who are here expos'd, and was the true Cause, of a Fable which the worthy *Tatler* was pleased to invent and publish a little after the Enquiry appear'd; though he thought fit to give another Reason when he was charg'd with doing what was so contrary to his Professions in many of his *Tatlers*, where he wou'd seem to pay Respect to Religion and Vertue'.

It is important to emphasize that this was a debate largely confined to the court. But Wotton, in his *Reflections*, that great antiquarian tome in defence of modern learning that made Sir William Temple's essay appear slight, had the temerity to venture republican views, and this may have been his temporary undoing. 'When the Romans once lost their Liberty', he declared, 'their Eloquence soon fell',[29] and he singled out Polybius as his favourite among the ancients.[30] In the event, his academic republicanism did not stand in the way of his being later hired by Queen Anne to tutor her son, William, Duke of Gloucester, but it may have been enough to raise the ire of the young princess and of Drake, her friend.

Drake's chief bone of contention is precisely Wotton's philology and history.[31] We know that Wotton applied modern philological techniques to the explication of Genesis 11:1–9,[32] the story of the peopling of the earth by Noah's sons, Shem, Ham and Japheth, which lay at the heart of Filmer's biblical patriarchalism and which also became the obsession of Newton. Wotton's 'Scandal' is that he appears to defend women's cause, but 'like a false Renegade fights under our Colours only for a fairer Opportunity of betraying us'.[33] In fact Drake is rather unfair to Wotton, who is generally favourable to women, praising Queen Christina of Sweden for her learning, for instance:[34]

Christina, Queen of *Sweden*, who, in other respects, was by no means the Glory of her Sex, did whilst she liv'd at *Stockholm*, send for the learnedest Men of *Europe*, to come to her, that she might converse with [them] about those things wherein they were most excellent. *Des Cartes, Salmasius, Nicholas Heinsius, Isaac Vossius*, were of that number: and her Profuseness, which knew no bounds, was scarce in any thing more visible than in her Marks of Respect to Men of Letters.

Drake, like Astell, believed that antiquarian displays like Wotton's were largely aimed at demeaning women, deprived of the classical education that had allowed men to monopolize learning: 'He levels his Scandal at the whole Sex, and thinks us sufficiently fortified, if out of the Story of Two Thousand Years he has been able to pick up a few Examples of Women illustrious for their Wit, Learning or Vertue, and Men infamous for the contrary'.[35] In fact, the passage in Wotton to which she refers appears in Chapter 30, *Reflections upon the Reasons of the Decay of Learning assign'd by Sir William Temple,* where he argues that classical eloquence was very fashionable for women at one time:[36]

It was so very modish, that the Fair Sex seemed to believe that *Greek* and *Latin* added to their Charms. And *Plato* and *Aristotle* untranslated, were frequent Ornaments of their Closets. One would think by the Effects, that it was a proper Way of Educating them, since there are no Accounts in History of so many truly great Woman in any one Age, as are to be found between the Years MD and MDC.

This remark was not likely to mollify Drake, however, for whom it was all too clear that a classical education in early modern Britain was a male monopoly used to exclude women, who could not have it, from public life.

3. Drake, the State of Nature and Freedom from Domination

Much of the interest in Drake's case concerns the way in which she holds up to ridicule state-of-nature arguments, arguing, like Astell, that rights pertain to minds, not bodies. Unlike Astell, however, she denies the Platonist theory of innate ideas, subscribing rather to the sensationalist psychology of Locke. She makes a series of arguments under the following headings: (1) *No distinction of Sexes in Souls*, (2) *No Advantages in the Organization of their Bodies*, (3) *Confirm'd from Experience of Brutes*, (4) *Experience of Mankind*, and (5) *Women industriously kept in Ignorance*. Their sum is the claim, the same as Astell's, that only custom and contingency keep women subordinate, something that can never be justified by reason. Declaring that 'the Ends . . . we aim at in all our Actions [are] in general only two, Profit or Pleasure', and that 'these are divided into those of the Mind and those of the Body', she goes on to dismiss the latter 'as having no Relation to the present Subject', confining herself rather to the mind. There is 'no such distinction, as Male and Female Souls' applies, she argues, 'there are no innate *Idea's [sic]*, but that all the Notions we have, are deriv'd from our External Senses, either immediately, or by Reflection'.[37] There is no natural advantage to men '*in the Organization of the Bodies*' either, she maintains: Their brains 'are contriv'd as well for the plentiful conveyance of Spirits, which are held to be the immediate Instruments of Sensation, in Women, as Men'.[38] In fact, as previously noted, she draws precisely the opposite conclusion to Hobbes and Locke on the physiology of the sexes: women, far from being the weaker sex, are intellectually superior.[39]

Drake parodies state-of-nature theories at length in the section of her book entitled *Confirm'd from the Experience of Brutes*, arguing against the relevance of such an artificial construct, using the benchmark of nature in the raw and the example of animals: 'In [animals] we may see Nature plainest, who lie under no constraint of Custom or Laws, but those of Passion and Appetite, which are Natures, and know no difference of Education, nor receive any Byass by prejudice'.[40] In other words, if we are arguing from bodies, and for the natural superiority of males over females, why not look at 'those Creatures that deviate least from simple Nature, and see if we can find difference in Sense, or understanding between Males and Females'? What do we find among the brutes but that 'a She Ape is as full of, and as ready at Imitation as a He; a Bitch will learn as many Tricks in as short a time as a Dog, a Female Fox has as many Wiles as a Male'?[41] No comfort for the physicalists there. Drake, perhaps unwittingly, highlights the tendency to conflate the state of nature as an analytic construct – as in Hobbes – with the state of nature as an anthropological description of the condition of primitive peoples – toward which Locke, and later Rousseau, influenced by accounts of indigenous peoples in the New World, tend – as well as calling into question the theory of progress that underpins the notion of the transition from status to contract as a sequential process.[42]

Proceeding up the ladder from brutes to the *Experience of Mankind*, Drake directs her imaginary interlocutor 'to observe the Country People . . . for amongst these, though not so equal as that of Brutes, yet the Condition of the Sexes is more level, than amongst Gentlemen, City Traders, or rich Yeoman.'[43] Or higher up the chain, and here Drake refers the princess to the position of women in the society of her kinsmen, William and Mary of Orange: 'Let us look a little further, and view our Sex in a state of more improvement, amongst our Neighbours the *Dutch*. There we shall find them managing not only the Domestick Affairs of the Family, but making, and receiving all Payments as well great as small, keeping the Books, ballancing the Accounts, and doing all the Business, even the nicest of Merchants, with as much Dexterity and Exactness as their, or our Men can do'.[44]

Drake, considering ways to reform the morals or manners by which women are subordinated, throws out a line of hope in the 'no honour among thieves' notion, observing of men that, 'like the Rebels in our last Civil Wars, when they had brought the Royal Party under, they fall together by the Ears about the Dividend'.[45] Drake, unlike Astell, professes to be uninterested in biblical history, 'leaving that for the Divines', and she finds her best case in an antediluvian people of whom 'Sacred History takes no notice', the famous Amazons of Herodotus – who in fact lived in Scythia – and would not suffer 'a Man to live amongst them, which cou'd be for no other Reason than their Tyranny'. Although surrounded by states inhabited only by men, 'the Conditions of their Society were not so easie, as to engage their Women to stay amongst 'em; but as liberty presented itself, they withdrew and retired to the *Amazon*'.[46]

Drake's appeal to the case of the Amazons as an example of women's liberation, reaching back into Herodotean pre-history as it does, represents a further satirical comment on state of nature arguments. It should come as no surprise that when it comes to the contest between the ancients and the moderns, Drake is firmly on the side of the moderns, although not without dispatching Wotton with the same contempt she reserves for Temple. In the event, Drake lambastes the pretensions of the entire Roman republican tradition under the heading '*Character of a Pedant*':[47]

For Schollars, though by their acquaintance with Books and conversing much with Old Authors, they may know perfectly the Sense of the Learned Dead, and be perfect Masters of the Wisdom, be throughly inform'd of the State, and nicely skill'd in the Policies of Ages long since past, yet by their retir'd and unactive Life, their neglect of Business, and constant Conversation with Antiquity, they are such strangers to, and so ignorant of the Domestick Affairs and manners of their own Country and Times, that they appear like the Ghosts of Old Romans rais'd by Magick. Talk to them of the *Assyrian*, or *Perssian* Monarchies, the *Grecians* or *Roman* Common-wealths. They answer like Oracles, they are such finish'd Statesmen, that we shou'd scarce take 'em to have been less than Confidents of *Semiramis*, Tutours to *Cyrus* the great, old Cronies of *Solon* and *Lycurgus*, or Privy Councellours at least to the Twelve *Caesars* successively; but engage them in a Discourse that concerns the present Times, and their Native Country, and they heardly speak the Language of it, and know so little of the affairs of it, that as much might reasonably be expected from an animated *Egyptian* Mummy.

Drake is rather indiscriminate in her attack on the antiquarians and their pretensions, noting, 'They are very much disturbed to see a Fold or a Plait ammiss in the Picture of an Old *Roman* Gown, yet take no notice that their own are thredbare out at the Elbows, or Ragged'.[48] 'They are excellent Guides, and can direct you to every Ally, and turning in old *Rome*; yet lose their way at home in their own Parish'.[49]

4. Astell and the Port Royal School

While Drake's feminism was too blatant to be passed off for what it was not, it was Astell's fate to be presented as a proto-Catholic quietist who wanted to resurrect the nunnery. It has escaped the notice of Astell's critics that it was not on a convent as such, even a Protestant convent, that *A Serious Proposal* was modelled, in fact. Astell had fortuitously to hand an institution for which her proposal was the perfect fit, the French Port Royal School, founded by a famous woman early in the thirteenth century, reformed by another late in the sixteenth, and specifically designated as a place of retirement for women who were not required to take religious vows in order to live there. Port Royal, a famous Cistercian abbey, had been established southwest of Paris in 1204 by Mahaut de Garlande, wife of Mathieu de Montmorenci-Marli, and singled out in 1223 by Pope Honorius III as a place of retreat for women who wished to withdraw from the world without taking the perpetual vows of a religious order. Its modern history commenced in 1598 under the leadership of Angélique Arnauld, sister of the famous Jansenist philosopher Antoine Arnauld (1612–94). Angélique Arnauld made contact in person with Jean Duvergier, abbot of Saint Cyran and chief promoter of Jansenism, a rigorous movement of Christian renewal with which her family and her convent became inextricably associated.[50] In 1648 the abbey had set up a school for the sons of Jansenist parents, but doctrinal skirmishing with the papacy consumed the next two decades, only concluded in 1669 by the Peace of Clement IX, who lifted the interdict on the school. The protection of Madame de Longueville, Louis XIV's cousin, gave the convent a decade of peace, but between her death in 1679 and the forcible removal of the Jansenists from Port Royal by the police in 1709, the king, enlisting papal support, exerted relentless pressure against them, eventually destroying their buildings and even their cemetery.[51]

As the nursery of such famous Jansenist philosophers and pietists as Antoine Arnauld, Pierre Nicole (1625–95) and Blaise Pascal (1623–62), whose philosophical arguments Astell promoted, it is hardly surprising that Port Royal should have been both a model and a warning for her project. Those who believe *A Serious Proposal, Part II* to be a curriculum proposal – mainly those who have not read it – therefore commit a double error. If the *Proposal* was not modelled on a nunnery, even a Protestant one, education as such was not Astell's project either, but rather those deep background philosophical and theological assumptions that deny women the capacity for improvement of the mind. Conceding that

'Education is a beaten subject and has been accounted by better pens' than hers,[52] Astell in the second part of her *Serious Proposal* specifically disavows any intention of laying out a curriculum, which she is happy to leave to those who 'have a more exact Knowledge of Human Nature, a greater Experience of the World, and of those differences which arise from Constitution, Age, Education, receiv'd Opinions, outward Fortune, Custom and Conversation, than I can pretend to'[53] – perhaps a reference to Locke's *Some Thoughts Concerning Education*. Rather, Astell is concerned to address philosophy of mind and the epistemological basis of female education. Already in her correspondence with Norris, Astell had debated the relative autonomy of human motivation and cognition, challenging Norris to accept the corollary of his argument that if God was the author of our pleasure, then he was equally the author of our pain – pleasure and pain being the twin motivational principles of Lockean sensationalist psychology. The theme she set in the opening letter of the Astell–Norris correspondence, described in Cartesian language what was to become a lifelong programme:

Sir, though some morose Gentlemen would perhaps remit me to the Distaff or the Kitchin, or at least to the Glass and the Needle, the proper Employments as they fancy of a Woman's Life; yet expecting better things from the more Equitable and ingenious Mr. Norris, who is not so narro-Soul'd as to confine Learning to his own Sex, or to envy it in ours, I presume to beg his Attention a little to the Impertinencies of a Woman's Pen. . . . For though I can't pretend to a Multitude of Books, Variety of Languages, the Advantages of Academical Education or any Helps but what my own Curiosity affords; yet, *Thinking* is a Stock that no Rational Creature can want.[54]

Following this line of attack in *A Serious Proposal, Part II*, she enters a metaphysical thicket far above the plane of educational theory, joining the company of Descartes, Malebranche, Arnauld, Nicole and Locke himself in a full-scale debate over the consequences of the Cartesian *cogito*. This work, presented as the second part of her famous proposal for a women's academy, in fact contains one of the most brilliant disquisitions of the age on Descartes's clear and distinct ideas,[55] the possibility of certitude, and the ethical and religious consequences of the Cartesian position, the very topics that had occasioned Locke's *Essay Concerning Human Understanding*, to the reception of which Astell's corpus belongs. For together with Masham's *Discourse*, Locke's *Reasonableness of Christianity* (1695) and his First and possibly Second Letters to Edward Stillingfleet, bishop of Worcester, which focused precisely on Descartes's notion of clear and distinct ideas and their implications for the Christian doctrine of the Trinity, are the specific works that occasion *A Serious Proposal, Part II*, in which Astell undertakes her first spirited rebuttal of Locke.[56]

Locke's *Letters to Stillingfleet*, like his *Letters on Toleration*, are in the epistolary style. Even his *Essay Concerning Understanding* is written in the first person, much as women writers of the period did, to indicate that his works were intended for a popular and not just an academic audience. In *The Christian Religion*, as we shall see, Astell replied to Locke's third letter to the Bishop of Worcester, which deals with 'Certainty by Reason, Certainty by Ideas, and Certainty by Faith; the Resurrection of the Body; the Immateriality of the Soul' and christology in general. But there is internal evidence in *A Serious Proposal, Part II* to suggest that she is already familiar at that early date with the arguments of the First and Second Letters to Stillingfleet, specifically concerned with 'a late Discourse of his Lordship's in Vindication of the Trinity' and that she is refuting them there. Moreover, marginal notes in *Moderation Truly Stated* of 1704, indicating the range of her reading, refer the reader to Stillingfleet's *The Mischief of Separation* (1680) and the *Unreasonableness of Separation* (1681), as well as to Thomas Edward's [*The Second Part of Gangraena . . . or*] *Further Discovery* (1646), his *Antapologia* (1644) and his *Epistle Dedicated to the Lords and Commons before his Gangraena* (1646).[57] Both Stillingfleet and Edwards were among Locke's most important contemporary critics.

If *A Serious Proposal* and *Reflections upon Marriage* are the best known of Astell's works and the most commented upon by contemporaries, they have so far escaped full analysis. The works stand to one another in an organic relationship, the central argument of Astell's work on marriage already foreshadowed in her proposal for a woman's place of academic retirement. But an important and undisclosed hiatus divides these works, as it also divides the first from the second parts of *A Serious Proposal*. Into that gap stepped Lady Damaris Masham. The chain of contingencies set in motion by Astell's *Letters Concerning the Love of God* and *A Serious Proposal, Part I* resulted in a curiously cerebral *ménage à trois* in which Astell proved to be the spiritual daughter of Ralph Cudworth but Masham, Cudworth's real daughter, the consort and advocate of John Locke. The situation is further complicated by the fact that in 1697, at the time of the publication of *A Serious Proposal, Part II*, Astell seems to have genuinely believed Masham's response to her *Letters*, the *Discourse Concerning the Love of God*, to be the work of Locke. But by 1705 and the publication of *The*

Christian Religion, Astell expresses doubts, suggesting that she may have known, or at least suspected, Masham's authorship:[58]

Whether [Locke] be the same Person who writ *A Discourse Concerning the Love of GOD*, or who is the Author, it is not my business to enquire, since he has not thought fit to discover himself. Nor am I about to complain or make reprisals, whatever occasion might be given by that *Discourse*.

The opening paragraph of *The Christian Religion* refers enigmatically to the press having 'help'd us to the Religion of a *Physician*, a *Layman*, a *Gentleman*, and a *Lady*, yet in my poor opinion, they have all of them but one Religion if they are Christians'.[59] The query, 'if they are Christians', may refer to the charge by John Edwards in *Socinianism Unmasked* (1696) that Locke was firstly a Socinian and secondly a Muslim.[60] This is a charge that Astell repeats, accusing defenders of Alcoran as a book of divine revelation of 'a Religion accommodated even to the lees and dregs of Sense, [that] obtains among too many sensual men'.[61] She is apt to target Locke as 'a sensual man', as for instance again in §29 of *The Christian Religion*, where she observes acerbically: 'Most Men are so Sensualiz'd, that they take nothing to be Real but what they can Hear and See, or which is some way or other the Object of their senses. Others who wou'd seem the most refin'd, make Sensation the fund of their Ideas, carrying their Contemplations no farther than these, and the Reflections they make upon the operations of their Minds when thus employ'd'. As E. Derek Taylor notes, the plural 'others' refers, of course, to the singular John Locke, author of the *Essay*.[62]

The peculiar intimacy of Masham and Locke – peculiar because its degree of Platonism has never been established – was public knowledge by 1697. John Edwards (1637–1716), son of the infamous and scurrilous Calvinist Thomas Edwards, author of *Gangraena* (1646), whom, as we have noted, Astell elsewhere quotes,[63] seems to have made it his life's work to expose Locke, with a series of books and even some scurrilous letters that impugned the man not only on technical grounds – attacking Locke's *Reasonableness*, his Socinianism and his *Some Thoughts Concerning Education* – but also for his private life. In 1697 Edwards published his *Brief Vindication of the Fundamental Articles of Christian Faith*, in which he referred to Locke as 'a lewd disclaimer', a 'raving tutor and reformer', a 'profligate scribe', a 'hater of women' and 'the governor of the seraglio at Oates' – where Locke resided with the Masham family.[64] Whether Astell knew of Edwards's specific allegations or not, she gives hints that she knows the Masham setup. She was probably aware, for instance, of the incident of the unsealed letter that is believed to have provoked Locke's animus against Norris, prompting him to write his rebuttal to Norris's occasionalism. For reasons of propriety, perhaps, given Locke's close association with William III, and his notorious reticence about his own work, Astell waited until Locke's death in 1704 to publish her open rebuttal of Locke's doctrines, whereupon she published *The Christian Religion* (1705), dedicated to refuting Masham's *Discourse* along with Locke's *Reasonableness of Christianity, Essay Concerning Human Understanding* and *Two Treatises of Government*, as if they were all by the same hand.

Masham had challenged the fundamental premise of the Astell–Norris *Letters Concerning the Love of God*: that the individual's dependence on her divine maker extended to cognition itself. Unmediated dependence on God as the disposition of the knowing subject entailed withdrawal from the world and denial of human sociability, leading to the nunnery as a logical consequence, Masham claimed.[65] Masham targeted the thesis under discussion in the Astell–Norris letters that 'we see all things in God', made famous by Malebranche and promulgated by Norris. It was not only the substance of the Masham challenge to which Astell responded in *A Serious Proposal, Part II*, a work enormously wide-ranging in its capacity to syncretize contemporary philosophical debate, but she took it as a personal attack, reading Masham's reference to 'a young Writer, whose Judgment may, perhaps be thought Byassesd by the Affectation of Novelty',[66] as implying that she, Astell, was no more than Norris's acolyte.

One has only to look closely at *A Serious Proposal, Part II* to see the lineaments of her mature arguments, along with the works that occasioned them, already there. Something of a revolution in her thought – hitherto unremarked – takes place between *A Serious Proposal, Part I* and *Part II*. Astell takes seriously Masham's claim that to deny the relative autonomy of individual cognition is gratuitous Platonist quietism. To deny the Creator who made us the power to endow us with independent cognition is both to deny God's essential attributes and to ignore New Testament exhortations to take responsibility for our own salvation, Masham argued. The consequence of seeing all things in God is a form of solipsism that allows the self as the only object of real knowledge. It thus denies the role of human interaction in understanding and implementing the programme for a Christian life and can end only in the nunnery, to which are confined the powerless subordinates of an omnipotent God. In *A Serious Proposal, Part II*, Astell appears to concede Masham's first charge and tries to address the second. She declares that the proposition of Malebranche endorsed by Norris, that we see all things in God, if not true, is at least pious.[67] And she denies that her house of retirement for women was ever intended as other than a primarily academic establishment. Astell's struggle to accommodate Masham's challenges has a happy outcome. Appealing to the Jansenist philosophers of the Port Royal school, Arnauld, Nicole and Pascal, who were so influential on Locke, Astell not only succeeds in improving the rigour of her model by abandoning Malebranche and endorsing the Port Royal logic of his critics, notably Arnauld, but she then holds Locke accountable to his own acknowledged sources. The task of *A Serious Proposal, Part II* is less to elaborate the specifications for an academy set out in *Part I* than to provide it sound epistemic, moral and Christian footings for women's autonomy. This involves Astell in laying out the foundations of her metaphysics, ethics, philosophy of education and religion systematically, a programme that she completes in *The Christian Religion* of 1705.

The brilliance of her exposition, and particularly her presentation of the Port Royal logic, is attested to by the extraordinary plagiarism of some 147 pages of Chapter 3, Sections 1–5 of the 1697 edition of *A Serious Proposal, Part II*, excerpted without acknowledgement in *The Ladies Library* of 1714. A devotional work targeted at Christian gentlewomen, it was widely circulated, being reprinted eight times up to 1772, and was translated into both French and Dutch.[68] 'Published by Mr. R[ichard] Steele', who supplied a preface, and purportedly 'written by a Lady', *The Ladies Library* was in fact compiled by none other than George Berkeley, the eminent cleric and philosopher. Reading between the lines, one can see in fact that Steele acknowledges that he has been given credit for a greater role in the work than he would claim for himself: 'I am only her [the Lady's] Gentleman-Usher', he wrote in the preface. *The Ladies Library* was only one of a number of works devoted to self-improvement, a genre targeting both sexes that included *The Ladies Calling, The Gentleman's Calling* and *The Gentleman's Library*, all three of which Astell cited. It was referred to by the author of the latter as 'having been read in most counties, though it was swell'd out into three volumes and sold at a pretty handsome price'.[69] Astell's pirated work appears in volume 1 alongside *The Ladies Calling* (1693 edn.),[70] as well as Fénelon's *Education of a Daughter*, in Hickes's translation, and her nemesis Locke's *Some Thoughts Concerning Education*.

Richard Steele (1672–1729) was until recently believed to be the compiler of *The Ladies Library*. Astell herself, in the 1722 Preface to *Bart'lemy Fair*, attributed the extensive plagiarism of *A Serious Proposal, Part II* to

him, having a bone to pick with him for having satirized her in the *Tatler*.
In the Preface to *Bart'lemy Fair* (1722 edn., Preface, p. A2a), she remarks
of Steele, with customary acerbic wit:[71]

The harmless Satyr does not bite; and tho' it shew'd its teeth against the *Proposal to the Ladies*, our honest *Compilator* has made an honourable Amends to the Author, (I know not what he has to the Bookseller) by transcribing above an hundred Pages into his *Ladies Library, verbatim*; except in a few Places, which if the Reader takes the Trouble to compare, perhaps he will find improv'd.

But *The Ladies Library*, according to the title page, 'published by Mr.
R[ichard] Steele', who supplied a preface, and 'written by a Lady', was
in fact compiled by Bishop George Berkeley, whose great contribution
to philosophy had been his critique of the materialism of Hobbes and
Locke, which he believed, like Astell, to be a negative consequence of
Cartesian dualism.[72] Accepting ideas in Locke's sense, as the immediate objects of mind in the cognition process, Berkeley had insisted that
ideas were not *outside* the mind, but constituted the world of reality *in* the
mind. Moreover, ideas were required as a translation language to interpret experience given by sensation. These are views with which Astell
could be expected to more or less sympathize, and it is surprising, perhaps, that she did not discover that the real perpetrator of the plagiarism
against her was more friend than foe.

5. Astell's Critique of Locke's Epistemology

In *A Serious Proposal, Part II*, Astell challenges objections raised by Masham
and Locke to her *Proposal* specifically and to her system of beliefs in general. The first, most fundamental and most successfully disposed of is her
challenge to any hopes of improving the condition of women raised by
Locke's sensationalist psychology and philosophy of environmental conditioning. She was not the first to lay such a challenge; and, indeed,
Norris, in remarks on Locke's *Essay Concerning Human Understanding*,
appended to the former's *Discourses upon the Beatitudes*, published the
year after Locke's *Essay*, had raised some of the topics Astell pursues.
In particular, Norris had claimed that Locke's empiricism can account
only for perceptions relating to the body and not higher-order metaphysical notions of truth, justice, order, good and so on, which are
products of the mind. Locke's dualism ruled out criteria to validate necessary as opposed to contingent truths and was therefore self-refuting,
Norris claimed. Given that Locke's entire system, from the *Essay*

Concerning Human Understanding, his *Thoughts Concerning Education,* through *The Reasonableness of Christianity* to his *Two Treatises of Government,* was devoted to proving the democracy of experience and the transparency of reason, this was no mean charge. Not only are all humans susceptible to the same sense impressions that the mind combines to produce ideas, Locke had argued, but they are in principle equally susceptible to reason, whose transparency is guaranteed by the cognitive apparatuses with which we have been endowed and sanctioned in the egalitarianism of the Christian life as set out in Scripture.

But what would seem to be democratic and egalitarian foundations for the emancipation of the poor and the downtrodden, as well as for women, Astell correctly perceived to be a bulwark for the *status quo.* If in fact the reception of ideas is largely dependent on environmental conditions, what Locke trumpets as reason is no more than custom. And if the reasonableness of Christianity sanctions this, then everything is left as it was. As long as the human psyche is environmentally conditioned, self-improvement is theoretically impossible and women are condemned to the tyranny of custom and convention, their jailers hitherto. A theory of environmental conditioning would cut the ground right out from under Astell's project for a women's academy. But Astell claimed to see through to the very foundations of Locke's system, arrived at expeditiously, like that of Hobbes on which it is based, as a strategy against religious sedition and the independence of puritanism and popery. Astell, like Descartes, by contrast, precisely targeted women and customary right, and her arguments would seem to follow rather closely those of the Cartesian François Poulain de la Barre[73] in his *De l'Égalité des Deux Sexes* of 1673, available in English in 1677 under the title *The Woman as Good as the Man,* although we have no direct evidence that she had read him.[74]

Astell's refutation of empiricism as sanctioning custom, that aggregate of material conditions that chains women to their posts, comprises one of the most important tasks of *A Serious Proposal, Part II.* Her case against custom foreshadows in general the arguments of *Reflections upon Marriage,* an attack on eighteenth-century morals and mores that demean marriage and reduce it from a sacrament to a form of servitude. It also casts specific light on Astell's famous rhetorical question.[75] Its substance, rephrased as a proposition, would read: 'only if men are born free can women be born slaves'. But the condition does not hold, for Astell denies the premise of Locke's *tabula rasa,* the slate wiped clean of hereditable obligations for persons, on three counts. First – and here she embraces the argument for sociability from Aristotle and Cicero through to the

Church Fathers, which Masham claims she had denied – individuals are born into families, countries, villages, towns and cities, and so do not come into this world shorn of hereditable obligations. Second, even if they did, given that women are persons, there are no earthly grounds for denying them the freedom enjoyed by men. For, third, Locke's rejection of hereditable obligations as regards one's person, but retention of hereditable obligation as regards one's property, is lamentably arbitrary, the more so because it makes women, who as legal minors cannot own property and are therefore dependent on men, mere chattels.

If to say that men are born free means accepting that they are born with rights, Locke is asserting a claim of the same order as the doctrine of innate ideas, which he rejects. Of course, these different claims are not mutually entailed, and Astell accepts the doctrine of innate ideas herself while rejecting the possibility that rights could be innate in an imperfect and hierarchically ordered world. She is able to argue a plausible case for innate ideas as emanating from the mind of God, whereas the case for rights as innate has always been merely rhetorical. Moreover, in her view, it serves to obscure the fact that women's servitude is the product of obdurate custom – and here Astell mounts the case against custom made so famously by Descartes. Because customary right belongs in a different zone, immune to reason, it is perpetuated by those very men who would claim for themselves the highest degree of enlightenment, who think it 'Honourable to break a Vow that ought to be Kept, and Dishonourable to get loose from an Engagement that ought to be broken'.[76] Astell, in *A Serious Proposal, Part II*, frames the *topoi* later to be discussed in *Reflections upon Marriage*. 'What do they think of Greatness who support their Pomp at the Expence of the Groans and Tears of many Injur'd Families?'[77]

A tissue of systemic ironies surrounds Astell's famous response to the argument for subordination from customary right. It frames a paradox that goes to the heart of Locke's doctrine and her own project. She sometimes appears to be seduced by her own rhetoric, as when, for instance, she suggests a master–slave analogue for the relations between God and his subjects:

For had we indeed that Esteem for GOD and Intire, Conformity to his Will, which is at once both the Duty and Perfection of all Rational Beings, we shou'd not complain of his Exercise of that Power, which a Prince or even an Ordinary Master has a Right to; which is, to set his Servants about such work as he thinks them fittest for. If we allow that GOD Governs the Universe, can we so much as imagine that it is not Govern'd with the Greatest Justice and Equity, Order and Proportion? Is not every one of us plac'd in such Circumstances as Infinite Wisdom discerns to be most suitable, so that nothing is wanting but a careful observation whither they lead us, and how we may best improve them? What reason then to complain of the Management of the world? and indeed except in the Morals of Mankind which are visibly and grossly deprav'd, I see not why we shou'd so much as wish for any alteration.[78]

But if this would seem to be a quietist argument, discouraging a program of social change, Astell here sanctions custom on grounds other than those of Locke. It is not because humans are subject to environmental conditioning that nothing changes or should be changed. It is because, although in principle capable of self-improvement and governing the will, humans give constant witness to the fallen state of human nature, from which Christ alone has the power to redeem them. Astell's religiosity fits a coherent system. The theodicy paradox, according to which God is the author of both good and evil, enjoins humans to strive for a perfection that the power of evil more or less guarantees they will never attain. These are all consequences of divine design, but they have little to do with reason as we conceive it.

Astell's epistemic assault on Lockean rationalism, sensationalist psychology and environmentalism allows her to deliver a moral diatribe against women who succumb to custom too easily. *A Serious Proposal, Part II* begins in Chapter 1 with an exhortation to women to abandon frivolity and get theologically serious. It is up to them to 'abandon the yoke of impertinent custom' and claim liberty back for themselves. As rational creatures, they can free themselves from the ghosts of irrational mechanism. What appears to be an inconsistency here is yet another paradox. To deny that men (or women) are born free is not to deny the case for liberty. Freedom Astell understands classically as the capacity to embrace a principle of conduct and follow it. The false deduction from the fact of existence to a right to freedom of which she accuses Locke – a violation of the is–ought distinction – far from liberating individuals, chains them to custom by virtue of the irrational mechanistic psychology imported to explain how material conditions impede freedom's exercise. Staying with freedom of the will as true freedom – and here Astell follows classical models since Aristotle on voluntary and involuntary conduct to which Locke also subscribed in fact – she resorts to moral pathologies to explain not only corruption of the will, but miscarriages of perception. And here her philosophy follows both Plato and the Stoics, for whom all thinking involves a degree of assent and for whom the disciplined will is a precondition to knowledge. Moral corruption is in her view all-pervasive.

Disease of the passions stands in the way of the proofs of Christianity, because the heart, not the head, is the seat of atheism.

In *A Serious Proposal, Part II*, Chapter 2, Astell sets out her own programme for freedom: a disengagement from prejudice, opinion of names, authorities and customs that

[c]ontract our Souls and shorten our views, hinder the free range of our Thoughts and confine them only to that particular track which these have taken, and in a word, erect a Tyranny over our free born Souls, whilst they suffer nothing to pass for True that has not been stampt at their own Mint.[79]

Once again, the apparent contradiction of her claim to dismantle a tyranny over 'free born Souls' is a function of irony, and once again, the target is Locke. We are cued by the long and convoluted argument that follows, beginning, 'But this is not all their mischief, they are really the root of Scepticism'. Astell claims that the weakness of Locke's original knowledge claims makes it imperative to draw false inferences to arrive at a predictable result, which is to claim certainty for nothing, that every-thing is probable and, in the end, believe nothing at all. This is not the only place where Astell turns against Locke a Platonist argument:

Were we to Poll for Truth, or were our own particular Opinions th' Infallible Standard of it, there were reason to subscribe to the Sentiments of the *Many*, or to be tenacious of our *Own*.[80]

But since this is not the case:

since Truth tho she is bright and ready to reveal her self to all sincere Inquirers, is not often found by the generality of those who pretend to seek after her, Interest, Applause, or some other little sordid Passion, being really the Mistress they court. . . .[81]

Self-styled authorities cannot stand in the way of what reflection reveals to the serious enquirer after truth. Locke, further developing the mechanis-tic psychology of Hobbes, had characterized human cognitive processes as the original black box that takes in sense data and puts out ideas. But if human agency has so little to do with behavioural output, then Locke's philosophy is just whistling in the wind, as vulnerable as any other to explanation as a form of interest-seeking.

Not surprisingly, Astell resorts to this sort of rebuttal of Locke wher-ever possible, for Astell is a serious Platonist, subscribing to the corol-lary of Socrates's rebuttal of Thrasymachus in the *Republic* 336b–54c. To Thrasymachus's challenge in *Republic* 338c that 'justice is nothing but the advantage of the stronger', which turns out to be a formula for tyranny of the majority, Plato had produced the rebuttal that if one is serious about knowledge claims, public opinion is irrelevant in deciding educational or any other political policy. But to concede with Thrasymachus and, more pertinently in Astell's case, with Locke, that people are primarily interest-seeking and that those policies win that attract the greatest number – whose interests they then serve – is to concede that politics and education can be no instrument for social improvement. But if such 'democrats' are wrong, and human perfectibility based on knowledge and disciplining the will is a duty-worthy project – Rousseau's later challenge to Hobbes and Locke – then democracy, as rule by the opinion of the greatest number, is out the window, and a true equality based on the equal capacity for perfectibility enters in its place, to which the principle of meritocracy appeals.

In Chapter 2, Astell is able not only to knock down Locke's theory of environmental conditioning as self-refuting, but to set a superior argument in its place. To this end she invokes the distinction between true and false forms of self-love, or interest-seeking, made famous by Pierre Nicole of the Port Royal school. She is not averse to the notion of the passions as an appetitive and motivating force, essential to maintenance of the animal spirits, to the degree that humans are so constituted. And here again she follows Plato. It is, of course, supremely ironic that she should turn against Locke the notion of true and false self-love, *amour-de-soi* and *amour propre*, set out in Pierre Nicole's *Essais de Morales*, the first four volumes of which reached an English audience from 1677 to 1680, translated by a Gentleman of Quality who may have been Locke.[82] The distinction between true and false forms of self-love opens a space for human control of the passions while allowing that malignant passions account for the corruption of the will. It allows Astell to hold out the hope of human self-improvement while accounting for why this hope is so seldom realized.

Astell's reasoning takes a straight line from her rebuttal of Locke to an attack on authorial *hubris* and self-proclaimed authorities in general. Distinguishing properly between rational and genealogical argument, she remarks that 'tho properly speaking all Truth is Antient, as being from Eternity in the Divine Ideas',[83] the genealogy of authority is no substitute for reason: 'our Forefathers were Men of like Passions with us, and are therefore not to be Credited on the score of Authority but of Reason'.[84] Only the church is exempted from Astell's wholesale attack on customary authority, on the grounds that ministers function as divinely appointed guides – once again the language of Platonism and of Descartes, the latter embracing what he felt to be the insight of Protestantism, that the tabernacle of the human heart was the shrine of reason and truth.[85]

6. Astell, Descartes, Stillingfleet and Locke on Ideas and Extension

The set of problems posed by the Cartesian *cogito*, and its consequences for individual piety, constituted the initial field of modern philosophy of mind and ethics. It is a discourse in which Locke and Stillingfleet, Astell and Masham are intimately involved, arguing and rehearsing arguments in the language of 'triangles', substance – the Indian 'I-know-not-what' of Locke's *Essay Concerning Human Understanding* – algebra and optics, language to which Descartes gave currency and that is still the idiom of modern philosophy of mind. For there is no denying the profundity with which Locke challenged Descartes. The deep-seatedness of his scepticism is nowhere more evident than in the correspondence between Locke and Stillingfleet, the first two installments of which Astell gives every indication of having read. The opening salvo of *A Serious Proposal, Part II*, delivered as part of an ongoing controversy about the Trinity, puts Astell with Stillingfleet on the theological implications of Lockean doubt.

Descartes had formulated his proposition that perception entails existence as one of the proofs for the existence of God. But by opening up a divide between thought and existence, in the categorical mind–body distinction, he cut away the proof for God that he sought. Perception entails existence, but certainty is established by reason. And reason, according to Descartes, inhabits a noncorporeal realm. In various imaginative ways, Locke, in the correspondence with Stillingfleet, explored the ramifications of this conclusion from Descartes' theorem, which he accepted and which calls into question the very notion of clear and distinct ideas that Descartes was at pains to establish.[86]

In his *Essay Concerning Human Understanding*, written in a colloquial first-person style to indicate his desire to reach the ordinary reader, Locke had endorsed Descartes' *cogito* as an observation even a child could make. But as easy as it was for a child to conclude from the reflexivity of thinking that he or she existed, was it impossible to go beyond the understanding of a child concerning what this 'existence' constituted:

[W]hen we talk of substances, we talk like children; who, being asked a question about somewhat which they knew not, readily give this satisfactory answer, that it is something.[87]

Locke had the temerity to compare the mysteriousness of existence in the Christian mind with the I-know-not-what of Indian pantheism. As we shall see, the charge of pantheism was to be very important:

[I]t is 'only an uncertain supposition of we know not what'. And therefore it is paralleled, more than once, with the Indian philosopher's 'He-knew-not-what; which supported the tortoise, that supported the elephant, that supported the earth: so substance was found only to support accidents.

The irreverence of Locke's chosen example brought to mind the problem of the Trinity, and the peculiar relation between substance and accidence that it posits, upon which Stillingfleet, and Astell following him, seized.[88]

In 1696–7 Stillingfleet embarked on his important controversy with Locke over the doctrine of the Trinity, which went to the heart of Locke's epistemology in *The Essay Concerning Human Understanding* (1690). Stillingfleet, whose position at court guaranteed him an audience, was a formidable opponent,[89] and Astell's critique of Locke on thinking matter in *The Christian Religion* shows an acquaintance with, and perhaps the influence of, Stillingfleet's critique. Locke's doctrine had put the Trinity out of reach, Stillingfleet insisted, because sensation concerns particulars, while God, the infinite being, is a complex idea, and ideas are inaccessible to sensation. Locke did not disagree and carefully restated his argument.[90] All simple qualities presuppose a substratum, or substance capable of supporting such qualities and of producing in us simple ideas, he maintained.[91] But in what precisely this substratum or substance of existence consists, 'not all the casuistry of the whole tribe of logicians put together has been able to tell us'.[92] Careful to distinguish between human cognitive apparatuses, subject to the experimental sciences and empirical method, and the ineffable divine mind, Locke drew a number of conclusions from his theorem that perception entails existence but does not presuppose certain knowledge. He denied the Platonist principle that ideas presuppose a class of particulars that participate in a common substance.[93] Ideas, he insisted, are generalizations produced by the operation of the mind and do not presuppose extension.[94] Locke thus forced Descartes, who denied extension to spirit, to more rigorous conclusions from his own dualism. Cognition is the necessary but not sufficient condition for establishing essence. Reason is a faculty of the mind like sight, enabling us to form ideas by abstracting from particulars.[95] Sensation suggests solid extended substances, just as reflection suggests thinking ones, but many things, including spirits, exist of which we have no ideas.[96] For if sensation and reflection are the foundation of all modes of thinking, Locke insisted, they are nevertheless only some of the modes of the mind, allowing for other words of experience that he does not specify.[97] He thus quite consistently believed that we can set out what we know but not what we do not know.

Unlike the Malebranchistes, then, who understood cognition as involving some degree of participation in the divine mind, Locke denied that substance was self-evident, insisting rather that substance was the product of an idea – the I-know-not-what that supported accidents, an incorrigibly childish idea but the best we can come up with. He debated with Stillingfleet over Cicero's and Quintilian's notions of substance, agreeing with Boethius that while the general idea of a man was obscure, ideas of particular men were clear.[98] Locke's examples have the charming concreteness of his later followers of the analytic school:

the country-man knows, that the foundation of the church at Harlem is supported by a rock, as the houses about Bristol are; or by gravel, as the houses about London are; or by wooden piles, as the houses in Amsterdam are; it is plain, that then having a clear and distinct idea of the thing that supports the church, he does not talk of this matter as a child; nor will he of the support of accidents when he has a clearer and more distinct idea of it, than that it is barely something. But as long as we think like children, in cases where our ideas are no clearer nor distincter than theirs . . . we must talk like them.[99]

Locke's revisions to the *cogito* have a compelling simplicity and rigour. Perceiving, reasoning and knowing, those activities that constitute reflection, leave everything as it is, Locke insisted. Just as colours, like the red of the cherry, are qualities in the object of perception independent of the sight or blindness of the perceiver, so our ideas concern the relation between powers and properties that do not disclose their essence.[100] Our sensations may be clear and distinct, but ideas about the objects of our senses are the product of inference and cannot be clear and distinct. Certainty does not obtain in the empirical realm, but only in the logical one: it pertains to relations between ideas expressed in propositions. Thus we may have certainty without clear and distinct ideas and vice versa – a point on which Astell vehemently disagreed.[101] But the main focus of her critique is the *reductio ad absurdam* to which Locke subjected the Cartesian *cogito* in the notion of thinking substance. If thinking posits substance, and the *cogito* proves the existence of mind (a spiritual substance), and further, if pure mind constitutes God, then the logic of the *cogito* was to infer from thinking substance (mind or soul) the possibility of eternal thinking substance (God), Locke argued. Following the storm raised by Stillingfleet and others, including Astell, over the notion of thinking matter, Locke claims in his *Letter to the Bishop of Worcester* to have introduced the idea in his *Essay* as an expression of scepticism that affirms one's faith in the omnipotent God.[102] Although thinking matter is a proposition intractable to reflection, it is not beyond the powers of God to super-add thinking to matter, he argues, supporting the idea with examples of Virgil's and Cicero's ideas of the soul as gross matter and spirit, *pneuma*, like the Hebrew spirit moving upon the waters. Such an incorrigible notion induces in us either dark doubt because of the limits of human understanding or an appeal to the deity out of faith, he concludes.[103]

In his letter to Stillingfleet, Locke steadfastly insists that the way of philosophy will not confirm thinking matter as immaterial, and he uses algebra as an example.[104] Moreover, Locke claims that Stillingfleet, who misrepresents him as a dogmatist, fails to see that the idea of God is a complex, not a simple, idea. Locke disagrees with Descartes that the idea of God is its own proof. Like algebra, which involves a number of clear ideas but gives rise to a thousand demonstrations, the idea of God, the infinite and ineffable, is a poor way to prove his existence, which is better confirmed by natural philosophy as a record of his works – witness 'Mr. Newton's wonderful demonstrations . . . that . . . were able to satisfy him with certainty, i.e. produce demonstration'.[105] Locke bases his explicit refutation of Cartesian certitude on that distinction that still stands today as the foundation of analytic philosophy: the distinction between analytic and synthetic propositions, between truth claims that appeal to logic compared with those that appeal to empirical evidence. And he makes it with reference to Newton's experimental science. Ordinary language, Locke claims, is not the language of ideas but has empirical referents, and here certainty does not belong. The ground of certitude is in the ideas laid out by reason – and Locke gives his famous example of the triangle.[106] Certainty is the function of agreement or disagreement between ideas expressed propositionally, as for instance 'when a man would show the certainty of this truth, that the three angles of a triangle are equal to two right ones'. However, Locke is careful to note that the truth expressed in propositions is not the *creation* of reason, which simply lays it out, without specifying where reason resides and in what relation to the deity.[107]

But to maintain that sensation and reflection produce *certain* ideas was to step beyond the constraints of the human cognitive apparatus and into the mind of God, in the opinion of both Stillingfleet and Astell. Astell turns Locke's scepticism against him as a sign of *hubris* disguised as humility. She charges him with the sceptic's dilemma – if we take his word about the impossibility of certitude, how are we to take what he says seriously at all? Moreover, she detects a fundamental contradiction in Locke's entire program, which asserts the 'reasonableness' of religion and the transparency of belief, on the one hand, and the intractability of things in themselves to clear and distinct ideas, on the other. Astell turns against Locke the *ad hominem* argument that he had used against the Malebranchistes: denying the rest of mankind access to certain truth, he then makes them dependent upon his own word, dependent on '*My* Discovery, *My* Hypothesis, the Strength and Clearness of *My* Reasonings, rather than the Truth',[108] typical of 'every little warm Disputer and Pretender to Reason, whose Life is perhaps a continual contradiction to it', she adds.[109] Once again, by appearing in his ordinary language philosophy to favour the man in the street, for whom he crafts images of the burghers of Haarlem or Amsterdam and the citizens of Bristol or London, Locke in fact disenfranchises him, in Astell's view.[110]

Astell stands by the principle that 'Truth in general is the Object of the Understanding, but all Truths are not equally Evident, because of the Limitation of the Humane Mind, which tho' it can gradually take in many Truths, yet cannot any more than our sight attend to many things at once'.[111] In this way she conforms to the Malebranchiste position that obstacles to knowledge are contingent and not necessary. She accepts Descartes' premises, endorsed by Locke, on the computational function of the mind. Those ideas not evident to us by intuition or introspection are relational, arrived at by the comparison of ideas we already hold or by searching for an independent criterion. Simple ideas are not false, but the way in which we compound them may be.[112] Not all ideas are given to us by God immediately, and uncertainty enters whenever a standard of comparison must be sought. Astell refers for a specific instance to the debate between Locke and Stillingfleet over the nature of the Trinity, 'of late very much controverted tho' to little purpose, because we take a wrong method, and wou'd make that the Object of Science which is properly the Object of Faith'.[113]

Astell challenges Locke on the impossibility of forming an idea of God, for whom there is no standard of comparison. Accepting his fundamental axiom that all knowledge is propositional, Astell goes on to hold Locke to account by his own stipulation that the comparison of ideas requires a measure or standard. 'All the Commerce and Intercourse of the World is manag'd by Equivalents, conversation as well as Traffick',[114] she declares, generalizing this principle in a marvelously Lockean way.[115] But knowledge of the infinite is something by definition beyond the structures of human cognition. Beyond the limits of human understanding lies not darkness but greater light, and Astell invokes a Platonist ecstatic metaphor to characterize God, who 'has folded up his own Nature, not in Darkness, but in an adorable and inaccessible Light'.[116] In the language of optics to which Descartes, Locke and Masham resort, Astell introduces the Stoic notion of assent. A strictly optical theory of cognition omits the will, but all human understanding involves a degree of assent. Thus, even in the very structures of cognition, a disciplined will is a condition of truth. In the realm of prejudice, passion and darkened eyesight, 'tho' Truth be exceeding bright, yet... it requires no little Pains and Application of Mind to find her out'.[117]

The logical impossibility of finding an equivalent for the infinite, causes Astell to conclude that faith, knowledge and opinion do not concern different modes of knowing so much as different degrees of evidence. 'Men of dry Reason and a moderate Genius, I suppose will think Nature has done very well in allotting to each Sense its proper employment'.[118] But these men (i.e., Hobbes and Locke) forget that the senses were made to tend the body, and not as 'Testimony in our Enquiries after Truth,' precisely because they elide their own distinction between the certain knowledge produced by logical deduction and the unreflected immediacy of sensation.[119]

In this enumeration of the several ways of Knowing. I have not reckon'd the Senses, in regard that we're more properly said to be *Conscious* of than to *Know* such things as we perceive by Sensation. And also because that Light which we suppose to be let into our Ideas by our Senses is indeed very dim and fallacious, and not to be relied on till it has past the Test of Reason; neither do I think there's any Mode of Knowlege which mayn't be reduc'd to those already mentioned.[120]

7. Astell's Critique of Locke's Psychology and Politics

Astell's critique of Locke's sensationalist psychology is wholesale. She appears to have caught him every which way. If sensations are cognitively prior, as he claims, then he is in no position to claim for himself a privileged position in expounding truth. But if truth is a function of propositional logic, as he also maintains, he cannot claim the priority of sense-based cognition, which must be submitted to the criterion of reason. He overstates the importance of sense data and understates the role of prudential or customary knowledge, by her book. It is not due to false sensations that women are enslaved, but to the tyranny of false opinion. Ironically, Astell once again turns against Locke, the proponent of plain speech and philosopher of common language, the charge that 'Many times our Ideas are thought to be false when the fault is really in our language'.[121] She is Aristotelian in according prudential knowledge such an important role. For if lack of prudence accounts for our vices, its practice perfects our virtues. Like Aristotle she understands virtue to be the yield of good attitudes and habits productive of good character. To this degree she accepts Aristotle's revision of Plato – that having the right ideas is not sufficient; it is the capacity to convert theory into practice that is the mark of good character. The realm of ethics is thus a prudential realm; moreover, it is a realm in which all have an equal capacity to excel. Locke, in *The Reasonableness of Christianity*, had made the case that the rhapsodic variety of Neoplatonism was excessively esoteric, arguing from the impossibility of making 'the Day-Labourers and Tradesmen, the Spinsters and Dairy Maids...perfect Mathematicians' to the equal impossibility of perfecting them 'in *Ethicks*'.[122] In *A Serious Proposal, Part II*, Astell willfully misreads Locke, accusing him of a category mistake in inferring an ethical incapacity from a lack of theoretical knowledge. Then she charges him with merciless insensitivity: 'a Mechanic who must work for daily bread for his Family, wou'd be wickedly Employ'd shou'd he suffer 'em to starve whilest he's solving Mathematical Problems.'[123] In *The Christian Religion* she clinches her case, declaring that her theology comprised only '*plain Propositions and short Reasonings about things familiar to our Minds, as* need not *amaze* any part of Mankind, no not the *Day Labourer and Tradesmen, the Spinsters and Dairy Maids*, who may very easily *comprehend* what a Woman cou'd write'.[124]

The full argument is foreshadowed in *A Serious Proposal, Part II*. There Astell treads a fine line, rejecting the simplicity of Locke's necessary knowledge as ruling out improvement of the mind, upon which salvation, 'the Grand Business that Women as well as Men have to do in this World', is conditional.[125] To this work of preparation an appropriate level of knowledge is requisite. Astell opts for a Platonist solution that is wholly Christian, a division of labour based on the distribution of talents, the very principle, ironically, on which Locke's Aristotelian economics in the *Two Treatises of Government* is founded. Astell makes an appeal to individualism against those very individualists, Hobbes and Locke, whose pragmatism she is confronting. She claims to 'see no reason why there may not be as great a variety in Minds as there is in Faces'.[126] This being the case, she asks, 'Why shou'd not every individual Understanding be in a more especial manner fitted for and employ'd in the disquisition of some particular Truth and Beauty?'[127] If 'Variety gives Beauty to the Material World . . . why not to the Intellectual?'[128]

But while Astell's attack on Locke was strong, her defence of her own position was weaker than it appears. For those areas in which evidence, in the nature of things, is relatively lacking, faith makes up the deficit – a poor basis for certitude in the technical philosophical sense, which was Locke's very reason for scepticism. To Astell, moral certitude is arrived at as a compound of faith and science to which no one is in principle denied access.[129] The notion of clear, as opposed to distinct, ideas[130] allows her to distinguish between those intangibles of which we can form certain ideas – the triangle and other mathematical and theoretical entities – and those for which we cannot, chiefly the nature of God and the Christian mysteries:

For that Idea which represents a thing so Clearly, that by an Attent and Simple View we may discern its Properties and Modifications, at least so far as they can be Known, is never false; all our Certainty and Evidence depends on it, if we Know not Truly what is thus represented to our Minds we know nothing. Thus the Idea of Equality between 2 and 2 is so evident that it is impossible to doubt of it, no Arguments could convince us of the Contrary, nor be able to persuade us that the same may be found between 2 and 3.[131]

In these discussions Astell uses a mathematical example, so evident, she claims, 'that it is impossible to doubt of it' and 'no Arguments could convince us of the Contrary'.[132] Turning to Descartes' own definition, she argues that whatever may be said to be 'Distinct . . . is so clear, Particular, and Different from all other things that it contains not any thing in it self which appears not manifestly to him who considers it as he ought'.[133] If distinctness is a function of the discreteness or singularity of an idea, as Descartes argued, then complex ideas like the concept of God are not likely to be clear. This Locke had already conceded to Stillingfleet. Astell argues to the contrary, and not very convincingly, that clear ideas entail distinctness, but that distinctness does not entail clearness,[134] thus yielding the conclusion that 'we may have a Clear, but not a Distinct and Perfect Idea of God and of our own Souls'.[135] It is easy to understand her reticence to reduce the psychological to the physiological, a category mistake of which she convicts Locke. She thus concludes concerning minds that 'their Existence and some of their Properties and Attributes may be Certainly and Indubitably Known' but that we cannot know their nature distinctly, 'for Reasons too long to be mentioned' or 'of God because he is Infinite'.[136] In fact, Astell could have clinched her case by arguing that we cannot have a clear idea of mind because it too is complex. But this she does not do.

There are other indications that Astell's position has not fully matured. Proceeding from her (unproven) assumption that we know enough about the structure of mind to adopt rules for its improvement, she turns to *The Port Royal Logic* for an exposition of what these rules are. Her exposition of the syllogism,[137] following that of Arnauld and Nicole,[138] leads her into strange territory, however. The example she gives seems to endorse Locke's hypothesis that the mind is 'thinking matter', which she was to demolish so brilliantly in *The Christian Religion*, once again willfully misreading his argument. Taking as her example the question 'Whether a Rich Man is Happy', Astell pleads Cartesian dualism and the inconvertibility of the two terms, 'riches' and 'happiness', as a reason for denying the derivation of a proper conclusion and therefore disqualifying the proposition 'the rich man is happy':

Now if we compare the Idea of Riches with that which we have of Man, we shall find in the former nothing but what's Material, External and Adventitious, but our Idea of the latter represents to us somewhat that Thinks, and so is of an Immaterial and more noble Nature. . . . [139]

If one accepts Descartes' principle of the inconvertibility of mind and matter, then material goods do not yield spiritual goods. So far so good:

by Consequence the less Noble cannot be the Good of the more, nor a Body or an Extended Substance, the Proper Good of the Mind, a Spiritual or Thinking Substance, So that upon the whole matter we find, that we cannot affirm a Man is Happy because he is Rich, neither can we deny it. . . . [140]

But while her conclusion that body, extended substance, cannot be the *good* of the mind or spirit is impeccable, her reading of Locke led her by a semantic lapse to endorse the principle of thinking matter that she was later to refute so resoundingly. In *A Christian Religion*, Astell makes a categorical distinction between material substance and immaterial nature. The latter, having no parts, is incorruptible and immortal, and therefore does not qualify as extension or substance at all.[141] This is a distinction as categorical as that between the triangle and the circle, she maintains, its acceptance a precondition for thinking as such.[142] Those who would allow thinking matter to fudge the mind–body divide are led to the ineluctable conclusion that 'if a body can think, thought must be the essence of body', which is to make of God himself a principle of extension![143]

8. Astell's Critique of Locke on Thinking Matter

In *The Christian Religion*, Astell is able to give some sense to the apparently vacuous claim of *A Serious Proposal, Part II* that clearness entails distinctness but not vice versa. And she scores points against Locke in the process. The claim that 'we may have a Clear, but not a Distinct and Perfect Idea of God and of our own Souls'[144] is not incompatible with the categorical intransitivity of mind and matter but rather a function of it. Turning back to Locke's assertion of *The Essay Concerning Understanding*, bk. 4, ch. 3, §29, Astell quotes, '"That in some of our Ideas there are certain Relations, Habitudes, and Connexions so visibly included in the nature of the Ideas themselves, that we cannot conceive them separable from them, by *any power whatsoever*"'.[145] For such complex ideas Locke gave the example of the triangle. Astell is not only with him, but turns the argument against him and his incongruous notion of 'thinking matter':

Now to be Distinct from a Thing is all one as not to be this Thing, so that since Thought and Extension are Different on their own Nature, as we may have seen, 'tis evident that a Thinking Being can't be Extended, and that an Extended Being does not, cannot Think, any more than a circle can Rave the Properties of a Triangle, or a Triangle those of a Circle.[146]

One cannot violate the fundamental distinction between thought and extension by having matter think. However, it does not follow that the conditions for a triangle being a triangle are violated by adding to it extension:

whatever Excellency, not contain'd in its essence, be superadded to a Triangle, *it does not destroy the essence of a* Triangle *if it leaves a Figure bounded by three* Right Lines, *for wherever that is there is the essence of a* Triangle.[147]

And just as the definition of a triangle is not exhaustive, 'so we may have a Clear but not a Distinct and Perfect Idea of God and of our own Souls'. Locke, she claims, believing that because we cannot conceive of something, it follows that God does not have the power to make it exist, has violated his own stipulation that we can set out what we know but not what we do not know:

shou'd I tell our Ingenious Author, That to deny GOD's *Power in this case, only because he can't conceive the manner how, is not less than an Insolent Absurdity; and a limiting the Power of the Omnipotent Creator.*[148]

Here she finds the answer for which she was reaching in *A Serious Proposal, Part II*: it is not the powerlessness of God to violate our conceptual categories, but our own powerlessness to get beyond them, that stands in the way of certitude. Our incapacity to hold more than one distinct idea in our minds at any given time is the reason we can be clear about distinct ideas because they are simple. But the relative lack of cognitive autonomy in beings who 'see all things in God' explains why distinctness does not entail clearness and why we can never be certain about the nature of complex ideas. Astell proposes to 'stick to [her] *Assertion*, that GOD *if He pleases can superadd Excellencies*' or qualities, even though humans discriminate between distinct ideas on the basis of one quality/one entity. In a bold stroke she turns her argument against Locke, arguing that '*if GOD cannot joyn things together by Connexions inconceivable to us, we must deny even the Consistency and being of Matter it self*'. Moreover, as she elsewhere points out, Locke's famous law of non-contradiction as a test of truth depends on our ability to make such connections and on assuming thinkable connections to be true.

Astell concedes what she earlier denied, that Locke was in fact willing to admit the intractability of complex ideas to be a mark of human finitude and not divine:

Shou'd I also add, That tho' the very Ingenious Mr. L. in his *Essay* tells us, That Connexions visibly included in Ideas, do not depend on any Arbitrary Power whatsoever, nor can be conceiv'd separably by any Power; yet in his *Third Letter to the Bishop of Worcester*,[149] he is of another Mind, his Reasonings there allowing us to conclude, That all the difficulties rais'd against a Speaking or Eating Triangle, and one that is equal to a Square, are *rais'd only from our Ignorance or Narrow Conceptions*,[150] but *stand not at all in the way of the Power of GOD, nor prove any thing against his having actually endued some* Triangles with those Properties (*tho'* every Triangle *as a* Triangle, *has them not*) *unless it can be prov'd that it contains a Contradiction to suppose it.*[151] Shou'd I argue at this rate, wou'd not that Great Master of good Sense, despise such sort of Discourses as the *Rhapsodies* and *strong Imaginations of* a silly Woman? And the World its like wou'd not allow them to pass any where as the *Philosophical Disquisitions* of a free Thinker, and a Lover of Truth, unless it pays a greater deference to Names than Things.

Astell's critique of that 'Great Master of good Sense', Locke, has in this case missed the irony or sarcasm of his argument. To allow God willful incongruity in the violation of human category distinctions makes no sense. That Locke's far-fetched notion of 'thinking matter' is a category mistake of the same order, suggests that this too was satirical, a divine slight, so to speak, and for this reason raised Astell's ire, or else a terrible lapse in one who despised 'such sort of Discourses as the Rhapsodies and strong Imaginations of a silly Woman'.

3

Astell on Marriage, Patriarchalism and Contractarianism

1. The Marriage Contract–Social Contract Analogue

Debate over the reception of Locke's anonymously published *Two Treatises of Government* (1690) has never given Astell her due. Her argument, in the first edition of *Reflections upon Marriage* (1700),[1] that the very men who press for liberty in the public sphere are the first to exempt themselves from constraints on the exercise of their power at home, is an important anticipation of the argument mounted against the social contract theory of 'Great *L–k* in his *Two Discourses of Government*' by Charles Leslie in 1703. It is an argument that Astell develops in high style in her famous 1706 Preface to *Reflections upon Marriage*. Not only is her critique more trenchant than that of Leslie, published in the Supplement to his *The New Association, Part II* of 1703,[2] but it is earlier on two counts, having been introduced not only in the body of the text of *Reflections upon Marriage* as early as 1700, but also implicit in *A Serious Proposal, Part II*, as we have seen. Introduction of the argument by Astell as early as 1697 has not been previously noticed. Nor has any account been taken of her bitter pleading in *A Fair Way with the Dissenters and Their Patrons* of 1704 against Leslie's getting credit for her earlier pamphlet of that year, *Moderation Truly Stated*, evidence enough, were any needed, that women who had to publish anonymously in her age could be plagiarized at will. However, as we shall see, Astell's works did not always go unacknowledged, and indeed, in the pamphlet skirmishing of 1704 in which she was involved, James Owen correctly assigns authorship.

Astell's *Reflections upon Marriage* (1700) is one of the earliest critiques of the cornerstones of early modern political theory: patriarchalism and contractarianism and the political philosophers who promoted them, Filmer, Hobbes and Locke. Marriage provided a juridical formula for the union of two wills, such that parties entering as free and equal individuals emerged in a relationship of domination/subordination. But problems lay in replicating these features in a social contract that was compatible with natural right and freedom as the contractarians defined it. Reason and power belonged to fundamentally different orders: if reason could not sanction tyrants, it could not disenfranchise them either. This Astell, addressing Locke, was able to demonstrate. The enduring significance of her critique lies, as Carole Pateman has correctly diagnosed,[3] in a prospective critique of contractarianism as the foundation of liberalism. But it is not for the 'trade in bodies' – conjugal right dressed up as equality – that Astell condemns the marriage contract–social contract homology. Rather, it is because contractarianism, as defining free and equal individuals, is predicated on models of contract in which these conditions do not apply. They do not apply in the social contract, which produces a political order of domination and subordination out of the initial freedom of the war of all against all; and they do not apply in marriage either, in which hierarchical social relations sanctioned by divine authority are merely *occasioned by* a 'contract' between the families designating partners to this estate. The power to authorize marriage, like the power to authorize a sovereign, is in her view a power assigned only to God. The power of his representatives is limited to designating incumbents to these respective estates.

Out of the many scores of works devoted to the subject of marriage, Hobbes's *Leviathan* had run a radical line in rendering family relations contractual.[4] Hobbes did so to deny categorical differences in social order theorized by Aristotle in the distinction between paternal, despotic and political power, institutionalized by feudal Christendom in general and the Catholic Church in particular. In this respect, he was at least more thoroughgoing than Locke in meeting the requirements that the marriage contract–social contract homology required. Astell made Locke's failure of nerve the butt of ridicule. But she did so not to transform social relations, but rather to critique eighteenth-century morals and mores that made a mockery of the sacrament of marriage. In richly rhetorical passages she mounted a vehement protest against the estate of marriage in her day, in language marked by images of freedom and slavery that her ontological commitments did not allow her to translate into political commitment. To this cry of protest against a cruel world corresponds her theology, marked by Cartesian rationalism and Platonist enthusiasm in which freedom of the spirit is given religious rather than political expression.

2. Marriage and Corporatism

Mary Astell came in at the end of a century dominated by corporatism, patriarchalism and contractarianism. Corporatism empowered family, king and church, as legatee to theories of governance that drew on Roman corporation theory to authorize collectivities. Enjoying the status of legally autonomous entities that could act as individuals by virtue of authorizing a representative, corporations could sue and be sued while their individual members enjoyed legal immunity.[5] Thomas Hobbes claimed erroneously to be the first to apply corporation to the polity. But in fact, corporation theory had afforded legal rights to feudal collectivities for at least a millennium, in particular the religious orders and universities and, by extension, great families and the Crown.[6] Patriarchalism, by contrast, was an organic theory of the power of collectivities that was biblically derived on the model of the dispensation of Adam and Moses, exemplified by Sir Robert Filmer's *Patriarcha, Or The Natural Power of Kings Asserted* of 1680.[7] Contractarianism, the third pillar of seventeenth-century political thought, was a response to patriarchalist theory that located the moment of political authorization in a social contract between individuals who entered the arrangement free and equal but exited into the state of civil society radically unequal. A theory as old as the Stoics, Epicureans and Plato, the theory of social contract was refined in early modern thought by Hobbes and Locke and inextricably connected to the continental civil law theories of natural rights.[8]

Interlocking but separate, these principles generated a three-cornered debate in and out of which political theorists moved. To those who feel it is anachronistic to term Astell a feminist, it is worth pointing out that she was the first to call into question in print the tissue of legal fictions around which early modern political theory was constructed. The marriage contract, as a juristic formula for the union of two wills, was the cornerstone of corporatism and patriarchalism and the model on which social contract theories were drawn.[9] Centuries of canon lawyers who had reflected on the institution of marriage had set this peculiar contract at the heart of the constitution of the state. Contracted by free and equal individuals, marriage necessarily produced asymmetrical power relations as a consequence. The freedom of the parties entering the contract was a condition on which the church insisted, given that coercion represented an impediment to legal marriage. But once transacted, the marriage brought into play institutions of family government whose terms were pre-given, defining relations of property, inheritance and power. The family as a corporate body was founded on a union that was deemed sacred, irrevocable and indissoluble by virtue of the holy vows that provided its sanction. It is not difficult to see how the marriage contract might provide an analogue for the social contract itself, but this is to underestimate the centuries of preparation that lay behind its creation.

The juridical complexity of the marriage contract and its ramifications in the seventeenth century require our attention. For it is the juridical efficacy of the marriage contract that made it such a handy vehicle, and not simply the fact that it legitimized the sexual trade in bodies.[10] Anthropologists and feminist political theorists have lately concurred that trade in women was probably among the first forms of social exchange, providing a bartering medium between competing tribes that satisfied the needs to widen the gene pool, replenish manpower lost in warfare, and enforce male control of sexuality.[11] The medieval church had long recognized the imperative of reproduction as the justification of marriage as a social institution, granting men and women a surprising degree of conjugal equality in terms of the rights each could enforce on the other. But it was not the official sexual equality within marriage – leaving aside the question of social practices – on which early modern thinkers focused, but the asymmetry of marriage as the foundation of corporate property rights and the vested power of the husband as head of the household.

Overstatement of the divide between medieval and early modern political theory risks attributing to the marriage contract–social contract analogue a false novelty. For certain features of the institution of marriage had made it inescapable. Among these are the conviction that marriage was a creation of positive law; distinctions between the contract made by the parties to each other and the separate vows made to God as guarantor of the pact; the indissolubility of the marriage bond due to obligations incurred by these vows that took precedence over the question of how the contract between the parties to it was honoured; and the corporate micro-society that this combination of contracts and vows created.

Hobbes and Locke were not the first to focus on the peculiar asymmetry of the marriage contract, by which free and equal individuals enter a relationship of domination/subordination. The church had long maintained that the primary reproductive function of marriage mandated a form of sexual equality whereby husband and wife had equal conjugal rights. Both were equally free to demand a redemption of the 'marriage debt' upon request. But as members of a civil union, husband and wife were socially unequal. A woman at marriage submitted to the 'government' of her husband, and only the most radical sects argued differently.[12] Centuries of debate over the institution of marriage and its relation to natural, divine and civil law had produced a general concurrence of opinion that marriage was a juridical creation. Some theorists were more explicit: the institution of marriage was not natural, in the sense of being a product of natural law or of ratiocination that would lead to natural law precepts. It was the creation of positive law, whether divine or civil. So, for instance, Duns Scotus had argued that 'it would not violate the law of nature for a woman or a man to give her or his body for a limited time – a year or a month – for one act or two were it not for the will of their superior Lord in imposing this law'.[13] Ambrosius Catharinus concurred. On the other side, Erastians such as Martin Bucer, John Milton and Thomas Hobbes argued from the premise that marriage was not an institution of natural law to the conclusion that it was the creature of civil law, and that therefore adultery and divorce were matters for the state to define.

It is well known that English common law, like Roman law, had spun public law out of private law. Thus, laws relating to persons and things generated laws relating to collectivities, as the rights of personhood were generalized to entities deemed to have a personality in the law.[14] The family was the first and primary of such collectivities, whose legal representative was the *paterfamilias* but whose internal affairs were a private matter, regulated by the grid of patriarchal authority. Religious sodalities, or registered cults, the *collegia*, had acquired such rights under the Roman Republic, partly due to the government's desire to control them, forming the first recorded corporations with publicly accountable official representatives in the West. The full extension of the concept saw the Roman Empire as the ultimate Great Corporation, for which the Latin term was *universitas*. Its official representative, bearing the *persona ficta* or fictitious personality of the collectivity, was the emperor himself.[15] And it was as the legacy of Roman civil law that corporation theory impinged on early modern European political theory.

The mindset that permitted personalities to collectivities, and that conceptualized them as animated by spirits or souls, is primarily religious in the most general sense and can be located in remote antiquity.[16] The corporate body Roma, the Eternal City, more than the pile of bricks and mortar that constituted it, was a moveable feast, at one time located on the Tiber, at another in Aachen, Charlemagne's capital. Corporations reflected their religious roots down to the seventeenth and eighteenth centuries, when they began to take on a modern secular character as joint-stock companies, flag bearers for the commercial empires of the new imperial age eventually theorized by Hegel and John Stuart Mill. In the Middle Ages religious institutions were the primary beneficiaries of corporate privilege, the monastic orders and the centres of learning they established, aptly named 'universities', enjoying the status of legal persons. If their public face was an official representative: their internal affairs were a private manner. Their members were juridically immune as individuals but collectively responsible, able to sue and be sued.

The monarchy too, deputizing for the 'mystical body of Christ', with sacred duties for the welfare of its subjects, enjoyed similar legal privileges, constituting a corporation in its own right, the 'corporation sole', of which the monarch was the single member.[17] It is small surprise that when Henry VIII made his break with Rome, his resourceful lawyers and propagandists formulated the new national entity that he created in corporation terms. The Tudor state now constituted a complex corporate entity, the king-in church one of its faces, the king-in Parliament another.[18] 'This Realm of England is an Empire', the famous preamble to the Act in Restraint of Appeals of 1533 declared. Thus mystical body language, referring to the larger-than-life persona of a collectivity, and first generated to account for the special relation of Christ to the church, later extended to the Christian empire, was now extended to account for the relation of the monarch to the national church and to the realm. Cardinal Pole, in a pamphlet addressed to Henry VIII actually opposed to the Henrician headship over the church, expressed it better than the king himself:[19]

> Your whole reasoning comes to the conclusion that you consider the Church a *corpus politicum*. . . . Great as the distance is between heaven and earth, so great is also the distance between the civil power and the ecclesiastical, as so great the distance between this body of the Church, which is the body of Christ, and that, which is a body politic and merely human.

But this view was not new either. From the days of the early church, monks and nuns had been thought of as divine spouses, later 'brides of Christ'. And since Gratian's decree (c. 1140), at least, bishops had been officially deemed to be 'married' to the church.[20] So when Elizabeth I claimed that the Commons loved her better than a step-dame, and the Commons referred to her both as natural mother and as wedded spouse, this charming metaphor was not uttered in innocence. James I declared to his Parliament of 1610: 'What God hath conjoined then, let no man separate. I am the husband, and the whole island is my lawful wife; I am the head, and it is my body; I am shepherd, and it is my flock'.[21]

Post-Reformation English monarchs were less wont to invoke the marriage metaphor, undoubtedly because of its canon law associations, than the French, who openly declared 'the king is the mystical spouse of the *respublica*'.[22] But when need arose they did so, Charles I also declaring himself husband and father of the realm. The marriage metaphor was widely serviceable. It had obvious applications to monarchy, where the royal family was projected as the icon of all the families of the realm, and where the familial relations of spouse and sibling had political ramifications. So, the notion of a *matrimonium morale et politicum* was used to claim for the prince the inalienability of fiscal property, construed as 'the dowry of the bridal *respublica*'.[23] But marriage, where the partnership of husband and wife was construed as one of corporate equality, might also be a mirror for aristocracy rather than monarchy, as depicted by Sir Thomas Smith in *De Republica Anglorum*, written under Elizabeth's reign:[24]

The man stern strong, bold, adventurous, negligent of his beauty, and spending: the woman weak, fearful, fair, curious of her beauty and saving; the man going out to work to earn money, the woman tarrying at home to distribute it among the family; for nature has forged men and women with complementary qualities so that each excels the other in the things belonging to their office; therefore where their wisdom doth excel therein it is reason that each should govern; each obeyeth and commandeth the other and they two together rule the house.... In the house and family is the first and most natural (but private) appearance of one of the best kinds of commonwealth, that is called Aristocracy.

3. Marriage and Patriarchalism

The marriage metaphor bespoke corporatism, mystical body language, but it also spoke the language of patriarchy. The seventeenth century was a century of explicit patriarchalism, in a manner that we no longer know, as Hegel diagnosed, just because the structure of the modern family is so different.[25] Attempts to legitimize the whole array of corporate entities, from the Crown to religious sects to families, on the model of the grant of power given from God to Adam and then to Noah, and to trace the filiations of that power in genealogies of Noah's sons as they peopled the whole earth, is a project long since abandoned.[26] But in some of its more arcane ramifications it occupied some of the greatest minds of the seventeenth and eighteenth centuries. Among those who examined the specific lineages by which Noah's son Japhet was said to people Europe, his son Shem to people Asia, and his son Ham to people Africa, assessing claims for the antiquity of those civilizations with respect to biblical, patriarchal, Israelite society, we find Gilbert Burnet and Sir Isaac Newton, whose volume of works devoted to ancient history in the latter case far outweighed his 'new science'.[27]

Biblical patriarchalism, the tradition of strict textual exegesis, and the aspirations of Protestant reformers to re-create the social relations of the Old Testament had political ramifications at all levels. Not only did such concerns animate those participatory puritan sects that tried to re-create the primitive democracy of the ancient Israelites and the civilizations in which they were embedded. They also contributed to the ethos of the emergent nation-state, pulled between the simple patriarchal theocracy of the original chosen people and the juridical complexity of feudal Christendom. As patriarchy stands to monarchy, so theocracy stands to absolutism. In the hands of the most explicit patriarchalists of the age, the French Jean Bodin and the English Sir Robert Filmer, all the marks of absolutism are present on the strictest terms of biblical fundamentalism. The king *was* the father of his people; the family *was* the state. God's will was absolute, and the king's will was too. As we are born into the family, so we are born into the state, and Aristotle's carefully constructed hierarchy of authorities, endorsed by medieval Christendom, which made political, matrimonial, patriarchal and despotic power (the last the power of a master over slaves) qualitatively different was conflated to produce one people, one realm and one source of power.

This argument was made more explicitly in the seventeenth century by Sir Robert Filmer in *Patriarcha* (1680) than ever before.[28] Circumstances were propitious. It was a period of uncertainty in which a strong monarchy was called for. Moreover, a literal reading of the Bible, which the Reformation favoured over medieval allegorizing, sanctioned biblical patriarchalism, in which the rule of kings was modeled on that of fathers. Nevertheless, patriarchalism, as one of the rarest and crudest examples of a genetic argument to receive wide public endorsement, met the early criticism of seventeenth-century thinkers, Astell among them. It is not difficult to see that a descriptive account of the devolution of power from father to son, in which the power of kings was melded to that of fathers, was unsatisfactory as an answer to the normative question, whence does political power derive? But perhaps it took the boldness of such an argument from sacred history to provoke the deliberately ahistorical rationalism of Locke – although not necessarily of Hobbes, who nowhere openly refutes Filmer, and for whom the fact of conquest in English history always provides a case of contract. Ironically, the explicit simplicity of Filmer's patriarchalism, unparalleled in the previous history of political thought, as Gordon Schochet argues,[29] provoked the very line of argumentation that, in the form of radical liberalism, was to undermine all claims to special entitlement in the distribution of rights, and to right by precedent more generally. But all that lay in the future. The power of genealogical argument, or argument from origins, to the extent that it constituted a mode of religious and political argument in the seventeenth century, was always vulnerable to the criticism that practice proves no title.[30] From the fact that something was once done, nothing strictly follows, or it if follows, it does so only contingently. To make a political precedent out of an historical event involves invoking an authority, if it is not done simply by political fiat. Analytic arguments concerning reasons always triumph over genetic arguments concerning origins unless the latter are specially assisted in this way.

Political patriarchalism foundered on the additional fact that if it was to fathers that God had given the original grant of power, then either this grant was subversive of kings or kings were subversive of fathers. It fell to Hobbes and Locke to exploit this particular vulnerability and to show that the right of kings was not by nature but by convention, in a word, by contract. In so doing, as Sommerville has succinctly shown, they resumed a debate about the contractual origins of government, as a principle derived from Roman law, that had been argued almost continuously from medieval times up to Richard Hooker and John Selden and defended by writers as different as John Pym, William Ames, Robert Mason and the Jesuit Francisco Suarez.[31] It does not follow, as the case of Filmer might suggest, that genetic arguments, from origins, versus contractual arguments, from reason, exhausted the possibilities in this debate. If Filmer's very simple-mindedness placed a weapon in the hand of his adversaries, few seventeenth-century advocates of customary right were this philosophically unsophisticated. Filmer's apparent simple-mindedness may, in any case, have been more in the nature of a desperate attempt at royalist propaganda on the part of one whose lifeline to the episcopacy and the court had been severed by imprisonment under the parliamentarians, and who was willing to defend at any cost a position that might ensure the return of the Stuarts – as surely such a strong argument for the role of lineage might.[32]

Mary Astell, sharing Filmer's dynastic allegiances, argued the case differently. Laying the subordination of women at the door of custom, Astell mocked the language of the Whigs who appealed to an ancient *constitu-tion* and ancient customary rights. The antiquity of institutions vouched for nothing unless they exhibited reasonableness and congruence with a divinely ordained social order. In this respect, Astell was like many of the common lawyers who, despite the fact that they made a living from appeal to precedent, made one principle 'peculiarly their own . . . the idea that ancient and rational customs should not, or could not be abrogated'.[33] More rigorous even than Hobbes or Locke, she argued precisely the dif-ference between the dictates of reason and the realities of empowerment as they did. Hobbes had made this distinction the very buttress of his theory of authorization, declaring that it was precisely because reason provides no *title* that a coercive instrument, the sovereign, is necessary to enforce contracts. Astell simply argued it the other way, declaring against Locke and all contractarians that they could not establish what they were required to prove: that the people were empowered to contract in the first place. Even the Bible could not establish that:[34]

For, allowing that the People have a Right to Design the Person of their Governour; it does by no means follow that they Give him his Authority, or that they may when they please resume it. None can give what they have not: The People have no Authority over their own Lives, consequently they can't invest such an Authority in their Governours.

4. Hobbes, Locke and Contractarianism

There was a distinction to be made between the general patriarchalism of a traditional society based on patriarchal families, monarchy as a form of super-family, and wider divinely sanctioned social hierarchies, on the one hand, and the radical patriarchalism of Filmer, on the other. To the more general patriarchalist tradition Hobbes and Locke also belonged. They differed from Filmer in believing that such patriarchalism is conventional, rather than by nature, but differed from each other in terms of the role that contract plays in establishing convention. It is fair to say that the plausibility of political patriarchalism in the seventeenth century had gained much from Church of England teaching on the Decalogue and specifically the Fifth Commandment: obedience to parents as a model for political obedience.[35] Patriarchalism also conspired with a perceived need of the state in this period for a strong hereditary monarchy to consolidate its political authority. The fiction of the marriage of monarchs to their commonwealths could only be maintained while kings did in fact act like fathers, making royal grants and concessions, guardians of

their people. But when Charles I began acting like a French despot and
James II, undeterred by the events of the interval, seemed to be repeating
the pattern, patriarchalism looked much less plausible. The interruption
in the genealogical line of royal succession, caused by the regicide of
Charles I in 1649, created a serious problem for patriarchal argument,
as subsequent oaths of allegiance to the House of Orange, conflicting
with prior oaths to the Stuarts, were to pose problems for theories of
obligation by social contract.

It is indeed difficult to overestimate the shock that the regicide created
for patriarchal theory or the degree to which radical contractarianism
represented a solution to the crisis of authority it created. The power
of Hobbes's argument, and that of Locke, was to preserve some of the
strengths of patriarchalism and corporatism, in the homology between
the marriage contract and the social contract, while shedding some of the
losses. The English Civil War had raised the spectre of anarchy, to which
Filmer had responded in a particularly pointed way. Hobbes and Locke
were both closer to the schoolmen they otherwise professed to abhor
than they were to Filmer in his solution to the problem. For Filmerian
father-right was a substitute for natural law as the source of patriarchy,
which both they and the scholastics rejected. In maintaining the primacy
of positive law as the law of contracts, they took the same line against
Filmerian father-right that they took against the divine right of kings.
Hobbes was careful to distinguish the peaceful power of the sovereign,
by covenant, from the violent power of the conqueror as the source
of patrimonial kingship. But even the despotic power of the monarch
established by conquest was institutionalized by covenant, he believed,
in this case in the form of a peace treaty. Following Aristotle, with whom
Hobbes otherwise finds little with which to agree (although more than
his rhetoric would lead one to suppose), he believed the presence of constraint on choice to be an irrelevance in assessing responsibility. In this
sense, even assent to a conqueror is freely given, he argued, the victor
empowered by the vanquished, whose choices are to flee, to die or to
submit.

Just this consent to the victor by the vanquished in civil war provided
Hobbes the analogue for marriage: as the peace treaty that concluded
the battle of the sexes. A freely entered contract of submission to the
husband by the wife was its consequent. Hobbes is adamant that men do
not rule women in marriage by natural right; they rule by contract, just as
fathers rule children and masters servants. The subordination of women
in marriage does not presuppose sex-right or the natural superiority of

men, any more than it supposes the natural submissiveness of women. It is born of necessity, the need of child-bearing women for protection; but its true sanction, as Hobbes noted, is civil law:[36]

And whereas some have attributed the Dominion to the man onely, as being of the more excellent Sex, they misreckon it. For there is not always that difference of strength or prudence between the man and the woman as that the right can be determined without War. In Commonwealths, this controversie is decided by the Civil Law: and for the most part, (but not always) the sentence is in favour of the Father, because for the most part Common-wealths have been erected by the Fathers, not by the Mothers of families.

Hobbes's argument against the rule of men over women as of right, or by natural law, Astell could endorse, but she was unwilling to soften the argument from necessity by dressing it up as freedom to contract. Consent, explicit in the marriage contract, Hobbes had argued, is tacit in the contract between fathers and children, masters and slaves. But in all these cases, whether between crowns and commonwealths or fathers and families, the reasons for contract remain the same: protection in exchange for allegiance. Just as the preservation of subjects from anarchy or civil war entails the empowerment of a sovereign, so the protection of the woman as a potential child-bearer entails the empowerment of the husband and the preservation of the child involves the empowerment of both parents as absolute preservers. By extending the ambit of contract to include not only rulers and ruled, but also domestic social relations, Hobbes reinstated the continuity of the family and the state insisted upon by Filmer, but on different grounds.

It was Hobbes's genius, setting aside questions of its justice, to incorporate the essentials of patriarchalism and the instruments of corporatism into his social contract theory. The power of fathers over their wives and children was as firmly entrenched, by contract, as the power of sovereigns over their subjects, and Hobbes claimed, unjustly, to be the first to see the efficacy of corporation theory for the modern nation-state, a claim that, as we have suggested, ignores the language of Tudor legislation in which the royal supremacy was established:[37]

...a corporation being declared to be one person in the law, yet the same hath not been taken notice of in the body of a commonwealth or city, nor have any of those innumerable writers of politics, observed any such union.

Hobbes isolated two aspects of the moment of contract: first, the motives to contract, which are the same for all covenants: self-preservation; and second, the sanctions to contract, which reside in the powers with which the authority is invested. These two aspects correspond in the case of the civil contract to two acts, the act of covenanting between citizens and the act of empowering a sovereign. The common concurrence of wills is not sufficient security to a common peace without the erection of a 'visible Power to keep them in awe, and tye them by feare of punishment to the performance of their Covenants and observance' of the laws of nature.[38] In the case of the civil contract, the free-rider problem, where many are depended upon to keep an agreement vulnerable to the delinquency of a few, is sufficiently serious to require the authorization of a sovereign with absolute and irrevocable power.[39] Resort to the coercive power of the sovereign has its analogue in the marriage contract, where authority falls to the husband by customary right, on the grounds of his purportedly superior physical (coercive) power.[40]

Hobbes's isolation of these two moments in the act of social contract is sometimes thought to be unduly artificial. But marriage itself had from earliest antiquity been understood to involve two separate acts, each of them involving a transfer of rights in the person, but the retention of proprietary rights, in a way that is quite similar to Hobbes's notion. In ancient Athens, for instance, the term 'to give in marriage', *ekdidosthei*, was the same as the term used 'to put out a baby to wet-nurse', 'to give out for apprenticeship' or 'to put out slaves to service'.[41] What it indicated was the transfer of usufruct in a person over whom one had control while retaining residual property rights in that person.[42] In this way, a woman was understood as being lent from one family to another to bear offspring but never finally transferred to the family of her husband. The marriage itself involved two separate acts of conveyancing: first, 'the disposing of', in the betrothal, and second, 'the receiving of', in the wedding. These acts would be separated by months, if not years, and accompanied by the appropriate securities in dowry and bride price. The legal entity that the marriage created was a family corporation, whose formal aspect was family property and whose longevity, like that of all corporations, lasted while there were legal incumbents. Only in the modern age, Hegel was to remark, did divorce or death mark the end of the family corporation, with the division of family property among its members.[43] The family corporation had its own representative, whose name, *persona ficta*, the word for the mask worn at funerals to impersonate dead family members, was lent to corporations more generally, which were derivative from it.

In the case of the social contract, the juristic vehicle that could accomplish the happy coincidence of simultaneous acts, covenanting and authorizing, was similarly the corporation. As Hobbes claimed to be the first to see, it was a device that recognized the state as a collectivity, at the same time permitting unity for collective action through the empowerment of a representative. The result was a mutual and binding obligation to follow the sovereign's bidding as of a representative (*persona ficta*) but irrevocable power inaugurated in perpetuity. Individual kings are mortal, but the *persona ficta* is eternal, its 'Artificiall Eternity ... that which men call the Right of *Succession*'.[44] It was precisely the protection/allegiance nexus, so elaborately expressed in the juristic formulae of corporation theory, that Astell and others were to question. John Locke could disagree with Hobbes on details while preserving a great deal of the substance of the social contract–marriage contract homology. To begin with, he denied that the state of nature was a state of war. The state of nature was a state in which families and conventions were already constituted. For Locke, as for Filmer and Hobbes, the family was central to politics. Like Hobbes, and unlike Filmer, he could distinguish between the power of the father as at once a *metaphor* for government, as the *origin* of government, or as the *source* of hereditable obligation. That men and women were *naturally* equal, and that marriage was intended for their mutual support and assistance, he agreed with Hobbes. He additionally agreed that, by convention, rule of the family falls to the man as the stronger. But on the same grounds that a slave cannot *contract* into subordination, he argued that a woman cannot *contract* away her natural freedom.

On the mutual role of husband and wife in procreation, Locke agreed with Hobbes, concluding something different: therefore, both share *parental* power. He argued with Hobbes that the source of parental power is a mutual need for protection/obedience, but he denied that this entails a binding or irrevocable power, any more than it leads by nature to an eternal relationship. Parental power, like sovereign power, is that of a guardian or trustee, and when the charges have reached their majority the power of trusteeship, in the case of the family, would appear to vanish. When the mutual assistance in procreation and child-rearing ceases to be necessary, the rationale for marriage ends. Were it not for the fact that marriage was an institution created by positive law, divine and civil, marriages might be terminated at will once children reached their majority.

John Locke, secretary to both the Lords Proprietors of Carolina (1668–75) and the Council of Trade and Plantations (1672–5), and therefore well acquainted with the institution of slavery, was, perhaps for that very reason, curiously sensitive to the rights of entitlement in one's own person. Not only could one not contract away what one did not have, entitlement in one's own person if one was a slave, but one could not contract away that upon which the very institution of contract was founded: freedom to dispose of oneself at will. One's rights and entitlements in one's own person, one's freedom, in a word, are such that, while one can inherit obligations and liabilities attaching to *property*, obligations and liabilities attaching to *persons* were not hereditable. Just as one could not be born into slavery, but only enslaved as a prisoner of war, so one could not be born into any set of hereditable obligations, whether as serf to a master, bondsman to a fief, wife to a husband or citizen to a king. Such obligations could only be undertaken as a duty freely contracted. Whether the contract was explicit, as in the case of the marriage contract, or tacit, as in the case of the social contract, the obligation was the same.

5. Astell's Critique of Contractarianism

As critics have widely concurred, such a version of the social contract puts a burden on consent that it was not apt to bear: if a highway man traveling through a territory was deemed, as Locke suggested,[45] by the use of its roads to assent to its form of government, the concept was so overextended as to be meaningless. Right gives way to might, as Astell percipiently remarked: 'And if meer Power gives a Right to Rule, there can be no such thing as Usurpation; but a Highway-Man, so long as he has Strength to force, has also a Right to require our Obedience'.[46] The image of the highway man was invoked again by Astell, in *Moderation Truly Stated*,[47] to make precisely the same argument, although this time with reference to Milton's defence of contract in the *Eikonoklastes in Answer to a Book Entitled 'Eikon Basilike'*. It seems very likely that she took it from Locke, with whom she had several scores to settle, believing, as she did, that his hostess, Lady Damaris Masham's, attack on her in two celebrated works were masterminded by Locke.[48]

Locke, invoking the authority of Aristotle and Cicero, saw property as an extension of personality, the resource in terms of which characteristic human powers and purposes are played out. While he believed hereditable restrictions on persons to be insupportable, his concept of freedom did not extend to the removal of hereditable restrictions on property. Moreover, on these two questions on which he lays so much emphasis, rights of entitlement in one's own person such that one cannot contract into subordination and rights to property as an extension of personality, women are in effect excluded. Although Locke was concerned to speak of 'parental', as opposed to 'paternal' or 'patriarchal', power, thereby denying father-right or the superior *rights* of the husband over his spouse *ipso facto*, at the same time insisting that the wife cannot *consent* to her own subordination, he nevertheless capitulated to *customary right* in both respects. What could not be garnered by natural rights was yielded to men by custom on the basis of physical superiority.

Astell, in perhaps her finest rhetorical piece, the 1706 Preface[49] to *Reflections upon Marriage,* locates the subordination of women precisely in custom. But custom, she properly argues, yields no right, going on to compare a woman's duties as a wife and housekeeper with those of a man who has contracted to raise hogs – something that should not reflect on the status of either of them![50]

That the Custom of the World, has put Women, generally speaking, into a State of Subjection, is not denied; but the Right can no more be prov'd from the Fact, than the Predominancy of Vice can justifie it. . . . '[T]is certainly no Arrogance in a Woman to conclude, that she was made for the Service of GOD, and that this is her End. Because GOD made all Things for Himself, and a Rational Mind is too noble a Being to be Made for the Sake and Service of any Creature. The Service she at any Time becomes oblig'd to pay a Man, is only a Business by the Bye. Just as it may be any Man's Business and Duty to keep Hogs; he was not made for this, but if he hires himself out to such an Employment, he ought conscientously to perform it.

It was the great accomplishment of Astell to kick away the chocks supporting the wheels of social contract and liberal democratic theory, its child as yet unborn. It was a ridiculous fiction to maintain, like Locke, that men are born free:[51]

If all Men are born free, how is it that all Women are born slaves? as they must be if the being subjected to the *inconstant, uncertain, unknown, arbitrary Will* of Men, be the *perfect Condition of Slavery?* and if the Essence of Freedom consists, as our Masters say it does, in having a *standing Rule to live by?* And why is Slavery so much condemn'd and strove against in one Case, and so highly applauded and held so necessary and so sacred in another?

The exclusion of half of the human race from the purview of natural right, in the denial to women of property and interests, casts serious doubt on the bold rationalist claim to freedom as a birthright. The widely circulated Leveller claim that 'men are born free', sometimes extended to women, had attracted extensive debate.[52] To the corollary, that it was only by contract that men could be bound, Filmer himself had provided an excellent rebuttal: the contractarians cannot have it both ways; either men are born free or not; if they are free they can never be bound, and if not there is no issue. Moreover, Filmer specifically applied his formula to children, whose relation to their parents Hobbes and Locke also construed contractually:[53]

For if it be allowed that the acts of parents bind the children, then farewell the doctrine of the natural freedom of mankind. Where subjection of children to parents is natural, there can be no natural freedom. If any reply that not all children shall be bound by their parents' consent but only those under age, it must be considered that in nature there is no nonage. If a man be not born free she doth not assign him any other time when he shall attain his freedom, or if she did then children attaining that age should be discharged of their parents' contract. So that in conclusion, if it be imagined that the people were ever but once free from subjection by nature, it will prove a mere impossibility ever lawfully to introduce any kind of government whatsoever without apparent wrong to a multitude of people.

Such an argument closed off the emancipation of women on the basis of natural right, as Astell was forced to agree. *Reflections upon Marriage* had been occasioned by the scandalous divorce of the Duchess of Mazarin, which Astell made the occasion for a cautionary tale, but not to sanction divorce. Astell defended the customary social order, much as she railed against it. Or else, as Filmer put it:[54]

where there is an equality by nature, there can be no superior power. There every infant at the hour it is born in, hath a like interest with the greatest and wisest man in the world ... not to speak of women, especially virgins, who by birth have as much natural freedom as any other, and therefore ought not to lose their liberty without their own consent.

Natural right entailed for Astell further false inferences, such as freedom of belief and freedom of the press, both of which she opposed. If freedom of belief is a 'natural right', it is subversive of the entire social order. J. Nalson, whom she cites in *An Impartial Enquiry*, had argued that religion was 'the only bond of union, the only maintainer and preserver of those respective duties which are owing from one to another, in those little primitive societies of mankind' that constitute the family. Without it 'neither the obligations of nature, education, or reason, are powerful enough to keep men within the limits of their duty'.[55]

Astell agreed. Human beings were born into a tissue of networks and obligations, and only the blind could pretend otherwise. Arguments for natural right were but thinly disguised arguments for might, and where might is right, men come up trumps (to paraphrase Hobbes):[56]

Men are possess'd of all Places of Power, Trust and Profit, they make Laws and exercise the Magistracy, not only the sharpest Sword, but even all the Swords and Blunderbusses are theirs, which by the strongest Logic in the World, gives them the best Title to everything they please to claim as their Prerogative; who shall contend with them? Immemorial Prescription is on their side in these parts of the World, Antient Tradition and Modern Usage!

Astell stood firm by her philosophical conviction that custom yielded no right. By the same token, she argued on Platonist grounds that, if might is right, rulers cannot press a title to rule in superior wisdom. Subjects ruled by governors whose title to rule is established customarily obey them customarily, and not for any other reason. The spiritual equality of all believers entitles subjects to keep their own counsel on the question of the duty-worthiness of their governors, passive obedience being the only form of resistance she will concede. What holds for the realm *eo ipso* holds for the family:[57]

But does it follow that Domestick Governors have more Sense than their Subjects, any more than that other Governors have? We do not find that any Man thinks the worse of his own Understanding because another has superior Power; or concludes himself less capable of a Post of Honour and Authority, because he is not prefer'd to it. How much time would lie on Mens hands, how empty wou'd the Places of Concourse be, and how silent most Companies, did Men forbear to censure their Governors, that is, in effect, to think themselves wiser. Indeed Government would be much more desirable than it is, did it invest the Possessor with a superior Understanding as well as Power.

6. Astell's *Reflections upon Marriage*, a Critique of Customary Right

Astell's *Reflections upon Marriage* began as a memoir of the Countess of Mazarin's scandalous divorce, prompted by the contemporary literature that it generated, as Astell freely confesses.[58] Hortense Mancini (1646–99), Countess of Mazarin, had been born in Rome, the fourth daughter of Lorenzo Mancini and apparently the favourite niece of Cardinal Mazarin. She went to Paris, where she attracted much attention for her beauty. The cardinal arranged her marriage to the Duc de Meilleraye, insisting that in return for an enormous fortune, the duc must assume the name of Mazarin. The marriage, however, was not a happy one, and the countess fled disguised as a man. In 1675 she accompanied the Duchess of York to England. King Charles II admired her greatly and possibly even considered marrying her. But Hortense was so charmed by the Prince de Monaco, then in England, that Charles angrily suspended temporarily the pension he had provided for her. William III continued her allowance, however, and she lived a comfortable life of exile in Chelsea as one of Astell's neighbours, where she remained until her death. She amused herself by playing bassette and hosting dinners for her aristocratic literary circle of friends. Her celebrated divorce produced a spate of publications in defence of both parties, mostly ghosted and of uncertain provenance.

Surprisingly, given Mazarin's prodigal life, Astell comes strongly to her support, her first line of attack the biblical 'he who is first to cast the stone' argument. But as the argument develops, Astell begins to reflect on marriage less as a Christian sacrament and more as a fallible institution in the customary realm. There the woman 'has been taught to think Marriage her only Preferment, the Sum-total of her Endeavours, the completion of all her hopes, that which must settle and make her Happy in this World, and very few, in their Youth especially, carry a Thought steadily to a greater distance'. Astell reflects on expectations raised by courtship: 'She who has seen a Lover dying at her Feet...whose Eyes have been daz[z]led with all the Glitter and Pomp of a Wedding...will find a terrible disappointment when the hurry is over, and when she comes calmly to consider her Condition, and views it no more under a false Appearance, but as it truly is.'[59]

Of course, there are as many ways of gilding the cage as there are snares and lures to entice one into it. Astell runs the gamut on the 'traps [men] lay...under so many gilded Compliments'[60] to give a fair catalogue of men and what motivates them to marry, 'Fops', 'Coxcombs', those who marry for beauty, those for wit, and those who marry for money. It all makes little odds, and women better know that '[s]he then who Marrys ought to lay it down for an indisputable Maxim, that her Husband must govern absolutely and intirely, and that she has nothing else to do but to Please and Obey. She must not attempt to divide his Authority, or so much as dispute it, to struggle with her Yoke will only make it gall the more'.[61]

In many respects a legacy of medieval society, the High Church Tory view to which Astell subscribed saw society as an elaborate artifice constituted by many-layered juridical institutions and their constituencies. Freedoms, like duties, were yielded from the specificity of laws, and freedom was not the great space that fills the political vacuum into which men step, or are born, as Hobbes and Locke would have it. Astell's position is not so different from that of Filmer and it is certainly not the freedom of

Locke, whose language she so heavily satirizes. Such freedoms as English common law and customary rights might guarantee threatened to be extinguished by the zeal of the parliamentarians and Independents[62] who fought over them, risking[63]

[t]he bringing *the Necks* of their Fellow Subjects, *Englishmen,* who *had the Spirit of a Free People!* under their own infamous *Yoke,* and *their Feet into* the most reproachful *Chains;* becoming themselves the Actors of those Arbitrary and Illegal Actions, which they had so loudly, and in great measure, falsely imputed to their Lawful Superiours. And the *Freeborn* People of *England,* for all their *Spirit of Honour and Genius to Liberty,* even those great *Fore Fathers,* whose *Off-spring we are,* had the *disdain of serving* in the most slavish manner and of wearing the heavy and shameful *Yoke* of some of the vilest of their Fellow Subjects: Till GOD was pleas'd to restore our Monarch, and with him the Exercise of our Religion, and the Liberties of the *English* Nation.

The universe is governed by a personal God, whose design for humankind includes the unfolding of history and situated social institutions, as well as the rights and duties they can command. It is not, Astell believes, a self-regulating mechanism composed of harmoniously arranged laws, from which divine intervention is absent, as the rationalists and Deists would have it. It is rather a universe of specific freedoms and specific constraints, historical rights and historical injustices. The cause of women, like that of all souls, is affected by the outcome of local struggles against local powers on particular issues. And just as reason is powerless to effect sweeping changes, so it is not going to be constrained by any particular construction placed upon it, such as the exclusion of women. Mystical body language still abounded. The outspoken and soon to be impeached Henry Sacheverell referred to the queen as the 'nursing mother' of the church, with an obligation to defend the church, just as the church owed the Crown the obligation of defence in turn, a role to which Anne as a High Churchwoman was personally inclined. Sacheverell, in his work, *The Political Union,* put it thus:[64]

The Civil and Ecclesiastical State are the Two Parts and Divisions, that Both United make up One entire compounded Constitution, and Body Politick, sharing the same Fate and Circumstances, Twisted and Interwoven into the very Being and Principles of each Other, Both alike jointly Assisting and being Assisted, Defending and Defended, Supporting and Supported, in the same vital Union, Intercourse and Complication.

But Astell was scathing against those who would conclude from the mystical body language of Paul to the Corinthians II, the inferiority of women, noting:[65]

that *the Head of every Man is Christ, and that the Head of the Woman is the Man, and the Head of Christ is GOD*; It being evident from the Form of Baptism, that there is no natural Inferiority among the Divine Persons, but that they are in all things Coequal. . . . The relation between the two Sexes is mutual, and the Dependance Reciprocal, both of them Depending intirely upon GOD, and upon Him only; which one would think is no great Argument of the natural Inferiority of either Sex.

The very sacredness of marriage, which in the Christian religion, unlike the pagan religions of antiquity, Islam, or even orthodox Jewry, is a sacrament, and not merely a special kind of contract, requires that women understand the form of dominion, irrevocable and absolute, they enter when they choose it, just as it is incumbent on subjects to understand the obligations they enter when they swear allegiance to the Crown:[66]

She who Elects a Monarch for Life, who gives him an Authority she cannot recall however he misapply it, who puts her Fortune and Person entirely in his Powers; nay even the very desires of her Heart according to some learned Casuists, so as that it is not lawful to Will or Desire any thing but what he approves and allows; had need be very sure that she does not make a Fool her Head, nor a Vicious Man her Guide and Pattern, she had best stay till she can meet with one who has the Government of his own Passions, and has duly regulated his own desires, since he is to have such an absolute Power over hers.

Family tyrants exhibit the monstrous ungovernability of the passions associated with *Leviathans* past and present. The unequal exchange of the marriage contract, which the social contract of Hobbes and Locke imitates, Astell seems to imply, is a travesty of trust. In exchange for government, a woman places herself willingly in sovereign hands, 'mak[ing] a Man the greatest Compliment in the World when she condescends to take him *for Better for worse*'.[67] The injustice is a double injury, for it rests on a false inference:[68]

when we suppose a thing to be made purely for our sakes, because we have Dominion over it, we draw a false Conclusion, as he who shou'd say the People were made for the Prince who is set over them, wou'd be thought to be out of his Senses as well as his Politicks.

Astell adopts the language of 'dominion', 'sense' and 'sovereignty' to mock Hobbes, whose monstrous *Leviathan* the husband-monarch resembles. Having courted his quarry into submission, the eighteenth-century husband in all respects resembles the seventeenth-century sovereign, to whose overtures unwitting subjects so easily acquiesced. It is not because she denies dominion that Astell objects to the social contract, but because of the empty promises such a concept makes and is never in a position to redeem. In this respect, the social contract and eighteenth-century conventions of marriage show the same lamentable frailty. Astell subscribes to Platonist notions of the educative function of superiors over inferiors as a justification for hierarchy in a society geared to achieving the common good. On the uses of dominion and divine order, she has this to say:[69]

Superiors indeed are too apt to forget the common Priviledges of Mankind; that their inferiors share with them the greatest Benefits, and are as capable as themselves of enjoying the supreme Good; that tho' the Order of the World requires an *Outward* Respect and Obedience from some to others, yet the Mind is free, nothing but Reason can oblige it, 'tis out of the reach of the most absolute Tyrant. Nor will it ever be well either with those who Rule or those in Subjection, even from the Throne to every Private Family, till those in Authority look on themselves as plac'd in that Station for the good and improvement of their Subjects, and not for their own sakes; not as the reward of their Merit, or that they may prosecute their own Desires and fulfil all their Pleasure, but as the Representatives of GOD whom they ought to imitate in the Justice and Equity of their Laws, in doing good and communicating Blessings to all beneath them: By which, and not by following the imperious Dictates of their own will, they become truly Great and Illustrious and Worthily fill their Place.

Astell mocks Hobbes's view that compliance with the commands of an absolute sovereign concerns only 'outward shews' in the public realm (*in foro externo*), and that freedom, enjoyed privately (*in foro interno*), is not compromised by conformity.[70] Lapsing momentarily into the protection/allegiance language of Hobbes and natural rights theorists, against which she otherwise inveighs, Astell points out that women have obligations too:[71]

And the Governed for their Part ceasing to envy the Pomp and Name of Authority, shou'd respect their Governours as plac'd in GOD's stead and contribute what they can to ease them of their real Cares, by a chearful and ready compliance with their good endeavours, and by affording them the Plesure of success in such noble and generous Designs.

But Astell is cynical enough about the uses of power in practice, observing of the subordinate wife:[72]

And if she shews any Refractoriness, there are ways enough to humble her; so that by right or wrong the Husband gains his Will. For Covenants betwixt Husband and Wife, like Laws in an Arbitrary Government, are of little Force, the Will of the Sovereign is all in all.

Astell's dismay at the injustices that the sacrament of marriage entailed for women in her age – an institution whose prospects for the mutual well-being of both partners she deemed in principle so great – is expressed in the bitterness of her portrait of the eligible bachelor. Adopting the language of Hobbesian sensationalist psychology, in which images transmitted to the brain by the retina must be raised to sense by imagination, Astell enjoins wives to see the husband as an emperor with no clothes: 'Strip him of Equipage and Fortune, and such things as only daz[z]le our Eyes and Imaginations, but don't in any measure affect our Reason, or cause a Reverence in our Hearts, and the poor Creature sinks beneath our Notice, because not supported by real Worth':[73]

alas there is nothing more contemptible then this trifle of a Man, this meer Outside, whose Mind is as base and Mean as his external Pomp is Glittering. His Office or Title apart, to which some Ceremonious Observance must be paid for Order's sake, there's nothing in him that can command our Respect.

The conclusion is a dismal one, passive obedience, since resistance is ruled out. In the yet more rhetorical Preface to the third edition of *Reflections upon Marriage*, Astell was careful to absolve herself of any charges of sedition, feigning 'with an *English* Spirit and Genius, [to] set out upon the Forlorn Hope, meaning no Hurt to any body, nor designing any thing but the publick Good, and to retrieve, if possible, the Native Liberty, the Rights and Privileges of the Subject'.[74] It is perhaps ironic that Astell's Tory commitment to expose social contract theory for a Whig conspiracy has now dropped from sight, and she is seen instead as simply a proto-feminist highly critical of marriage as an institution. It is true that although pessimistic about the prospects for female emancipation, if it is even a duty-worthy cause in her eyes, Astell cannot contain her emancipatory rhetoric. Her feminist legacy is testimony both to her passionate protest against the injustice of marriage mores and her powerful argument against the very foundations of liberal theory, the marriage contract–social contract analogue.

7. Astell and Milton

In the first edition of *Reflections upon Marriage*, which ran to four editions in her lifetime, Astell had made an ironic argument for female slavery and male despotism implicit throughout that work, to be later amplified in the famous 1706 Preface:[75]

...how much soever Arbitrary Power may be dislik'd on a Throne, not *Milton* himself wou'd cry up Liberty to poor *Female Slaves,* or plead for the Lawfulness of Resisting a Private Tyranny.

Astell considers for a moment, and then dismisses, liberation, as belonging to the logic of slavery, falling back on passive obedience, the good old Tory substitute for the Lockean right of resistance – although not for long, as we shall see:[76]

[B]ut Patience and Submission are the only Comforts that are left to a poor People, who groan under Tyranny, unless they are Strong enough to break the Yoke, to Depose and Abdicate, which I doubt wou'd not be allow'd of here. For whatever may be said against Passive-Obedience in another case, I suppose there's no Man but likes it very well in this....

John Milton (1608–74), the poet and the butt of Astell's remarks, offended against her principles not only on the subject of marriage, but politically, regarding the monarchy and the episcopacy. In 1641 Milton had produced three pamphlets that vehemently attacked episcopacy on historical grounds and, taking no active part in the Civil War, Milton in 1643 had married a seventeen-year-old girl. The marriage, which lasted only a month, led Milton to write on the need for divorce, which further angered the clergy. His *Tenure of Kings and Magistrates,* which argued for the right of the people to judge their rulers, appeared immediately after the king's death, and the newly formed Council of State invited Milton to become their Latin secretary. Pamphlets written by Milton in this period show that he favoured strict republicanism, complete separation between church and state, and the permanent rule of the chiefs of the army and the Council. In 1650 Milton was commissioned to write in defence of those attacked as responsible for the king's death. The work, *Pro Populo Anglicano Defensio,* caused him to be arrested in 1660, but Milton was subsequently immune to prosecution by the terms of the Indemnity Act.

Astell had multiple reasons then for attacking Milton, 'who was a better Poet than Divine or Politician', she says, and whose attack on Charles I, the martyr king, in his *Eikonoklastes in Answer to a Book Entitled 'Eikon Basilike'*[77] deeply offended her. David Norbrook, in his recent book, *Writing the Republic,* has succeeded in moving Milton to centre stage as a seminal republican theorist – and quite deservedly so. So hostile was Milton to monarchy that even his ecclesiology was affected. For instance, as Norbrook points out, 'Milton says that if God gave the people episcopacy "he did it in his wrath, as he gave the Israelites a King"',[78] a reference to Sulpicius Severus, who described the people as insane for wanting a king, and a frequent republican trope. The Apostles, 'like those hero-ick patricians of Rome (if we may use such comparison) hasting to lay downe their dictatorship, they rejoys't to call themselves and to be as fellow Elders among their brethren. Knowing that their high office was but as the scaffolding of the Church yet unbuilt, and would be but a trouble-some disfigurement, so soone as the building was finisht.'[79] Furthermore, Milton actually described the primitive church as 'democratic', or at least aristocratic', its officers elective so that the 'voyce of the people' was heard.[80]

But that same Milton, democrat and defender of divorce on the grounds of non-domination, dared to put into print the claim: 'in vain does he prattle about liberty in assembly and market-place who at home endures the slavery most unworthy of man, slavery to an inferior'.[81] It was an inconsistency that Astell would not allow, and she argued her case precisely on the grounds that Milton had grandly staked out for freedom in the opening of his *Tenure of Kings and Magistrates* of 1649, God-given right. No one, he maintained, 'can be so stupid to deny that all men naturally were borne free, being the image and resemblance of God himself'.[82] There is, therefore, more point than commentators have noted to Astell's incredibly perspicacious remark that 'how much soever Arbitrary Power may be dislik'd on a Throne, not *Milton* himself wou'd cry up Liberty to poor *Female Slaves*, or plead for the Lawfulness of Resisting a Private Tyranny'.[83]

Astell was no contractarian and no patriarchalist either. The Preface to *Reflections upon Marriage* is a litany of biblical references affirming the power of women, in answer to the patriarchalists who would argue from the creation of Eve from Adam's rib to her inferiority.[84] However, corporatism features quite importantly in her thought. Not only is Astell quite consistent in maintaining the real constraints imposed on men and women by the institutions and structures into which they are born, but her views accord much more with the widely held perceptions of marriage and the family in her day than those of Hobbes and Locke, which were considered far-fetched and outlandish.[85] Astell turned the tables on them:[86]

Again, if Absolute Sovereignty be not necessary in a State, how comes it to be so in a Family? or if in a Family why not in a State; since no Reason can be alledged for the one that will not hold more strongly for the other? If the Authority of the Husband so far as it extends, is sacred and inalienable, why not of the Prince? The Domestic Sovereign is without Dispute Elected, and the Stipulations and Contract are mutual, is it not then partial in Men to the last degree, to contend for, and practise that Arbitrary Dominion in their Families, which they abhor and exclaim against in the State? For if Arbitrary Power is evil in itself, and an improper Method of Governing Rational and Free Agents it ought not to be Practis'd any where; Nor is it less, but rather more mischievous in Families than in Kingdoms, by how much 100000 Tyrants are worse than one.

It was Astell's genius to see that society has drawn a veil over the face of justice in the fiction of the social contract. The reason women must submit to this domination, and had better love it, is simply an issue of power. And those nice distinctions that divide the public and private spheres in early modern liberal theory of the state are just so many tricks to disguise it. As Rousseau and Marx were later to argue so powerfully, it matters not that the man is ugly – power will make him handsome – or lame – money will give him the power to walk.[87] Man is king – or as Rousseau put it, he is *citoyen*, and that is also an entitlement in the private sphere, whether he is a *bourgeois* or not.[88] Astell discusses at length the difficulties an industrious wife faces in meeting the demands and expectations of such a tyrant.[89] The case is well nigh hopeless. A woman 'who does not practice Passive Obedience to the utmost, will never be acceptable to such an absolute Sovereign as a Husband'.[90] Astell is tempted to resort to state-of-nature arguments herself: 'Tho' we live like Brutes, we wou'd have Incense offer'd us that is only due to Heaven it self, wou'd have an absolute and blind Obedience paid us by all over whom we pretend Authority. We were not made to Idolize one another, yet the whole strain of Courtship is little less than rank Idolatry.' In fact, of course, the manners and mores of marriage belong to the customary realm where the division of power between the public and private spheres is secured by social practices. Might is converted into right, and the right to power in the public sphere is read as an entitlement to tyranny in the private:[91]

But how can a Woman scruple intire Subjection, how can she forbear to admire the worth and excellency of the Superior Sex, if she at all considers it? Have not all the great Actions that have been perform'd in the World been done by Men? Have not they founded Empires and overturn'd them? Do not they make Laws and continually repeal and amend them? Their vast Minds lay Kingdoms wast, no bounds or measures can be prescrib'd to their Desires. War and Peace depend on them, they form Cabals and have the Wisdom and Courage to get over all the Rubs which may lie in the way of their desired Grandeur. What is it they cannot do? They make Worlds and ruine them, form Systems of universal nature and dispute eternally about them; their Pen gives worth to the most trifling Controversie; nor can a fray be inconsiderable if they have drawn their Swords in't. All that the wise Man pronounces is an Oracle, and every Word the Witty speaks a Jest.

It is a Woman's Happiness to hear, admire and praise them, especially if a little Ill-nature keeps them at any time from bestowing due Applauses on each other! And if she aspires no further, she is thought to be in her proper Sphere of Action, she is as wise and as good as can be expected from her!

Dominium in the private sphere matched by *imperium* in the public one tilt the playing field impossibly. All the arguments in terms of which the power of husbands over wives is justified are just so much flimflam, and Astell cocks a snoot at the hoary old argument, to be found in Hobbes and Locke alike, that power falls to the man by the convention of rule by the stronger:[92]

Besides, it were ridiculous to suppose that a Woman, were she ever so much improv'd, cou'd come near the topping Genius of the Men, and therefore why shou'd they envy or discourage her? Strength of Mind goes along with Strength of Body, and 'tis only for some odd Accidents which Philosophers have not yet thought worth while to enquire into, that the Sturdiest Porter is not the Wisest Man!

Warming to her subject, Astell goes on to mock the achievements of men in the public sphere that are said to justify women's being 'taken to be Man's Upper-Servant'.[93]

As therefore the Men have the Power in their Hands, so there's no dispute of their having the Brains to manage it! Can we suppose there is such a thing as good Judgement and Sense upon Earth, if it is not to be found among them? Do not they generally speaking do all the great Actions and considerable Business of this World, and leave that of the next to the Women? Their Subtilty in forming Cabals and laying deep Designs, their Courage and Conduct in breaking through all Tyes Sacred and Civil to effect them, not only advances them to the Post of Honour, and keeps them securely in it for twenty or thirty Years, but gets them a Name, and conveys it down to Posterity for some Hundreds, and who wou'd look any further? Justice and Injustice are administred by their Hands, Courts and Schools are fill'd with these Sages; 'tis Men who dispute for Truth as well as Men who argue against it; Histories are writ by them, they recount each others great Exploits, and have always done so. All famous Arts have their Original from Men, even from the Invention of Guns to the Mystery of good Eating. And to shew that nothing is beneath their Care, any more than above their Reach, they have brought *Gaming* to an Art and Science, and a more Profitable and Honourable one too, than any of those that us'd to be call'd *Liberal!* Indeed what is it they can't perform, when they attempt it? The Strength of their Brains shall be every whit as Conspicuous at their Cups, as in a Senate-House, and when they please they can make it pass for as sure a Mark of Wisdom, to drink deep as to Reason profoundly; a greater proof of Courage and consequently of Understanding, to dare the Vengeance of Heaven it self, than to stand the Raillery of some of the worst of their fellow Creatures.

The manners and mores of marriage belong in the field of customary law, and it is only here that hope for reform lies. Even in the first drafting of *Reflections upon Marriage*, Astell realizes the seditious force of her arguments. Observing, in conclusion, 'perhaps I've said more than most Men will thank me for, I cannot help it, for how much soever I may be their Friend and humble Servant, I am more a Friend to Truth', Astell goes on to insist that she does men 'more Honour than to suppose their lawful Prerogatives need any mean Arts to support them'. Stealing a line from Filmer, she notes, 'They may fancy I have made some discoveries which like *Arcana Imperii*, ought to be kept secret'. Quite so, for what she has discovered is that the logic of slavery applies to marriage as it does to all institutions, if it applies at all:

> If they have Usurpt, I love Justice too much to wish Success and continuance to Usurpations, which tho' submitted to out of Prudence, and for Quietness sake, yet leave every Body free to regain their lawful Right whenever they have Power and Opportunity. I don't say that Tyranny *ought*, but we find in *Fact*, that it provokes the Oppress'd to throw off even a Lawful Yoke that sits too heavy: And if he who is freely Elected, after all his fair Promises and the fine Hopes he rais'd, proves a Tyrant, the consideration that he was one's own Choice, will not render more Submissive and Patient, but I fear more Refractory.

In the famous Preface to the 1706 edition of *Reflections upon Marriage*, Astell, provoked by the critical reception of previous editions, stakes out her claim even more forcefully, as we have seen. The burden of her argument, once again, is to expose as fictions the appeals to natural right, in the name of which women are subjugated. With characteristic irony, 'She hopes it is no Presumption to insist on this Natural Right of Judging for her self, and the rather, because by quitting it, we give up all the Means of Rational Conviction'.[94] Showing that she can turn an argument as well as the next man, Astell accuses those who argue for women's natural slavery of violating the is–ought distinction: 'That the Custom of the World has put Women, generally speaking, into a State of Subjection, is not deny'd; but the Right can no more be prov'd from the Fact, than the Predominancy of Vice can justifie it.'[95] Moral arguments disguised as history, like the arguments for patriarchalism of Sir Robert Filmer and William Whiston,[96] get equally short shrift as genetic arguments that once again confuse facts and values. The law of nature must extend to women the same rights it extends to men, although they may not be fully realized on this earth, rights that attach to humans as mind rather than body. Fictions of the state of nature to the contrary – in fact, just because the conventions of marriage do fall under the laws of nations, or *ius gentium*,

and not *ius naturale*, or natural law – 'the Service she at any
oblig'd to pay to a Man, is only a Business by the Bye'.[97]

The homology between the marriage contract and the s
does not hold, Astell insists, and the subjection of women ca
from no law of reason; it comes down to a question of powe

Our Fathers have all along both Taught and Practis'd Superiority over the weaker
Sex, and consequently Women are by Nature inferior to Men, as was to be Demon-
strated. An Argument which must be acknowledg'd unanswerable, for as well as
I love my Sex, I will not pretend a Reply to *such* Demonstration!

But unable to forebear, reply she does:[99]

Only let me beg to be inform'd, to whom we poor Fatherless Maids, and Widows
who have lost their Masters, owe Subjection? It can't be to all Men in general,
unless all Men were agreed to give the same Commands; do we then fall as Strays
to the first who finds us? By the Maxims of some Men, and the Conduct of some
Women one wou'd think so.

Sheer power may explain, but it cannot justify, such an arbitrary dispensation. And, stealing an example from Hobbes's and Locke's books, Astell
makes the powerful argument that 'if mere Power gives a Right to Rule,
there can be no such thing as Usurpation; but a Highway-Man so long as
he has strength to force, has also a Right to require our Obedience'.[100]
And if right, and not might, is to rule, there is no justification for anyone's being subjected to the *'inconstant, uncertain, unknown arbitrary Will'*
of another man, which defines the *'perfect Condition of Slavery'*.[101]

The law of nature, assimilated in the Christian era to the law of God,
does not rule on earth. But were it to, it would require consistency in both
the public and private domains. Carried away by the force of her own
rhetoric, in the paean to Queen Anne that concludes the preface, Astell
hails a future heaven on earth, 'those Halcyon, or if you will *Millennium*
Days, in which the Wolf and the Lamb shall feed together':[102]

Adieu to the Liberties not of this or that Nation or Region only, but of the Moiety
of Mankind! To all the great things that Women might perform, Inspir'd by
her Example, Encourag'd by her Smiles, and supported by her Power! To their
Discovery of New Worlds for the Exercise of her Goodness, New Sciences to
publish her Fame, and reducing Nature itself to a Subjection to her Empire! To
their destroying those worst of Tyrants Impiety and Immorality, which dare to
stalk about even in her own Dominions, and to devour Souls almost within view
of her Throne, leaving a stench behind them scarce to be corrected even by the
Incense of her Devotions! To the Women's tracing a new Path to Honor, in which
none shall walk but such as scorn to Cringe in order to Rise, and who are Proof
both against giving and receiving Flattery! In a word, to those Halcyon, or if you

will *Millennium* Days, in which the Wolf and the Lamb shall feed together, and a Tyrannous Domination which Nature never meant, shall no longer render useless if not hurtful, the Industry and Understandings of half Mankind!

What prompted Astell's extraordinarily prospective critique of Locke, and how can we be sure that he was really her target? Critics may question the extent to which Astell would have been specifically concerned with Hobbes or Locke, who in twenty-first-century political theory are too often taken to subsume all the complex views of their age. In Astell's case, however, we can cite special reasons for her interest in the form of personal antagonisms roused by Locke and Damaris Masham and, more importantly, the machinations of Locke and the Shaftesbury circle in the lead-up to the Glorious Revolution of 1688 and the settlement on William and Mary. Not only does she refer to Hobbes and Locke, the latter by name on several occasions; but she probably knew that it would do little for Locke's personal standing to class him with the notorious Hobbes,[103] even if it tended to efface Hobbes's monarchism and Locke's Whiggish party affiliations that she was otherwise at pains to stress.

4

Mary Astell and the Settlement of 1689

1. Astell's *An Impartial Enquiry*: The Context

Astell's *An Impartial Enquiry into the Causes of Rebellion and Civil War* of 1704 is, of all her works, the most polemically partisan, a classic set piece of Tory rhetoric, in which the events of 1649 become a surrogate for discussion of the constitutional provisions of 1689. It was occasioned by the sermon of the Whig bishop White Kennett (1660–1728) preached on 31 January 1703/4 to commemorate the anniversary of the death of Charles I, entitled 'A Compassionate Enquiry into the Causes of the Civil War'. The very notion of a 'Compassionate Enquiry' on such an occasion was offensive to a royalist, and Astell leapt to the defence of 'the Royal King and Martyr'. Glorification of the royal martyr had long been a calculated Tory strategy, and Tory iconography depicting England's most absolute monarch 'as a mythological but appealing figure'[1] dates in fact to the work *Eikon Basilike* of 1649 – a sentimental and embroidered version of Charles's last reflections, the provenance of which became entangled in Civil War debates. But after 1688 the memory of Charles, and even commemorative sermons, were no longer sacred, and on this occasion, the anniversary of 31 January 1703/4, no less than four prominent Whig divines had preached sermons that damned the royal martyr with faint praise. Some measure of the vitriol the memory of Charles could command may be gained, for instance, by the antics of the Calves Head Club, to which Astell refers in *An Impartial Enquiry* in the context of Kennett's sermon. A club established shortly after the death of Charles I to mock his death, its meetings were also held on his anniversary, 30 January. The dishes served were a cod's head, to represent Charles the man, a pike to represent tyranny, a boar's head to represent the king preying on his subjects, and calves' heads representing Charles and his followers. An axe and a toast celebrated the regicide, and a copy of *Eikon Basilike* was burned. After the Restoration the club met secretly, and in 1734 the diners were mobbed, which put an end to further meetings.[2]

Of the four commemorative sermons preached on 31 January 1703/4, by George Hooper, Bishop of Bath and Wells, by William Binckes, Dean of Lichfield, and by William Sherlock, Dean of St. Paul's, the sermon of White Kennett, Bishop of Peterborough and respected ecclesiastical biographer, was the most famous, and it was to his sermon that Astell responded. Some measure of those who preached these sermons, all Whig divines, eminent and erudite men, is important to appreciate just what a provocation to the High Church Tory position they represented. Kennett had taken holy orders at Oxford and worked as a curate, but his dislike of James II's ecclesiastical policy had modified his political views, prompting him to preach against popery and openly support the Revolution. In his commemorative sermon he implied that there had been some errors in Charles's reign, due to a 'popish' queen and a corrupt ministry 'whose policy tended in the direction of an absolute tyranny'. A toned-down version of his sermon was printed – with 'exaggerations corrected', as it was so nicely put – but it still elicited angry replies from Kennett's High Church opponents. Astell, in *An Impartial Inquiry*, noted indeed that Kennett, in company with Hooper, Binckes and Sherlock, had preached 'upon this Day such antiquated Truths as might have past upon the Nation in the Reign of K. *Charles* II. or in Monmouth's rebellion'.[3]

*George Hooper, the erudite Bishop of Bath and Wells, had also preached a commemorative sermon for Charles to the two houses of Parliament on 31 January 1703/4, to which Astell refers. *William Binckes, also included in Astell's comment, had preached to the lower house of convocation on 30 January 1701, on the martyrdom of Charles I. In this sermon, indulging in the type of outrageous hyperbole that was among the techniques of irony in the rhetorical armoury of the day – famously employed by Daniel Defoe, as we shall see – Binckes had argued that the execution of Charles I was an act of even greater enormity than the crucifixion of Jesus Christ, because Charles I was in actual possession of his crown, whereas Jesus Christ was merely the uncrowned king of the Jews. He suffered no reprisals for publishing this sermon, and in 1703 was made dean of Lichfield and in 1705 appointed as prolocutor to convocation.

*William Sherlock, the fourth figure mentioned in Astell's cryptic remark, was altogether a more complicated figure. In 1681 Sherlock was collated to the prebend of St. Pancras in St. Paul's Cathedral, where he wrote his *Case of Resistance* of 1684, in which he argued for the divine right of kings and the duty of passive obedience on scriptural grounds. Yet he declined to read James II's 1687 declaration for liberty and conscience and continued to attack Catholics. He was made master of the Temple in 1685. During the Revolution he opposed alterations in the prayer book to gain dissenters, sided with the nonjurors and encouraged others to refuse the oath to William and Mary. As a result, he was suspended from all his preferments. In 1689 Sherlock published the most popular of his works, the *Practical Discourse concerning Death*, but the following year he switched allegiances and took the oath to William and Mary. He was promptly rewarded with the restoration of his preferments and in addition was granted the deanery of St. Paul's in 1691. Sherlock is also important as the addressee of remarks by Locke concerning the entitlement of kings, as we shall see.[4]

If White Kennett's sermon preached on the anniversary of the death of Charles earned notoriety for Whig tepidness on the merits of Charles, Astell's reply is one of the famous set pieces of the Tory canon, appealing to standard authorities, the Bible, the first Earl of Clarendon and *Henry Foulis. Kennett is referred to by Astell as a writer in the Convocation Controversy who had assisted Archbishop Tenison to assert William's prerogative forbidding the convocation of the lower clergy in Parliament. Astell, a firm supporter of the autonomy of the Anglican hierarchy, like her High Church authorities, represented what Goldie has suggested to be the real roots of Tory constitutionalism in the revolt against James: the choice of church over king.[5] Her analysis, which patterns the problems of 1689 on those of 1649, is not merely an elaborately crafted ruse to bypass the censor. It reflects the perceptions of contemporaries, who could overlook the hiatus between the Civil War and the Restoration and see real parallels in the two successful attempts in one century to unseat Stuart kings. Astell thus vindicates the trend of recent historiography to take seriously the claims of contemporary critics of the Restoration who analyzed the Revolution of 1688 against the benchmark of 1641.[6] Excuses for resistance were the same (popery and arbitrary government); so were the fears – civil war without cease, on the one hand, or capitulation to the forces of continental counterrevolution, spearheaded by the French, on the other. Astell attacks Kennett for inflating fears of popery and the French threat – classic scare tactics of the Shaftesbury circle, to which

Locke belonged, in her view. Here, of course, Astell was less than just. If one could say that the threat from France was exaggerated for political purposes in 1640–2, or even in 1679–81, one could not claim the same of the wars of 1689 to 1713, which, if lost by England, could have resulted in James II or his son being installed as a French puppet. The political instability of the period owed much to the frailty of the Stuart line, and the crisis of 1701, for instance, was due in large part to the death of the Duke of Gloucester, Queen Anne's last surviving child, which created uncertainty about the succession and led to passage of the Act of Settlement. Astell too easily blames these crises on scapegoats: the Presbyterians and *Pym in 1640–2, Locke and the Shaftesbury circle in 1679–81 and Defoe and the dissenters in 1701–5.

Astell's references are to the published, somewhat toned-down (as he tells us) second edition of White Kennett's sermon, a slim pamphlet of twenty-eight pages, which attracts from Astell a rebuttal of more than double the length.[7] She creates a sort of pastiche out of his pamphlet in which hardly a word he wrote goes unquoted, but not necessarily in context, and succeeds in making him sound more Whiggish than the text would allow. Astell renders him a surrogate for Locke, making much of his passing reference to motives of self-preservation and fears of citizens for their liberties and estates[8] when in fact, the most sustained passages of his political theory suggest a rather old-fashioned view of the well-ordered polity that relies on the metaphor of the body.[9] What is most remarkable about Astell's work is not only its perspicacity in analyzing the basic tenets of Whig political theory, and specifically Locke's, but also the degree to which it is representative of arguments that came to characterize the Augustan Tory position. It is sometimes forgotten that Sir Robert Filmer's *Patriarcha* was first and foremost a refutation of scholastic arguments for popular sovereignty as they were, in the 1630s, already infecting Protestant political thought.[10] The great debates that had raged under James I between Cardinal Bellarmine and fellow Counterreformation defenders of the right to depose unlawful kings against supporters of the English Protestant kingdom had their efflux in the later debates between Hobbes and Filmer, Filmer and Locke. Filmer was republished between 1679 and 1680 during the *Exclusion Crisis to support the Tory cause. It was highly desirable for theorists like Hobbes and Locke to be able to establish distance between their theories and those of the patriarchalist, whose very fundamentalism posed a problem in times of dynastic uncertainty. Locke, needless to say, was not keen to be classed with the scholastics. It was up to him to give the lie to Filmer and later exponents of his views, such as Henry Foulis, that popular sovereignty had roots independent of popery. Most notable in Astell's *An Impartial Enquiry* is the genealogy of theories of popular sovereignty that it records, taken from Foulis, where Jesuits and defenders of papal power are thrown together with Calvinists and Whigs. Thus once again the Jesuits, Mariana, Suarez, Molina and Bellarmine, were declared to be in an unholy alliance with the radical Protestant sects, the Diggers, the Levellers, Milton and Locke.[11]

Two years later, White Kennett once again preached a commemorative sermon on the occasion of Charles I's death, on January 30, this time to both houses of Parliament. He was one of only four Whig bishops ever to do so.[12] On that day he delivered a very mild set piece, and finally seemed to capitulate to the Tory cause in 1715 with a sermon on resistance to the king as a species of witchcraft, citing the articles, canons and homilies against rebellion that constituted the Tory litany, and on which Astell also draws, concluding with an exalted argument for divine right: 'Kings and Princes do in a more especial Manner represent the Majesty of God himself; are his Viceregents and Deputies here on Earth'.[13] Whether this is testimony to Astell's persuasive powers or evidence for the inconstancy of a bishop whose affiliations until 1700 had been Tory is debatable. As a moderate Tory herself, the distance between Astell and the bishop was less great than the tone of her pamphlet would suggest.[14]

2. Astell, Locke and the Problem of Resistance

If Astell's *Impartial Enquiry into the Causes of Rebellion* is about the Civil War of the mid-seventeenth century, it belongs no less to the Exclusion Crisis, the Glorious Revolution and the succession crises in the reign of Anne. Political surrogacy was a strategy by which it was possible to discuss present problems with reference to analogues in the past, and this is how the English Civil War was seen. Works purporting to discuss 1649 were surrogates for the analysis of events in 1689, and vice versa. Scholars have shown how the constitutional debate that post-dated the Revolution of 1688 rehearsed the arguments of the *Engagement Controversy forty years earlier.[15] The works of Anthony Ascham (1649), Philip Hunton (1643), George Lawson (1660), Henry Parker (1643, 1650) and John Milton (1689, 1690) were republished.[16] The arguments of John Goodwin, Richard Baxter, whose *Five Disputations of Church Government* of 1659 were mentioned by Astell in *A Fair Way with the Dissenters* (1704),[17] and *James Owen, author of *Moderation a Virtue* (1703), to which Astell replied, were re-rehearsed. The latter were radicals condemned in the

Oxford Decree of 1683. Thus Locke's and Astell's works belong to the same political milieu, a politics that, from the Exclusion Crisis to the end of Anne's reign, is in many respects a seamless whole, but from this literature Locke was in fact absent, at least by name. A matter of some interest, as we shall see.

The greater issues on which these particular debates turned were the following. The ultimate source of law: was it customary right enshrined in common law or in the will of the prince? The true guardian of the law: was it Parliament, as representative of the people, or the Crown, with its duty of protection in exchange for allegiance? The provenance of the ancient constitution: did it lie in immemorial custom or the institutions of the Crown? The nature of the relationship between the Crown and its subjects: was it contractual, or was it defined by submission to providential rights or rights of conquest? The entitlement rights of subjects in their own person and to their property: were they by nature or by contract? The respective antiquity of the institutions under contest and their historical status, whether relatively indigenous, native to Englishmen, feudal, originating in Roman law or ahistorical, originating in natural right, was another set of questions. As John Pocock has shown,[18] the long contest begun in the 1640s between Parliament and the Crown had seen a desegregation of customary rights and the ancient constitution. The upshot of the contest was the hijacking of customary right by the parliamentary party (later the Whigs) and of the ancient constitution by the royalists (later the Tories). And if such a characterization seems too crude, it is worth noting that party politics in the age of Anne, in which Astell participated, turned on just such formulations and are barely comprehensible without them. From Sir Edward Coke's time on, juridical thought had conceived of the ancient constitution as comprising the Crown, its institutions and the entirety of common law, as well as statutory law enacted by Parliament sitting as a high court. But the heightening conflict between the Crown and Parliament over the royal prerogative brought with it a contest over their antiquity and, therefore, the superior claims of one against the other. The long process of disaggregating the ancient constitution and customary rights marked the juridically most sophisticated, perhaps the politically most participatory, certainly the party politically most polarized, and the most vigorous pamphlet paper war in the history of the early modern English state. It was ultimately won by the Whig side, with the limitations on royal prerogative put in place successively from 1649 to 1702. Goldie, in his review of politics and the press for the period, concludes, 'Between 1689 and 1714, newspapers apart, the figure of five to six thousand, or on average four per week, would not be an unrealistic guess at the total number of polemical pieces coming off the presses'.[19]

Astell was implacably opposed to the removal of James II from the throne and hostile to William and Mary as impostors. Her friends numbered prominent nonjurors, and her early works are replete with double entendres aimed at William III and his apologists. Much of Astell's case against the fickleness with which men treat their marriage vows in *Reflections upon Marriage* (1700) can be read at another level as criticism of the fickleness of those who took oaths of allegiance to William and Mary despite solemn and binding oaths to James II still in force. In this way, Astell characteristically turned to her advantage the marriage contract–social contract homology. So, for instance, in the famous 1706 Preface to *Reflections upon Marriage*, Astell combines insistence on the rule of queens, as affirmed by Salic law in general, and endorsement of the rule of Queen Anne in particular, with jibes at Locke, Defoe and William's propagandists who, in forsaking James II, forsook the lineage of the great Queen Elizabeth I:[20]

If they mean that *some* Men are superior to *some* Women this is no great Discovery; had they turn'd the Tables they might have seen that *some* Women are Superior to *some* Men. Or had they been pleased to remember their Oaths of Allegiance and Supremacy, they might have known that *One* Woman is superior to *All* the Men in these Nations, or else they have sworn to very little purpose. And it must not be suppos'd, that their Reason and Religion wou'd suffer them to take Oaths, contrary to the Law of Nature and Reason of things.

Mark Goldie, in his analysis of the structure of political argument in 1688, has shown that only the radical Whigs, among whom Locke of the *Two Treatises of Government* belongs, along with Tyrrell, Samuel Johnson, Atwood, Blount and Defoe, 'used a natural law case for resistance or right of deposition' – although a Whig middle group used contractual resistance in some form.[21] Astell mounts against them a brilliant case, calling upon distinctions between authorization and designation that are to be found in Hobbes and Filmer, drawn ultimately from scholastic debate and now put to similar use by thinkers otherwise very much at odds to deny a right to dethrone kings, even bad kings.

In this, as in other instances, Astell demonstrated her consistency and care in argumentation preparatory to her great attack by ridicule on the social contract–marriage contract analogue in *Reflections upon Marriage* and *An Impartial Enquiry*. The attempt in scholastic theory to drive a wedge between authorization and consent as sanctions for institutions public and private had its legacy in Hobbes's finely crafted theory of simultaneous authorization and consent in the moment of social contract. If for Hobbes popular consent was the necessary but not sufficient condition for legitimacy, the fabric of social institutions could nevertheless not be allowed to hang by such slender threads. Mainstream scholastic theory had sought to secure the social power of even secular institutions, the magistracies of state and semi-secular ones, notably the family, by separating out as different acts the authorizing of an institution and the appointment of an incumbent to it. Authorization fell to God alone, but in the act of designation the people had their day. Where the papalists Bellarmine and Suarez took the more radical position that only a community could authorize the transfer of power from a community to a ruler, Hobbes fell back on the older scholastic position that vests power to authorize with the author (in this case God), leaving only the designation of an incumbent to popular choice.[22] Hobbes's extension of contract theory to the recesses of household and family was not necessarily inconsistent. Scholastic theory held, correspondingly, that entry into the estate of marriage could only be divinely authorized, as registered in the marriage vows, but that the choice of incumbents could be left to consent, as recognized by the marriage contract between the parties.

Astell, who tipped her hand against the marriage contract–social contract analogue in *Reflections upon Marriage*, argued her case systematically in *An Impartial Enquiry* and *The Christian Religion*. Themes from contemporary parliamentary and pamphlet controversy dominate these works, notably the distinction between authority and title on which her case depended. In *An Impartial Enquiry*, she proceeded to invoke Paul, Romans 13,[23] although not by name, the very text canonically recited by the rationalists and pragmatists of her day, who claimed as a practical necessity of government that God, while ordaining good governors, also permitted bad ones to be obeyed. It was once again an argument only permitted on the grounds of the scholastic distinction between *ordinatio commissionis* and *ordinatio permissionis*,[24] which absolved the deity of whatever bad choices the people might make in choosing incumbents to offices. Since these were offices that only God could authorize, and because their continued stability was in his care, the consent of the people was a nonrevocable act: once made, it could not be withdrawn. This was precisely the argument made by Hobbes. It was also the basis for the Christian case against divorce, and Astell in *Reflections upon Marriage*, by no accident, had used the opportunity of a celebrated divorce case between the courtesan Hortense Mancini and her husband to reflect on duty and contract in the public and private spheres.

3. Astell and the 'Glorious Revolution' of 1688

Astell's *An Impartial Inquiry into the Causes of Rebellion* (1704), the weightiest rebuttal that White Kennett's inflammatory sermon to commemorate the death of Charles I ever received, is firmly anchored in the politics of the Glorious Revolution, as her deconstruction of the French threat and the fiction of contract demonstrate. When William, the Dutch Prince of Orange, and his wife, Mary, daughter of the deposed James II, came to power, it was widely known that Locke had been involved as a propagandist. It is ironic that Locke's *Two Treatises*, written, it is now argued, between 1681 and 1683, constantly revised and secretly guarded until their release was safe after 1689, may have been disguised as the mysterious work *Tractatus de Morbo Gallico* – 'Concerning the French Disease', which had a double meaning: syphilis in one sense, despotism in another, both considered by the English to be peculiarly French.[25] Locke's involvement in the Shaftesbury circle pressuring for the abdication of James II, and his widely acknowledged role as propagandist for William III, attracted Astell's bitter invective. She saw the much vaunted threats of a French alliance, popery and despotism as trumped-up Whig justifications for the deposition of James II and the basis for their case against the Pretender's being reinstated. Presbyters, not popes, were the greatest threats to the prevailing civil order, she charged, and Presbyterians were more than popish in their tactics. In this respect Astell adopted uncritically the attitude of Henry Foulis, author of *The History of the Wicked Plots and Conspiracies of Our Pretended Saints* and *The History of the Romish Treasons and Usurpations* and among her most frequently cited sources. For just as Whigs charged Tories with popery and Francophilia, Tories charged Whigs with Presbyterian–Calvinist plots against church and state, and among them Foulis was canonical. Some indication of the grounds for Astell's view may be found in the Bill of Rights, which, in its first wording, had raised the spectre of 'Jesuits and other wicked persons' having advised James II 'to subvert the constitution of the kingdom by breaking the original contract between king and people'.[26] It was on the basis of such charges, admittedly moderated somewhat in the final form of the bill, that clerics, mindful of their oaths to the Stuarts, had been deprived of their livings.

Political events in 1701 had conspired to give Lockean arguments a rerun, heralded by the reissue of radical tracts from 1649 and 1689. Attempts by the Tories to impeach Lords Somers, Halifax, Portland and Oxford for their role in the partition treaties provided the conditions. The Kentish petitioners, who demanded that the Crown fund a new war with France and were gaoled for their efforts, were the catalyst.[27] In 1701 a petition had been presented to Parliament by Kentish men in favour of supporting William in a war against France. When the petitioners were imprisoned by the Tory majority in the House of Commons, Defoe responded with the *Legion Memorial* – so-called because of the signature: 'Our name is Legion, and we are many' – which he presented to the House. The petitioners were released and much debate ensued. But Somers and the indefatigable Defoe, a publicist for Locke, continued the defense of the right of subjects to petition. Somers, citing Locke's *Two Treatises,* argued precisely for government as a pact between property-owners, whereby consent of the governed to government as a species of protection agency entailed that the people might also submit grievances where their liberties seemed to be jeopardized. Charles Davenant, in *Essays upon Peace at Home and War Abroad* (1704), on which Mary Astell comments in the long prefatory discourse to her pamphlet *Moderation Truly Stated* (1704), pointed out that, not since the Civil War itself, had radical proponents of consent so loudly proclaimed rights of resistance and parliamentary accountability.[28] Davenant, preoccupied with Machiavellian theories of corruption, followed up with the trenchant *True Picture of the Modern Whig,* which showed modern Whigs to be careerists prosecuting war with France to gain political place and personal profit,[29] just the line of argument pursued by Astell in *An Impartial Enquiry.* This was also the argument she made in *Moderation Truly Stated,* where her target appears to be Locke, although her tract was read by contemporaries as a refutation of Davenant.[30]

The Kentish petitioners had raised in the minds of pamphleteers on both sides constitutional issues that never lay far beneath the surface. Whig strategies to keep alive the threat of French despotism and the Pretender as a pretext for war cast serious doubt on their credentials as defenders of immemorial rights, while 'Tory writers manipulated the ancient constitution myth by leveling it at its perpetrators'.[31] Hence we have Charles Davenant, and even Astell herself, declaring the English constitution to be a mixed constitution consisting of 'the harmony of a prince, who is Head of the Republick, the lords and the commons'.[32]

Davenant, using Machiavellian language, speaks of a constitution balanced between arbitrary government and democracy (Crown and Commons), arguing that a fourth estate of the common people with separate rights, such as the Kentish petitioners had pressed for, would be destabilizing. Astell, in *An Impartial Enquiry*, argues similarly against 'the People's Supremacy':[33]

And since our Constitution lodges the Legislative Power in the Prince and the Three Estates assembled in Parliament; as it is not in the Power of the Prince and one of the Houses, to Make or Abrogate any Law, without the Concurrence of the other House, so neither can it be Lawfully done by the Prince alone, or by the two Houses without the Prince.

Astell cogently argues the Tory case, interspersing her exegesis of the Tory canon, in the form of authorities, the Bible, the first Earl of Clarendon and Henry Foulis, with broadsides in all directions. On the subject of factiousness she lashes out at fanatics: the 'Malignants, High-flyers and what not'.[34] She takes a shot at Hobbesian mechanism as voiced by White Kennett: 'we are told, that the *Prime Engines* were *Men of Craft, dreadful Dissemblers with GOD* (what is meant by adding *and Heaven*, I know not, for the Dr. is too zealous against Popery, to suffer us to imagine that he takes in Angels and Saints)'.[35] Then she dares to turn against dissenters and regicides Hobbesian charges of demonology: 'They shou'd not suffer Men to infect the Peoples Minds with evil Principles and Representations, with Speeches that have double Meanings and Equivocal Expressions, *Innuendo's* and secret Hints and Insinuations'.[36] It is not the only time that she uses explicitly Hobbesian language to hoist the famous author on his own petard. Nowhere is her parody of Hobbes more explicit than in her defence of popery against the worst charges of the Presbyterians, whose own popishness brooks no mercy, where she echoes the great master's comments about hay and stubble and straw men:[37]

Now they who are curious to know what Popery is, and who do not rail at it at a venture, know very well, that every Doctrine which is profess'd by the Church of *Rome*, is not Popish; GOD forbid it shou'd, for they receive the Holy Scriptures, and teach the Creeds. But that Superstructure of Hay and Stubble, those Doctrines of Men or Devils, which they have built upon this good Foundation, this is Popery.

Having beaten up her case against faction, Astell recommends against democracy: 'For we have the sad Experience of our Civil Wars to inform us, that all the Concessions the King and his Loyal Subjects cou'd make to the Factious and Rebellious, cou'd not satisfie'.[38] She even suggests that the outspoken, and presumably the press, should be muzzled: 'Governours therefore may very justly animadvert upon, and suppress it. For it is as much their Duty, and as necessary a Service to the Public, to restrain the Turbulent and Seditious, as it is to protect the Innocent, and to reward the Deserving'.[39]

Astell's charge that the Scots, John Pym and the French Cardinal Richelieu (1585–1642) had conspired to trump up the French threat is a constant refrain. At one point she even enlists Grotius against 'factious, turbulent, and Rebellious Spirits', Pym and company, otherwise known as '*Presbyterians*, or *Whiggs*, or whatever you will call them'.[40] Having given a litany of offenders against political obedience and supporters of passive resistance outstanding in this particular debate, she proceeds to give an equally impressive list of evil ministers, intent on 'appeas[ing] the Party...obstruct[ing] the King's Business, and...weaken[ing] his authority'; the cause, as Foulis instructs us, of 'perpetual Hurly-burly...and...Leap-frog Government'.[41] With characteristic reflexivity, she compares the role of the Whig pamphleteers in the political skirmishing that brought about the Glorious Revolution with the contribution to theories of non-resistance of the Jesuit casuist Parsons, and with Buchanan and Milton.[42] And if she saw Locke in the same mould, we have an indication, in his anonymous and only recently published Minute to Edward Clarke, that he too could vent the full ideological armoury of the Whig pamphleteers, declaring:[43]

Every one, and that with reason, begins our delivery from popery and slavery from the arrival of the prince of Orange and the compleating of it is, by all that wish well to him and it, dated from King William's settlement in the throne. This is the fence set up against popery and France, for King James's name, however made use of, can be but a stale to these two! If ever he returne, under what pretences soever, Jesuits must governe France and be our master. He is too much wedded to the one and relyes too much on the other ever to part with either. He that has ventured and lost three crowns for his blinde obedience to those guides of his conscience and for his following the counsels and pattern of the French King cannot be hoped, after the provocations he had had to heighten his natural aversion, should ever returne with calme thoughts and good intentions to Englishmen, their libertys, and religion. And then I desire the boldest or most negligent amongst us, who can not resolve to be contemned popish convert and a miserable French peasant, to consider with himself what security, what help, what hopes he can have, if by the ambition and artifice of any great man he depends on and is led by, he be once bought to this market, a poor, innocent sheepe to this shambles; for whatever advantageous bargains the leaders may make for them selves, tis eternally true that the dull heard of followers are always bought and sold.

These do not sound like the words of a democrat or even of an abstract political theorist. Locke's reputation for being overly philosophical is not something he necessarily enjoyed in his own day. Astell quite clearly sees him as a polemical political theorist, whatever the undoubted merits of his psychological theory might be. As Farr and Roberts note, even passages in the *Two Treatises* apparently concerned with obligation in the abstract take on a different significance, seen in the light of this private document.

Whatever Locke's position on the ancient constitution may have been – and, given his role in drafting the constitution of the Carolinas, we can guess that he had one – Mary Astell was quick to convict him of opportunism. She observed the antinomy between the reductionism of his sensationalist psychology that placed collectivities forever out of reach and his predilection for the fictions of the state of nature and natural rights that were peculiarly intractable to empirical analysis, constantly parodying appeals to the rights of freeborn Englishmen made by Locke, Defoe and John Tutchin (1661?–1707).[44] Certain it is that if Locke did endorse a 'mixed constitution', as Martin Thompson[45] and Lois Schwoerer[46] believe, he would not have endorsed that peculiar version of 'mixarchy' promoted by Lord Clarendon or Astell, a version of the ancient constitution as comprised of king, Lords and Commons. For Clarendon, like the bishops who promulgated the theory under Charles II, the Lords included the bishops of the Anglican Church, jealous in the protection of their ecclesiastical power,[47] something Astell supported and Locke denied. If Locke's constitutional monarchy looked down the centuries in its anticipation of modern constitutional forms, it did so precisely by virtue of a lack of commitment to the constitutional niceties of which Astell and Clarendon, along with those Whigs who tried to reconcile contract and conquest, were zealously protective.

4. Astell, Hobbes, Locke, Filmer and the Title to Rule

Astell's political pamphlets focus on the twin pillars of Toryism: abhorrence of the doctrine of right of resistance and of nonconformity. They also represent a response to the upsurge of Lockean language occasioned by the two events already mentioned as critical: the demands of the Kentish petitioners, who raised again the question of ancient liberties, a constitutional myth that the Whigs defended and the Tories manipulated; and the Occasional Conformity Bill, introduced into Parliament in 1703 but not passed until 1711. For Mary Astell, the occasional conformity crisis presented the true test of theological seriousness. On this subject two of her three important pamphlets of 1704 turn. In *Moderation Truly Stated* (1704), her 185-page rebuttal of James Owen's pamphlet, *Moderation a Virtue* (1703), whose defence of occasional conformity was not unreasonable, Astell adopts the extreme tactic of representing this sort of reasonableness as treason. If the Church of England was established by law, then attempts to bypass the requirement that office-holders must be communicating Anglicans were unconstitutional at the very least, she maintained. Astell dealt a particularly stinging and belittling riposte to Defoe, himself a dissenter, whose string of satirical pamphlets on the hysterical harangues of Sacheverell, Leslie and others drew her ire in *A Fair Way with Dissenters and Their Patrons*.

On the issue of occasional conformity, Astell was at one with some of the most conservative writers. Goldie has suggested that the real roots of Tory constitutionalism in the revolt against James lay in the choice of church over king.[48] The language of toleration was, to Astell, the language of schism: schism in religion and schism in politics. Occasional conformity meant opening the door to religious and patriotic slackness, one of her most sustained objections to it. Thomas Edwards (1599–1647), author of *Gangraena* and 'the most voluble opponent' of the religious sects,[49] is among her most frequently cited sources. Edwards, a Cambridge-educated Puritan divine who was referred to as the 'Young Luther', had been imprisoned for his outspoken views and had recanted, but nevertheless found himself among those 'suppressed or suspended' by Laud. Permitted to preach again, he campaigned against 'popish innovations and Arminian tenets' and was prosecuted in the high commission court. Under parliamentary rule, Edwards proved a zealous supporter, who also contributed money to the cause. He achieved real prominence in his crusade against the Independents with the publication in 1644 of *Antapologia, or a full Answer to the Apologeticall Narration of Mr. Goodwin, Mr. Nye, Mr. Sympson, Mr Burroughes, Mr Bridge, Members of the Assembly of Divines* and the yet more virulent *Gangraena; or a Catalogue and Discovery of many Errours, Heresies, Blasphemies and pernicious Practices of the Sectaries of this Time, vented and acted in England in these four last Years* of 1646. The sheer venom of Edwards's attack produced a host of replies, among them tracts from John Lilburne, John Goodwin (author of the anonymous *Cretensis; or a briefe Answer to an Ulcerous Treatise . . . intituled 'Gangraena'*) and Jeremiah Burroughes (*Vindication*, 1646). These prompted *The Second Part of Gangraena; or a fresh and further Discovery of the Errours, Heresies, Blasphemies . . .*, and another round of replies. To this Edwards replied with *The Third Part of Gangraena; or a new and Higher Discover of Errours....* Resentment by Independents, now the dominant party, was at this point so great that Edwards wisely retired to Holland, where he promptly died from an ague. Edwards's *Gangraena* is frequently cited by Astell, who makes reference to his *Antapologia* as well. For Astell agrees with Nalson, whom she cites in *An Impartial Inquiry*, that religion, in the household as in the commonwealth, is what makes people observe the covenants they have made. The moderate first Earl of Clarendon, Astell's source, who also lay the disorder of the Great Rebellion at the door of the Protestant sects, saw the same consequences: 'Children asked not blessing of their parents.... The young women conversed without any circumspection or modesty.... Parents had no manner of authority over their children'.[50]

Biblical patriarchalism had never been more baldly stated than in Sir Robert Filmer's *Patriarcha* of 1680, the work of a man desperate to preserve his standing with the Crown.[51] Filmer categorically denied the position that different power sets establish qualitatively different spheres, argued by Aristotle and entrenched by Aristotelianism. Aristotle in his distinctions in the *Politics*, between paternal, marital, despotic and political power – as the powers of a father, husband, slave owner and magistrate, respectively – had created a distinction between private and public spheres that Hobbes and Locke, for different reasons, were keen to revive. Ignoring Aristotle's caution against confusing the rule of a large household with that of a small kingdom,[52] Filmer claimed in fact that men were born into states by being born into families, and that the power of kings was the power of fathers and nothing more. Such a claim raised the counter-claim that if fathers were indeed kings, the sovereign was superfluous.

Not only was such a notion intolerable to Hobbes and Locke, but so were the assumptions of biblical fundamentalism associated with Puritanism that underpinned it. Moreover, the separation of public and private spheres on which they insisted had a larger purpose. The great stress Hobbes laid on the state's being artificial rather than natural was designed to erode any self-authenticating powers the Scriptures may have been claimed to have in the Protestant community of believers. At the same time, it prepared the way for an analysis of the particular artifice in terms of which the creation of the state was brought about: a contract. Scripture had its uses in acclimating people to negotiation by covenant or contract, of which marriage was the most immediate experience in the everyday life of most people. For the marriage contract to function as an analogue

for a social contract as an institution-creating artifice, the spheres had to
be categorically distinct.

Astell, who had much in common with Filmer, and whose mentor,
Archbishop Sancroft, had assisted Edmund Bohun in arranging the
1685 publication of *Patriarcha*, was nevertheless gravely offended by his
patriarchalism. She shared Filmer's concern to distinguish the separate
moments of authorization and designation, noting, however, the propen-
sity of the Presbyterians to borrow scholastic casuistry:[53]

Yet upon the grounds of this doctrine both Jesuits and some over zealous favourers
of the Geneva discipline have built a perilous conclusion, which is 'that the people
or multitude have power to punish or deprive the prince if he transgress the laws
of the kingdom'. Witness Parsons and Buchanan. . . . Cardinal Bellarmine and Mr
Calvin both look asquint this way.

Like Filmer she supported the notion of a unitary state, divided not
into spheres but into power zones in which power was distributed hierarchically. But she marshaled an impressive line of biblical women to
remonstrate against the misogyny of the Apostle Paul and those adherents
who argued the natural inferiority of women.[54] And here Astell appealed
to canons of reason established by Descartes and vouchsafed by Hobbes
and Locke, for whom men and women were naturally equal but made
radically unequal by the marriage contract, as the model for the radical
inequality of citizen and sovereign powers achieved by the social contract.

5. Astell, Locke, Sherlock and the Allegiance Debate

Astell, with characteristic irony, enlisted the support of William Sherlock,
Dean of St. Paul's, against Locke.[55] Named by Astell among the three
Whig bishops who preached the 31 January memorial sermon for Charles
I,[56] he took a position on Locke's dismissal of innate ideas surprisingly
close to that of Stillingfleet and Norris. And Locke in 1697 rightly viewed
with apprehension the prospect of public criticism from yet another
prominent clergyman, this time a Whig, noting that 'a man of no small
name, as you know Dr Sherlock is, has been pleased to declare against
my doctrine of no innate ideas, from the pulpit in the Temple, and, as
I have been told, charged it with little less than atheism'.[57] Seven year's
later, Anthony Collins, James Tyrrell and Robert South were separately
to warn Locke of the impending publication of an attack on him by
Sherwood, the very attack on Locke's position on 'innatism' that the
churchman had preached from the Temple pulpit in 1697 and that now

appeared as 'A Digression concerning Connate Ideas, or Inbred Knowledge' in Sherlock's *A Discourse Concerning the Happiness of Good Men.* If Sherlock's critique contained very little that was new, restating arguments already voiced by Stillingfleet and by John Norris in the second volume of his *An Essay Towards the Theory of the Ideal or Intelligible World* of 1690, his determination to expose Locke's doctrine as 'directly *Tending* to, if not also necessarily *implying,* or at least *Inferring* Atheisme'[58] was particularly worrying. In the event, Sherlock's book came too late to do Locke much harm, but it did prompt the anonymously published defence of Locke, *A Philosophick Essay Concerning Ideas According to Dr. Sherlock's Principles* (1705), which not only exposed Sherlock's critique as inept, but differentiated his position carefully from that of Malebranche and Norris.

It is likely that Astell was aware of Sherlock's critique of Locke and altogether possible that it contributed to her own. But it is not for his critique of Locke's theory of ideas that she invokes Sherlock against him, but rather for the distinction between authority and title, again rather messily made by Sherlock. Astell phrases the distinction thus:[59]

For, allowing that the People have a Right to Design the Person of their Governour; it does by no means follow that they Give him his Authority, or that they may when they please resume it.

Astell could not have known that Locke had actually penned a rebuttal of Sherlock's distinction, which he considered it important to refute. Sherlock had argued quite cogently that the necessity of government was logically prior to the title of any particular sovereign. If authority was the right to command obedience, decided, it turned out, on *de facto* grounds, legitimate title was a question of constitutional law, *de jure.*[60] Sherlock then carefully distinguished three modes of political empowerment: first, patriarchal, on the grant of authority made to Adam, Noah, Moses and all subsequent fathers; second, by divine command (as to a chosen people); and, third, by consent. He had dismissed the patriarchal argument and the argument from consent – the former because it ignored all the usurpations, beginning with Nimrod, the latter because consent, once given, could be withdrawn. He dismissed any historical arguments concerning legitimate title as 'carrying men into such dark Labyrinths of Law and History, etc, as very few know how to find their way out of again'.[61] He came down rather on the side of the Hobbist reciprocity of protection/ allegiance, citing Paul, Romans, 13, and concluding, 'If the prince can't Govern, the Subject can't Obey',[62] a view shared by the secular

Engagers,[63] Anthony Ascham and Marchamont Nedham. Sherlock tried to distance himself from the controversial Hobbes, however, for whom 'Dominion is naturally annexed to Power', whereas he, Sherlock, was at pains to stress the *moral duty* of allegiance.[64]

6. Astell, Sherlock and Locke on Authority and Title to Rule

Sherlock's exposition was not inconsequential. Both Gottfried Leibniz (1646–1716) and Locke commented on *The Case of Allegiance due to Sovereign Powers*, the latter in detail, although not in public.[65] Leibniz, less squeamish about *de facto* power and less Hobbist than Sherlock, argued explicitly: 'And one can say that loyalty being relative to protection, there is a *quasi-contractus* between the government and him who enjoys the advantages of public security'.[66] The exchange of obedience for protection lay at the heart of Hobbes's theory of social contract. Moreover, thorough-going contractarian that he was, Hobbes extended the principle to account for contractual relations within the family, claiming that wives contracted explicitly in marriage to obey their husbands in exchange for protection in their child-bearing years, while children tacitly contracted with their fathers to enjoy protection in their minority. Astell rejected these legal fictions as making a mockery of marriage as a sacrament.

Locke, whose comments on Sherlock constitute his only recorded remarks on political obedience postdating the *Two Treatises* of 1689, ridiculed Sherlock for attempting to separate legal title and God's authority – as if the law could breach the latter – seeming certainly to subscribe to obedience and non-resistance in this instance:[67]

Q. Does not god['s] authority whch the actuall K[ing] has bar all other human claims & are not the subjects bound to maintain the right of such a prince as far as they can.

Locke, like Sherlock, distanced himself from Hobbism, but this time Sherlock's 'submission' was not enough for legal title; it had to be consent:[68]

Where there is noe reistance ther is a generall Submission. but there may be a generall submission without a general consent wch is an other thing.

Sherlock had argued, quite to the contrary, and indistinguishably from Hobbes on conquest: 'All Mankind have this natural Right to submit for their own preservation'; a submission that 'is a voluntary Consent, tho' extorted by Force'.[69] Astell does not even deal with Sherlock's argument, but she demolishes Locke's, turning against him exactly the argument he uses against slavery, on which his case for freedom was based:[70]

For a Man, not having the Power of his own Life, *cannot*, by Compact, or his own Consent, *enslave himself* to any one, nor put himself under the Absolute, Arbitrary Power of another, to take away his Life, when he pleases. No body can give more power than he has himself; and he that cannot take away his own Life, cannot give another power over it.

This is just the argument that Astell uses to make the case for a distinction between authority and title, but on assumptions that are otherwise directly contrary to Locke on authorization. People may choose the person of the governor, but they cannot empower him, because[71]

[n]one can give what they have not: The People have no Authority over their own Lives, consequently they can't invest such an Authority in their Governours.

The argument with which Astell then proceeds against Locke is in fact proto-Hobbist:[72]

And tho' we shou'd grant that People, when they first enter into Society, may frame their Laws as they think fit; yet these Laws being once Establish'd, they can't Legally and Honestly be chang'd, but by that Authority in which the Founders of the Society thought fit to place the Legislature. Otherwise we have been miserably impos'd upon by all those Arguments that were urg'd against a Dispensing Power.

Locke makes the apparently contradictory claim in his criticism of Sherlock's *The Case of Allegiance Due to Sovereign Powers* that 'Allegiance is neither due nor paid to Right or to Government which are abstract notions but only to persons having right of government'.[73] While such a statement might seem to deny all attempts to provide a *de jure* rather than *de facto* basis for government, when more closely scrutinized it reads differently. The 'Right' or 'Government' deemed abstract are in fact divine right and hereditary monarchy. The virtue of the Williamite settlement was that it could be presented as a virtual elective monarchy if the right construction was put upon the empowering oaths. Much of Locke's effort in the memorandum to Clarke was to ensure that this would be done and the project of the Whigs to convert a *de facto* into a *de jure* settlement accomplished.[74] Such a purpose casts Locke's claims in the *Two Treatises* concerning *de facto* power and the basis of citizenship in a new light. There he asserted that 'An Usurper . . . [can never] have a Title, till the People are both at liberty to consent, and have actually consented',[75] and concerning how individuals 'come to be *Subjects or Members of [any]*

Commonwealth', he insisted that 'Nothing can make any Man so, but his actually entering into it by positive Engagement, and express Promise and Compact'.[76]

Nor did Locke's critique of Sherlock fly in the face of his claim in the *Two Treatises* that 'there cannot be done a greater Mischief to Prince and People, than the Propagating wrong Notions concerning Government'. It is a position he reinforced in the Minute to Clarke with his demand that *de jure divino* claims be treated with 'public condemnation and abhorrence'.[77] There is no inconsistency here. The statement in the critique of Sherlock merely affirms what is elsewhere asserted: that oaths of allegiance took precedence over hereditary right as supplying the element of consent that allowed the notion of social contract to fly. However, for those who were not willing to swear allegiance, the alternative was 'separation from the Government'[78] – a position perilously close to the sanctions against occasional conformity that Locke could not have approved. The more immediate problem was to cut a swathe through the conflicting oaths that tied the nonjurors to the Stuart dynasty, and this Locke could do.

It had been the accomplishment of Thomas Hobbes to justify government on non-providential grounds.[79] Locke was in this respect a successor to Hobbes, but one who argued less for the necessity of government than for its conventionality – both prongs of the Hobbesian position – emphasizing not the injunction of reason on citizens to obey, but the motivations for governments to contract and citizens to consent. The elaborate juridical artifice by means of which citizens, like wives, children and servants, were deemed voluntarily to have contracted into subordination had as little credibility in the late seventeenth and early eighteenth centuries as now, but for different reasons. In the early modern era, providential arguments still reigned supreme; in ours, different conclusions are drawn from contractarian arguments, which seem to have won the day.

Astell's challenge to Locke to extend to women against domestic tyrants the liberty he claimed for subjects against the Crown was a deliberately subversive stratagem. Its object was to expose to ridicule the tenets of contractarian liberalism and certainly not to endorse the space they appeared to open up. She challenged the division into spheres – a public realm of freedom over against which the private confinement of the family was set – on which Lockean liberalism was predicated. In this respect she dared Locke at least to follow Hobbes, who, having ousted patriarchalism from the public space, was unwilling to readmit it in the private sphere. Her rationalism, as ruthless as that of her adversaries, impressed on her the contingency of all social institutions. Reason could no more empower citizens to authorize or delegitimize a sovereign than it could empower husbands as monarchs in their families or enfranchise women to overthrow them. Relying on age-old Scholastic distinctions between the authorization and delegation of power she believed that only God could authorize, even if it fell to men to designate an incumbent. Such was the kingdom of this world; only in the hereafter, as deathless and sexless angels, would women enjoy the freedom to which they so rightly aspired.

A Fair Way with the Dissenters and Their Patrons

1. Locke, Toleration and Dissent

A Fair Way with the Dissenters and Their Patrons of 1704 was Astell's answer to Daniel Defoe's anonymous *More Short-Ways with the Dissenters* of the same year. Like *An Impartial Enquiry* it is a pamphlet difficult to read out of context, and indeed, this context is important to review, if for no other reason than to demonstrate how inextricably Astell's contribution is bound up with those of Tory High Churchmen known as the 'High Flyers', *Charles Leslie and *Henry Sacheverell, and yet how anxious Astell is to distance herself from them and receive acknowledgement for her own work. As we shall see, she had to protest in print against the crediting of her pamphlets to these more visible men. Defoe had fired the opening shots in the pamphlet warfare over occasional conformity with a series of pamphlets, among them *The Shortest Way with the Dissenters* (1702), in which he had parodied Leslie and Sacheverell precisely. Their responses, of Leslie in particular, suggested that he had not been wide of the mark, as he pointed out in *More Short-Ways with the Dissenters* (1704), to which Astell herself responded with *A Fair Way with the Dissenters* (1704). While serving a jail sentence for libeling the church, Defoe in 1704 started the *Review*, a regular periodical devoted to politics, which attracted vigorous debate from Charles Leslie in the *Rehearsal* and provided the forum for a critique of John Locke, in many respects Defoe's mentor.[1]

If religious conformity was the test of state power in a realm in which religion was officially established, it was also the issue on which Locke's most central writings had turned. The situation is a complicated one and worth reviewing, if for no other reason than Mary Astell's lifelong animus against dissent and career-long hostility to Locke. Persistent terminological confusions, compounded by chronological uncertainties about the dating of important tracts and leading to historical anachronism, clouds the debates over toleration and dissent. The first and most obvious feature of church–state relations created by the English Reformation was that religion was irredeemably politicized. This put theologically serious thinkers like Astell in a double bind, and to some extent the division of her *oeuvre* between philosophical-theological and political writings is a reflection of the tension this situation could induce. Changes of register are signaled by clear differences in the idiom and tonal quality she employs: anywhere from the humble to the ecstatic in the homiletic register; authorial and dispassionate in the philosophical; shrill and verging on the scurrilous in the political. The range of registers is symptomatic not only of Astell's literary repertoire, but also of the range of debates in which she participated and upon which the central issues of religious toleration turned, issues that were decided not just for the day but for the future, and not just for England but for Europe and the Americas as well.

The very fact of an established state religion divided religion between issues of conscience and issues of conformity. The Church of England had dealt with the problem in terms of the concept of 'indifferency', claiming that those issues of worship on which God, as recorded in the Scriptures, was silent were the very issues on which the state had the right to enforce conformity and command obedience. This salient fact was registered by political theorists like Hobbes and Locke, who reformulated it in terms of 'conscience' and 'will': matters of central belief were decided *in foro interno*, or in the internal court of conscience, as opposed to those subject to political will, decided *in foro externo*, or by the state.[2] The issue on which the whole problem turned was that of 'religious freedom', a term, it is worth noting, that was infrequently used.[3] In this period 'toleration' and 'rights' were much more often understood as privileges granted than as a birthright; they were 'objective', as the specific concessions of a conceding power, and not 'subjective', as pertaining by natural right to the subject. This is a situation that it was Locke's accomplishment to assist in reversing, but it is nevertheless still registered in the authoritative vocabularies of the day. So, for instance, 'test acts', royal acts of 'indulgence' and 'toleration', presupposed the interrogative power of the state on religious matters, assuming an active grant of immunity by the state and passive acceptance by citizens.

The problem for the nonconformists was that what the Church of England defined as indifferent issues of worship, for them were often

central, but state power officially foreclosed debate. From the point
of view of the state, conscience was dangerous because morally implacable and incoercible, making demands for liberty that it could not
see itself meeting. In practice it arrived at a saving formula on which
its policy of religious inclusivity was based: 'for conscience could be
"informed" and "instructed" without being violated, and the "will" could
be "engaged" while that instruction was taking place'.[4] Indifferency took
care of those dissenting Protestants ranging from Presbyterians, who had
no objection in principle to being members of the established church but
were kept out by scruples of conscience, and the separatists, comprising
Independents – doctrinally close to the Presbyterians, in fact – Baptists,
and Quakers, as well as those smaller sects that objected in principle
to an established church and organized themselves in 'loose confedera-
tions of "gathered congregations"'.[5] The various measures designed to
accommodate dissenters from the 1660s to 1689 concerned them. Dating
at least from Richard Hooker's *Laws of Ecclesiastical Polity* (1592/3), this
formula for incorporation applied to dissenting Protestants but not to
Roman Catholics, whose doctrinal differences on the matter of ecclesiastical authority were too great – Andrew Marvell's comment in 1678
that 'popery and arbitrary government' traveled together was generally
accepted – and so toleration was not generally thought of as extending
to them.[6]

But in the Stuart period Catholic-leaning kings confused the issue.
For religious toleration tested not only the faith of subjects but also the
power of kings. When on 15 March 1672 Charles II, apparently acting
on the advice of his chancellor, the first Earl of Shaftesbury, and Locke's
patron, had reissued a Declaration of Indulgence that 'suspended', by
his 'will and pleasure', all ecclesiastical penalties 'against whatsoever sort
of nonconformists or recusants', he specifically included Catholics. This
caused him to be reprimanded by Parliament, when it met a year later,
as being '"very much misinformed" about the nature of his prerogative
rights, "since no such power was ever claimed, or exercised, by any of
your maj.'s predecessors"'.[7] Charles wisely withdrew the act, agreeing
to the anti-Catholic first Test Act, which not only drove Catholics from
office and effectively destroyed his ministry, but also forced James, Duke
of York, to disclose his Catholicism and resign as Lord High Admiral.
When in 1687 James tried his hand at reinstating Catholics, he did so by
reasserting the power to suspend the penal laws against dissenters that
had been denied to Charles, ordering that his Declaration for Liberty of
Conscience be read in every parish in the country. It was at this point that

Archbishop William Sancroft, despite his High Church Tory convictions, along with six fellow bishops, petitioned James to excuse them on the grounds that the 'suspending power' he claimed was illegal, a power that was finally and effectively removed by the Bill of Rights of 1689. The trial and subsequent acquittal of the 'seven bishops' that followed created an unbridgeable rift between James and the episcopacy, but improved his relations with the Presbyterian dissenters led by Richard Baxter and created a moment at which reunion might have seemed possible.[8]

James had explicitly used the term 'liberty of conscience', and it seems that it was a principle to which he sincerely adhered, largely for political reasons, because he considered religious conformity an impossible project. Constraining conscience, he declared, 'in matters of meer religion has ever been directly contrary to our inclination, as we think that it is to the interest of the government, which it destroys by spoiling trade, depopulating countries, and discouraging strangers; and finally, that it never obtained the end for which it was employed ... to reduce this kingdom to an exact conformity in religion'.[9] James's case is not so different, in fact, from that first made by Locke in his earliest political writings, the two tracts concerning the right of the magistrate to impose religious practice on the basis of indifference, written between 1660 and 1661. There he supported the principle of indifference with arguments that verge on casuistry, arguing that 'the whole liberty of conscience' fell under the rubric 'liberty of judgment', which he distinguished from 'liberty of will' and which could 'be removed without infringing the liberty of the conscience'. He concluded, much as Hobbes did, that the zones of conscience and state compliance were sufficiently distinct, arguing 'that all the magistrate's laws, civil as well as ecclesiastical, those that concern divine worship as much as those that concern civil life, are just and valid, obliging men to act but not to judge; and, providing for both at the same time, unite a necessity of obedience with a liberty of conscience'.[10]

By 1667 Locke had changed his mind on the appropriateness of the indifferency principle to set the limits of state power over religion,[11] however, and in subsequent writings, as the issue of dissent heated up, he saw the zones of conscience and political will further insulated from one another along Hobbesian lines. So he could argue in the *Letter Concerning Toleration* of 1685, published in 1689, that 'the business of true religion' concerns 'regulating men's lives in accordance with virtue and piety', which is not at all a matter of 'outward pomp', 'ecclesiastical dominion' or 'force'. Locke, like Hobbes, argues from *raison d'état*: if care is not taken 'to distinguish between the business of civil government and that of religion, and to mark the true bounds between the church and the commonwealth . . . no end can be put to the controversies between those who truly have or pretend to have at heart a concern on the one hand for the salvation of souls, and on the other for the safety of the commonwealth'.[12] The church, Locke declared, 'is absolutely separate and distinct from the commonwealth, and civil affairs. The boundaries on both sides are fixed and immovable. He mixes heaven and earth together, things most remote and opposite, who confuses these two societies, which in their origin, their end, and their whole substance are utterly and completely different'.[13] It is not surprising that Astell should have seen Locke and Hobbes as bedfellows. Such a pragmatic separation of church and state bespoke a *Realpolitik* that threatened the very foundations of the established church and cast aside the entire question of inclusivity.

The textual history of Locke's *Letter Concerning Toleration* is itself instructive as regards timing. It was originally written in Latin in 1685, it is believed, the year of James II's accession and the ill-fated Monmouth rebellion, which had been followed by the Bloody Assizes, James II's insistence on installing Catholic officers in the army, and his prorogation of Parliament rather than face the consequences. But the *Letter* was published in the Netherlands only in 1689. Between publication in April by Philip van Limborch, to whom it had originally been addressed, and June of that year, when Locke received copies, Parliament had already passed, and William III had already approved, the Act of Toleration.[14] Given what we know of the timing of the text, then, there is no way that Locke's *Letter* could have related to the Toleration debates of 1688–9, much less be read as a response to the Toleration Act of 1689. But no such direct link was necessary, for this was an issue that consumed Locke, who had been writing about toleration and dissent throughout his entire career, so that Astell and others were not wide of the mark when they made the association between Locke and the new constitutional order that the Revolution of 1688–9 had brought into being.[15]

The Act of Toleration, like the Bill of Rights, did not achieve all that their promoters had hoped. William, on 16 March 1688/9, had addressed Parliament on the need to include formerly excluded Protestant dissenters in public office in order to fulfil a promise made in 1687 '[t]hat no Christian ought to be persecuted for his Conscience, or be ill used because he differs from the publick and established Religion'. Depriving them from office was construed as persecuting dissenters but, once again, not Catholics, who were considered beyond the pale. In any event, the storm of Tory protest with which the measure was greeted ensured that

'comprehension' would be put off for another day. The occasional conformity debates lay in the future, and William's Act of Indulgence, which
permitted dissenting Protestants to worship behind locked doors without
penalty or reprisal, was narrower in scope than even James's 'prerogative
indulgence' had been.

2. Astell, the Dissenters and *Short-Ways*

Astell entered the debate at this later stage, where measures to circum-
vent the restrictions on the exercise of public office by dissenters were
at issue. The Astell–Defoe exchange belongs to the complicated pamphlet skirmishing over the occasional conformity debate, initiated by the
introduction of the parliamentary bill in 1702 to permit dissenters who
attended the Anglican Church at least once a year to enjoy the privileges of government office. Although the Corporation and Test Acts
of 1673 had not been repealed, an entire generation of occasional
conformists had grown up, to whom no serious objections were made
until the flagrant conduct of Sir Humphrey Edwin, a Presbyterian Lord
Mayor of London, drew attention to the matter when he attended in full
regalia both dissenting and Anglican services on the same Sunday. Daniel
Defoe's pamphlet, *An Enquiry into the Occasional Conformity of Dissenters* of
1698, dramatically increased the tension by opposing any conformity
on the dissenters' part as a political ploy. In 1701 the new Lord Mayor
of London, Sir Thomas Abney, repeated the performance of his predecessor, providing the occasion for republication of Defoe's tract. But
this time, as a conciliatory measure, Defoe replaced his earlier preface
to the mayor with one to John Howe (1630–1705), pastor of the dissenting church to which Abney belonged and a supporter of occasional
conformity.

Defoe was in fact no conciliator, and his anonymous *The Shortest Way
with Dissenters* (1702), which followed, burlesqued the High Flyers:
Charles Leslie, the nonjuror, and the later-to-be-impeached Henry
Sacheverell. Defoe's ironical ploy was to 'out-Herod Herod' by advocating draconian punishments for dissent, recommending 'Gallows instead
of the Counter, and the Gallies instead of the Fines' as a way of drawing
matters to a head.[16] Certain incautious High Flyers fell for it, chagrined
when the authorship of these views was later revealed to them – Astell
refers to Defoe's pamphlet's having been taken for a work of Sacheverell,
as Defoe himself claimed.[17] When Charles Leslie fired back with *Reflections upon Some Scandalous and Malicious Pamphlets, viz. I The Shortest Way*

with the Dissenters, and then issued an anthology of the exchange in the form of *The New Association, Part II*, Defoe's tone became more serious. What he had originally painted as an extreme scenario, the persecution of dissenters and closure of the dissenting academies, he now presented as normal Tory policy. It was in defence of Tory policy that Astell responded with her *Fair Way with the Dissenters*, in which she defends the positions of Leslie and Sacheverell, arguing that one does not have to be an extremist to hold that obedience to the English constitution required conformity to the Anglican Church. Thus the point of her subtitle: 'Not Writ by Mr. *L–y*, or any other *Furious Jacobite*, whether Clergyman or Layman; but by a very Moderate Person and Dutiful Subject to the QUEEN'.

3. Astell, Leslie and the High Flyers

A Fair Way with the Dissenters was in fact Astell's second foray into the occasional conformity debate. Her first had been the pamphlet *Moderation Truly Stated: or a Review of a Late Pamphlet, Entitul'd Moderation a Virtue, or, The Occasional Conformist Justified from the Imputation of Hypocricy* . . . (1704), written in response to James Owen's *Moderation a Virtue* (1703). Astell's second pamphlet on occasional conformity (her third of the year 1704), *A Fair Way with the Dissenters and Their Patrons*, had the addendum: 'Not Writ by Mr. L–y, or any other Furious Jacobite . . .', to make more than one point. It refers directly to the claims of Defoe in *The Shortest Way* of 1703, and *More Short-Ways* of 1704, as well as to Owen's claim in his pamphlets, of 1703 and 1704, that Leslie and Sacheverell were 'furious Jacobites', while they themselves were 'Men of Moderation'.[18] But it is also designed to ensure that Leslie does not get credit for her second pamphlet, as he had for her first. We are given the clue in the Postscript to *A Fair Way with the Dissenters*,[19] where she complains that authorship of her *Moderation Truly Stated* had been credited to the High Flyer Leslie. In the Postscript it is also clear that she is piqued that Owen should have given her (anonymous) *Moderation Truly Stated* only passing mention, conflating it with Leslie's *The Wolf Stript of His Shepherd's Cloathing* (1704), which he gave close scrutiny.[20] As we shall see, this is not the first time that arguments of Astell and Leslie become inextricably entangled.

Charles Leslie, an Irish-born nonjuror and pamphleteer, had in 1692 commenced a series of controversial pamphlets in which he attacked the king, Whig divines, Quakers, Deists, Jews and dissenters. His *The New Association of those Called Moderate-Church-man, with the Modern-Whigs and Fanaticks to Under-mine and Blow-up the present Church and Government* . . .

(1702), was cited by Defoe in *A Brief Explanation of a Late Pamphlet* (1703) as one of the provocations that inspired Defoe's *The Shortest-Way with the Dissenters*. Addressed to the pamphlet *The Danger of Priest-craft to Religion and Government* (1702) by John Dennis (1657–1734), Leslie's *New Association* responded to Lockean ideas, inveighing against 'that *Whig-Principle* (strenuously Asserted in this *Pamphlet*) That all Men are Born *Free*'.[21] Leslie's *Cassandra*, number 1, even more explicitly anti-Locke, opened by declaring, 'The Root and Foundation of all our *Republican Schemes*, and Pretences for *Rebellion* is this suppos'd Radical Power in the *People*, as of Erecting *Government* at the beginning, so to *Overturn* and *Change* it at their Pleasure'.

In *The New Association, Part II* . . . (1703), Supplement, 4, one of the first published critiques of Locke's *Two Treatises*, Leslie presented the argument against the hypocrisy of Whigs – that they claimed a freedom in the public sphere that they would never tolerate in the private one – which Astell had foreshadowed in the first edition of *Reflections upon Marriage* (1700) and made more explicit in her famous 1706 Preface. That Leslie has been credited with these arguments is probably due to Astell's anonymity and to the direct reference he made to 'The Great *L–k* [who] in his *Two Discourses of Government*, makes the *Consent* of every *Individual* Necessary', one of the first print references to the *Two Treatises*, the authorship of which had also been kept anonymous. We have an indication of how incendiary a character Leslie really was, and why Astell might not have cared to be too closely associated with him, from his subsequent career. In 1704 Leslie began publishing the periodical *The Rehearsal*, in opposition to Defoe's *Review*, while continuing to carry on his ecclesiastico-political warfare. A warrant was issued in 1710 for his arrest following the publication of a pamphlet which supposedly maintained that the queen was a usurper. Leslie escaped to St. Germains in 1711 and in 1713 accepted a place in the Pretender's household at Bar-le-Duc. After the suppression of the Monmouth rebellion, Leslie accompanied the Pretender to Avignon and Rome, hoping to extract from him a letter promising to maintain as inviolate the rights and privileges of the Church of England should he be restored to the throne.

Not less incendiary was the High-Flying hell-fire and brimstone preacher Henry Sacheverell. His pamphlets and sermons pushed the High Church and Tory cause, abusing dissenters, Latitudinarians and Whigs. His views were aired in *Character of a Low Churchman* (1701), *On the Association of . . . Moderate Churchmen with Whigs and Fanatics* (1702) and *The Rights of the Church of England* (1705), the latter, a sermon preached before the University of Oxford of 2 June 1702, which is among the publications that prompted Defoe's parody, *The Shortest Way with the Dissenters*. In the later *More Short-Ways*, with reference to this sermon, Defoe declares: 'Mr. *Sacheverell* of *Oxford* has blown his second Trumpet, to let us know he has not yet taken down his Bloody Flag, and that he was the Real Author of the *Shortest Way*, tho' another was Punish'd for it, and we see he has the face to let them know, he is still of the same mind'.[22] This passage is a clever piece of dissembling that perpetrates the fiction that his pamphlet had indeed been written by the High Flyers, as Defoe originally claimed, or, if that was too hard a pill to swallow, that it accurately represented Sacheverell's position. Defoe goes on to craft a skilful example of what pretends to be an Anglican confession to extremism. It reads:[23]

When in King *James* the Second's Time his Majesty found, that in order to reduce the Church, it was his business to Caress the Dissenters, and accordingly publish'd an Immediate Indulgence, a great many of the Dissenters made warm by their former sufferings, clos'd eagerly with the Proposals, and would willingly have set their Hand to the work; but when the Men of Temper, *for we do not deny to have some too violent Spirits among us,* came to consider the Case, they found the design struck at the whole Body of the Church of *England*, they considered them as Protestants and Brethren, they considered the Methods useing with them as Destructive to the Laws, as to the Church, and a Plot as well on Liberty as Religion....

Defoe describes Sacheverell's preaching not unjustly as '*a Fury* made up of a Complication of Malice, intollerable Pride, bigotted Zeal, and bloody Hellish Unchristian Principles'.[24] Sacheverell's sermons of 1709 at Derby and St. Paul's, London, arguing in favour of non-resistance and condemning toleration and occasional conformity, were sufficiently extreme to be declared by the House of Commons seditious libels on her majesty and her government. Sacheverell was impeached, although the feeling of the country was strongly on his side, in proceedings that drew John Toland (1670–1727), John Dennis (1657–1734) and *Gilbert Burnet (1643–1715), Bishop of Salisbury, into the debate. During his trial there were riots, meeting houses were attacked and the houses of several leading Whigs were threatened. Although found guilty, his only punishment was a ban on preaching for three years. Such a light sentence was viewed as a triumph for the High Church and the Tory Party, and the Tory victory in the general election in 1710 was recognized as being largely due to the ill-judged impeachment of Sacheverell, although many Tories also despised him.

Defoe denied the charges made by Sacheverell against the dissenters of 'Phanaticism' and 'Diabolical Prejudices'.[25] He accused Sacheverell of staking out an exclusivist position that none of the 'Eminent Persons' of his own church would support: 'none of 'em would ever Advance a Notion so Black, so full of Malice, and so empty of Charity, that we are under *Diabolical Prejudices,* and consequently *cannot be sav'd out of your Church,* this is Popery in its Exalted Extreams. . . .' Defoe's ingenious self-defence in the opening sentence of his pamphlet, to have exposed the High Flyers as fomenters of sedition, and to have done so on behalf of the dissenters who were the defenders of, and not the aggressors against, peace, was not without justice:[26]

It is not without just Ground, a Challenge of Peace was made to the Nation in the Name of the Dissenters, that the World might know who were the Men, in spight of her Majesty's frequent Invitation to *Union,* and the pressing Exhortations she made from the Throne for *Peace,* are constantly the Aggressors, on every occasion Insult their Brethren, and prompt the Nation to Unite in their Destruction.

4. Astell, Defoe and the Dissenting Academies

Defoe had come clean about the trick he had played in his parody, *The Shortest Way with the Dissenters* (1702),[27] but his defence in *More Short-Ways* was once again ironic. He protested that his only crime in *The Shortest Way* had been to take too seriously the High Church polemic demanding the destruction of the dissenters, for which he begs 'pardon of the Church of *England* . . . that he, like a too credulous Fool, gave any heed to such slight and cursory things as *Preaching,* and *Printing* of Books'.[28] Tossing back Sacheverell's slurs on the dissenters as 'Double-dealing *Practical Atheists,* whose *Gain* is their *Godliness,* whose *Profit* is their *Religion,* and whose *Interest* is both their *God* and *Conscience!* Who can Betray and Sell their *Saviour* for *Money*',[29] Defoe goes on to accuse the High Church party of cheap politicking:[30]

What tho' the Author of whom we are now treating has declar'd from the Pulpit, that a Man can't be a true Son of the Church of *England,* but he must lift up the bloody Flag against the Dissenters; yet since Printing Books is but a Modern Contrivance *to get a Penny,* and ought to be prepar'd so as may best suit the Market, and Sermons are only long Speeches directed to, and made to please the Auditory, and consequently suited to their Circumstances and Humour, it does not therefore follow, that because they have Preach'd and Printed these things, they really Intended and Design'd the thing, *no, Good Men,* it was far from their Thoughts. The Author therefore was most justly punish'd for his Folly, in believing any thing they said and pretending to Alarm the Dissenters for the little insignificant Performances of the Pulpit or the Press.

Astell countered with the obvious response that it was Defoe who was the opportunistic party man and that the Tories were deadly serious in demanding the destruction of the dissenting party. In *An Impartial Inquiry*, she refers again to 'those Mercenary Scriblers whom all sober Men condemn, and who only write after the Fact, or in order to it, to make their own Fortunes, or to justifie their own Wickedness', probably with reference to Defoe, who, along with Tutchin, was sued for libel in 1704.[31] It is symptomatic of the style of debate that Astell should systematically satirize Defoe by using the very language he had reserved for the High Flyers, in a pastiche of quotations taken from Defoe's attack on both Sacheverell and Leslie.[32] Astell takes a scattershot approach to Defoe's text, picking epithets from here and there without textual acknowledgement, partly because Defoe himself repeats the epithets so often. She scissors and pastes the quotations, twisting and turning his arguments in a merciless parody of what was originally itself a parody, an eighteenth-century form of invective that is fortunately now foreign to most of us – the passions and hatreds roused in these debates over religious freedom are not easy to recover now that that freedom has been won.

In his sermon of 9 March 1703/4, 'Preach'd at St. Mary's in Oxford at the Assizes', *The Nature and Mischief of Prejudice and Partiality Stated*, Sacheverell had launched a vitriolic attack on the dissenting academies, referring to them as '*Schools* and *Nurseries* of *Rebellion* [which] have *Spawn'd* That Multitude of *Factions, Hetherodoxs, Atheistical, Lewd* Books, and *Seditious* Libels, which are every day *Publish'd* against *Monarchy*, and the Establish'd *Hierarchy*, and *Religion*'.[33] Sacheverell had enumerated five causes of the dissenters' 'prejudice': 'I. *Education* and *Custom*. 2. *Ignorance* and *Affectation*. 3. *Conversation* and *Company*. 4. *Authority* and *Example*. 5. *Interest* and *Party*'.[34] Citing I Timothy 5:21, he had begun his sermon with charges against the dissenters of base and mercenary partiality, fourteen in number, which are later repeated by Astell herself.[35] Sacheverell began *The Nature and Mischief* as follows:[36]

As all Government is Built upon Law, and all Law is Supported by the due Execution, and regular Administration of Justice, which is the Grand End and Design of Both: So there's Nothing that does more effectually Overturn Its Foundation, Countermine and Defeat Its good intention, and utterly Disappoint and Evacuate Its Force and Power, than a *Personal Prejudice*, or a Blind, Mercenary, and Base *Partiality*.

Defoe countered by charging Sacheverell with 'positive Untruths, I am loath to say *L–s*, of which I'le prove, you have in this one

Sermon debauch'd the Pulpit with about Fourteen', which he goes on to enumerate:[37] 'What tho' a Reverend B–op had frequently said we shou'd never be well in *England*, till all the Dissenters were serv'd as the *Huguenots* in *France*? What tho' Esq: *M* – has given it under his Hand, that he heartily prays God would give her Majesty the Grace to put all that was wrote there in the Book call'd *The Shortest Way* in Execution? What tho' Dr. H – frequently has Preach'd and Printed too, that the Dissenters were a Brood of Traytors, and the Spawn of the Rebels, and not fit to live?'. Defoe does not identify the bishop here or in *The Shortest Way*,[38] where he discusses the Huguenots; nor does he identify Dr. H. or Esq. M. But clearly Henry Sacheverell is Dr. H. and Henry Morton is Esq. M.

Astell structures her case against Defoe in terms of Sacheverell's fourteen points in turn, seeming to close what distance she had tried to establish between herself and the High Flyers.[39] Once again the debate moved between the poles of the 1640s and 1680s. Defoe in *More Short-Ways* had accused Sacheverell of falsehood, charging, 'To fill up that one Page of Scandal, and make it pass for a true Libel, you go back to *the never to be forgotten* Year of 41'.[40] Here he was referring to the fifth charge of Sacheverell's sermon against the dissenters, promotion of '*Interest* and *Party*'.[41] Sacheverell, speaking of the 'Malignant Virulence and Implacable Rancor of *Phanaticism*', at this point restated the argument that dissenters had borrowed Jesuit theory and practice in resisting the king:[42]

For if We were to Consider its Progress, in all that *Series of Rebellions*, from its *Odious*, and *Never-to-be-forgotten Aera* of Transcendent Villainy, in the Year *Forty-One*, We shall find the same *Jesuitical Principles*, like a *Plotter in Masquerade*, only Changing the Name, but carrying on the same Machinations and Wicked practices in *Church* and *State*, to the Subversion of our Constitution in Both, down to this Present Day.

Defoe had gone so far as to refer to Sacheverell as a hired gun – 'a Mercenary Renegado . . . hir'd to expose the private Accademies of the dissenters' – claiming:[43]

I could easily run a parallel between these Gentlemen's Proceedings, and the present *French* King's, when he first went the *Shortest Way with the Protestants of* France, and could tell them that they seem exactly to follow his blessed Example, *viz.* First to deprive them of all Offices or Imployments in the State, then to take from them the Education of their Children, and then to the pulling down of their Churches, *Etc.* and so on to Gallows and Gallies.

Charles Morton (1627–98), a Puritan divine, had established a dissenting academy at Stoke Newington in the 1670s, of which Defoe was a proud pupil, as he admits in *More Short-Ways*.[44] *Samuel Wesley had written a letter that had been published without his permission, criticizing the dissenting academies as anti-monarchical,[45] which Defoe addressed, coming strongly to the defence of the academies. He correctly noted that Wesley had been a pupil of Morton, like himself, and that he, Defoe, was personally able to testify on Morton's behalf:[46]

I must do that learned Gentleman's memory that Justice to affirm, that neither in his System of Politicks Government and Discipline, or in any other Exercises of that School, was there any thing Taught or Encourag'd, that was Antimonarchical, or Destructive to the Government, or Constitution of *England*; and particularly among the Performances of that School, I find a Declamation relating to the benefit of a single Person in a Common-Wealth, wherein it is declar'd and prov'd from History and Reason, that Monarchy is the best Government, and the best suited to the Nature of Government, and the Defence of Property; which Discourse, together with the said Manuscripts, System of Politicks and Government, as Read in that School, and which are now above twenty-five Years old, are left at the Publishers of this Book for any one to peruse, as a Satisfaction of the truth of Fact.

Defoe had been joined by Samuel Palmer, whose *Defence of the Dissenters' Education in their Private Academies in Answer to Mr. W——y's disingenuous and Un-Christian Reflections upon 'em* (1703) attracted Wesley's rebuttal, *A Defence of a Letter on the Education of Dissenters* (1704), followed in turn by Palmer's *A Vindication of the Learning, Loyalty, Morals of the Dissenters. In Answer to Mr. Wesley* (1705). Defoe declared on behalf of the dissenters:[47]

We own the design to enjoy our Liberty of Worshiping God according to our Consciences, which, to your great mortification, is now our Right by Law, and which her Majesty, to your yet greater Disappointement, has promis'd us to Maintain and Continue. . . . We own also the Design of maintaining our just Rights and Privileges as English-men, and by all lawful Means to oppose and suppress all sorts of Tyranny and Oppression, as well Ecclesiastical as Civil.

5. Astell, Burnet, Toleration and the Tolerationists

Astell refers to one of the arguments against dissent reported by Defoe: 'That this design of suppressing their Schools does not Affect the Dissenters, they may serve God according to the Toleration their own Way, it only prevents Posterity following their Method'.[48] Against which Defoe had protested: 'this is such jesting with the dissenters, and such a civil way of telling them they are all Fools, that it can hardly be allow'd to pass without a little Satyr upon the Nonsense of it'. It is an argument that, undeterred, Astell nevertheless repeats. Defoe had promised in the closing sentence to *More Short-Ways* to expose calumnies against the dissenters:[49]

And I design once a Month to give a particular of the Mis-representations and base Treatment the Dissenters receive from this Party, till I have gone thro' the whole History, so I shall produce such unanswerable Proofs, such just Authorities and plain Matter of Fact, that I have no Apprehension of being disprov'd, having no need to help out our Cause with so weak and disadvantageous a shift as the refuge of Lyes.

Astell claimed that Defoe merely proved the Tory case, and in *Moderation Truly Stated*, produced earlier in the same year as *A Fair Way with the Dissenters*, she had given 'Precedents of Dissenters' from the New Testament, quoting John 4:20, 5:22 and Christ's opinion of the Samaritans, that '*they Worship'd they knew not what*'.[50] One of the major lines of argument in Astell's *Moderation Truly Stated* is once again that the Anglican episcopacy is constitutionally established and that to slander it is treasonous. She attacks William Prynne (1600–99), the Rev. Henry Burton (1578–1648) and Dr. John Bastwick (1593–1654), Puritans who had opposed the episcopacy, for which in 1637 they had been jointly tried, convicted and pilloried. John Tutchin, the Whig pamphleteer to whom Edward Ward's notorious *Secret History of the Calves' Head Clubb* was dedicated, had criticized the monarchy and defended Defoe over *The Shortest Way with the Dissenters*. And William Stephens (1647?–1718), a divine with strong Whig principles, had recommended discontinuing the observance of the anniversary of the execution of Charles I. This put them all in the same camp in Astell's eyes.

The Toleration Act, allowing freedom of worship for Protestant dissenters, had been passed in 1689, nevertheless. John Howe (1630–1705), a Puritan divine, had argued for a radical separation of church and state, as promoted by Locke in his *Letter on Toleration*, which would leave religious doctrine to conscience and private belief and disempower the clergy.[51] Astell, vehemently opposed to toleration, took up Defoe's discussion in *More Short-Ways* of *The Bishop of Salisbury's* [Bishop Gilbert Burnet's] *Speech in the House of Lords, upon the Bill against Occasional Conformity* (1704, 2), in which Burnet claimed that Elizabeth I had given precedents for religious toleration.[52]

Gilbert Burnet is a curious case, as a tolerationist with a Presbyterian background, who campaigned against absolutism on all sides. His remarkable tract on the economic success of the Protestant states, compared with the misery of those lands that had embraced Counter Reformation absolutism, *Some Letters containing an account of what seemed most remarkable in Switzerland, Italy, etc.* of 1685, was a *succès de scandale* at the court of James, whose agents banned it, seized it, and only succeeded in promoting it. It became a set piece both in England and the Americas on popery and absolutism as twins and poverty as the outcome. In 1686 Burnet had accepted an invitation to reside with the Prince of Orange at the Hague, and he it was who urged William to have his fleet ready to invade England, obtaining from Mary, consort of the prince, a promise to place all power in William's hands should they succeed in attaining the throne. Burnet personally drafted William's declaration and accompanied him to England in 1688. He was rewarded for his services with the bishopric of Salisbury and took his seat in the House of Lords, where he zealously advocated toleration. He preached the coronation sermon and in 1689 was placed on the commission for comprehension, where he hoped to bring about an accommodation between the Anglican and Presbyterian churches. In 1698 Burnet was appointed to attend Peter the Great, and his laborious work *Exposition of the Thirty-Nine Articles of the Church of England* was published. Indeed, Burnet's involvement in English politics was unceasing, even from afar. In the event, he returned to England to attend William on his death bed in 1702 and in 1703 strongly opposed the bill against occasional conformity, publishing his speeches on this and the Sacheverell impeachment. It is in this context that he is mentioned by Mary Astell in *A Fair Way with the Dissenters*.[53] Burnet's most important work, the *History of My Own Time*, was not published until after his death. Due no doubt to the intolerance of the Scottish church and Scottish law, which permitted the torture of prisoners, witnessed by Burnet in the case of his uncle, the Covenanter Lord Warriston, and threatened in his own case by the agents of James II, Burnet was steadfast in his support of liberty of conscience. His 1689 tract, *An Enquiry into the Measures of Submission to the Supream Authority: and of the Grounds upon which it may be Lawful or necessary for Subjects, to defend their Religion, Lives and Liberties*, the most liberal of all his writings, published before Locke's *Two Treatises* (1690), takes as its first precept the principle that 'men are born free'.[54]

6. Defoe, Burnet and Clarendon

Defoe claimed Burnet as a champion of toleration, for which there were precedents as far back as Elizabeth I, declaring: 'my Lord of *Salisbury*, . . . in his Speech to the House of Peers . . . [proves] 'twas the practice of Queen *Elizabeth* to admit of Persons of Different Religions into Places of Trust'.[55] Burnet's speech had understandably provoked controversy, evident from Charles Leslie's scurrilous reply, *The Bishop of Salisbury's Proper Defence from a Speech Cry'd about the Streets in his Name* (1704). Once again, it is typical that the toleration debate should be argued through surrogates, this time Elizabeth I, almost a century earlier. So Defoe concurred with Burnet:[56]

It is certain she treated the Papists all along with a very particular Indulgence. She would have the Peers excused from the Obligation to take the Oath of Supremacy. She employed Papists in all Her Affairs: They were Privy-Councellors and Lords Lieutenants. Her Lord-Treasurer protested against all the Acts for the Reformation; and was known to be a Church-Papist, or an *Occasional Conformist*; and yet he continued in that great Post Fourteen Years, till he died. She encouraged the *Occasional Conformity* of Papists, and apprehended no Danger in that, even from them: And yet I hope, it will be acknowledged, that there was more reason to be afraid, considering both their Numbers, and the Hopes they had for many Years of a Popish Successor, than we have now to be afraid of the Dissenters.

Defoe tried to turn the tables on the High Flyers by claiming that it was they who were the aggressors, while the dissenters practiced passive resistance.[57] 'We have always been upon the Defensive with you; we have ever been attack'd, and have only resisted your Violence', he claimed; to which Astell replied:[58]

10. Whether Dissenters were only on the Defensive and not the Aggressors, shall I say, in 41? I need not go so far back, even within this two years? Now to *State this*, I hope I may as freely *have recourse* to a *New Test of the Church of* England's *Loyalty*, as *Short ways* has to the *Occasional-Bill*. And we find in that Temperate and Uniting Treatise, writ a few months after her Majesty's Accession to the Throne, and before there was a word of a Bill, or any thing had been done or said against Dissenters; *that* "tho' *Names* of Contempt have been often changed on either side; as Cavalier and Roundhead, Royalist and Rebels, Malignants and Phanaticks, Torys and Whigs, yet the Division has always been barely *the Church and the Dissenter*, and there it continues to this Day."

Defoe had worked hard to defend the dissenters against the argument of treason, claiming that they did not 'do any thing to King *Charles* I. but what you [the Tories] did to his Son'[59] – here Defoe was referring to Charles II's indulgence toward dissenters and the opposition he faced from the Tory Party and particularly Clarendon. It is a challenge to which Astell responded by reminding him of the moves against the Crown of 1641: the passing of the *Grand Remonstrance; the debating of the *Root and Branch Bill; resistance to the taxing powers of the Crown in the form of ship money; abolition of the *Star Chamber and High Commission[60]

and the Ulster insurrection.[61] Defoe's defence was to appeal to the authority of Edward Hyde, first Earl of Clarendon and Tory doyen, whose fall
and exile under Charles II in 1667 attested to already dubious loyalty,
in Defoe's view. Defoe even presented Clarendon as a critic of Charles I:
'has not a noble Lord vouchsafing to turn Author, and write the History
of that Rebellion, has he not told us in the first part of his first Volume,
that the ill Conduct of that Prince brought all the Calamities of Civil War
upon his Head[?]'.[62]

But Astell leapt to Clarendon's defence, correctly citing his *History of
the Rebellion and Civil Wars in England* on the pacific moments of Charles
I's reign. Clarendon had concluded sanguinely that, 'after some unquiet-
ness of the People, and unhappy assaults upon the Prerogative by the Parliament, which produced its Dissolution, and thereupon some froward
and obstinate disturbances in Trade; there quickly follow'd so excellent
a Composure throughout the whole Kingdom, that the like Peace and
Plenty, and universal Tranquillity for ten years was never enjoy'd by any
Nation'.[63] Again, in a lengthier and more finely nuanced statement, he
had affirmed:[64]

It was now a time of great Ease, and Tranquillity; the King (as hath been said
before) had made himself Superior to all those Difficulties, and Streights, he had
to contend with the four first years he came to the Crown, at Home; and was now
Reverenced by all his Neighbours, who needed his Friendship, and desired to
have it; the Wealth of the Kingdom notorious to all the world, and the general
Temper, and Humour of it, little inclined to the Papist, and less to the Puritan.
There were some late Taxes, and Impositions introduced, which rather angred,
than griev'd the People, who were more than repair'd by the Quiet, Peace, and
Prosperity they enjoy'd; and the Murmur, and Discontent, that was, appear'd to
be against the Excess of Power exercised by the Crown, and supported by the
Judges in *Westminster*-Hall.

Clarendon cites the wording of the Bill for a Triennial Parliament,
where the Commons claimed 'to have sufficiently provided for the Security of the Common wealth; and that there remain'd nothing to be done,
but such a return of Duty and Gratitude to the King, as might Testify their
Devotions; and that their only End was to make Him glorious' – to which
Clarendon makes the aside, 'those Fits of Zeal and Loyalty, never lasted
long'.[65] Astell's last citation to Clarendon here concerns the passing of
the Bill of Attainder and the act for the continuing of Parliament, upon
which he comments:[66]

After the Passing these two Bills, the temper and spirit of the People, both within
and without the walls of the two Houses, grew marvellous calm and composed;
there being likewise about that time Pass'd by the King, the two Bills, for the

taking away the Star-chamber Court, and the High Commission: So that there was not a Grievance or Inconvenience, Real or Imaginary, to which there was not a through [*sic*] Remedy applied.

Astell in *Moderation Truly Stated* reviews those events in England and Scotland of 1642 leading up to the Civil War, which began the erosion of episcopal power completed in its course. In February 1642, several months before the outbreak of war, the king had reluctantly given his assent to the Bishops' Exclusion Bill, which prohibited not merely members of the episcopate but all clergymen in holy orders from occupying temporal offices in the state. It represented a triumph for the laity over the intrusion of clergymen into state positions, both at the centre of government and in the localities, which had been such a prominent feature of the 1630s under Laud. Shortly afterwards Parliament had taken even more drastic action by abolishing the episcopal office itself. In January 1643 both houses of Parliament approved a bill that swept away any form of diocesan administration in England and Wales, and in October 1646 the offices of archbishop and bishop were formally abolished by parliamentary ordinance. Violation of the episcopacy was tantamount to violation of the monarchy in Astell's eyes, and both added up to treason.

7. Astell, Owen and *Moderation Truly Stated*

Arguments in support of toleration that invoked international precedent were not uncommon in the debate. James Owen, for instance, in *Moderation a Vertue* (1703),[67] to which Astell responded with *Moderation truly Stated* (1704), had presented 'a short View of the *four great Empires* of the World, the *Assyrian*, or *Babylonian*, that of the *Medes* and *Persians*, of the *Grecians* and *Romans*, in all which, *Dissenters* from the Publick Religion have been prefer'd'.[68] But a defence of dissent that invoked the four-empire theory of early modern European thought, famous since Montesquieu, was tantamount to using a sledge hammer to crack a nut, in Astell's view. Owen was as rabid on the dissenters' side as Leslie and Sacheverell were on the High Church side, and his pamphlet in support of occasional conformity, *Moderation a Virtue*, to which Astell responded, had in fact drawn fire from Leslie, whose pamphlet *The Wolf Stript of his Shepherd's Cloathing etc.* (1704) set the tone for the debate. Owen countered with another pamphlet, *Moderation still a Virtue: in Answer to Several Bitter Pamphlets: especially Two, Entituled 'Occasional Conformity a most Unjustifiable Practice', and 'The Wolf Stripp'd of his Shepherd's Cloathing'.* There he referred to Leslie, 'the Wolf-stripper', as one of those who '*harangue us with tedious Narratives of the late Civil Wars, and the Confusions that followed; and they impute all to the present Dissenter, who were most of them unborn*'.[69]

Sacheverell too, in *The Nature and Mischief of Prejudice and Partiality Stated*,[70] in a passage singled out by Defoe in *More Short-Ways*,[71] had included a reference to Isaiah 65:25 with the rhetorical question: 'Are these the *Wolves in Sheep's Cloathing*, that are to be *Invited* and *Complemented*, even by Our *Superior Pastors*, into *Christ's Fold*, to Worry and Devour it?'. And Defoe in the same tract, with clear reference to the titles of Leslie's and Sacheverell's tracts, had declared:[72]

if your *Woolf Stript*, your *Associations*, your *Peace and Union*, be of any weight, then 'tis no Scandal to affirm that there is a barbarous Design on foot, in, and among some who call themselves the Members of the Church of *England*, to Extirpate and Destroy the Dissenters. . . .

The text of Isaiah had already been given a famous gloss by Locke, attacking the Tory alternative to resistance, passive obedience, in chapter 19 of the *Second Treatise:* 'Who would not think it an admirable peace betwixt the mighty and the mean when the lamb without resistance yielded his throat to be torn by the imperious wolf?'. In the conclusion to Astell's celebrated 1706 Preface to *Reflections upon Marriage*,[73] and in the title of Leslie's pamphlet *The Wolf Stripp'd of His Shepherd's Cloathing* (1704), the words of Isaiah echo together with the old aphorism 'a wolf in sheep's clothing'.

In the Postscript to *A Fair Way with the Dissenters*, Astell replied to Owen's reply, *Moderation Still a Virtue*. It was undoubtedly a matter of disappointment to her that Owen had not subjected *Moderation Truly Stated* to the scrutiny he gave Leslie's 'Wolf', as she referred to it.[74] The attention Owen pays Leslie's pamphlet, whose authorship he seems only to have discovered in time for the Preface and Postscript,[75] may well have been additional cause then for the disclaimer in the subtitle of Astell's pamphlet, 'Not Writ by Mr. *L—y*, or any other *Furious Jacobite*' – to ensure that Leslie did not get the credit for her pamphlet. Astell complained in her Postscript[76] that the arguments of *Moderation Truly Stated*, quoted anonymously by Owen in *Moderation Still a Virtue*,[77] had been largely overlooked and, to the extent that they had been treated, classed with those of Leslie. The latter's *The New Association, Part II. . . . An Answer to some Objections in the Pretended D. Foe's Explication in 'the Reflections upon the Shortest Way* (1703) was after all a reply to Defoe's earlier pamphlet. And it was in the Supplement to this work that Leslie had introduced the arguments against Locke for which he was to become famous but that Astell had anticipated in her *Reflections upon Marriage* (1700).

Nevertheless, Owen had in fact acknowledged Astell's contribution to the debate, and Astell quotes, almost verbatim, the charge Owen[78] leveled precisely against her when he claimed: '*Some of them violently oppose all* Moderation, *and confound it with* Lukewarmness *in the* Essentials *and* Vitals *of Religion; so the verbose and virulent Author of* Moderation Truly Stated (5, 24)'. Owen correctly referenced his source, which was indeed *Moderation truly Stated*, 5. To give some idea of Astell's sensitivity, however, Owen had referred to one of his adversaries (unnamed) as 'rank[ing] Schism *in the same degree of Guilt with* Adultery *and* Murder, *and think[ing] the* Blood of Martyrdom *can't* wash *away its Guilt*'.[79] Astell gives the impression that it is she to whom Owen refers, but this is not the case. Undaunted, she goes on to point Owen to [53–]54 of her text, *Moderation Truly Stated*, where she had demonstrated, precisely to the author of *Moderation a Vertue*, 27, these to be the views of the Presbyterian divine Thomas Edwards (1599–1647), in his *Further Discovery*, 197. The same Edwards, in his *Epistle Dedicated to the Lords and Commons before his Gangraena*, had confessed himself to being a schismatic, and Edwards's works are discussed in Astell's *Moderation Truly Stated*.

Understandably zealous in seeking acknowledgements for her views, when Owen refers to *Reflections* Astell also assumes this to be a reference to her work by that title, whereas in fact the reference appears to be to the title of Charles Leslie's *Reflections upon Some Scandalous and Malicious Pamphlets* (1703). And again, on page 4 of *Moderation Still a Virtue*, which Astell accurately cites, Owen seems not to be referring to *Moderation Truly Stated*, but rather to the anonymous author of *Occasional Conformity a Most Unjustifiable Practice*, who, along with Leslie, bears the burden of Owen's critique in this pamphlet. However, Astell takes the opportunity to vindicate herself by referring the reader to page 81 of *Moderation Truly Stated*, a particularly virulent and witty passage (including a poem 'in the manner of the *French* Satyrist') that 'justly', she claims, charges the dissenters with responsibility for the regicide.

Particularly difficult to read out of context, Astell's Postscript to *A Fair Way with the Dissenters*, when related to the relevant arguments of the earlier pamphlets, gives a very good indication of the mood and texture of pamphlet warfare, full of allusion, satire, invective, and, at times, high style. Astell took the opportunity in the Postscript to restate the arguments of her *Moderation Truly Stated*, despite the fact that Owen had paid them only cursory attention. Closely read, it provides an abstract of her earlier pamphlet, for which there is no modern edition, as well as a digest of the literature to which she responds. The occasional conformity debate, conducted over the life of the three bills introduced between 1702 and 1705, up to the passing of the act in 1711 and its repeal in 1719, had brought to light the full panoply of arguments for and against religious toleration. In *Moderation Truly Stated*,[80] Astell had taken up the 'Dissenters Arguments against Schism and Toleration', deferring to 'what has been writ upon this Subject by much better Pens'.[81] Astell refers to Owen's reflections on the differences between ministers in the 'Episcopal Church' and the dissenting churches in *Moderation a Virtue* (1703), pages 18–21, which at page 19 seem harmless enough. But she probably has more serious objections to what he has to say at pages 20–1, where he singles out the nonjurors and Jacobites (among whom she numbered friends).

In these pages of *Moderation Truly Stated*, Mary Astell reviews some forty items from the parliamentary debates and pamphlet literature on occasional conformity. The texts to which she refers, as indicated in the marginal notes, include Edward Stillingfleet's *The Mischief of Separation* (1680) and the *Unreasonableness of Separation* (1681); [Thomas] Edwards's [*The Second Part of Gangraena... or*] *Further Discovery* (1646), his *Antapologia* (1644), and his *Epistle Dedicated to the Lords and Commons before His Gangraena* (1646) [possibly *The Third Part of Gangraena...* in response, *inter alia*, to William Dell's *Right Reformation... In a Sermon... preached to the honourable House of Commons, November 25, 1646*]; 'Pryn's *Full Answer to J. Goodwin*' [William Prynne (1644), *A Full Reply to Certaine Briefe Observations and anti-Queries... Together with Certaine Briefe Animadversions on Mr. John Goodwins Theomachia*]; Samuel Rutherford's *Free Disputation* [*against Pretended Liberty of Conscience*] (1649); and Daniel Cawdrey's *Independency a Great Schism* [1630].

Owen, in *Moderation a Virtue* (1703) had asserted seven propositions, which constitute the chapters of the work. It is to these propositions, as restated in his *Moderation Still a Virtue*, that Astell systematically refers.[82] Owen's principal argument is from *raison d'état*, that 'Princes who understood their own Interest [know] better than to exclude Persons from publick Places, for their being Dissenters from the Religion of the State; And that there is danger too in excluding Dissenters'.[83] Astell's response in *Moderation Truly Stated* was to reformulate the argument as two questions: 'First, *In fact*, whether the Dissenters have either been Friends to the *Church of England*, or good Subjects to their Prince, when it was in their power to be otherwise?... And, Secondly, Whether by their Principles they can be so?'.[84] To these (rhetorical) questions she had given an extended reply in the form of a history of Puritanism and Parliament in the Civil War period in her *Impartial Enquiry* of early 1704.[85]

Astell's discussion of the conduct of the dissenters in the reigns of Elizabeth and Anne produces some of her finest political analysis, including disquisitions on the maxims that 'the *Little Finger* of an Usurp'd Power, is heavier than the *Loins* of a Lawful Prince'[86] and that 'a Wise Prince ought to put himself in no bodys hands, nor should he put it in any Man's Power to Ruin him'.[87] These arguments are made, at the pages indicated, in *Moderation Truly Stated*, to rebut Owen's fourth proposition, 'That the employing of [dissenters] in Public Trusts, strengthens the Church'.[88] 'So says the Independent to the Presbyterian in the *Pulpit Incendiary*, 1648', page 45. Astell replied: 'He who would be further Inform'd in their Apothegms may consult Different Sayings, 1683.'[89]

Astell is at her best in this argument, maintaining that occasional conformity in religion correlates with occasional conformity in government and is by any account unconstitutional, given that allegiance to the Church of England is legally established. In *Moderation Truly Stated* Astell had given a sample from Bancroft's '*Dangerous Positions*, Book 2, Chapters 12 and 13' and 'Case's *Sermon*, 30 Sept. 1543, page 45, *Etc.*,' of the full range of invective against dissenters, variously described as '*false, bastardly Governours of the Church, Incarnate Devils, Cogging, Confining Knaves, Impudents, Shameless Dolts, Hogs, Wolves, a Troop of Bloudy Soul Murderers, Idle Shepherds, Dumb Dogs, Greedy Dogs, Vile Wretches*, and what not'.[90] And at pages 72–3 of *Moderation Truly Stated* Astell gives an impressive list of examples of refusal to extend toleration to their enemies, and determination to subordinate the monarchy to the yoke of their confession, by some of the staunchest advocates of toleration and dissent. She proceeds to quote from the *Declaration of England and Scotland. 30 Jan. 1643*, as cited in *Moderation Truly Stated*,[91] where

they took care "to give publick Warning to all *Neuters*, to rest no longer upon their Neutrality, but that they address themselves speedily to take the *Covenant*, and joyn with all their Power in defence of this Cause against the Common Enemy, (*The Term by which they were pleased to denote their Sovereign King*, Charles Ist), *etc.* Otherwise (say they) we do declare them to be Publick Enemies to their Religion and Country; and that they are to be Sentenc'd and punish'd as profess'd Adversaries and Malignants. In *Scotland* he who should not take, or who deferr'd taking the *Covenant*, was to have all his Rents and Profits confiscated, was not to enjoy any Office or Benefit, and to be cited before the next Parliament, *Etc.*"[92]

But the web of conflicting oaths that office-holders had taken under the Stuarts in fact posed a problem, as Locke was not the first to see. Owen had made a telling point against divine right and hereditary monarchy when he claimed:[93]

I cannot see how those Gentlemen that so fiercely condemn the *Parliament* in 1642, can approve the Revolution in 1688, which was founded in the Invitation of the Pr. of O. by a certain Number of *Lords*, and *Gentlemen, out of Parliament.* And they that disapprove of the Dethroning of K. *J.* II. cannot be true to the Present Government, which is Establish'd on the same Foundation with that of K. WILLIAM.

6

Astell, Locke and the Highway Man

A Test Case

1. Locke and the Settlement of 1689

Locke's contribution to the constitutional debate of 1688–9 has gradually been reevaluated.[1] For some time it had been minimized, due to the anonymity of the *Two Treatises*, written between 1681 and 1683, published in 1689 but with 1690 on the title page, and officially acknowledged by Locke only in the codicil to his will of 1704. Peter Laslett, in a pioneering work of textual excavation, developed the thesis that Locke's *Two Treatises on Government* were not in fact a rationalization of the Glorious Revolution of 1688, as had hitherto been believed, but a work written in the Exclusion Crisis of 1679–83, during which the principle of Stuart dynastic rule was formidably challenged.[2] For the Glorious Revolution is generally seen as the *coup d'état* that brought to fruition the steady erosion of James II's legitimacy over this period. Among Whigs, James had so thoroughly discredited himself that opposition to his removal is said to have been negligible. It was the terms in which he was removed that were fought over. These ranged from Tory theses of James's moral incapacity to rule, evidenced by his tyranny;[3] to loyalist 'theses of contract, non-contractarian resistance, possession, conquest and abdication'; to Whig political arguments with roots in the radical reformation thinkers Calvin, Luther and Melancthon.[4] Among the works in which these positions were debated, only two references to Locke's *Two Treatises* are to be found, both by Whig radicals. Samuel Johnson, who was flogged while Locke fled, Algernon Sidney, executed in 1683, and Tyrrell, were more famous for Lockean arguments than Locke,[5] who received a brief notice in Le Clerc's *Life* and a notice by Tyrrell but was otherwise unmentioned by name as author of the *Treatises* until 1705. Richard Ashcraft, who reinstates the view that Locke's *Two Treatises* relate principally to the Exclusion Crisis, gives an explanation for the secrecy surrounding the authorship of the *Two Treatises*:[6]

> The *Two Treatises of Government* reflects the language of Shaftesbury and the Rye House Plot and of Monmouth's Rebellion, and not the language of the Whig and Tory magnates who managed the Glorious Revolution. The individuals most deeply involved in marshalling the social, economic, and political forces necessary to settle the crown on William and Mary were, with very few exceptions, the very men who had prosecuted the Rye House conspirators and who led the army and militia against Monmouth's troops. It is hardly surprising that they preferred not to be reminded of the events and ideas associated with the radicals' activities in the 1680s. It is from this standpoint, I shall argue, that we can understand the reception given to the *Two Treatises*, and the gulf that stands between the arguments of that work and the posture adopted by the defenders of William III's government and by those who tried to create an official Whig ideology in the 1690s.

But Locke had also joined cause with the Whig magnates involved in the Glorious Revolution, and he too hoped to settle the Crown on William III as a dynastic closure to the perennial threat of popery and arbitrary government under the Stuarts. Is this why he was so reticent about the authorship of the *Two Treatises*? And was it for this reason that contemporary commentators, familiar with the establishment Locke, who had sailed over with Princess Mary and who had been offered two government jobs, hesitated to pin the authorship of such a radical work on such a trimming man? Locke, after his immersion in the conspiracies of the Shaftesbury circle against Charles II in the 1680s, had fled to Holland, living on the periphery of William of Orange's court. Although personally absent from the Revolution of 1688, through the good offices of Viscount Mordaunt, who had been a Shaftesbury supporter in the House of Lords, he had found a place on Princess Mary's ship in February 1689.[7] If the Whig magnates who had prosecuted the Revolution of 1688 did not want to be reminded of the radicalism of the early '80s, perhaps Locke did not either.

Unnamed and perhaps redrafted, refocused to vindicate William, as the Preface suggests, Locke's *Two Treatises* entered a flow of pamphleteering in 1689–93 to the extent of some 200 items, equaled only at other political turning points – in 1642, 1648, 1660 and 1710. Its reception as part of the allegiance controversy had important consequences, whatever Locke's original intentions may have been. While in length and degree of philosophical abstraction the *Two Treatises* may stand apart from other items in the allegiance debate, they represent a radical Whig tendency that had other adherents. Identifying six types of justification for the Glorious Revolution in the corpus of pamphlets, Goldie goes on to analyze eight political positions on the Revolution, defined by doctrines and interests of the adherents, assigning to the radical Whig position Locke's *Two Treatises*, along with the works of Tyrrell, Samuel Johnson, Atwood, Blount and Defoe.[8]

Recent scholars have firmly reinstated Locke at the centre of the debates of 1688–9, finding confirmation in rediscovered documents in which Locke is to be found advising contemporary politicians and commenting on constitutional and dynastic issues. These documents, together with evidence that Locke's political advice was sought and that he was offered two government posts during the 1690s,[9] have caused revision of the judgment that Locke's political philosophy was more philosophical than political.[10] Locke becomes visible in the politics of the Convention and the Allegiance Oath of 1689, even if, so to speak, behind the arras.[11] From the 1670s to the 1680s he was already prompting from behind the chair, as in the case of Shaftesbury's famous *Delenda est Carthago* speech of 5 February 1673 to the Commons, to which Astell alludes. She refers sarcastically to Shaftesbury as 'a Leading Peer among the *Whiggs*, and who consequently wou'd be thought a Great Patriot and Friend to Liberty, and very much in the Interest of his Country, [who] took the freedom to say in the House of Lords, *Delenda est Carthago*'.[12] Locke was also perhaps advising Somers behind the scene on the Bill of Rights in the spring of 1689;[13] he addressed his minute to Clarke some time after March 1690;[14] and he was to be found commenting in an unpublished paper on Sherlock's *Case of Allegiance* some time in the 1690s.

2. Astell's Rebuttal of Locke: The Case

But still no satisfactory answer has really been given to the question of 'why it took until 1703 before "any Tory or Jacobite considered it worth their pains to engage in a critical examination of the Treatises"'[15] or why the first extensive critique of the second treatise awaited the anonymous *Essay upon Government* of 1705. The argument is made here that scholars are still looking for the wrong person in the wrong place. Not only did the systematic refutation of Locke not await the works of 1703 and 1705 customarily cited, but reasons lie in the centrality of religion to politics as the great issue on which constitutionality itself turned. It is in the response to Locke's religious works that we must look for answers to the *Two Treatises*, which were correctly treated with his theology as a seamless whole. Here we find not only Leslie, already credited with the first systematic response to the *Two Treatises*, but Astell, who in works that purport to be educational, theological and homiletic, proves to be more single-mindedly devoted to the refutation of Locke than any of her contemporaries.

It is, moreover, a Locke who until recently has been eclipsed by the Locke of the American Revolution, the Locke of possessive individualism – or of the political economists – and other post-Enlightenment Lockes. Astell's Locke, in fact, provides a test of authenticity that only very recent scholarship has met. It is for this reason, perhaps, that her pioneering critique was for so long overlooked. The issues on which it focuses are the following: Anglicanism, Trinitarianism and the settlement of 1689; contracts, oaths and political allegiance; biblical patriarchalism and the claims of dynastic monarchy; and the rights of freeborn Englishmen versus the ancient constitution. On religion and the settlement of 1689, Astell negotiates the issues of unitarianism, socinianism and dissent, all with reference to Locke. On the question of oaths, contracts and political allegiances she has no difficulty in seeing Locke's purpose as undermining the traditional sources of hereditary monarchy – something perceived by William III as well, who saw himself hostage to the consent of people in a way that did not please him.[16]

Locke's attack on Filmerian biblical patriarchalism was also a target. Father-right Locke could easily show to be the most simple-minded basis for hereditary monarchy. Filmer's relentless defence of patriarchal lineage may have represented a desperate attempt at royalist propaganda on the part of one whose lifeline to the episcopacy and the court had been severed by imprisonment under the parliamentarians, and who was willing to defend at any cost a position that might ensure the return of the Stuarts.[17] In any event, *Patriarcha* had become the bastion of post-1688 Tory orthodoxy. But not for Astell, who invoked a long line of powerful biblical women against the proverbial patriarchs. Although Filmer's particular genius in marrying natural law and monarchical theory appealed to a wide range of royalists, including, most notably, Robert Brady, the royalist position did not depend on Filmer. Defence of sovereignty in terms of Romans 13 and other biblical quotes that sanctioned local constitutional arrangements, as made by Astell, was typical and deemed sufficient.[18]

It was the umbilical cord between patriarchalism and hereditary monarchy that Locke had set out to sever, which he could easily do, given the inherent weaknesses of genetic arguments as opposed to arguments from reason.[19] On the question of contracts and constitutionalism he took the high road of reason, once again to bypass the constitutional complexities of legal case and countercase.[20] The upshot is a doctrine of natural rights that lends to his work the much-noted philosophical abstraction, erroneously interpreted by some as a detachment from politics.[21] Astell, not taken in, makes the doctrine of natural rights the frequent butt of her ridicule. If she was no advocate of the rights of freeborn Englishmen, spurning traditional appeals to the ancient constitution, denying even the salience of Magna Carta, she was no supporter of biblical lineage either. To argue from heredity, as such, was to resort to contingency, but Astell defended monarchy on the basis of divine design. As a Cartesian rationalist and Cambridge Platonist, she paradoxically participated in a 'rationalist' movement that was ultimately to allow Whig encroachments on Tory territory and to erode the very constitutional position she supported.

The relation between contracts, covenants and the constitution was not a simple one. The constitutional politics of Locke were by no means straightforward either. A supporter of popular sovereignty during the Convention Parliament of 1689 – to which he may have been an informal advisor[22] – and of the Bill of Rights in 1689, in 1690 he nevertheless advocated the Allegiance Oath against James II, demanding that all citizens take an oath of allegiance to William instead. It is generally believed that the anomalies of Locke's constitutional position did not become apparent until subjected to intense scrutiny in the debate over the American colonies in the 1760s.[23] But these very anomalies undoubtedly account for Locke's own failure to commit himself on constitutional specifics, the significance of his silences having become a matter of recent debate.[24] Lois Schwoerer believes that Locke's 'praise of "our ancient government", expressed in a letter to Clarke of February 1689, is foreign to his theoretical work, which of course is cast in the non-historical idiom of reason and natural rights'; but that he was personally committed to the constitution as comprised of King, Lords and Commons, which the missing portions of the *Two Treatises* might have told us.[25] Thompson,[26] while conceding that Locke is grappling with the technical problem of resistance in mixed monarchies, believes that he wished to extricate politics from the teeth of constitutional lawyers, and for this reason he did not commit himself on the details, preferring the rationalist Hobbesian and Grotian state-of-nature model of the social contract – which was not a contract at all but a peculiar amalgam of social anthropology and ancient history with parallels in the biblical Fall.

Like commentators in her day, Astell cast Locke with Hobbes. Whig state-of-nature arguments similar to Locke's, which emerged during the Exclusion Crisis, were routinely treated as Hobbist by the Tories, and it was only after 1760 that the differences between them became of general interest. Moreover, her characterization of the Whig position, which Locke represents, suggests that appeals to the rights of freeborn Englishmen were vaguely expressed generalities intended to be deliberately evasive on constitutional technicalities. This was typical of airy references to English liberty by the country Whig John Tutchin, by White Kennett and by Defoe, with whom the phrase becomes a Whig catch-cry. Astell intuited that Locke, by his very vagueness, had succeeded in disaggregating the ancient constitution and customary right that a generation of Whigs, including Atwood and Burnet, had tried to preserve by melding contract to conquest – a technically impossible project. So, in *An Impartial Enquiry*,[27] Astell mocks the language of the country Whig, exemplified in particular by John Tutchin, who combined reverence for the ancient constitution, Parliament and native right with patriotism, declaring of the constitution that 'she's as well beloved now by all true *Englishmen*, as she was by our Forefathers a Thousand Years ago'.[28] Tutchin's views, set out in the *Observator* from 29 September to 7 November 1703, focused on resistance and were targeted at Charles Leslie. They were bound for this reason to have come to Astell's attention. Tutchin, it is true, admired 'those two great men, Mr. Sidney and Mr. Lock', defenders of ancient liberty, 'the one against Sir Robert Filmer, and the other against a whole Company of Slaves'.[29] This, the only occasion on which Tutchin names Locke, rhetorically couples defence of liberty with opposition to slavery, but by then Astell's *Reflections upon Marriage* had already been written.

3. Astell's Rebuttal of Locke: The Evidence

What is the evidence for the claim that Locke is Astell's consistent target, given that Lockean arguments mounted by Tyrrell, Blount and Sidney were more widely known, and given that Astell's full critique of Locke did not appear before 1705? The story is a curious one and worth rehearsing. Astell's first published work, *A Serious Proposal to the Ladies for the Advancement of Their True and Greatest Interest* (Part I, 1694), had been initially taken for the work of Masham, as typical of the daughter of Ralph Cudworth.[30] But when in 1696 Masham's *Discourse Concerning the Love of God* was published, it was read as criticizing both Astell's *Serious Proposal* and the *Astell–Norris Letters Concerning the Love of God* of 1695. Norris replied directly to Masham's pamphlet in the fourth volume of his *Practical Discourses* of 1698, assuming it to be the work of Locke, an assumption that Astell also made. The Masham intervention explains what commentators have hitherto had difficulty explaining: the content of *A Serious Proposal, Part II*. There, on closer examination, Astell departs from the simplicity of her original project for a full-scale rehabilitation of the Port Royal school, whose ethics, rhetoric and logic are all called into play to refute the sensationalist psychology and empiricism of the now detested Locke.

Astell responded openly to Masham only after Locke's death with *The Christian Religion as Profess'd by a Daughter of the Church* of 1705. This, Astell's 400-page *magnum opus*, was a systematic treatment of the then known works of Locke: *Essay Concerning Human Understanding* (1689), *The Reasonableness of Christianity* (1695), *Vindication of the Reasonableness of Christianity* (1695), and *Two Treatises of Government* (1690), and some not by Locke, namely, the anonymous *A Ladies Religion* (1697) and Masham's *Discourse*. Astell was able to complete in a systematic treatise the rebuttal of Locke she had earlier undertaken by elaborate subterfuge. Initially attributed by Lord Stanhope to her Chelsea neighbour and acquaintance the Tory Francis Atterbury,[31] Astell's *The Christian Religion* diagnosed the central tenets of Locke's doctrine only much later established with the discovery of hitherto unpublished texts.[32] They are three. The first is the principle of self-preservation, which Locke shares with Hobbes on the basis of a remarkably similar theory of human psychology. Its target was scholastic metaphysics. The second is the right of freedom from hereditable encumbrance as regards one's person but not one's property. Its target was hereditary monarchy. And the third is the old principle of popular sovereignty – that the power of government is based on popular consent. Its purpose was to legitimate dynastic change. These principles are systematically under attack in Astell's three Tory pamphlets of 1704, *Moderation Truly Stated*, *A Fair Way with the Dissenters*, and *An Impartial Enquiry into the Causes of Rebellion and Civil War*.

In making my case for the centrality of Locke to Astell's enterprise, let me take the explicit references first. Astell's first named reference to Locke, in *Moderation Truly Stated*,[33] is to his theory of the association of ideas:

then Lukewarmness and Indifferency in our Profession, is the only sense in which *Moderation* can be taken in the present context; if with the *Great* Mr. *Locke*, it be our constant care to annex to the word a determinate Idea.

Her remarks preface a long diatribe on the tactics of the classical Whig: a Low Churchman who puts party above all. To effect the balance he will throw Presbyterians into the scales, 'and if this is not sufficient, we can add *Independents, Anabaptists, Socinians,* and what not, to make a dead weight upon occasion' and deny 'the Prince a Prerogative'.[34] If these inducements are not enough, she says, perhaps lumping Locke with Hobbes, 'whoop the Government is almost shatter'd to pieces, and we're within a hair's breadth of being once more in a State of Nature!'.

Astell's second named reference to Locke occurs in *An Impartial Enquiry*.[35] Ostensibly a reference to his sensationalist psychology, it again connects his epistemology to his politics, this time with a sarcastic comment on Locke as party to Shaftesbury's manoeuvring against Charles II and the 'French threat' during the Exclusion crisis:[36]

Only let me recommend to all such Thinkers, Mr. *Lock's* Chapter *of the Association of Ideas*; they need not be afraid to read it, for that ingenious Author is on the right side, and by no means in a *French* Interest! And indeed, till People will observe the excellent Precepts of our Holy Religion, and that in particular, of calling no Man Master upon Earth, of following no Popular Speaker and Leader of a Party, they will easily be persuaded to *think*, as every Cunning and Factious Man will have them.

Astell's reference to John Locke for a Whiggish theory of the relation between ideas and evidence is a stroke of genius. Chapter 33 of Volume 2 of Locke's *Essay Concerning Human Understanding*, entitled 'Of the Association of Ideas' – Sections 4 and 5 being entitled 'A degree of madness' and 'From a wrong connexion of ideas', respectively – was among the chapters added by Locke for the fourth edition of 1700.[37] Astell notes that Locke was a model for White Kennett, and the passage must be read as an elaborate satire of Locke's views. Locke, while professing to 'observe the excellent Precepts of our Holy Religion', was a Latitudinarian, if not a Deist; while claiming to call 'no Man Master upon Earth' and follow 'no Popular Speaker and Leader of a Party', he was, of course, the follower of Shaftesbury, who exactly fitted that description. This kind of double talk is facilitated, she seems to be suggesting, by Locke's sensationalist psychology, which easily allows people 'to *think*, as every Cunning and Factious Man will have them'.

Locke is not Astell's only possible target and some of her strongest invective is reserved for Defoe, acknowledged as Locke's popularizer and yet more than just his man.[38] In *A Fair Way with the Dissenters*,[39] Astell remarks that were it not for the Christian injunction to charity, she would vent 'all that Contempt that is due to little Scriblers and Busiebodies, who, either for Bread, and to deserve their Wages of the Party, or out of an innate Love to Mischief, alarm the Mob, and impose upon the Ignorant and Careless Reeader [*sic*], by venting bold Slanders and notorious Untruths, in a plausible Stile and with some shews of Probability, with an Insolence peculiar to themselves, and a matchless Effrontery'. Similar accusations later in the same year seem also to be aimed at Defoe, again classed among 'those Mercenary Scriblers whom all sober Men condemn, and who only write after the Fact, or in order to it, to make their own Fortunes, or to justifie their own Wickedness'.[40] Astell's phraseology is close to that of a work published in the following year by an anonymous Jacobite/nonjuror, *An Essay upon Government. Wherein the Republican Schemes Reviv'd by Mr. Lock, Dr. Blackal, &c are Fairly Consider'd and Refuted*,[41] which refers to them as 'licentious, mercenary and ignorant scribblers'. And in 1704 Defoe and Tutchin had been sued for libel.[42]

The third set of explicit references to Locke is in *The Christian Religion*,[43] where Astell argues against self-preservation with explicit reference to the *Two Treatises*, Book 2, §149, claiming:

139. Suppose our Enemy is a Persecutor, and does invade that *Fundamental, Sacred and unalterable Law of Self-Preservation* (*Two Treatises of Government*, B.2, S.149.), as some call it. . . . A Persecutor who wou'd deprive us of our dear and desirable Estates, Offices and Employments, our dearer Lives perhaps, (over which we our selves *have no power* (*Treatise of Government*, B.2, S.23.), therefore how shou'd he come by't, tho' we invested him with all the power we had, on condition he kept his compact?) . . . .

And again:

312. What then is *Self-Preservation*, that Fundamental Law of Nature, as some call it, to which all other laws, Divine as well as Human, are made to do Homage? and how shall it be provided for? Very well; for it does not consist in the Preservation of the Person or Composite, but in preserving the Mind from Evil, the Mind which is truly the Self, and which ought to be secur'd at all hazards. It is this *Self-Preservation* and no other, that is a *Fundamental Sacred and unalterable Law*, as might easily be prov'd were this a proper place; which Law he obeys, and he only, who will do or suffer any thing rather than Sin. *No Man having a power to deliver up this Preservation, or consequently the means of it, to the absolute Will and arbitrary Dominion* [306] *of another, but has always a Right to Preserve what he has not a Power to part with* (*Two Treatises of Government*, B.2, S.149.), as a certain Author says in another Case where it will not hold.

So far, it appears, we have no significant critique of Locke by Astell before 1703, the date of Leslie's critique. In *An Impartial Enquiry*, she attacked the case for self-preservation mounted by Locke and Hobbes,[44] cautioning

White Kennett about what she considers to be Locke's religious apostasy in *The Reasonableness of Christianity*, a constant refrain with her:[45]

Beware of every one who wou'd draw you into *a necessity* of *believing*, that your *Liberties and Estates are in some danger*, who wou'd give you such a *Prospect*, and work you into such a *Persuasion*, and so draw you in by the old Cant of *Self-Preservation*, tho' they seem to demonstrate ever so great a *necessity* (page 18). Much more ought you to abhor being *drawn in* by the bare *meaning* of it, at least if you have any regard to real Self-Preservation, and think your Souls of greater moment than your Lives or Estates.

This is a paraphrase, Astell's quotation of Locke's words indicated by italics, of the central passage §209 of the *Two Treatises*,[46] in which he asserts the right of resistance with clear reference to James II and his Catholicism:[47]

But if either these illegal Acts have extended to the Majority of the People; or if the Mischief and Oppression has light only on some few, but in such Cases, as the Precedent, and Consequences seem to threaten all, and they are perswaded in their Consciences, that their Laws, and with them their Estates, Liberties and Lives are in danger, and perhaps their Religion too, how they will be hindered from resisting illegal force, used against them, I cannot tell.

Astell's case is that the right of conquest, which Locke denied to James, he was willing to assert with respect to the people, who are granted the right to resist the lawful king and place their own candidate on the throne. Locke's subsequent endorsement of William III seems to bear out her charge. Commentators early and late have noted that if self-preservation is the motive to contract in Locke's system, tacit consent is too frequently the means, a vehicle too weak to do the job. But Astell's argument is a different, and in some respects a more compelling, one. The weakness of the push of consent against the pull of self-preservation is simply indicative of the sleight of hand by means of which *de facto* conquest is converted into *de jure* rule. Self-preservation dictates that right give way to might, as Astell percipiently remarked: 'And if mere Power gives a Right to Rule, there can be no such thing as Usurpation; but a Highway-Man so long as he has strength to force, has also a Right to require our Obedience'.[48] The argument appears to be a clever play on Locke's famous argument for freedom of the highway as the test of tacit consent made in the *Second Treatise*, §119,[49] where, having established that 'man is born free', Locke sets out the conditions on which one can be bound to a civil authority:

And to this I say, that every Man, that hath any Possession, or Enjoyment, of any part of the Dominions of any Government, doth thereby give his *tacit Consent*, and is as far forth obliged to Obedience to the Laws of that Government, during such Enjoyment, as any one under it; whether this his Possession be of land, to him and his Heirs for ever, or a Lodging only for a Week; or whether it be barely travelling freely on the Highway; and in Effect, it reaches as far as the very being of any one within the Territories of that Government.

4. Astell and the Highway Man: A Test Case

Astell may be seen as cueing us for her arguments against Locke by the play she makes of the highway man. It is a test case for her method of refutation employed against Locke's theological arguments and against his epistemology, particularly evident in her critique in *The Christian Religion* of Locke on 'thinking matter', as we have seen. Locke's strenuous disavowals of the right of conquest endorsed by Hobbes were to no avail with Astell.[50] The pre-eminent Whig theorist of popular sovereignty, who completed his career by promoting a Dutch conqueror on the English throne and defending royal prerogatives against a Tory parliament, had in her view destroyed the credentials of his own argument. In *An Impartial Enquiry*,[51] she declares rogue government to be the consequence of Locke's right of self-preservation:

But now, if *Doubts and Suspicions, a Thought, a necessity of Believing, a Prospect and Persuasion, a Meaning of Self-Preservation*, or even Self-Preservation, when Life is really in Danger, can lessen the Guilt of this *Unnatural Rebellion*, and all the *Horrid Facts* it produc'd; what will they not excuse! He who robs upon the High-Way, has his *Prospects*, and *Persuasions*, and *Necessities*; and when he resists the Officers of Justice, he only *means Self-Preservation*.

Astell casts Locke with Hobbes, rebutting them both: 'And if a Thief meets me on the High-way and goes off with my Purse, therefore he has a Right to it, and GOD Approves the Action!'.[52] Finally, in *An Impartial Enquiry*, in an ironic parody of Locke on resistance and self-preservation, Astell uses the image again:[53]

He who robs upon the High-Way, has his *Prospects*, and *Persuasions*, and *Necessities*; and when he resists the Officers of Justice, he only *means Self-Preservation*.

In an extraordinary series of manoeuvres Astell succeeds, by the use of this single metaphor, in conflating separate and incompatible arguments of Locke, collapsing the difference between Locke and Hobbes and consolidating a case against the Whigs in the popular mind as opportunists, if not bandits. This very vulgarization of the Whig position, on which

the polarity of party politics to a certain extent depended, had its counterpart in the case that Milton, Locke and Sidney had mounted against
the loyalists, and on the same ground: as supporters of absolutism, *de
facto* power and conquest.[54] For while the idiom of the highway man
appears in Locke's phraseology of the argument for tacit consent, he
employs it elsewhere as a synonym for the rogue government of absolute
monarchy. For his part, the vulgarized Tory position, as Locke paints it,
traces a trajectory from the obscurantism of patriarchalism, to the veneration of lineage, to the irrationality of *de facto* power and the violence of
conquest.

The image of the highway man did sterling service for this constellation
of ideas. In Chapter 16 of the *Second Treatise*, §176, Locke had laid out his
case against right of conquest with clear reference to James II, claiming
'That the *Aggressor*, who puts himself into the state of War with another,
and *unjustly invades* another Man's right, *can*, by such an unjust War,
never come to *have a right over the Conquered*', any more than 'Robbers and
Pirates have a Right of Empire over whomsoever they have Force enough
to master'.[55] To complete the metaphor he asks: 'Should a Robber break
into my House, and with a Dagger at my Throat, make me seal Deeds to
convey my Estate to him, would this give him any Title?' And he answers:
'Just such a Title by his Sword, has an *unjust Conquerour*, who forces me
into Submission'. Without doubt Locke is making his case in opposition
to Hobbes, for whom conquest established legitimate contracts, and who
first introduced the metaphor of the highway man with the claim that
'amongst men, till there were constituted great Commonwealths, it was
thought no dishonour to be a Pyrate, or a High-way Theefe'.[56] Hobbes
had reflected on the case of the highway man in making his case for the
inviolability of contracts: 'And even in Common-wealths, if I be forced to
redeem my selfe from a Theefe by promising him money, I am bound to
pay it, till the Civill Law discharge me'.[57]

With unmistakable reference to his own case and the treatment by
Charles II of the Shaftesbury circle in the wake of the Rye House Plot,
Locke, in §202 of Chapter 13 on tyranny, defended an individual's right
to self-preservation against arbitrary arrest, a symptom of arbitrary government, once again compared to highway robbery:[58]

He that hath Authority to seize my Person in the Street, may be opposed as a
Thief and a Robber, if he indeavours to break into my House to Execute a Writ,
notwithstanding that I know he has such a Warrant, and such a Legal Authority
as will impower him to Arrest me abroad.

To make it clear, indeed, that his case is aimed at defenders of absolutism, Locke in §177 of the same chapter boldly states: 'They that found Absolute Monarchy upon the Title of the Sword, make their Heroes, who are the Founders of such Monarchies, arrant *Draw-can-Sirs*', employing a proverbial phrase from the Duke of Buckingham's much-played play *The Rehearsal*, of 1663/4, for characters who kill off everybody around them.[59] Locke may be taking a poke at Hobbes, for whom title by the sword is matched by the power of the crosier, both grasped firmly in the hands of the sovereign in the frontispiece to *Leviathan*. Locke concludes the passage by reminding him of the people, whose legitimacy a theory of sovereignty modelled on conquest neglects: '[They] forget they had any Officers and Soldiers that fought on their side in the Battles they won, or assisted them in the subduing or shared in possessing the Countries they Master'd'.

In §182 of the same chapter Locke further employed the image of the highway man to define the precise limits of the rights to self-preservation and the protection of one's property:[60]

For though I may kill a Thief that sets on me in the Highway, yet I may not (which seems less) take away his Money and let him go; this would be Robbery on my side. His force, and the state of War he put himself in, made him forfeit his Life, but gave me no Title to his Goods.

Possibly here too the analogue of royal usurpation is in Locke's mind. In §186 of Chapter 16 the theme is replayed: 'He that forces my Horse from me, ought presently to restore him, and I have still a right to retake him'.[61] But now the highway man is furnished with a pistol, rather than a knife:[62]

Nor does it at all alter the case, to say to I *gave my Promise*, no more than it excuses the force, and passes the Right, when I put my Hand in my Pocket, and deliver my Purse my self to a Thief, who demands it with a Pistol at my Breast.

In point of fact, Locke consistently uses the image of the highway man to illustrate the conditions under which the right of resistance may be exercised. They are conditions in which the writ of legal redress does not run. This he clearly spells out in §207 of the chapter on tyranny, where he expands on his thesis that rule of law is a form of malpractice insurance for the sovereign – it guarantees the loyalty of his subjects. But Locke notes an anomaly: that the protection of the law against a violation of trust that endangers one's life runs out when it comes to protection of one's property. Expressed in the metaphor of highway robbery, it is an anomaly that is systemic, given Locke's insistence that violence must be met by passive resistance where appeal to the law is available. This principle, designed to protect the sovereign once legally instated, ensures that the '*Doctrine* of the lawfulness of *resisting* all unlawful exercises of his Power, *will not* upon every slight occasion indanger him, or *imbroil the Government*'.[63] This is because 'where the injured Party may be relieved, and his damages repaired by Appeal to the Law, there can be no pretence for Force, which is only to be used, where a Man is intercepted from appealing to the Law'. So far so good, but as Locke freely admits, this leaves the honest citizen hostage to free riders and outlaws, if not to highway men as such. Reading it, one can understand why Astell might have deliberately conflated Hobbes's 'high-way theefe', who was a bandit, with Locke's highway man, who was not. Such a disparity in the security offered the sovereign by rule of law, compared with the citizen, held to ridicule the new political order the social contract was said to enstate:[64]

A Man with a Sword in his Hand demands my Purse in the High-way, when perhaps I have not 12'*d.* in my Pocket; This Man I may lawfully kill. To another I deliver 100.*l.* to hold only whilst I alight, which he refuses to restore me, when I am got up again, but draws his Sword to defend the possession of it by force, if I endeavour to retake it. The mischief this Man does me, is a hundred, or possibly a thousand times more, than the other perhaps intended me, (whom I killed before he really did me any) and yet I might lawfully kill the one, and cannot so much as hurt the other lawfully. The Reason whereof is plain; because the one using *force*, which threatned my Life, I could not have *time to appeal* to the Law to secure it: And when it was gone, 'twas too late to appeal. The Law could not restore Life to my dead Carcass: The Loss was irreparable; which to prevent, the Law of Nature gave me a Right to *destroy* him, who had put himself into a state of War with me, and threatned my destruction. But in the other case, my Life not being in danger, I may have the *benefit of appealing* to the Law, and have Reparation for my 100 *l.* that way.

These sections of the *Two Treatises* at which we have looked (§§ 176, 182, 202, 207), drafted during the Exclusion Crisis of 1679–81, are recognized to contain specific references to James II.[65] By the 1690s, however, the situation looked considerably different. It was not the prospect of James invading with the power of France behind him, but the reality of a Dutch interloper on the English throne, with which the parties were now confronted. Suddenly the caricature of defenders of the last Stuart king, painted by Sidney, Tyrrell and Locke, bore a strange resemblance to the Whig defence of unconditional allegiance to the House of Orange endorsed by Locke.

5. Political Demagogues and Domestic Tyrants

Whether by coincidence or not, Astell and Charles Leslie arrived at the same test of veracity for Locke and the Whigs, challenging them to show their sincerity by implementing in the family the criteria for public accountability they applied to the state. In the Preface to *Reflections upon Marriage*, in the passage immediately following the remarks about the highway man, Astell drew the analogue between rogue government in the state, scarcely veiled by the fiction of tacit consent, and rogue government in the family, to which no fig leaf is attached, with specific reference to Locke:[66]

Again, if Absolute Sovereignty be not necessary in a State, how comes it to be so in a Family? or if in a Family why not in a State; since no Reason can be alledg'd for the one that will not hold more strongly for the other? If the Authority of the Husband so far as it extends, is sacred and inalienable, why not of the Prince? The Domestic Sovereign is without Dispute Elected, and the Stipulations and Contract are mutual, is it not then partial in Men to the last degree, to contend for, and practise that Arbitrary Dominion in their Families, which they abhor and exclaim against in the State?

This appears to refer to an argument made by Locke on the right of resistance in §209 of Chapter 13 of the *Second Treatise*, 'Of Tyranny', a passage widely agreed to be directed at James II,[67] where Locke, drawing the analogy to the family, notes of tyrannous acts:

This is an *Inconvenience*, I confess, that *attends all Governments* whatsoever, when the Governours have brought it to this pass, to be generally suspected of their People; the most dangerous state which they can possibly put themselves in: wherein they are the less to be pitied, because it is so easie to be avoided; It being as impossible for a Governour, if he really means the good of his People, and the preservation of them and their Laws together, not to make them see and feel it; as it is for the Father of a Family, not to let his Children see he loves, and takes care of them.

Charles Leslie, in his 'Supplement', dated 25 March 1703, to *The New Association, Part II*, had given what is believed to be the first systematic commentary on Locke's *Two Treatises*.[68] There Leslie made precisely the argument against Locke that Astell makes here, drawing the conclusion that she implies:[69]

These Men whose chief *Topick* is the *Liberty* of the *People*, and against *Arbitrary Power*, are the most *Absolute* of any other in their *Families*, and so Proportionably, as they rise *Higher*. . . . And can any Believe, that a *Tyrant* in a *Family* would not prove the same upon a *Throne?* It has ever prov'd so. And I desire no other *Test* for these Publick *Patrons* for *Liberty,* than to look into their *Conversation* and their *Families.* Then let any Man *Believe* them if he *Can*; and *Trust* them, if he *please.*

The same argument was made first by Astell in the 1700 edition of *Reflections upon Marriage* and later amplified in the famous 1706 Preface:[70]

For if Arbitrary Power is evil in itself, and an improper Method of Governing Rational and Free Agents it ought not to be Practis'd any where; Nor is it less, but rather more mischievous in Families than in Kingdoms, by how much *100000* Tyrants are worse than one. What tho' a Husband can't deprive a Wife of Life without being responsible to the Law, he may however do what is much more grievous to a generous Mind, render Life miserable, for which she has no Redress, scarce Pity which is afforded to every other Complainant. It being thought a Wife's Duty to suffer everything without Complaint. If *all Men are born free*, how is it that all Women are born slaves?

Astell's famous concluding question, italicized to indicate quotation, seems to make direct reference to Locke's *Two Treatises.* The *First Treatise* had set out to rebut Sir Robert Filmer's *Patriarcha,* founded, Locke claims,[71] on two principles, the first '*That all Government is absolute Monarchy*'; the second '*That no Man is Born free*'. To the refutation of these principles the entire *First Treatise* is dedicated, while the principle that 'men are born free' is asserted in the *Second Treatise* in §§4, 22, 87, 95, 113, and so on.

Locke was by no means the only thinker of his day to make the case for liberty as a birthright, a claim renowned among the radical sects[72] and endorsed by his contemporary, Gilbert Burnet, in his 1689 tract, *An Enquiry into the Measures of Submission to the Supream Authority,* also a possible source for Astell. The most liberal of Burnet's writings and published – although probably not written – before Locke's *Two Treatises* of 1690, this work appears to be the source for Astell's later sarcastic reference in *A Fair Way with the Dissenters* to '*my Lord of Salisbury*'.[73] Burnet's work begins by specifically excluding women from the natural right to freedom enjoyed by men, allowing voluntary enslavement, also permitted by Hobbes, but denied by Astell and Locke. As Locke put it:[74]

I. It is certain, that the *Law of Nature* has put no difference nor subordination among Men, except it be that of *Children* to *Parents,* or of *Wives* to their *Husbands*; so that with Relation to the Law of Nature, all Men are born free: and this Liberty must still be supposed entire, unless so far as it is limited by Contracts, Provisions and Laws. For a Man can either bind himself to be a Servant, or sell himself to be a Slave, by which he becomes in the power of another, only so far as it was provided by the Contract: since all that Liberty which was not expressly given away, remains still entire: so that the plea for Liberty always proves it self, unless it appears that it is given up or limited by any special agreement.

What allows us to establish with more or less certainty that Astell is in fact quoting from Locke and not Burnet? In the continuation of her passage Astell incorporates further quotations from the *Two Treatises*, once again italicized. As an aside on her rhetorical question 'If *all Men are born free,* how is it that all Women are born slaves?', she comments:[75]

as they must be if the being subjected to the *inconstant, uncertain, unknown, arbitrary Will* of Men, be the *perfect Condition of Slavery?* and if the Essence of Freedom consists, as our Masters say it does, in having a *standing Rule to live by?* And why is Slavery so much condemn'd and strove against in one Case, and so highly applauded and held so necessary and so sacred in another?

Here Astell seems to be quoting from two different sections of the *Two Treatises.* The first is Book 2, §22:[76]

A Liberty to follow my own Will in all things, where the Rule prescribes not; and not to be subject to the inconstant, uncertain, unknown, Arbitrary Will of another Man.

The second is Book 2, §149:[77]

For no Man, or Society of Men, having a Power to deliver up their *Preservation,* or consequently the means of it, to the Absolute Will and arbitrary Dominion of another; whenever any one shall go about to bring them into such a Slavish Condition, they will always have a right to preserve what they have not a Power to part with; and to rid themselves of those who invade this Fundamental, Sacred and unalterable law of *Self-Preservation,* for which they enter'd into Society.

This last is the source for the passage in *The Christian Religion,* already stated, where Astell quotes from the *Two Treatises* with acknowledgement.[78] Does this mean then that Leslie takes the argument concerning the hypocrisy of advocates of liberty in the public sphere, who deny it in the private one, from Astell? Or is it merely a coincidence? If sheer density of argumentation were considered, the systematic rebuttal of Locke that Astell undertook throughout her corpus would constitute not only the first, but perhaps also the most sustained, contemporary critique of Locke's *Two Treatises,* crossing back and forth from the *Reasonableness of Christianity* to the *Essay Concerning Human Understanding,* the *Letters on Toleration* and Locke's Letters to Stillingfleet.

6. Astell's Critique of Locke: The Significance

The function of Locke's argument in the very fluid situation leading up to 1688 was not lost on Astell – it was to disentangle political obligation from dynastic allegiance and break the knot of conflicting oaths undertaken to the Commonwealth, to the Stuarts and, subsequently, to William III. The image of the highway man was perhaps unfortunate, a sign of rogue government of which Astell made the most. But dynastic uncertainty and fears of a relapse into civil war and anarchy were very real from the 1660s to the establishment of the Hanoverians. Locke and the Whigs had their own solution to the dynastic problem, which combined pragmatism and conciliation of the religious parties, a cost too high for the Tories. Locke's priority in the 1680s, the subject of recent scholarly scrutiny, had been to cut a swathe through the conflicting oaths that tied subjects to the Stuart dynasty by endorsing the right of citizens to give or withhold their consent to dynastic change. He rested his case on the eloquently expressed argument against slavery: that 'a Man, not having the Power of his own Life, *cannot* by Compact, or his own Consent *enslave himself* to any one, nor put himself under the Absolute, Arbitrary Power of another, to take away his Life, when he pleases'.[79]

Astell uses Locke's argument against him to make the case for a distinction between authority and title, on assumptions that are otherwise directly contrary to Locke on authorization, restating scholastic arguments for a distinction between authorization and designation in the capacity of the people to empower a government. These were the very arguments put to Locke by William Sherlock, on whose views Locke commented in the draft essay that has survived, as already discussed. Although Astell could not have known about this document, it gives some indication of the recycling of scholastic argument still common in the seventeenth century, with which Locke himself was charged. People may choose the person of the governor, but they cannot empower him, Astell argued. And Locke by 1690 had in fact come to agree, insisting on the oath of allegiance to William as a condition of citizenship and threatening ostracism to nonjurors or those who refused to take it. Astell, on the other side, shows Locke and the radical Whigs to have been opportunists who did not stoop to exaggerate the threats posed to the regime by those who refused to swear allegiance – ironic, given the official freedom to consent that Locke endorsed:[80]

The *Innuendo* (if one may be so bold as to unveil it) is, that Men in Office and Power, are of the same Principles of the Present *Non-jurors*, if there are any such, and minister to some Design, which we are pleas'd to fansie for them; tho' the poor Men have neither Power to Accomplish, nor if we will believe them, the Will to contrive any. But that *Innuendo* is a Calumny as ridiculous and unreasonable, as it is groundless and without any manner of Proof, scarce any Colour, but that which the good Fore-heads of the Inventors give it. Because whatever the Pretended Reasons of Revolutions may be, the true Reason is always the Change of hands; that Party which was neglected endeavouring to get into the Saddle.

In *Moderation Truly Stated*, Astell seems to trace the contours of Locke's career – at first supporter of the Anglican establishment, then, as he fell under Shaftesbury's influence, a proponent of resistance, and finally a propagandist for William III. Who but Locke made such 'a bustle about Liberty and Property' after all?[81]

And for what End and Purpose is all this ado? for what do they Rent the Church of Christ, and tear the Bowels of their Country by intestine Broils? for what but to advance themselves to gratify their Passions and their Vices! The People never get by Divisions and Revolutions, they lose their Peace and Quiet, their Money is exhausted in Taxes, and their Blood in War, only to raise a few *New Men*, and that the cunning Folks who manage all, may make their Markets. So that all their goodly Pretences of Redress of Grievances, and their bustle about Liberty and Property, have no other meaning, no other Conclusion, but their Own Advancement.

Locke was presented as the typical Whig who at all times put party and preferment over principle. Astell would seem to refer to Locke's counsels to William III when she continued:[82]

The truth is, as he can be no Friend to a Prince, who fills his Head with projects of Arbitrary Power, and carries him beyond those bounds the Laws have set him; for whether or no the People *ought* to Resist in such a Case, yet to be sure they *will*: so on the other side, he is no true Patriot who would invest the People with a Power they know not how to manage, teaching them to Mate their Superiors, and by withdrawing their necessary Subjection from their Lawful Prince, certainly tho' slily, and under the specious name of Liberty, enslaves them to a few seditious Demagogues, and Popular Haranguers.

In *The Christian Religion*, published a year later and perhaps already underway, there are frequent and unmistakable references to Locke as a party man whose politics drive his theology. In this work, in which Astell treats together *The Essay Concerning Human Understanding*, Locke's Letters to Stillingfleet on the *Essay*, *The Reasonableness of Christianity* and the *Vindication of the Reasonableness of Christianity*, Masham's *Discourse Concerning the Love of God*, the anonymous *A Ladies Religion*, and Locke's *Two Treatises*, as if all were by the same hand, she characterizes Locke as a Socinian,

an Epicurean, a party man and a defender of liberty, property, choice
and dissent. Her characterizations usually begin with a satirical denial
and then immediately proceed to assume the proposition that has been
denied. So in the very passage in which she acknowledges treating these
works indiscriminately as Locke's, she disingenuously disavows slander:[83]

§87. I do not accuse that Author of *any tang of Prepossession or Phansy; any footsteps
of Pride or Vanity; any touch of Ostentation or Ambition, any thing tending to his own
bye-interest, or that of a Party;* as if these had *tempted* him *to mix any conceits* with the
Christian Religion, or to give any wrong turn to the Faith of the Gospel. And I
hope I have not treated him otherwise than becomes a Christian, whose Charity
is the substance of what Good-breeding is only the shadow and counterfeit.

Astell betrays her great cleverness in later levying the charge against her
nameless opponent, clearly Locke, representative of the country gentleman, of 'unsufferable Insolence . . . from which even Good-breeding, the
only Religion that some People have, shou'd methinks restrain them,
if Reason and Religion do not weigh with them', thus canceling her
disavowal.[84] She openly accuses the author of the *Discourse* of tailoring
his – in fact it was Masham's – theology to his politics:[85]

every thing is not True which we find in the *Discourses* of our Modern Authors,
who not only refine upon Philosophy, by which they do Service to the World;
and upon Politicks, by which they mean to Serve their Party; but even upon
Christianity it self, pretending to give us a more *Reasonable* Account of it, by which
they mean somewhat more agreeable to their Genius and own Conveniency, for
their Systems, so far as I can find, do no manner of *Service to decaying Piety, and
mistaken and slander'd Christianity.*

Other references to the defence of liberty, property, interest, reputation,
sensibility and status are to be found in *The Christian Religion*, §§128, 180,
182 224, 239, 341 and 386.[86] At §386 Astell declares:[87] 'We think our
selves Saints if we are Zealots for a Party; and that we do GOD great
Service when we labour to make Proselytes, not to Religion but to our
Faction'. The ascription of this view to Locke seems likely from the drift
of her following remarks that ideologues are prone to idol smashing and
sacrilege, all in the name of reasonableness, to dramatize their cause.
Elsewhere Astell suggests that politicians who dared to 'dispossess Lawful
Sovereigns, who destroy GOD's Heritage, and root up the Order and Government of His Church *shall Rot*', in hell, presumably, as if she subscribed
to mortalism, which she does not.[88]

Allowing for her own partisan position, the picture that emerges
of Locke and the typical Whig in Astell's writings is a window on an

eighteenth-century Locke that, in the absence of much contemporary reference, we have been for too long lacking. It is not a pretty picture and is undoubtedly only one among many partisan portraits, but it is certainly a necessary antidote to the sanitized Locke, father of liberalism, of more recent acquaintance. The answer to the question, 'did Astell know the authorship of the *Two Treatises*?' in 1700 is probably yes. Locke's authorship was a widely circulated secret in the 1690s. Charles Leslie, to whose *The New Association*[89] Astell made reference in *A Fair Way with the Dissenters*,[90] had in the supplement to *The New Association, Part II*, dated 25 March 1703, undertaken one of the first critiques of the *Two Treatises*.[91] Earlier, Leslie had observed Locke's hand in the work of Molyneux, *The Case of Ireland's being bound by Acts of Parliament in England, Stated* (1698), which ran the Lockean argument that Irish parliaments had 'consented' to English rule by swearing allegiance to William and Mary in 1692 and 1695.[92] Astell's own use of Lockean language and metaphor of the *Two Treatises* as early as 1700, and her reuse of the same material with acknowledgement in *The Christian Religion* of 1705 along with other known works of Locke, suggest that she considered this work to be by her adversary as well.

Questions have been raised about the reasons for Astell's ceasing to write after 1709,[93] the completion date of *Bart'lemy Fair*, her critique of the *Letter Concerning Enthusiasm* (1708) by Anthony Ashley Cooper, the third Earl of Shaftesbury. Addressed to Lord Somers (whose name is not given) and occasioned by the 'French prophets', Astell pretends her work to be that of Wotton. Anthony Ashley Cooper, grandson of Locke's patron, the first Earl of Shaftesbury, had been Locke's pupil, and here too she probably saw an extension of Locke's legacy. It is my surmise that when Locke and his projects died, Astell's urge to write died with them. The Tory cause became ascendant in 1710 and no longer required such embattled defences. Only after 1714 was it to succumb to Locke and the Whigs, ultimate winners of the struggle for constitutional and historical hegemony.

Astell's position on Locke sets her apart from later feminists, Judith Drake, Catharine Macaulay and Mary Wollstonecraft, who found in his refutation of the doctrine of innate ideas hope for women's education and emancipation. But, Astell's attack on Locke notwithstanding, her reception today is in terms of a concept of freedom from domination that she shares with him. This passionate defence of liberty no more makes her a republican than it does Locke, but it does underscore her contribution to human rights. The exigencies of party politics and personal animosities based on circumstance set thinkers apart whose commitment to freedom brought them together. But in their day these differences were overriding, and indeed, no contests were more closely and bitterly fought than those over occasional conformity and toleration, which found Astell and Locke on different sides. Their metaphysics and epistemology further divided them. In the event, it was Locke's position that prevailed over the long haul, an inspiration to feminists for the possibilities of education and advancement that his empiricism and doctrine of rights opened up, while Astell was almost forgotten.

7

Astell, Drake and the Historical Legacy of Freedom

1. Freedom from Domination in the Civil Law and Natural Rights Traditions

Mary Astell had an overwhelming concern to persuade general citizens of the sanity of Tory arguments and the dangers to the public interest of theories of social contract and resistance, theories that had ever gained but limited advocacy. But new ideas were abroad unsettling to old Tory views, and it is a mark of the complexity of Astell's thought that she reflects these tendencies also. Whig arguments for specified freedoms – particularly religious toleration – to be constitutionally protected reflected the inroads made in the second half of the seventeenth century by doctrines of natural right.[1] To this Continental legal tradition belonged the great European natural rights theorists, Hugo Grotius and Samuel Pufendorf (1632–94), the former of whom Astell cites,[2] along with their English counterparts, Hobbes and Locke, whose periods spent in Europe had brought them within the orbit of the civil law tradition. Rights discourse intruded into an environment of fairly parochial English argument about the legitimacy of monarchy, where case and counter-case were typically argued in terms of British history, the ancient constitution, whether king or Parliament was the true repository of immemorial custom, claims made for English common law as a fund of equity and justice, and on behalf of the lawyer practitioners who articulated it. But it would over-simplify the position to argue that the English legal tradition had been parochial for long. As Pocock in his *Ancient Constitution and the Feudal Law* well shows, the Continental feudal law tradition had early been inserted into the debate against the common law parliamentarians. The ancient constitution lived on as a conceit, which it may always have been, against the onslaught of the rationalists, whether they be canon law proponents of popular sovereignty or Whig adherents of natural rights, whom Astell lumps together. And many conservative arguments, including those of Astell, were philosophical, not historical, grounded rather in an appeal to reason.[3]

Rights doctrines were to prove especially corrosive of Tory causes. Drawn in initially as resources in the constitutional crisis of 1688 and developed in the refinement of the Whig position, they opened a new chapter in political debate. To the extent that Astell championed the equality of women by attacking customary right as such, she worked to undermine the Tory position. The same could be said of Hobbes and Locke, although both resorted to custom to explain hard cases, in partic- ular the inferiority of married women. Astell is among the most trenchant critics of Locke and Hobbes, yet she participated in the philosophical tra- dition out of which Hobbism and Lockeanism grew. It is an historical irony that she should be best remembered as an advocate of women's rights – a term that she would never herself have used – because for Astell what passed for rights were rather the God-given entitlements that accrue to all human beings by virtue of the nature of their souls, entitlements that Christianity teaches will not be fully realized on earth.

Astell, like Drake and, later, Wollstonecraft and a number of early mod- ern feminists, was positionally situated to see that what passed for natural rights were in fact the rights of men.[4] Incorporated into society through their fathers, husbands and sons, women lived in a limbo between the state of nature and civil society, excluded from citizenship – hence the long discursus on the state of nature in Drake's *Essay*.[5] Society and the state create a systemic inequality that does not exist, in fact, in the state of nature, she argued, and they do so in the name of natural rights – as none was more forcefully to demonstrate than Jean-Jacques Rousseau half a century later. But this was a conclusion early modern women were in a position to draw. As Carole Pateman has eloquently argued:[6]

A great, but unacknowledged, insight of the feminists of the early modern period was that 'rights' were two-dimensional. The familiar civil and political rights form the first dimension. The second dimension – as both opponents of natural rights, like Astell, and advocates, like Mary Wollstonecraft in the 1790s, were aware – gave men the power of government over women, whether in marriage or in the state. Men's special rights, as I have called this dimension of 'rights', depend on the denial that women were born free, or possessed the requisite form of rationality and other capacities to take part in public and political life.

Mary Astell's reputation in the twenty-first century largely rests on her famous question whether freedom for men necessarily means slavery for women, and she is folded into the rights tradition of theorizing freedom – a tradition from which women had hitherto been more or less excluded. The latest installments of that tradition are being written by John Pocock, Quentin Skinner and Philip Pettit as chapters in the history of republicanism,[7] and Pettit uses Astell's famous rhetorical question to argue her support for republican ideals. Skinner, in particular, focuses on the transmission of certain Roman notions of positive freedom and their reception in the early modern period, endorsing as central to classical republican thought the notion of freedom as moral autonomy, or the absence of domination.[8] Freedom from a *dominus* or lord, 'freedom from servitude', as Philip Pettit puts it, is positive freedom, as opposed to the negative 'freedom from interference' that would tolerate a 'friendly master',[9] and this is the notion of freedom Astell is said to exemplify. Pettit quotes a number of early modern sources, including James Harrington in the seventeenth century, who argued tautologically: 'The man that cannot live upon his own must be a servant; but he that can live upon his own may be a freeman',[10] and *Cato's Letters*, in the eighteenth, which argued more substantively:[11]

Liberty is, to live upon one's own Terms; Slavery is, to live at the Mercy of another; and a Life of Slavery is, to those who can bear it, a continual State of Uncertainty and Wretchedness, often an Apprehension of Violence, often the lingering Dread of a violent Death.

Pettit, in a brief discussion of Astell reproducing her famous question on freedom and slavery, notes that it 'testifies to the appeal of non-domination as a feminist ideal'.[12] But Astell and her contemporary, Judith Drake, despite the centrality of the freedom–slavery antithesis to their arguments, stand in a paradoxical relation to the tradition of republicanism as Pocock, Skinner and Pettit define it. Not the least consideration is the fact that they were both royalists, addressing their works to Princess, later Queen, Anne. More importantly, given the constitutional role of the monarch as head of the established church, they understood republicanism to be a species of heresy. And they immediately saw how academic – and how hollow – the freedom–slavery argument really was in the seventeenth century, a time at which Britain was active in the slave trade abroad and in which indentured servitude annulled the freedom of many at home. The sixteenth and seventeenth centuries saw the great scholastic debates on freedom and slavery, undertaken, not coincidentally, in those very nations principally involved in slaving, the Dutch Republic, Portugal and Spain.[13]

Why, then, should the royalist Astell and her contemporary Judith Drake, by supporting a theory of freedom and equality for women, be deemed republican? It is true that they are both famous for the way they posed the freedom–slavery antithesis with respect to women. But, as we shall see, this antithesis was central to early modern, as it was to Greek and Roman, definitions of freedom, because it was the most fundamental distinction underpinning the class structure in what were slave societies.[14] Pettit notes that Machiavelli, that great early modern classical republican, 'gave pride of place to the liberty – servitude opposition', claiming in the *Discourses*, that 'men [who] are born free and not slaves' live 'without fear that [their] patrimony will be taken away from [them]', confident 'that by means of [their] abilities they can become prominent men'.[15] But we should take note that Machiavelli, that learned and percipient observer of human conduct, quickly introduced property and power as the corollary of the freedom–servitude antithesis. For *libertas* in the Roman republican tradition, even defined against the foil of slavery, did not stand alone as some abstract moral principle. It belonged rather within a range of highly contextualized legal concepts: *ius*, right; *dominium*, property; *imperium*, power – and their refinements.

Some idea of the richness of this tradition of freedom and its definitional complexities may be obtained from an examination of the context for Astell's question. There is, in fact, no better starting point for an examination of neo-republican claims than an examination of the natural rights tradition as it grew out of republican and imperial Roman law and its scholastic natural law legacy.[16] These are the tasks of this chapter, as an assessment of the significance of Astell's critique of the liberal foundations of the early modern state – for it is precisely as an alternative to liberalism that the neo-republican tradition is asserted. The Skinner–Pettit case for a peculiar nexus between freedom and republicanism suffers from the fact that it is heavily reliant on Roman historians and rhetoricians who make ambit claims in an adversarial tradition of overstatement. But to reduce republicanism to the claims for freedom of its rhetoricians is to abridge a living institutional and legal tradition in a highly abstract way. The 'best practice' arguments of rhetoricians are significant, but as a guide to institutional norms they need to be measured against outcomes. As we shall see, they do not really allow us to differentiate between republicanism and liberalism at all. Indeed, with all the refinements of Roman law and its successor, ecclesiastical natural law, stripped away, early modern republicanism is barely distinguishable from liberalism – if we may use that term to characterize the early modern tradition beginning with Locke, which placed liberty at its heart.[17] Perhaps, in fact, republicanism so denaturalized *is* liberalism, as its trajectory in the ideology of modern republics would suggest. An impressive series of women writers, including Astell, Drake and later Wollstonecraft, in major polemical works, had no compunction about exposing freedom in the liberal tradition as a sham. Such pressures, combined with the nineteenth-century German theorization of freedom as subjective right, contributed eventually to an attempt to recover some of the richness of the Roman law and natural law traditions in modern notions of natural rights as universal norms.[18] But the feminist contribution to the prehistory of modern civil society, founded on universal human rights, has hitherto received very little attention.[19]

Let us turn to the claim that early modern republicanism was indistinguishable from liberalism on the issue of freedom – a case that Skinner and Pettit explicitly deny. At the very least, we can establish that in the minds of feminist critics the difference was immaterial. What caught their eye was the fact that liberty, whether articulated by Hobbesian absolutists, Filmerian patriarchalists, Lockean liberals, Miltonian democrats or Harringtonian republicans, left everything more or less as it was. This perception was not due to general pessimism about life, because these women were for the most part impossible optimists. It was due rather to their reflection upon the important categories of *dominium*, property, and *imperium*, power, categories that the early modern treatment of the freedom–servitude antithesis conveniently ignored but without which it was meaningless. In making this case, as Astell and Drake implicitly do, Hobbes and Locke were much more significant adversaries than the proto-republicans, Milton and Harrington, if only for the reason that these women, unlike us, did not suffer from the hindsight of the Whig view of history.[20] For the likelihood of republicanism, as an institutional form defined by the absence of monarchy, winning the day seemed slight at the turn of the seventeenth and eighteenth centuries.

Let us reiterate that Astell's famous claim incorporates the precise form of words used by Locke on liberty, flagged in fact by her use of italics to indicate quotation. Locke was no republican, and this was a debate between royalists and proto-liberals. In the *Second Treatise*, Chapter 4, 'On Slavery', in answer to Robert Filmer, Locke says:[21] '*Freedom* then is not what Sir R. F. tells us, *O.A.* 55 [224]. *A Liberty for every one to do what he lists, to live as he pleases, and not to be tyed by any Laws*'. In other words, it is not the freedom from interference that we associate with that other royalist, Hobbes. Hobbes's definition of freedom as freedom from interference is a paradigm case. As we shall see, however, it is not incompatible with Roman law definitions. In Chapter 21 of *Leviathan*, 'Of Liberty of Subjects', Hobbes asserts:

LIBERTY, or FREEDOM, signifieth properly, the absence of opposition; by opposition, I mean external impediments of motion; and may be applied no less to irrational and inanimate creatures, than to rational. . . . And according to this proper, and generally received meaning of the word, a FREEMAN, *is he, that in those things, which by his strength and wit he is able to do, is not hindered to do what he has a will to.* But when the words *free,* and *liberty,* are applied to any thing but *bodies,* they are abused; for that which is not subject to motion, is not subject to impediment. . . . So when we *speak freely,* it is not the liberty of voice, or pronunciation, but of the man, whom no law hath obliged to speak otherwise than he did. Lastly, from the use of the word *free-will,* no liberty can be inferred of the will, desire, or inclination, but the liberty of the man; which consisteth in this, that he finds no stop, in doing what he has the will, desire, or inclination to do.

Given that he is a determinist, Hobbes's freedom can only be the absence of impediments. But Locke concedes free will:

Freedom of Men under Government, is, to have a standing Rule to live by, common to every one of that Society, and made by the Legislative Power erected in it; A Liberty to follow my own Will in all things, where the Rule prescribes not; and not to be subject to the inconstant, uncertain, unknown, Arbitrary Will of another Man.

Locke's definition of freedom as the absence of a *dominus* combined with rule of law has a quintessentially modern ring. It was, however, the standard definition of freedom in the Roman law tradition of *ius naturale,* or natural right. As Richard Tuck remarks, 'the ancient jurists had been unwilling to allow that men might naturally have *dominium* over other men (slaves) or goods'.[22] So, for instance, Ulpian had famously remarked that 'everyone was born free under the law of nature' – and slavery only came in with *ius gentium,* or the law of nations.[23] Like Locke, whose opening arguments follow much of the structure of Roman law glosses, the jurists maintained that under *ius naturale* all things had been held in common, but under the regimes of *ius gentium,* 'wars arose, nations became separate, kingdoms were founded, property was privatized, land enclosed, habitations were grouped together, commerce began', and so on.[24] Much of the language of Hobbes too appears to be derived from the civil law tradition. For instance, his use of the terms *civitas, dominium* and *imperium,* and his famous references to *meum* and *tuum,* all cue us to the jurists and notions of sovereignty alien to the common law tradition, to which, as a weapon in the hands of the parliamentary side of the English Civil War, Hobbes was implacably opposed.[25] It is inconceivable that a philosopher as well versed as he in Roman imperial historiography and the Patristic tradition could have borrowed this legal terminology in ignorance.[26] In England of his day, civil lawyers were still plentiful, among them his early patron Francis Bacon, and on the Continent the theories of the civil lawyers, Grotius and Pufendorf, were dominant. But little, to my knowledge, has been written on Hobbes and the civil law tradition[27] and even less on Locke, who opened the *Second Treatise* with an account of the distinct orders of power, political, paternal, despotic and matrimonial, straight out of Aristotle's *Politics*[28] but, when it came to an account of the formation of civil society, followed the Roman jurists.[29] Hobbes, in *Behemoth,* claimed to be the author of 'the science of just and unjust' as a demonstrative science, accessible to those even of the meanest capacity, stating explicitly that *Leviathan* was the text in which he set it out.[30] A project in civil education, it faced two formidable obstacles, Hobbes believed, the first being the universities, ecclesiastical and sometimes papist bastions, and the second those 'democratical gentlemen' and classical republicans dominating Parliament.[31] When he claimed that 'just and unjust' are equivalent to 'lawful and unlawful', he was not, as is frequently assumed, merely asserting a nominalist or legal positivist position. He arrived at this conclusion rather as the third term of a practical syllogism, the first term of which is that *ius*, or right, is the foundation of justice; the second, that justice only obtains among individuals in society; and the third term, or conclusion, that because justice can only obtain where *ius*, or right, has been converted into *lex*, or law, justice is therefore synonymous with lawful, injustice with unlawful. *Leviathan* was precisely an exercise in converting *jus* into *lex*, explicated in terms of theories of natural right and Roman law. This view, which I have expounded at length elsewhere, has not been argued by others, to my knowledge.

2. Republicanism and Freedom from Domination

Astell makes peculiar use of the freedom and slavery trope in *The Christian Religion*, arguing:[32]

If we are not thus Impartial, 'tis plain we are not led by the Holy Spirit of GOD, and by consequence, are not Living Members of His Son; but are Slaves to our Passions, and under the bondage of Sense and corrupt Inclinations. For *where the Spirit of the Lord is, there is Liberty*; true Liberty, which consists in making a right use of our Reason, in preserving our Judgments free, and our Integrity unspotted, (which set us out of the reach of the most Absolute Tyrant) not in a bare power to do what we Will; much less in a petulant Censuring and Judging our Governors, which is not Liberty but Licentiousness, whereby Seducers make us the Instruments of their Passions, under appearance of indulging our own. But subjection to our Passions is of all Slaveries the most grievous and ignominious; because the Mind it self puts on its own shameful yoke, and we are willing Slaves to the vilest Masters. Whereas in other cases, our Bodies only are Slaves by constraint, and perhaps to an Honourable Person, whilst the Mind may be freer than his whose Chain we wear. And therefore did not Compassion restrain one, who could help Laughing to hear a Vicious Man exclaim against Slavery, and harangue for Liberty, he himself being all the while, the most contemptible Slave! He and he only is a Freeman who acts according to Right Reason, and obeys the Commands of the Sovereign Lord of all, who has not put the Liberty of His Creatures in any ones power but in their own. And as Prejudice and the Dominion of Passion is a sign that we are not led by the Spirit of GOD, so it also deprives us of His Influence and Assistance, and prevents the Good he wou'd otherwise do us.

Here Astell expresses the conventional Christian view that freedom, like grace, is a divine gift that, mediated through the agency of reason, allows us 'to preserve our Judgments free and our Integrity unspotted'. Directed at Hobbes and Filmer, according to whom freedom is 'a bare power to do what we Will', their voluntarism, she argues, leaves the determination of the will to the passions, which 'make me a necessary, instead of a free Agent'. And here she echoes Locke, for whom a free agent is one who has the 'power to suspend any particular desire, and keep it from determining the Will'. Locke had adopted the classic Aristotelian position on voluntary and involuntary behaviour,[33] to which Astell also clearly subscribes, where appetition is checked by the power of reason as a guide, permitting deliberation to mediate between desire and action. If, in Astell's case, this guide is none other than 'the Spirit of the Lord', this simply brought her closer to Anglican orthodoxy than Locke, who placed more emphasis on the deliberative process, arguing:[34]

Examination is *consulting a guide*. The determination of the *will* upon enquiry is *following the direction of that Guide*: and he that has a power to act, or not to act according as such determination directs, is a *free Agent*; such determination abridges not that Power wherein Liberty consists.

The Christianized Stoic concept of freedom, defined as the ability to choose good over evil despite one's interests, was still pervasive, and it is this tradition that both Astell and Locke represent. For this reason, I tend to disagree with Skinner and Pettit that the master–slave analogue bespoke a general commitment to freedom from domination. Rather the opposite. Human beings were seen as bound in all sorts of ways. They were constrained by their passions, but through the agency of the redeeming Christ, they were bound to a special path to salvation. On this path, reason and will were the instruments of their moral freedom. In the political sphere, they were socially bounded by the grid of rights and duties that the familial, economic and political structures into which they were born dictated. If moral freedom ranked highest, it was a spiritual achievement that had no obvious political corollary in freedom from domination as freedom from a worldly master; for political freedom, as we find it articulated in early modern rights theory, still took the form of specific objective rights, and not 'subjective freedom', or freedom as a birthright. Only after the demonstration effect of the American and French revolutions, one might say, did 'subjective right' become a duty-worthy formula for freedom, anticipated in the theory of Jean-Jacques Rousseau but not, I believe, in that of Astell or Locke.

In this respect, one could truly say that late-seventeenth-century doctrines of rights looked back to Roman models, but not quite in the way that the theorists of classical republicanism argue. Neo-Romanism as Skinner identifies it seems to conflate two different traditions that are, admittedly, sometimes difficult to disaggregate. One is the Roman law juridical tradition and its late medieval/early Renaissance accretions in the work of the glossators and the post-glossators.[35] The other is what we think of as the Renaissance humanist tradition in general – and this had a heavily Roman component, influenced by Cicero and the Roman historians as it was. It seems to me that Skinner's neo-Roman tradition comes closer to describing Renaissance humanism – by the seventeenth century seamlessly melded to the English vernacular – than to describing classical republicanism, for the reason that it is a tradition in which republicans and monarchists, libertarians, and absolutists participate. In this respect Astell and Drake are a test for the thesis freedom from domination equals republicanism, which it fails.

The reception of the European Renaissance went in waves – roughly from its epicentre in Italy in the fifteenth century to France and the Low Countries in the sixteenth century and England mainly in the seventeenth century. To my mind Thomas Hobbes, for instance, is a classically Renaissance humanist figure, who began and ended his life translating the classics, as well as being a contributor to the new sciences, and particularly optics, after the model of Leonardo da Vinci and Galileo, the latter whom he is reputed to have met. Hobbes was a cosmopolitan, widely traveled on the Continent. As an encyclopaedic philosopher, his corpus almost exactly mirrors the contours of that of Lorenzo Valla – his model, as he more or less admits, and probably the crib, for his early translation of Thucydides – except that Hobbes also ventured into the experimental sciences. Not only did Hobbes and Valla both produce translations of Thucydides and Homer, but both published works on the problem of the will, and Valla's famous exegetical work, the *Commentary on the New Testament*, edited by Erasmus, is clearly imitated by Hobbes, who borrows some of his philological examples from Valla in the long chapters of *Leviathan* devoted to biblical exegesis.[36] Hobbes, as one who subscribed to the quintessentially humanist project of classical modeling,[37] and for whom history was an advice book according to the maxim '*historia magistra vitae*' ('history is the teacher of life'), was in many respects a transition figure between antiquity and modernity, which the label 'Renaissance' nicely captures.[38] He betrayed many neo-Roman traits in the tradition of Machiavelli and others:[39] he referred to the state as *civitas*, and he was clearly a rights theorist in the Roman law/natural law tradition. His notion of freedom as the absence of impediments might, at a stretch, even qualify as freedom from domination. But he was no classical republican.

There is no doubt that Astell and Drake were both acquainted with the neo-Roman humanist tradition, and even contributed to it in their interventions in the battle between the ancients and moderns, begun in France and transmitted to England by Wotton, Temple and Swift. But they came down on the side of the moderns precisely because of their reservations about the use to which the classics had been put. Astell, like Drake, was scathing on the way in which the classics and a classical education shut women out of public discourse, and for this reason I am sceptical of the attempt to meld Astell to the classical republican tradition.[40] That their language might be infected by neo-Roman concepts is not implausible, however, just because, by the seventeenth century, humanist thought with its heavily Latin idiom was pervasive in England. This raises two issues. First, is the definition of freedom as freedom from domination a quintessentially republican concept? And second, is this the definition of freedom to which Astell subscribed? In answer to the first question, I would say that such a definition is neo-Roman without being necessarily republican. Roman republican rhetoricians, belonging to an adversarial forensic tradition, often spoke of freedom in these broad general terms, if it is true. The same men would even be prepared to defend such ambit claims in the courts. In the Roman law tradition, freedom as a natural right (*ius naturale*) is defined as freedom from a *dominus*, or lord, but with the proviso that under the positive law regimes of nation-states (*ius gentium*) it does not necessarily obtain. Is this the meaning that Astell and Drake give freedom? I seriously doubt it, in the first place because they were not much acquainted with the Roman law or Roman republican rhetorical tradition. What they knew of it they wrote off as representing a tradition from which women were excluded. And they mercilessly ridiculed English customary law and the rights of freeborn Englishmen.

It seems to me that the claims made for the English classical republican tradition face problems that can only be resolved by disaggregating the different elements that the theoreticians conflate. The Latin formula '*liber non servus*', 'a free man is he who is not a slave', is a basic distinction regarding the law of persons as set out in the opening sentences of Justinian's *Digest*. It was implicit, but unstated, in the early law code of the Roman Republic, *The Law of the Twelve Tables*, which then went on to treat familial and patron–client relations as belonging to a grid of rights and duties that covered the free space that the freedom–slavery antithesis demarcated.[41] It is my sense that when the innumerable writers of the seventeenth century, to some of whom Astell refers, spoke of the rights of freeborn Englishmen – figures ranging from the Levellers to country Whigs like John Tutchin, for instance – what they had in mind was not freedom as the birthright of Englishmen, but rather the set of considerably restricted liberties set out in the Magna Carta – where the rights of women were at best folded into those of men. When women compared themselves to slaves, and even to slaves in the new colonies, they were simply noting that the formula *liber non servus*, which is anyhow stated in the masculine, did not apply to them, and that they therefore fell into the class of slaves – or remained in the state of nature and were 'outside' society in a different sense, as slaves to the anarchic world of unbridled passion, as the state of nature was characterized by Hobbes, for instance.

Quentin Skinner in *Liberty before Liberalism*, an elegant essay that charts the history of neo-Roman notions of liberty in early modern England, gives an impressive list of sources for the notion of freedom as freedom from domination in this period. But cutting away the rhetoric, it seems to me that his sources often argue different things. To begin with, as Skinner notes, the concept of slavery is initially discussed in the *Digest* under the rubric *De statu hominis*,[42] where clearly slavery is conceived of as a *status* rather than as the consequence of coercion, meaning that the fact of domination is a necessary but not a sufficient condition for slavery. The notion of a *status* indicates something altogether more complicated, however, describing asymmetric power relations that have been institutionalized, rather than an act, or any collection of acts, of *ad hoc* domination. The condition of slavery, which may have had its origins in violence or conquest, as a *status* designates a specific juridical condition: lack of ownership in one's person. In the *Digest* the slave is defined in fact as 'someone who, contrary to nature, is made into the property of someone else' – contrary to *ius naturale*, that is, but, once again, a practice that does not necessarily offend against *ius gentium*, or the law of particular nations.[43] Slavery put one *in the power of another*, and this was a more salient fact than the coercive exercise of domination. Seventeenth-century writers, including Hobbes, Locke and Drake, tended to talk about *dominium* or *dominion*, emphasizing an institutionalized power of ownership, rather than *domination*, the exercise of coercive force.[44] While the former can be constitutionally limited, the latter notoriously cannot. 'Freedom from domination' has been the catch-cry of revolutions that both succeeded and failed, but all of them seem to have failed in this, at least in part because it promises a psychological freedom that institutionalized hierarchies can never guarantee to deliver.

The Roman law *Digest* defined the essential feature of slavery as being *in potestate domini*, within the power of a master, but this also emphasized the institutional aspect of ownership, understood as a *status*, and did not necessarily translate into 'domination' as we understand it, or the malevolent use of power.[45] As Skinner notes, even when translated into the darker concept of *obnoxius*, or the condition of being 'perpetually liable to harm or punishment', the jurists used this term 'almost exclusively to refer to the condition of legal liability'.[46] Moreover, Roman and early modern writers, in disaggregating the free individual and the free state, at the same time broke the nexus between coercion and unfreedom, or dependence.[47] The liberty of a 'free republic' lay in institutional freedoms that it guaranteed under the rule of law and did not translate directly into the personal freedom to do as one willed. Public liberty had institutional consequences, economic, social and political, that had no necessary corollary for the individual as such. Conversely, the morality of freedom, involving the choice of good over evil, could be exercised, and most heroically exercised, even under tyranny. So, for instance, the Roman Sallust and the Florentine Machiavelli both emphasized the institutional features, conceiving of freedom as a precondition for *imperium*, which afforded state expansion and glory.[48] But Sallust, less sanguine, reflecting upon the career of the Roman consul and dictator Lucius Sulla, observed that glory abroad often meant tyranny at home,[49] an argument that English republicans like James Harrington were quick to turn against Cromwell.[50] It was a version of this argument that Astell and Drake, by applying it to the family, directed against English republicans in turn, especially Milton.

In many instances, both ancient and early modern, freedom is defined over against dependency, but usually in rhetorical or forensic contexts, and it is here that the association was made between republicanism and freedom, monarchy and tyranny. So Livy, for instance, arguing for free states, conceives of freedom as non-dependence and dependence as servitude, the condition that the Romans escaped when they rid themselves of the Tarquin kings.[51] Livy's case for republican liberty resonated with early modern English thinkers reflecting on the petty tyranny of Stuart kings.[52] Marchamont Nedham, for instance, in the Introduction to his *Excellency of a Free Nation*, referred to both Sallust and Machiavellian republican arguments, noting first, 'it is incredible to be spoken (saith Sallust) how exceedingly the Roman commonwealth increased in a short time, after they had obtained liberty', and going on to deliver a classic eulogy to the anti-monarchical republic:[53]

The Romans arrived to such a height as was beyond all imagination, after the expulsion of their kings, and kingly government. Nor do these things happen without special reason; it being usual in free states to be more tender of the public in all their decrees, than of particular interests: whereas the case is otherwise in a monarchy, because in this form the prince's pleasure weighs down all considerations of the common good. And hence it is, that a nation hath no sooner lost its liberty, and stooped under the yoke of a single tyrant, but it immediately loseth its former lustre.

Many of the early modern examples that Skinner gives of the freedom–slavery antithesis are expressions of a rhetorical strategy aimed at the royal prerogative. So, for instance, Milton, in his *Readie and Easy Way to Establish a Free Commonwealth*, claims that the subjects of monarchy live in 'detested thralldom' under 'regal bondage and the yoke of slavery', arguing the case for 'a free nation' with specific reference to Charles I's use of the veto as rendering England 'a nation enslaved'.[54] This language was used to describe the various abuses by Charles I of the royal prerogative, for instance in the case of ship money and, most signally, his attempt to arrest five members of Parliament in January 1642, which provoked Milton's excoriation in the *Eikonoklastes*:[55]

If our highest consultations and purpos'd lawes must be terminated by the Kings will, then is the will of one man our Law, and no subtletie of dispute can redeem the Parliament, and Nation from being Slaves, neither can any Tyrant require more then that his will or reason, though not satisfying, should yet be rested in, and determine all things.

In another great set piece of the *Eikonoklastes*, Milton inveighed in the name of freedom versus tyranny against Charles I's claim to the right to control the militia:[56]

As for sole power over the *Militia* . . . give him but that, and as good give him in a lump all our Laws and Liberties. For if the power of the Sword were any where separate and undepending from the power of Law, which is originally seated in the Highest Court, then would that power of the Sword be soon maister of the law, & being at one mans disposal, might, when he pleas'd, controule the Law, and in derision of our *Magna Charta*, which were but weak resistance against an armed Tyrant, might absolutely enslave us.

This is the kind of hyperbole that Astell might well have been mocking when she accused Milton of hypocrisy in failing to extend the principles he pressed against arbitrary government in the public sphere to women enslaved in marriage in the private.[57] But Milton was not alone in such polemical displays, and the case against the royal prerogative was taken up in similar terms by Harrington, who in *Oceana* asserted, in vindication of Parliament's decision to bring Charles I to trial, that to 'boast, as we doe, to be a free Nation, and not have . . . the power to remove or abolish any governour supreme or subordinat' is 'to please their fancy with a ridiculous and painted freedom, fit to coz'n babies; but are indeed under tyranny and servitude; as wanting that power, which is the root and sourse of all liberty'.[58] Algernon Sidney in the *Discourses*, in one of the most explicit statements of the freedom–slavery analogue, similarly claimed against the one-man rule of Charles I:[59]

For as liberty solely consists in an independency upon the will of another, and by the name of slave we understand a man, who can neither dispose of his person nor goods, but enjoys all at the will of his master; there is no such thing in nature as a slave, if those men or nations are not slaves, who have no other title to what they enjoy, than the grace of the prince, which he may revoke whensoever he pleaseth.

This is an argument that Lord Bolingbroke repeated in his *Dissertation upon Parties* to denounce the long leadership of Sir Robert Walpole in the 1730s. But when rhetoric and forensics are laid aside, the substantive freedoms men such as Milton, Nedham and Bolingbroke were promoting cashed out in terms of political participation and representation, liberties of the objective kind that could be constitutionally guaranteed, as compared with freedom from domination, which could not. So, for instance, Nedham in *The Excellency of a Free State* insisted that for the people to have 'real liberty', they must be 'possessed of the power' of 'enacting and repealing laws' and 'duly qualified with the supreme authority'.[60] Nedham did not consider it appropriate for 'the confused promiscuous body of the people' to participate in government directly, and in his case, like that of Milton, the question of freedom came down to the issue of representation.[61]

From the heterogeneous claims to liberty as freedom from domination that Skinner presents, it is in fact hard to extract a coherent neo-Roman theory of liberty as such. Orators like Cicero and Cato might be read this way, perhaps, but their forensic displays were in any event always with respect to the defence of specific rights justiciable in the courts. The historians, particularly Tacitus in the *Germania*, who characterized some peoples as freer than others, notably the Germans, did so to make a moral point that in fact some peoples were more disciplined, tougher or nobler than others, in individuals, a discipline, toughness or nobility that expressed their customary mares. But such a concept of freedom is neither freedom from domination nor the right to non-interference in a zone of freedom. Hobbes was the first to introduce such a spatial concept of freedom – an extension of his theories of matter in motion – with the consequence that, from this point on, freedom was conceived less as the moral enterprise of erecting a rule and following it than as the political condition of freedom from the intrusive will of others. He did so by mocking self-governing republics like Lucca, which cherished illusions of personal freedom, in an attempt once again to disaggregate freedom of the individual from freedom of the state.[62] Hobbes's conception of liberty is perhaps the best, but negative, case for an early modern neo-Roman concept of liberty, against which he personally campaigned, because he read it as the demand for constitutional liberties asserted by parliamentarians against the Crown.[63]

As Skinner himself warns, to interpret the antithesis between freedom and slavery as a case for freedom from domination risks a sort of anachronism. When it comes to citizenship, freedom from domination has never been pressed as a justiciable right, but rather more specific freedoms, such as freedom of speech, freedom of the press, freedom of assembly and so on. These freedoms, women who were not to win the vote for over a century, and despite draconian laws against seditious libel, were still in exceptional cases able to enjoy. It is ironic that Astell, who explicitly denied the right to freedom from censorship and freedom of the press, in fact was among those privileged to exercise them. The right to participate in the intense early modern political forums of debate created by the pamphlet skirmishing of 1649 and 1689, precisely centring on issues of dissent and toleration, should surely not be devalued as a form of civic freedom even where freedom from domination did not obtain – and even if we more readily associate this right with liberalism than republicanism. In any event, freedom from domination sets too high a threshold for compliance, and even today few can meet it. It would be a delusion to imagine that any of the formal freedoms we have won in fact is a guarantee against the small tyrannies and petty coercion of family life, much less against the silent coercion of the disciplined workplace, despite laws against discrimination and harassment.[64] If in the private sphere, subject to the grid of public rights and duties, the psychological freedom that such a notion promises is chimerical, there is no law proof against domination in the international system either, and we live in a world in which the sovereignty and independence of states are increasingly violated, often in the name of human rights and freedom. How can we guarantee non-dependence, given that no right to non-domination as such obtains?[65] Should we not rather settle for a definition of freedom that entails rights that are justiciable? But is this not the very heritage we associate with liberalism and its promise of toleration and civility? Casting my mind over the panoply of republics that modernity has brought into being, from the American and French republics of the eighteenth century to the social democratic, national socialist and people's republics of the twentieth, it seems to me that, like the curate's egg, they are mixed – good in parts, bad in parts, and sometimes simply awful. Their goodness or badness is less a function of their institutional arrangements as republics than it is a question of the institutionalized rights they guarantee their citizens for personal freedom, institutional representation and legal redress.

3. *Ius, Dominium* and *Imperium*: Right, Dominion and Power

The contrast between freeman and slave that Astell invokes was not just rhetorical, then. It was the language on which freedom of the subject turned in her day, as Skinner and Pettit have demonstrated.[66] It put Locke, who maintained it, in a notoriously paradoxical position. Locke endorsed the natural law principle on which the jurists were unanimous: that everyone is born free. 'For a Man, not having the Power of his own Life, *cannot*, by Compact, or his own Consent, *enslave himself* to any one, nor put himself under the Absolute, Arbitrary Power of another, to take away his life when he pleases'.[67] There is a certain strain in Locke's argument, evident in the fact that he bases this principle on the consideration that 'No body can give more Power than he has himself', which he then translates into the weakened form: 'he that cannot take away his own Life, cannot give another power over it'. Having denied the right of suicide, on the one hand, he immediately concedes it, on the other, as the only expression of freedom the slave enjoys: 'For, whenever he finds the hardship of his Slavery out-weigh the value of his Life, 'tis in his Power, by resisting the Will of his Master, to draw on himself the Death he desires'. As Astell surely observed, there was not much comfort here for men who are naturally born free – a cautionary tale for women who are not! Furthermore, Locke's *Fundamental Constitutions of Carolina* (1675), §CX, Locke, *Works* ([1693] 1823), Vol. 10, 175,[68] had concluded with the declaration that every freeman 'shall have absolute power and authority over his negro slaves'. This document, which comprised a plan to transplant European-style feudalism to America, establishing eight lords proprietors as a hereditary nobility with absolute control over their serfs, called 'leet-men', expressly designed, as stated in the preamble, to 'avoid erecting a numerous democracy' in Britain, is evidence enough that Locke's concept of freedom as ownership in one's own person, if it applied at home, did not apply abroad. Its provisions included the following explicit violations of his generally accepted principle that ownership in one's person could not be compromised by hereditable obligations of status or servitude, and did not even allow manumission.

XIX: Any lord of a manor may alienate, sell, or dispose to any other person and his heirs forever, his manor, all entirely together, with all the privileges and leet-men there unto belonging.

XXII: In every signory, barony and manor, all the leet-men shall be under the jurisdiction of the respective lords of the said signory, barony, or manor, without appeal from him. Nor shall any leet-man, or leet-woman, have liberty to go off from the land of their particular lord, and live anywhere else, without license from their said lord, under hand and seal.

XXIII: All the children of leet-men shall be leet-men, and so to all generations.

From another point of view Locke was lamentably consistent, maintaining after the jurists that slavery, intolerable under *ius naturale*, where everyone was born free, came in with *ius gentium*, which saw wars, slavery and so on. His appeal to natural law principles to rule out voluntary slavery, by contract, which Hobbes had endorsed, was nevertheless weak, as his formulation demonstrates, if for no other reason than that the law of nature no longer has teeth. The notion of consent, pivotal in the marriage contract–social contract analogue on which he relies, is not the only casualty of his theory. The gravest injury is that dealt to freedom. By historicizing *ius naturale*, Locke made a mockery of liberty as freedom from domination. His empty protests that *ius gentium* should ensure the enjoyment of life, liberty and property as an extension of legal personality meant freedom for men, patriarchy for women and slavery for leet-men, as both Astell and Drake immediately saw.

There are no arguments from nature and none from experience that would support the subordination of women, Drake insisted. The issue is rather one of power, '*Women* [are] *industriously kept in ignorance*' out of fear and by means of tyranny, she claims: 'For nothing makes one Party slavishly depress another, but their fear that they may at one time or other become Strong or Couragious enough to make themselves equal to, if not superiour to their Masters. This is our Case.'[69] Drake follows Astell in arguing that men, having enslaved women, then require them to love their chains:[70]

and consequently make them tamely give up their Liberty, and abjectly submit their Necks to a slavish Yoke. As the world grew more Populous, and Mens Necessities, whetted their Inventions, so it increas'd their Jealousie, and sharpen'd their Tyranny over us, till by degrees, it came to that height of Severity, I may say Cruelty, it is now at in all the Eastern parts of the World, where the Women, like our Negroes in our Western Plantations, are born slaves, and live Prisoners all their Lives.

The notorious East is not alone in enslaving women in this way: 'Nay, so far has this barbarous Humour prevail'd, and spread in self, that in some parts of *Europe*, which pretend to be most refin'd and civiliz'd, in spite of Christianity, and the Zeal for Religion which they so much affect, our Condition is not very much better'. And Drake takes as an example France, 'a Country that treats our Sex with more Respect than most do', but where women are nevertheless 'by the *Salique Law* excluded from Soveraign Power'.[71] This is another case of tyranny bred of fear, Drake argues, fear that women on the throne 'would favour their own Sex, and might in time restore 'em to their Primitive Liberty and Equality with the Men, and so break the neck of that unreasonable Authority they so much affect over us'.[72] In England the situation was more insidious for being less transparent, 'since our Sex can hardly boast of so great Privileges, and so easie a Servitude any where as in *England* . . . tho' Fetters of Gold are still Fetters, and the softest Lining can never make 'em so easy, as Liberty'.[73]

It is unlikely that Astell or Drake was much acquainted with natural law principles in the Roman law tradition, although they were familiar enough with their seventeenth-century historicized versions in the form of state of nature arguments. Both women immediately grasped the fallacy of arguing from facts to values, the genetic fallacy exemplified so fully in Filmer's patriarchalism.[74] They both focused on the customary manners and mores by which women were subordinated under *ius gentium* without possibly ever having heard the term. The transition from objective natural rights theory of positive law to a subjective understanding of rights as pertaining to the human subject was made, I believe, under these sorts of pressures. The law of nations, divorced by history from natural law as a universal norm with the abolition of the ecclesiastical courts and the sequestration of the Roman law tradition, presented obvious arbitrariness and glaring injustices, which these women immediately saw.

Astell's rhetorical cry resounded. And it was indeed rhetorical just because she denied Locke's claim to property in one's person, a claim that in his day applied only to men. In Locke this right is crucially important in the negative: as the incapacity of individuals to incur hereditable impediments to their freedom or voluntarily to enter into slavery. Since Astell denied property in one's person, vouched for in Locke by the right of real property (a right to which women were denied), she could not technically argue the slavery of women compared with the freedom of men. Astell believed all creatures were God's possessions. On the issue of freedom she took a different tack, appealing to the equality of woman as mind rather than body along Cartesian lines. The domestic enslavement of women offended against Christian principles of the equality of all believers, but it referred more to souls than to bodies. Astell dared Locke and Milton to apply in the domestic sphere the criteria to which kings were forced to submit in the public: resistance to tyranny. But she did so satirically, knowing that they could not respond. For all that she derided the marriage contract–social contract analogue as the merest fiction – but one that justified the enslavement of women as it did the subordination of subjects – Astell herself subscribed to a Christian view of natural hierarchies on earth that only heaven could efface.

Her successors did not show the same reticence, however, generalizing Locke to produce a claim for subjective rights – or rights pertaining to the subject as a birthright. They read Astell literally: If all men are born free, how is it that all women are born slaves? And they answered with a critique of prevailing manners and mores as aberrations from a Christian norm. Judith Drake is, as we have seen, a very good case. Drake takes seriously the comparison between slaves and married women that for Astell can only be rhetorical, likening the condition of wives in the East, and increasingly in Western countries, with that of 'our Negroes in our Western Plantations'. If Astell's rhetoric had a double edge – on the one hand, a plaintive resignation to the quietism of Christian teaching, on the other, a rebellious protest at the indignity of subordination – Drake's biting satire made no such concessions to Christian hierarchies. Her claim for the right to equal education, her cost–benefit analysis of the resource inefficiency involved in educating only one-half of the human race, and her account of the contribution to society of women intellectuals despite the lack of a formal education system are all worthy of Astell. But in Drake's case, like that of Wollstonecraft after her, they are directed at claiming equality for women as a right that attaches to the human subject. In Astell's, by contrast, these are provisions to improve the female soul, as worthy of perfectibility through education and the life of the mind as that of any man.

Slavery is an organizing theme of Wollstonecraft's *Vindication of the Rights of Woman* (1792), as the legal expression of unfreedom exemplified in its most extreme form in colonial slavery.[75] But even Wollstonecraft is closer in spirit to Astell, in her emphasis on freedom as primarily instrumental for duty and virtue as final goods, than she is to the notion of freedom as non-domination *tout court*. It is true that she refers to the 'enslaved state of the labouring majority', and to marriage as enslavement, even where subjection of the wife is to a benevolent master. As Lena Halldenius notes: 'Female subjection is not a special case, but a token of the type: liberty-loss through enslavement'.[76] Virginia Sapiro has commented on the degree to which Wollstonecraft's *Vindication of the Rights of Women* is in fact about virtue and duties, rather than rights, to which Halldenius responds by noting that for Wollstonecraft, where there are no rights there can be no duties.[77] She points out that the logic of Wollstonecraft's question 'Why . . . expect virtue from a slave?' is to point out the immorality of ascribing duties to those denied rights.[78] Such a grid of corresponding rights and duties belongs, however, to the Roman law conception of objective rights, and not to the modern conception of subjective rights ushered in by Rousseau. It is significant, for instance, that in the initial debates on the protocols of the United Nations Charter of Human Rights, both the Spanish and French had argued that without a corresponding schedule of duties there could logically be no schedule of rights – the legacy of a pre-modern conception of rights that has now been lost.

The story of the transition from objective to subjective rights is really the story of German jurisprudence and the contributions of Kant, Fichte and Hegel. Rousseau's famous protest, 'Man is born free and everywhere he is in chains',[79] coming a full fifty years after that of Astell, marks a step in the transition. Rousseau, who willingly admitted his debt to Locke and Hobbes, was explicitly republican on the Roman model, but the texture of his argument does not differ significantly from that of these forebears.[80] The radical rhetoric of his *Discourse on the Origins of Inequality*, which gives way in *The Social Contract* to the language of constitutionalism, in fact departs little from natural law theory. Rousseau's state of nature in both works represents an historicized *ius naturale*, exited by means of the social contract for the regime of *ius gentium*, or the state of civil society. In the *Second Discourse*, it is true, the primitive condition of mankind in which the writ of natural law runs much more closely resembles the classical golden age of the Stoics, the Epicurean Lucretius and Ovid. These were classical sources for linear theories of social and technological development that charted human progress from the state of nature to a gradually evolving and institutionally more complex civil society. Such theories had an ancient pedigree, first of all in the pre-Socratic Democritus, in Plato himself, and in the Hellenistic Chrysippus and Epicurus.[81] But they were most fully developed in the work of the Roman Stoics and Epicureans, notably in Seneca's *Ninetieth Letter* on progress and Lucretius' *De Rerum Natura*.[82]

It is worth noting that modern natural rights theory represents yet another attempt to inject into the law of nations natural law principles as a universal norm. Germany, which could at once be the seat of the Holy Roman Empire, could also adapt Roman law to local conditions. Gilmore has observed the apparent ease with which the Germanic peoples took over the precepts of the Roman jurists as their own.[83] And in Wilsonian democracy and the protocols of the United Nations, these principles have had another run, this time in international law. Given the ease with which the American founding fathers, like the Germans, melded Roman law to indigenous common law traditions, it is perhaps not surprising that the rhetoric of natural law should have resurfaced with Woodrow Wilson. The great revolutions, namely the American, French and Russian revolutions, are often seen as the triumph of subjective right, but the American and French actually took place before the transition had been fully made, and one still sees traces in the eighteenth century of objective rights to specific entitlements and positive law preoccupations. The human rights protocols of the League of Nations, and subsequently of the United Nations, represent, at least at one level, an attempt to make subjective rights justiciable in the Roman law tradition. And with a large measure of success if one considers the force of human rights rhetoric in the late twentieth century and experiments with international war tribunals.[84]

4. Towards a Subjective Concept of Freedom and Universal Human Rights

It is not difficult to show that the notion of liberty which Pettit and Skinner identify as freedom from a *dominus,* or lord, had a firm footing in Roman law, but with an important proviso that applies also to Locke. And this is that the jurists' concept of rights was still, despite the rhetoric, objective rather than subjective. It concerned specifications of positive law justiciable in the courts. Even property in one's person, defined as *persona sui iuris,* was 'corporeal' and not 'incorporeal', the aggregate of a sum of positive rights and duties and not subjective, a birthright attaching to the subject *sui generis.* It was, I think, in the logic of the *ius naturale–ius gentium* distinction to see the latter as a set of conventions that assigned specific objects to specific persons in an interlocking web that covered the civil space. It is for this reason that Locke moves so quickly from the assertion of one's property in one's own person to the labour theory of value, with no discussion of the metaphysical or ethical dimensions of personal autonomy beyond the issue of slavery. And it is also why, I believe, Milton and Locke both proclaimed freedom for men from the housetops, yet felt they could assign the subordination of women to convention, as if that settled the matter. Rights were specific conventions mapping the boundaries of social interaction, rather like modern torts, and they could be expected to have a certain arbitrariness about them.

The real arrival of the subjective notion of freedom awaited Kant, Hegel, von Humboldt and German legal theory of the nineteenth century.[85] But it had harbingers in the critiques of Astell and Drake. For, as Astell and her followers intuitively grasped, Hobbes and Locke, by historicizing *ius naturale,* had, intentionally or not, relocated slavery in the private sphere.[86] Women, and particularly married women, were quite simply deemed natural slaves, a condition to which they were consigned by liberals and republicans alike. That they arrived there by contracting out of freedom in the single state only compounded the injustice. Deprived of the right to own property until the various married women's property acts of the 1880s, European and transatlantic married women lacked legal personality because of the terms in which this was defined. As we have seen, there was always an intimate relationship between freedom and property ownership, as there was between *dominium* and *imperium*. If property was the objectification of personality according to Locke, it was also the field in which legal personality has free play, a position endorsed later by Hegel.

Hegel, in the *Philosophy of Right*, devotes Part 1, Subsection 1, to property as the objectification of personality, 'characterized as subjective individuality in opposition to the universal'.[87] Beginning from the Stoic standpoint of freedom of the will, he treats possession as the moment at which freedom of the will becomes objective to the subject, so that 'property, acquires the character of private property'.[88] Devoting considerable space to Roman law and distinctions between *proprietas, dominium directum* and *dominium utile* in Justinian's *Institutes*,[89] Hegel in §169 claims: 'The family, as person, has its real external existence in property; and it is only when this property takes the form of capital that it becomes the embodiment of the substantial personality of the family'.[90] Hegel was harshly critical of Roman law on the point of the enslavement of children, although, characteristically, he had nothing to say about the position of wives: 'One of the blackest marks against Roman legislation is the law whereby children were treated by their father as slaves. This gangrene of the ethical order at the tenderest point of its innermost life is one of the most important clues for understanding the place of the Romans in the history of the world and their tendency towards legal formalism'.[91]

The condition of married women, who were passed by the marriage contract, as an instrument of legal conveyance, from father to husband, was clearly one of servitude in the eyes of a succession of early feminist theorists. What held them in thrall was an entrenched distribution of power that excluded women from public life but enabled men to translate their public power into private leverage, allowing them to rule their families as tyrants. And it was precisely for condoning this arrangement that Astell pilloried Milton and Locke, republican and liberal alike. If Hobbes and Locke may be seen as yet another phase in the reception of Roman law, historicizing the distinction between the law of nature and the law of nations by means of the social contract, the paradoxical result was, as stated, to consign subjects to the regimes of *ius gentium* without appeal to natural law. What this meant, as radical critics saw,[92] was to create of the state a mythical public sphere in which the writ of natural law still ran, and where men were free and equal creatures, while allowing the

arbitrary inequalities of *ius gentium*, or statutory law, to flourish unabated
in the private sphere. For the force of the distinction between *ius naturale* and *ius gentium* always lay in the contrast between the laws of natural
reason and the contingency and arbitrariness of national law. It was this
arbitrariness, and the injustices to which it gave rise under the law of particular nations, that ensured that the law of nature would always remain
at best a residual norm, and not an active court of appeal. The sleight
of hand by which Hobbes and Locke, under the social contract – and in
the wake of the dissolution of the ecclesiastical courts – consigned subjects to *ius gentium* was not lost on Astell or her successors. The upshot
was to transfer to women the status of natural slavery so famous from
Aristotle.

The works of Astell and Drake are a healthy reminder that, as the
Roman law tradition tells us, *ius* and *dominium* were always hedged about
by *imperium*. The rise of civil society, predicated on a public–private split,
appeared to create a zone of freedom in the public sphere. If, given the
realities of political power, this freedom could in fact be realized, which
is doubtful in the period that Pocock, Skinner and Pettit take as their
best case – the early modern British state – inhabitants of the private
sphere were for the most part worse off. Whatever freedom men enjoyed
in the public sphere gave them more leverage in the private, where they
tyrannized over families. This was not accidental but systemic. Astell, by
singling out the works of Milton and Locke as the *locus classicus* of the
freedom fallacy, saw that in this respect it mattered little whether the
thinker in question was a liberal, a republican or an absolutist like Hobbes.
From the perspective of those worst off, women and children, the whole
enterprise – to use a deliberate anachronism – was like shuffling chairs
on the decks of the *Titanic*.

Astell's claim that if all men are born free all women are born slaves
may not be empirically defensible. It is questionable whether, given the
denaturalization of freedom as a universal norm under the pressure of
liberal theory, and the decline of the ecclesiastical courts where natural law was justiciable, anyone in Britain in this period really enjoyed
freedom from domination and whether, if we read domination as the
constraint of a master, even a friendly master, they enjoy it yet. As Hegel,
in his famous critique of the English parliamentary reform bill of 1832
remarked, unwritten constitutions lack transparency and hand over to the
lawyers and the courts the whole issue of civil rights. Perhaps, as Astell
and Drake suggest, the very seductiveness of discourse on the ancient
constitution,[93] the rights of freeborn Englishmen under the Magna Carta

and invocation of the classical republican tradition were in fact impediments to liberty. Polemical but academic traditions of discourse, they
created an ideological climate that permitted a form of liberty to flourish
that could tolerate the worst excesses of the class system and the rele-
gation of married women to the status of legal minors. Republicanism,
understood in its other sense, as abolition of the monarchy and the substitution of a republican written constitution, may hold some hope for
reforms that guarantee greater freedom and more transparency in government. But this would be institutional republicanism of a type that most
early modern women could not imagine.[94]

But this was no mere failure of imagination. One has to credit early
modern thinkers with the subtlety they deserve and a sensibility about
their environments that we can never hope to recover. One of the most
offensive aspects of modern conceptions of civil society and the state – if
it is not plain ridiculous – is the way in which it reduces the complexity of
political arrangements to a simple binary abstraction – and here, I believe,
we have a lot to learn from conservative political thought and in particular
that of Michael Oakeshott.[95] Curiously enough, Oakeshott's critique of
social engineering and the sanctimoniousness of political utopianism,
which rides roughshod over centuries'-old, fine-tuned social arrangements on the ground, finds a substantive convergence in elements of
Karl Marx's critique of the myth of the state. *Étatism*, one might say, has
become a modern religion, or at least a substitute for religion, just as Marx
diagnosed[96] – and Marxism too suffered the fate of becoming a religion,
and an apocalyptic and particularly terrible one at that.[97] The first commandment of *étatism* of the liberal-democratic variety is the separation of
civil society and the state – along the lines of the separation of church
and state – and modern societies pass the test of modernity or not according to whether they meet this requirement. If not, they are candidates
for 'modernization' and 'forced to be free' – with consequences that the
utopian Rousseau, luckily for him, could never possibly have foreseen.
As a German philosopher with a surprisingly sensitive anthropological
nose, Marx provided an analysis of the myth of the state precisely in
terms of the obfuscation of the civil society–state distinction, which modern policy makers seem compelled to revalidate day after day in country
after country, either in ignorance of the perspicacity of Marx's analysis
or because of an unwillingness to heed its wise warning. Nation after
nation is being dragged by its bootstraps (to use Marx's language) into
a modernity marked by the sterility and *ennui* that only a policy of social
engineering based on futile abstractions could be calculated to produce.

Nomadic societies, Islamic societies, Latin societies and all those forms of human life dedicated to living 'uneconomically', or on the terms they choose, for whatever uneconomical reasons they choose them – if this is not already too voluntarist a way to frame ways of life that are the products of millennia of small and inadvertent choices! – are threatened with the dreadful leveling of modernity and its juggernauts.

And if this statement smacks of the apocalyptic against which I inveigh, make no mistake. There is nothing new about the project of modernity at all. It is a process of cultural transformation involving the technology transfers at which hegemons are adept.[98] (Discussions of *imperium* and *ius* are never innocent: if there is no smoke without fire, there is no *imperium* without a hegemon!) Forcing people to be free was a program for which the Romans were particularly renowned and they did it, cleverly, in the name of the Greeks. It was the 'freedom of the Greeks' that they forced upon the citizens of Egypt and Asia Minor, and we cannot doubt that there were eventual benefits to citizens reorganized in town councils under democratic constitutions and a remote *imperium*, even if these reforms were not freely chosen.[99] Human institutions are like the curate's egg, and given enough time, human beings can take nourishment from the good parts. Moreover, technological constraints did not allow hegemons of the past to reach down into a society to achieve its purification to the degree to which modern hegemons are capable. By the same token, constraints of communication and transportation did not admit of 'ethnic cleansing' in the modern sense either. Ancient peoples were more or less forced to get along with their neighbours whom they lacked the technological means to remove, except by genocide, to which they sometimes dreadfully resorted.

Oddly enough, or perhaps not oddly at all if one thinks about it carefully, some early modern thinkers were surprisingly attentive to the sort of prospective critique that characterizes Marx's critique of the liberal-democratic state; and sometimes their worst nightmares ran to apocalyptic outcomes. Astell herself could strike a stridently apocalyptic tone, and not just because she lived in an apocalyptic age. One has to try to imagine how much Anglicanism and the Stuart social order meant to a theologically serious woman who lived under the perennial political instability induced by the Civil War and its aftermath, and who personally escaped being made socially *déclassé* by political and economic forces beyond her control only by her writings. She was not alone; literary theorists have noted that the early modern novel, often the work of women, gained its universal edge by intimations of a wider imperial world, a foil for the microcosms it described that somehow enhanced them, suggesting the fragility of 'the world of small things' by hinting at the menace of the international system of states.[100] At the same time, visions of empire provide vistas of hope, a larger-than-life canvas on which to paint the small intimacies of the lived world. Jane Austin, whose brother served in the Royal Navy, providing a personal link to the world of empire, is of course the classic example.[101]

It may go deeper. Writing is sometimes an existential act for individuals who can only cope with the instability and menace of the external world by writing it out, so to speak. But for individuals dedicated to understanding their life-worlds by description and itemization of the particulars of which they are constituted, turning them this way and that to see how they might look under a different light, the application of theoretical abstractions provides no help.[102] To the contrary, such thinkers could be extraordinarily attentive to cant and puff, just because in their practice they daily faced rhetorical strategies designed to obscure and obfuscate the durable realities with which they were struggling. Mary Astell was one of these peculiarly *sensible* thinkers – and here I use the term in its European form to elide Jane Austin's curiously local distinction between 'sense' and 'sensibility'. Largely due to the environment in which she operated, Astell just so happened to confront the liberal-democratic myth of the state at the moment of its formation. With a pamphleteer's ear for rhetoric, she set about to deflate proto-Whig universalist democratic claims for 'the rights of freeborn Englishmen' as just so much cant in a world in which most people enjoyed nothing that resembled freedom in their everyday lives. By the logic of Hegel's master–slave parable[103] – if one may dare – and as a woman, from that half of the human race entrusted with making sure that life goes on while men make history,[104] she was particularly outraged at the way in which Whigs could transgress against church and state in the name of a freedom they refused to concede in the world in which most people lived: the family.

High-minded folly is all about us. One of its most amusing forms, to my mind, is the attempt to redeem the apparent incongruousness of Astell's High Church Tory feminism by making her a proto-republican, thus making a silk purse out of a sow's ear. But classical republican theory, when indiscrimately applied, is simply a further theoretical abstraction that perpetuates the myth of the state – by specification. I am mindful of the sensible remarks by Noel Malcolm on the efforts of historians to view the European Enlightenment Republic of Letters as an exercise in creating 'civil society' or the 'public space'. Malcolm, in his excellent essay

'Hobbes and the European Republic of Letters', observing that 'modern studies of the Republic of Letters tend to read back into the seventeenth century those ideological descriptions of it that they find in the writings of the Republic's spokesman in the early eighteenth', goes on to comment on a magnificent case of the historicist self-fulfilling fallacy.[105]

These are then combined with a curiously teleological version of Jürgen Habermas's argument about the emergence of a 'public space', to create the impression that from an early stage the participants in the Republic were striving to establish a quasi-political entity, a public realm over and against the State. The very use of the term 'Republic', harped on by early eighteenth-century publicists such as Jean Le Clerc and Pierre Desmaizeaux, seems to encourage this. . . . It is true that some writers in the sixteenth and seventeenth centuries did make use of the political connotations of 'respublica' in the phrase 'respublica literaria'; but they usually did so ironically, often self-deprecatingly, to emphasize the *non*-political nature of the world of scholars, its detachment from the political – and confessional – world. . . . The 'public' my scholars cared about was each other. . . . If 'ideology' is a system of justification for politics, then the ideology of the seventeenth century Republic of Letters was a peculiarly negative one, an ideology of the non-political.

Redemption by republicanism piles irony upon irony in Astell's case, given that it is the very pretentiousness of republican puff against which she is inveighing. Rhetorical strategies like the melding of Whig purposes to the grand strategies of the Roman Republic – which indulged in just such rhetorical strategies in the name of an aggrandizing oligarchy itself – were not lost on Mary Astell, herself an adept at the rhetoric of the Grubb Street gutter press.[106] Once again there is nothing strange about all this, nor does it bespeak fundamental bad faith on the part of republicans, who ride a hobby horse that is normatively privileged, usually for the best of all possible reasons.

The search for institutional solutions to the human predicament is fraught with paradox that arises from the endless capacity of individuals to outwit institutions and of institutions to betray their purposes. And perennial hope makes all of us vulnerable to utopianism, which is the modern form of religiosity that redemption-by-institutions takes. One of the nice sides to the story of historical contingency is that history can sometimes outwit us. (By this I mean that the lived world sometimes transgresses in a grand way against the abstractions we have created to frame our life-worlds – abstractions such as the public–private and civil society and the state!) The history of early modern women is part of that story. Lacking formal education and legal standing, some of them nevertheless carved out for themselves a public role, participating in the dominant philosophical and political discourse that sought to exclude them. Mary Astell is one of them. Her contribution to the print debate that surrounded the constitutional battle over toleration and dissent in Britain, one of the most vigorous and democratic of early modern political debates, to judge by the sheer volume of pamphlets and their provenance, was among Astell's signal public achievements – and we do not need to create a vacuous public sphere to dignify it. Her contribution to the critique of morals and mores surrounding women's education and marriage was another. Her role in the reception of Descartes and the Platonist philosophical debate that met the challenges of Hobbes and Locke is of great importance, not only in the history of early modern philosophy, but for the philosophical underpinnings it provided to Anglicanism, of which she was a most dedicated advocate.

Provoked by the apparent paradox of her persistent feminism compatible nevertheless with High Church Toryism, I have tried to recover the contexts for Astell's thought, divided as it is among philosophical, theological, political and literary genres. This study is a companion to the editions of her writings that I have already completed in the hope that she will reach a new and wider public in the new millennium. Among the considerable number of early modern women philosophers, dramatists, novelists and pamphleteers whose work is being revived, Astell is surely one of the most profound, as well as being a high stylist of the English language. But this study is not simply a tribute to individualism and the capacity of exceptional figures to surprise us. In important ways it discloses institutional paths, some of which were lost as historical contingencies forked and branched. It addresses the perennial hope of freedom, in particular, and some of the many and subtly different ways this aspiration is imagined, as well as the social and institutional frustrations to its realization.

Appendix

Glossary and Select Biographical Notes

Arminianism. The doctrines of Jacobus Arminius (1560–1609), Dutch Reformed student of the Genevan Calvinist Theodore Beza (1519–1605), as formulated by his followers in the Remonstrance of 1610, had made the following modifications to Calvinist doctrine: Christ died for all men, not just the elect; his saving mission is God's most important work on earth; the individual is involved in his/her own salvation through free will; consequently, through dereliction of duty, the individual may fail to be saved. Aimed at the heart of Calvinist doctrines of predestination of the elect, Arminianism was publicly debated at the Sydnod of Dort of 1618–19, summoned to condemn it. Arminian doctrines were declared inadmissible or heretical, and the Arminians were given the choice of recantation or exile. Although they were viewed as radical reformers, their advocates were also leaders of the established church, such as Archbishop William Laud. However, this did not prevent them from being accused of popery. Laud, who stressed the importance of church ceremony, was thought to be a Roman sympathiser.

Atterbury, Francis (1662–1732), Tory Bishop of Rochester, was made chaplain to King William and Queen Mary even though he was regarded as controversial for his opposition to state ascendancy over the church and his strong advocacy of the rights of the clergy. Queen Anne made him her chaplain in ordinary and, in 1704, Dean of Carlisle. Atterbury had been an active participant in the lower-house convocation assemblies, and he soon became almost as prominent in the House of Lords. In 1713 he was made Bishop of Rochester and Dean of Westminster. Atterbury ended his life as a Jacobite, was imprisoned in the Tower in 1722 for his alleged role in the attempt to restore the Stuart line, and was found guilty, stripped of all his ecclesiastical offices and banished forever from the realm. He entered the service of James II's son, the old Pretender, in Paris. However, James did not treat him well, and in 1728 Atterbury retired to the south of France, where he later died.

Baxter, Richard (1651–91), was a Presbyterian divine. Ordained in 1638, he took neither a clearly conformist nor non-conformist stance. In 1641 he was made lecturer (preacher) in Kidderminster in Worcester. When the Civil War erupted in 1643, the people of Worcester sided with the king, while Baxter sided with Parliament, and he was driven out of Worcester. In Coventry he officiated as chaplain to both the towns-people and soldiers. He said of the Civil War that 'both sides were to blame . . . and I will not be he that will justify either of them.' In 1647 he retired from his duties as army chaplain due to ill health. He returned to Kidderminster and resumed his prolific writings. In 1660 he went to London as one of the king's chaplains, but retired from the Church of England on the passing of the Act of Uniformity, and suffered much ill treatment under Charles II and James II. When the tumult of the Restoration was past, he left London and continued to write and preach until he was jailed along with other non-conformists. He was released in 1686 after serving around eighteen months, and in 1688 pursued his lifelong principles by entering enthusiastically into the coalition of Protestant dissenters and the clergy of the Church of England against the Catholic James II. Mary Astell, in *Moderation Truly Stated* (1704, 71), referred to the 'godly Mr. *Baxter*' as an Occasional Conformist: 'one of those *Moderate Dissenters*, that . . . *sometimes receiv'd the Lord's Supper in the Communion of the Church of England*'.

Berkeley, George (1685–1753), Bishop of Cloyne, in Ireland, philosopher and polymath, as a young man in Dublin formed a society of 'new philosophy' with some friends to study the works of Descartes, Hobbes, Locke, Malebranche, Leibniz and Newton. His early works were compared with those of Norris and Malebranche, but on moving to England in 1713, he became associated with the 'wits', Steele, Addison and Pope.

Binckes, William (d. 1712), Dean of Lichfield, was educated at St. John's College, Cambridge, and graduated with an M.A. in 1678. He was made prebendary of Lincoln in 1683, and of Lichfield in 1697, and took the degree of D.D. in 1699. He is most known for his commemorative sermon, to which Mary Astell makes reference in *An Impartial Enquiry* (16/146).

Bolingbroke, Henry St. John (1678–1751), Eton and Oxford educated, entered Parliament in 1701, joined the Tory Party, and became prominent as an orator. In 1712, he was called to the House of Lords with the title of Viscount Bolingbroke and, against the wishes of nearly the entire nation, concluded the Peace of Utrecht in 1713. Having previously quarreled with his old friend Robert Harley, now the Earl of Oxford and his most powerful rival, he contrived his dismissal in July 1714. Bolingbroke immediately proceeded to form a strong Jacobite ministry, prompted by the inclinations of his royal mistress. The accession of George I was a death blow to Bolingbroke's political prospects; he was deposed from office and in March 1715 fled to France. For some time he held the office of secretary of state to the Pretender, but after an unsuccessful attempt to return to British politics by obtaining a royal pardon, he retired to a small estate that he had purchased near Orleans.

Boyle, Robert (1627–91). Boyle, a prominent member of the Royal Society, advanced the inductive reasoning of Francis Bacon to focus on a philosophy that he called 'new, corpuscularian, atomical, Cartesian or Mechanical', which was built on two foundations: 'reason and experience'. He is best known for the discovery, arrived at through detailed experimentation, that the volume of a gas is inversely proportional to its pressure, known as 'Boyle's law'. Boyle was among the group of seventeenth-century 'Virtuosi', a term used by Astell to describe men of leisure who used their free time to engage in an esoteric examination of nature. But in *The Christian Virtuoso* (1690–1) Boyle redefined the term to describe a person who is interested in the investigation of natural science. The Christian Virtuoso is one who is 'dispos'd to make use of the knowledge of the Creatures to confirm his Belief, and encrease his Veneration, of the Creator'. Boyle's early work, based on his knowledge of the original biblical languages (in addition to Latin, Aramaic, Syriac, French and Italian), expressed his concern for a proper English translation that would result in a proper communication of the sense of the Hebrew and Greek texts. This, in turn, would encourage people to study the Bible for themselves. Astell referred to Robert Boyle's *Some Considerations Touching the Style of the Holy Scriptures* (1661) in a marginal note to *A Serious Proposal, Part II*, 226/208.

Burnet, Gilbert, Bishop of Salisbury (1643–1715), born in Edinburgh, and educated at Marischal College, Aberdeen, was pivotal in the cause of William III and toleration. In 1661 he had been made probationer of the Scottish church, visiting England in 1663, where he became acquainted with the Cambridge Platonist Ralph Cudworth, the orientalist Edward Pococke, the mathematician John Wallis and the scientist Robert Boyle. In 1669 Burnet was appointed professor of divinity at Glasgow University and set about to promote 'comprehension' to bring the Presbyterians back into the established church. But this, to be feasible, required a reduction of the power of bishops. During this period Burnet wrote the *Modest and Free Conference between a Conformist and a Nonconformist,* which expressed his liberal views regarding church government. In 1673 Burnet wrote *Vindication of the Authority, Constitution, and Laws of the Church and State of Scotland,* which supported the cause of episcopacy, however diminished, and the illegality of resistance purely on religious grounds. In the same year he and Edward Stillingfleet, in James, Duke of York's presence, were called to consult on ecclesiastical policy and succeeded in impugning Charles II's integrity, a bold measure that earned Burnet banishment from the court. During the Popish Plot of 1678–80, Burnet protested against the persecution of the Catholics, incurring the ire of both the court and the extreme anti-popery party, the circle of the first Earl of Shaftesbury. Meanwhile the first volume of his *History of the Reformation in England* was published in 1679, followed by the second volume in 1681. The Rye House Plot of 1683, which resulted in the death of Burnet's two best friends, Arthur Capell, first Earl of Essex (1631–83), and Lord William Russell (1639–83), prompted him to flee in 1684 to France, where his warm reception angered James. Returning to England, Burnet was dismissed from his posts as chaplain at the Rolls and lecturer at St. Clements for preaching a vehemently anti-popish sermon. He then traveled extensively throughout Europe, including Rome, where he was warmly received by Pope Innocent XI, and Geneva, where he played his anti-popery card. (See Bruce Lenman, 'The Poverty of Political Theory in the Scottish Revolution of 1688–9', in Lois G. Schwoerer, ed., *The Revolution of 1688–1689, Changing Perspectives* [Cambridge: Cambridge University Press, 1992], 246–7; and John Jay Hughes, 'The Missing "Last Words" of Gilbert Burnet in July 1687', *Historical Journal,* 20 [1977], 221–7).

Cambridge Platonism. A group of influential Cambridge philosopher-theologians who flourished between 1633 and 1688, led by Benjamin Whichcote, including Ralph Cudworth, Henry More and John Norris – although the last was in fact educated at Oxford, and in many respects shared more with Malebranche than with this school. Often educated as Puritans, the Cambridge Platonists reacted against the Calvinist emphasis on the arbitrariness of divine sovereignty, arguing that ritual, church government or elaborate dogmas are not essential to Christianity. Because of their toleration of religious diversity they were referred to as 'Latitude men', and were even condemned as Unitarians or atheists because they stressed morality above dogma.

Charles I, King of Great Britain (1600–49). The second son of James I and Anne of Denmark, Charles had become heir apparent on the death of his brother, Prince Henry, in 1612. In 1614 James I's quarrel with his second Parliament had persuaded him to enter marriage negotiations on Charles's behalf with Philip III of Spain for his daughter, the Catholic Infanta Maria, negotiations broken off in 1618 and finally abandoned in 1624. But the death of James I on 27 March 1625, gave the matter of succession urgency, and on 1 May of that year Charles was married by proxy to Henrietta Maria, sister of Louis XIII, the Catholic king of France. That the head of the Anglican Church had intermarried with a powerful Catholic Continental dynasty was undoubtedly provocation enough, but without foreign policy setbacks it would probably have been insufficient reason to remove Charles from the throne. But foreign policy setbacks, including military disasters at Cadiz (1625) and the Isle of Rhé near La Rochelle, bedeviled his first three Parliaments of 1625, 1626 and 1628–9, and the dissolution of Parliament in March 1629 marked the beginning of eleven years' personal rule, during which he used forced loans, like ship money, and other unpalatable practices to raise revenue. These years saw a rapprochement with Spain abroad and the ascendancy of Archbishop Laud, perceived as High Church if not Anglo-Catholic, at home. Discontent culminated in the armed revolt of the Scots against Laud's ecclesiastical programme in the Bishops' War. Recalling Parliament, first the Short and then the Long Parliament in 1640, Charles forced through a series of bills for constitutional change. The Civil War broke out in 1642. Charles surrendered to the Scots in 1646 and began parleying with various groups for his reinstatement. The army intervened in 1648, and the Rump Parliament appointed a high court that found Charles guilty of treason. Charles was executed on 30 January 1649.

Cooper, Anthony Ashley, first Earl of Shaftesbury (1621–83). Although in 1643 an avowed supporter of the royalist cause who led horse and troop regiments in defence of Charles I at Weymouth and Dorchester, by 1644 Cooper had switched allegiance, resigned all his commissions under the king and gone over to the Parliament side, even commanding parliamentary forces in Dorsetshire. He initially supported Parliament's decision to hand over power to Cromwell, and in 1653 was made member for Wiltshire under Cromwell's Parliament, serving on the Council of State. But when he realized that the Protector planned to rule alone, Cooper led the coalition of Presbyterians and republicans opposed to him in the 1656 Parliament. Despite having fought against the king, Cooper was admitted to the Privy Council and received a formal pardon in 1660. He urged leniency for the regicides. In 1661 he was raised to the peerage as Baron Ashley of Wimborne St. Giles, and was appointed Chancellor of the Exchequer and Under-Treasurer. He took a liberal line against the measures designed to consolidate royal power promulgated by Edward Hyde, first Earl of Clarendon, opposing the Act of Uniformity and the Militia Act, for which Clarendon had campaigned. He also advised and supported Charles II in his first Declaration of Indulgence for Protestant dissenters in 1662–3. With the fall of Clarendon in 1670, Cooper supported the more tolerant Buckingham and became a strong partisan of the scheme to legitimize Monmouth as the successor to the throne. In 1672 he approved Charles II's Declaration of Indulgence and also in that year was made Earl of Shaftesbury and Baron Cooper of Pawlet, as well as Lord Chancellor. In 1673 Shaftesbury supported the Test Act, which made it impossible for Catholics to hold office, leading to the forced dismissal of several of the king's favourite ministers. While embarked on his own course of anti-Catholic agitation, Shaftesbury nevertheless urged prosecution of war against the Protestant Dutch as rivals in trade and enemies of the monarchy, nowhere more famously than in the '*Delenda est Cathargo*' speech, for which Locke 'had to stand at his elbow with the written copy as prompter' (*DNB*, 1959–60, 12, 29), and to which Astell so contemptuously refers (Astell, *An Impartial Enquiry*, 41/178). Placing himself at the head of the parliamentary opposition to the court, he excited popular feeling by his loudly expressed fears of a Catholic uprising, and in 1674 he was dismissed from the Privy Council and ordered to leave London. Upon his refusal to do so, he was imprisoned in the Tower and was released only after begging pardon in February 1678. In 1679 Shaftesbury supported the Exclusion Bill to exclude James from the throne on account of his Catholicism and introduced the Habeas Corpus Act. He continued to support Monmouth's bid for the throne over that of James and in 1681 was once again committed to the Tower, this time on the charge of high treason, but released the following year when a Whig grand jury dismissed the charges. Hearing of further warrants for his arrest, he fled in 1682 to Holland, where he died the following year.

Cooper, Anthony Ashley, third Earl of Shaftesbury (1671–1713), moral philosopher and grandson of the first Earl of Shaftesbury, Locke's patron, was the target of Astell's *Bart'lemy Fair*. Elected member of Parliament for Poole in King William's second Parliament in 1695, he became Earl of Shaftesbury in 1699, attending the House of Lords regularly until William's death, and was an ardent Whig. He did his best to influence elections and to support the war party, and it was rumoured that William wanted to make him Secretary of State.

Cumberland, Richard (1631–1718), English philosopher, was bishop of Peterborough from 1691. In his *De legibus naturae* [*On Natural Laws*] (1672) he both propounded the doctrine of utilitarianism and opposed the egoistic ethics of Thomas Hobbes.

Dacier, Anne Lefevre (1651–1720), wife and collaborator of the translator and bibliophile André Dacier, published her own edition of fragments from the Alexandrian poet Callimachus (Paris, 1674), translations of Anacreon and Sappho (Paris, 1681), and plays by Plautus and Aristophanes, (1683–4) and Terence (1688), as well as collaborating with her husband on translations of Homer's *Iliad* (1699) and *Odyssey* (1708).

Defoe, Daniel (1661?–1731). A leading dissenter, journalist and the famous author of *Robinson Crusoe*, Defoe had a long history of dissent, attending meetings to protect witnesses from intimidation during the Popish Plot, and joining William of Orange's army in 1688. He became prominent in William's reign as a writer in defence of the king's character and policy. Like many of the early dissenters he did not object to the established church on principle, maintaining rather that it was a necessary barrier against popery and infidelity, but he was violently anti-Jacobite and was prosecuted for libel several times.

Descartes, René (1596–1650), French philosopher and mathematician who disputed with Hobbes. Descartes never left the Catholic fold, although his *Discourse on Method* incurred the displeasure of both Catholic and Calvinist ecclesiastical authorities and was eventually placed on the Papal Index of Prohibited Books. Perhaps to allay suspicions of heterodoxy, he published two editions of *Meditations on the First Philosophy*, which nevertheless represented a genuine attempt to provide a *modus vivendi* for science and religion, and to which Hobbes, at the request of his patron, Marin Mersenne, contributed his series of published 'Objections'.

Engagement Controversy is the name given to the controversy that raged around the secret treaty, or 'engagement', negotiated at Carisbrooke in 1647 between Charles I and commissioners representing the Scottish government.

Exclusion Crisis (1679–81) refers to the political skirmishing over the awkward question of whether Charles II's younger brother and heir, the Roman Catholic James, Duke of York, could be trusted as his successor. The Whigs and Tories, divided over the issue of excluding the Duke of York from the royal succession, emerged as political parties in the process.

Foulis, Henry (c. 1636–69). The son of Sir Henry Foulis, who entered England with James I and was made a knight in 1603 and created baronet in 1619, he was an Oxford royalist, educated at Queen's College, and was after elected Fellow at Lincoln College, Oxford, in 1659. He wrote *The History of Wicked Conspiracies* and *A History of the Romish Treasons and Usurpations* before his early death in 1669. Anthony A. Wood, in his *Athenae Oxoniensis*, says of him that 'the products of his writings shew him to have been a true son of the Church of England'.

The 'Grand Remonstrance', drawn up by the Commons in 1641, comprised a review of the personal government of Charles I as well as an account of measures already passed by the Long Parliament. The full text can be found in Samuel Rawson Gardiner, ed., *The Constitutional Documents of the Puritan Revolution, 1625–1660*, 3rd ed. (Oxford: Clarendon Press, 1906).

The Green Ribbon Club seems to have been founded about the year 1675, meeting at the King's Head Tavern, the locale for politicians hostile to the court. Its members wore a green ribbon to identify themselves. It was associated with the extreme faction of the Country Party, the men who supported Titus Oates, and who were involved in the Rye House Plot and Monmouth's rebellion. Thomas Dangerfield supplied the court with the names of forty-eight members in 1679, many confirmed from a corroborating list given to James II (Harleian MSS. 6845). A number of other members are mentioned in *The Cabal*, a satire published in 1680. From these sources it seems that the Duke of Monmouth himself, and statesmen like Halifax, Shaftesbury, Buckingham, Macdesfield, Cavendish, Bedford, Grey of Warke and Herbert of Cherbury, were among the members, along with writers such as Richard Scroop, Lord Mulgrave and Thomas Shadwell, with remnants of the Cromwellian regime like Falconbridge, Henry Ireton and Claypole.

Harley, Robert, first Earl of Oxford (1661–1724), English statesman and bibliophile, like Bolingbroke, entering Parliament in 1689, was first associated with the Whigs and introduced the Triennial Bill (1694), requiring regular parliamentary elections to the House of Commons. But by the time of the accession of Queen Anne in 1702, he had become a leader of the Tories. He was Secretary of State from 1704 to 1708 but was forced out of office by John Churchill, first Duke of Marlborough, because of his intrigues against the predominantly Whig government. When the unpopularity of the War of the Spanish Succession and the uproar caused by the trial of Henry Sacheverell brought about the fall of the Whigs in 1710, Harley returned to power with Henry St. John (later Viscount Bolingbroke). He survived an attempt on his life in 1711 and was made Earl and Lord Treasurer. Consolidating his power, he undertook secret peace negotiations that led to the Peace of Utrecht (1713) and founded the South Sea Company, involved in the notorious stock market bubble. His position was undermined by the intrigues of St. John, and he lost office just before Queen Anne's death (1714). After the accession of George I, he was imprisoned (1715) and impeached (1716) for his conduct of the peace negotiations and for dealings with the Jacobites but was acquitted. See Brian W. Hill, *Robert Harley: Speaker, Secretary of State and Premier Minister* (New Haven, Conn.: Yale University Press, 1988).

Hobbes, Thomas (1588–1679). Hobbes, philosopher and scientist, was a public figure, if demonized for his religious views, and remained a force to be reckoned with after his death both in England and on the Continent, where some of his works were first published. He had traveled abroad as tutor to the Cavendishes in Derbyshire, and is reputed to have met Galileo and Paolo Sarpi (1552–1623), the Venetian. We know that in 1623 Hobbes acted as amanuensis to Lord Chancellor Francis Bacon, providing a conduit for English scientific ideas to the Venetians through Sarpi, critic of the papacy and author of an important work on the Council of Trent. Hobbes's Continental links were strengthened by his further sojourns abroad, and from 1635 he was associated with Marin Mersenne, Pierre Gassendi and French philosophers in Paris, including Descartes, to whose *Méditations* he provided written 'Objections'. In 1642 his *De Cive* was published in Paris, where he sat out the Civil War, returning to England in 1652, a year after the publication of *Leviathan*. Both works were considered politically and religiously seditious, and Hobbes was excluded from the court of the future Charles II from 1651. From 1666 he lived under threat of prosecution for atheism, which prompted him to write several works on heresy, probably with the intention of exonerating himself. In 1679 he drafted a manuscript on the Exclusion Crisis for the third Earl of Devonshire's son, supporting a moderate Whig position, and died at Hardwick Hall in the same year.

Hooper, George (1640–1727), Bishop of Bath, Wells and, briefly, St. Asaph, had graduated as a doctor of divinity from Oxford in 1677, having studied Hebrew, Syriac and Arabic under the renowned orientalist Edward Pococke, and his promise as an antiquarian had prompted Archbishop Selden to engage him as his chaplain. Upon the marriage of Princess Mary to the Prince of Orange, Hooper went with her to the Hague, where he incurred the displeasure of the prince, who leaned toward the dissenters, by persuading the princess to read Hooker and Eusebius. Hooper was twice offered, and twice declined, the Regius Professorship of Divinity at Oxford. He was chaplain to Charles II in 1685, Dean of Canterbury in 1691, and prolocutor of the Lower House in 1701. He declined the primacy of Ireland but accepted the see of St. Asaph in 1703, resigning it in the same year to take the dioceses of Bath and Wells, which he held until his death in 1727. Hooper went on, in 1706, to preach against the union of England and Scotland, to defend the cause of the Scottish Episcopal Church and to defend the relentless High Church Tory, Henry Sacheverell, against impeachment.

Hyde, Edward, first Earl of Clarendon (1609–74). Hyde, made Lord Chancellor in January 1658, was opposed to severe treatment of Protestant non-conformists, pressing for the passing of the Act of Indemnity – which only caused both Catholics and Presbyterians to petition for his removal. He was, however, firm in enforcing the Act of Uniformity in 1662 and, by 1667, had succeeded in alienating not only the House of Commons and the courts but also the king, who was incensed by his opposition to the policy of a more generous religious toleration. Charles II dismissed him as Chancellor in 1667, but Clarendon's enemies were not satisfied and the House of Commons impeached him on seventeen counts, including one of high treason. After first protesting his innocence, Clarendon was forced to flee to France, where he died seven years later.

Laud, William, Archbishop of Canterbury (1573–1645). Educated at St. John's College, Oxford, of which he became president in 1611, Laud rapidly became associated with pro-Catholic opinions and was promoted by James I to a series of important benefices as Bishop of Bath and Wells in 1626, Dean of the Chapel Royal as well as Privy Councillor in 1627, and Bishop of London in 1628. On Laud's advice, Charles, in 1628, prohibited controversial preaching and declared that all questions of the external policy of the church were to be decided by convocation. Elected chancellor of the University of Oxford in 1629, Laud was appointed Archbishop of Canterbury in 1633. He continued to enforce strict conformity in ecclesiastical affairs and, when in 1639 the first Bishops War erupted, the Scots resorted to arms to resist the conformity he forced on the Scottish Church. His insistence that churches should be decorated and the communion table separated from the congregation smacked of Catholicism, causing Laud to be (unfairly) suspected of intending to facilitate a reunion with Rome, which united important Protestant circles against him. Laud used the prolonged sittings of convocation in 1640 to pass a new body of canons formulating the doctrine of the divine right of kings in such a way as to imply that bearing arms against the king was an offence against God. He was thus perceived as tying the established church to absolutism in the state, impeached for treason, imprisoned in the Tower and, after a lengthy trial and in spite of a pardon by the king, was beheaded in January 1645.

Leland, John (1691–1766), was a Presbyterian minister and author of theological works. Born in Wigan, Lancashire, he was educated in Ireland, where he entered the ministry. He was opposed to Deism, attacking proponents of Deist ideas, such as Matthew Tindal.

Leslie, Charles (1650–1722), was born in Dublin and graduated with an M.A. from Trinity College in 1673, studied law and was ordained a priest in 1680. Through the good auspices of his patron, the second Earl of Clarendon, he was made Chancellor of Connor in 1686. But his loyalty to James II was unshakable, and when he refused to take the oath of allegiance to William and Mary, he was removed from his post, finding employment as chaplain to Clarendon, his patron, and officiating at Ely House, a magnet for nonjurors. In 1721 Leslie returned to Ireland, where he died the following year.

Locke, John (1632–1704), philosopher and political secretary, was educated at Christ Church, Oxford, where he was appointed Greek lecturer in 1660, lecturer on rhetoric in 1662 and censor of moral philosophy in 1663. Locke rejected both Aristotelian philosophy, then dominant at Oxford, and the Puritanism of his upbringing and presented the most persistent challenge to Astell's views.

Malebranche, Nicholas (1638–1715), Neoplatonist. Malebranche, who had studied theology at the Sorbonne and was ordained a priest in 1664, set himself the project of integrating the Platonist orientation of the Augustinian order, to which he belonged, with the scientific ideas of Descartes. Malebranche's doctrine, centred on a theory of reason as immutable and eternal and part of God's wisdom and on the notion that human powers were only an occasion for the exercise of divine power, had an important reception in England; his *Recherche de la Verité* was translated twice in Astell's lifetime. John Dunton, the English Malebranchiste and publicist, had published a translation of Malebranche's *Traité* under the title *Malebranche's search after truth: or a treatise of the nature of the humane mind* in 1694–5, undoubtedly the translation that Astell used given the connection between Dunton and Norris, while Thomas Taylor's *Father Malebranche his treatise concerning the search after truth. The whole work complete* was published in 1700 in a revised translation.

Manley, Mary de la Riviere (c. 1663–1724). The daughter of Sir Roger Manley, governor of the Channel Islands, according to her autobiography, entitled *The Adventures of Rivella, or the History of the Author of the Atalantis by Sir Charles Lovemore* (1714), she was orphaned at the age of sixteen and then married off to a relative who deserted her. Leaving Jersey for patronage at court, she belonged for a short time to the circle of the Duchess of Cleveland and wrote an unsuccessful comedy, *The Lost Lover* (1696). Her tragedy, *The Royal Mischief* (1696), was more successful. She is the probable author of *The Secret History of Queen Zarah and the Zarazians*, a satire on Sarah, Duchess of Marlborough, in the guise of romance, which appeared in 1705, and the certain author of the infamous *Secret Memoirs . . . of Several Persons of Quality* (1709), a scandalous chronicle purportedly from 'the New Atlantis', an island in the Mediterranean, a spurious narrative designed to expose the private vices and intrigues of government ministers in the circles of Bolingbroke and Harley. Manley was arrested in the autumn of 1709 as the author of this libelous publication but discharged. During the political campaign of 1711 she continued to write critical pamphlets, as well as many articles for the *Examiner*. Her later tragedies include *Lucius* (1717), *The Power of Love, in Seven Novels* (1720) and *A Stage Coach Journey to Exeter* (1725).

More, Henry (1614–87), Cambridge Platonist. In his many works, and most notably in his *Enchiridion ethicum* (1667), he argues for the essential goodness of human nature, translated into virtuous action under the direction of the 'boniform faculty', through which the principles of morality are imprinted on the soul. More elaborated a philosophy of spirit that explained all the phenomena of mind and of the physical world as the activity of spiritual substance controlling inert matter. He conceived of both spirit and body as spatially extended, but defined spiritual substance as the obverse of material extension: whereas body is inert and solid, but divisible, spirit is active and penetrable, but indivisible. It was in his correspondence with Descartes that he first expounded his view that all substance, whether material or immaterial, is extended. As an example of non-material extension he proposed space, within which material extension is contained. He went on to argue that space is infinite, anticipating Newton. More also argued that God, who is an infinite spirit, is an extended being (*res extensa*). There are, therefore, conceptual parallels between the idea of God and the idea of space, a view that he elaborates in *Enchiridion metaphysicum*, where he argues that the properties of space are analogous to the attributes of God (infinity, immateriality, immobility, etc.). More attempted to answer materialists like Thomas Hobbes, whom he perceived as an atheist on account of his dismissal of the idea of incorporeal substance as nonsensical. Astell had almost certainly read More's *The Immortality of the Soul and An Account of Virtue* (1690), which she cites, and had probably also read More's Correspondence with John Norris in *The Theory and Regulation of Love* (1688). Although More's philosophical project was mainly devoted to demonstrating the existence and providential nature of God by proving the existence of incorporeal substance, or spirit, he was also interested in contemporary science. For More, as for Cudworth, seventeenth-century physics (the so-called mechanical philosophy) offered the most satisfactory explanation of phenomena in the physical world. For that reason he seized on Descartes' physics, recommending that Cartesianism be taught in the universities.

Owen, James (1654–1706), born in Carmarthenshire, Wales, had been ordained by Presbyters in 1677, and in 1690, with the help of money from the London Presbyterian fund, had established an academy for training students for the ministry at Oswestry. In 1700 he became minister of High Street Chapel, Shrewsbury, where he continued his academy. His works include a pamphlet written in defence of occasional conformity in 1703 entitled *Moderation a Virtue*, to which Mary Astell responded with her *Moderation Truly Stated* (1704), twice the length. Owen replied to a number of his critics, making reference to Astell among them, in his preface to *Moderation Still a Virtue* (1704), to which Astell once again replied in the postscript to *A Fair Way with the Dissenters* (1704).

Pym, John (1584–1643), parliamentary statesman. In the first Parliament of Charles I in 1625, Pym sat as member for Tavistock, and helped compose the articles against Catholics that were adopted with some modifications. In 1628 Pym warmly supported the Petition of Right, which sought to obtain from Charles strict definitions of the limits to arbitrary taxation and arbitrary imprisonment. In the Short Parliament of 1640, Pym began to play the part of unacknowledged leader of the House of Commons. During 1640 he moved for the impeachment of Laud and Strafford and in 1641 supported the Root and Branch Bill for the abolition of episcopacy. In July 1642, Pym was one of fifteen members of the newly formed Committee of Safety, a rudimentary government acting in the interests of Parliament, which took on the role of organising military action once the Civil War had begun.

The Root and Branch Bill, said to have been drawn up by St. John and presented to Parliament by Vane and Cromwell in May 1641. The bill was dropped in the House of Commons and finally abandoned after long debates in August.

The Rye House Plot of 1683 was an alleged Whig conspiracy to assassinate or mount an insurrection against Charles II because of his pro-Catholic policies. The plot drew its name from Rye House at Hoddeston, Hertfordshire, near which ran a narrow road where Charles was supposed to be killed as he traveled from a horse meet at Newmarket.

Sacheverell, Henry (1674?–1724), was born in Wiltshire and educated at Magdalen College, Oxford, where in 1708 he was created D.D. and was made bursar the following year. He resumed preaching in 1713 and accepted the queen's offer of the rich living of St. Andrew's, Holborn. He died from complications of an accident. A fanatical High Churchman from whom, along with other 'High Flyers', Astell was keen to distance herself, Sacheverell played a prominent role in the occasional conformity debate.

Sancroft, William, Archbishop of Canterbury (1617–93). Educated at Emmanuel College, Cambridge, the college in which Cambridge Platonism was later centred, he was elected a Fellow in 1642, holding the offices of Greek and Hebrew Reader. In 1658 an English translation of a Latin work of his, *Fur Praedestinatus*, was published, attacking Calvinism. Shortly afterwards, Sancroft published *Modern Policies taken from Machiaval, Borgia and other choise Authors by an Eye-witness*, an indictment of the religion and politics of the Commonwealth written in highly inflammatory terms. In 1657 he traveled abroad, studying at Padua and, learning of the Restoration in Rome, returned to England in 1660. In 1661 he was appointed one of Charles II's chaplains, and the following year he was made D.D. at Cambridge and Master of Emmanuel College. After a series of preferments, including the deanery of St. Paul's, Sancroft was appointed Archbishop of Canterbury in 1678 and in this position tried unsuccessfully to win back James, Duke of York, to the Anglican Church. A churchman who exhibited extraordinary integrity, to his own cost, in the subsequent political manoeuvrings that established William and disestablished James, Sancroft, upon James II's accession in 1685, had refused to take part in the high commission court James had established and subsequently was forbidden to appear at court. In 1688, in consultation with other senior clergy, Sancroft stated that the order that the king's declaration of liberty of conscience be read in church was illegal, whereupon he and the five bishops who had signed the petition against the order were committed to the Tower for seditious libel, although eventually found not guilty. On his release, Sancroft headed a deputation to James that advised him to revoke all his illegal acts. Later in that same year, believing James now incapable of governing, he signed a declaration calling on William of Orange to assist in procuring peace and a 'free Parliament'. However, he favoured appointing William merely *custos regni*, not king, and in 1689 Sancroft excused himself from attending William's coronation. He was suspended later that year and deprived his benefices the following year, along with the five bishops and about 400 clergy. Soon afterwards, he joined the other nonjuring bishops in circulating a flysheet that denied all sedition or intrigue with France. He appears to have joined in the preparation for the consecration of new nonjuring bishops and, until his death in 1693, communicated only with nonjurors.

Sherlock, William (1641?–1707), Dean of St. Paul's, was born in Southwark and educated at Cambridge, graduating with an M.A. in 1663. After taking orders he did not obtain a preferment until 1669, when he went to a rectory in London where he soon gained a reputation as a preacher. His first publication, *The Knowledge of Jesus Christ, and Union with Him* (1674), started a war of words by attacking John Owen, who had argued that divine mercy was known only through Christ, the second person of the Trinity. Other controversial writings by Sherlock include *Preservative against Popery* (1688), *Vindication of the Doctrine of the Trinity* (1690) and *Present State of the Socinian Controversy* (1698) (*DNB* and *British Biographical Archive*).

The **Star Chamber** developed from the judicial proceedings traditionally carried out by the king and his council, and was entirely separate from the common law courts of the day. Faster and less rigid than the common law courts, its scope was extended by the Tudors. Under Chancellor Wolsey's leadership (1515–29), the Court of Star Chamber became a political weapon, bringing actions against opponents to the decrees and edicts of Henry VIII. The court remained active throughout the reigns of James I and Charles I but was abolished by the Long Parliament in 1641. See J. R. Jones, *Charles II: Royal Politician* (London: Allen & Unwin, 1987), ch. 7.

Steele, Richard (1672–1729), essayist, dramatist and politician, began his career in April 1709 by establishing the *Tatler*, which was to develop into a collection of essays on social and general topics. It ceased publication abruptly in 1711, probably due to its satirization of Harley, who had become head of government. Only two months later, however, Steele launched the even more successful *Spectator*. From 1712, Steele's writings took on a more overtly political tone, and in 1713 he openly challenged the Tory paper the *Examiner* in a new publication, the *Guardian*. In 1713 Steele was elected member of Parliament for Hampshire, and the following year he published a pamphlet entitled *The Crisis*, which reviewed the whole question of the Hanoverian succession. As a result, he was accused of seditious libel and was expelled from the House of Commons. With the death of Queen Anne later that year, however, his fortunes changed. Among the rewards King George I bestowed upon him for his loyalty to the Hanoverian cause was the license of the Theatre Royal of Drury

Lane. Shortly after this, Steele published *The Ladies Library* and *Mr. Steele's Apology for himself and his Writings.*

Stillingfleet, Edward (1635–99), Bishop of Worcester, was born in Dorset. He was educated at St. John's College, Cambridge, where he graduated with an M.A. in 1656 and, having gained fame for his writings, was incorporated at Oxford in 1677. From 1654 he worked as a tutor in Nottingham, and around this time was ordained. In 1657 he was made rector of Sutton. He was appointed preacher at the Rolls Chapel in 1664 and rector of St. Andrew's, Holborn, in 1665, and was also made Reader of the Temple. He was collated to the prebend of Islington in St. Paul's Cathedral in 1667, graduated with as D.D. in 1668 and became a canon in Canterbury Cathedral the following year. He soon became a popular London preacher and was made a royal chaplain. His writings against both Socinians and Catholics were extremely popular, and in 1677 he was made Archdeacon of London. In 1678 he was appointed Dean of St. Paul's and was also prolocutor of the lower house of convocation of Canterbury. He was less prominent during the reign of James II, but with the Revolution he again found royal favour. Stillingfleet's later views departed a conciliatory line for a defence of intolerance in his works the *Unreasonableness of Separation* (1680) and *The Mischief of Separation* (1680). In 1689 he was consecrated as Bishop of Worcester, and was placed on the commission to consider the revision of the prayer book and the possibility of 'comprehension' to bring dissenters into the fold. His views on the duties and rights of the parochial clergy were published in his *Ecclesiastical Cases* in 1695. Despite illness, Stillingfleet spoke frequently in the House of Lords and advised Archbishop Tenison as well as other bishops.

Swift, Jonathan (1667–1745), Dean of St. Patrick's and satirist, epitomized these debates in his first famous work, *The Battle of the Books* of 1704, which lampooned Fontenelle's position in the debate over the ancients and the moderns. Reared in Dublin, where he spent the greater part of his life, Swift, soon after completing a B.A. at Oxford, was adopted by the statesman Sir William Temple, who used him as a go-between with William III, the same Temple who in 1692 had published an essay that introduced to England the debate over the ancients and moderns, begun in France.

Tenison, Thomas, Archbishop of Canterbury (1636–1715). Tenison, as William III's appointee and Sancroft's replacement, was an uncompromising crusader against Catholicism in such works as the *Discourse of*

Idolatry of 1678. As the author of *The Creed of Mr Hobbes Examined* (1670), he would have informed Astell directly of the evils of Hobbesian 'atheism'. Educated at Corpus Christi College, Cambridge, where he became a Fellow in 1659, he was subsequently obtained from Charles II the benefice of St. Martin's-in-the-Fields. There, according to Gilbert Burnet, Tenison endowed schools and set up a public library, projects close to Astell's heart. Under William III, Tenison was appointed in 1689 to the ecclesiastical commission responsible for preparing a reconciliation of the dissenters, and here, of course, Astell parted ways with him. Indeed, it was his generally liberal religious views that commended him to the royal favour, procuring for him the posts of Bishop of Lincoln in 1691 and Archbishop of Canterbury in 1694. Along with Burnet, he attended the king on his death bed and crowned Queen Anne, but during her reign he was not in much favour at court. A strong supporter of the Hanoverian succession, he was, upon the death of Anne, one of the three officers of state entrusted with the duty of appointing a regent until the arrival of George I, whom he crowned on 31 October 1714.

Warburton, William (1698–1779), Bishop of Gloucester and author of *The Alliance between Church and State; or the Necessity and Equity of an established Religion, and a Test Law demonstrated, from the essence and End of civil Society upon the fundamental Principles of the Laws of Nature and Nations* (1736), while taking the high ground, as the title indicates, maintained that the state church should tolerate those who differed from it in doctrine and worship. From 1737 to 1741 his *magnum opus* on Deists appeared, *The Divine Legation of Moses, Demonstrated on the Principles of a Religious Deist, from the Omission of the Doctrine of a Future State of Rewards and Punishments in the Jewish Dispensation.*

Wesley, Samuel (1662–1735), divine, father of the Methodist leader Charles, although attending Morton's dissenting academy, became strongly anti-dissent, and in 1703 he published *A Letter from a Country Divine to his Friend in London, concerning the Education of Dissenters in their Private Academies* which attacked the dissenting academies. Defoe, in *More Short-Ways*, 5, referred to 'The Reverend Mr. *Wesly* Author of two Pamphlets, Calculated to blacken our Education in the Academies of the Dissenters'.

Notes

Introduction

1. Mary Astell, *Reflections upon Marriage, To which is added a Preface in Answer to Some Objections* (London: Printed for R. Wilkin, at the King's Head in St. Paul's Church Yard, 1706), xi. Reprinted in Patricia Springborg, ed., *Mary Astell (1666–1731): Political Writings* (Cambridge: Cambridge University Press, 1996), 18–19. Henceforth citations will be given to both the 1706 and 1996 editions of this work, divided by a forward slash.
2. See Philip Pettit, *Republicanism: A Theory of Freedom and Government* (Oxford: Clarendon Press, 1997), 139. For my critique of Pettit, see Springborg, 'Republicanism, Freedom from Domination and the Cambridge Contextual Historians', *Political Studies*, 49, 5 (2003): 851–76. For the wider issue of classical republican theory, see J. G. A. Pocock, *The Machiavellian Moment: Florentine Political Theory and the Atlantic Republican Tradition* (Princeton, N.J.: Princeton University Press, 1975); Quentin Skinner, 'Thomas Hobbes and the Proper Signification of Liberty', *Transactions of the Royal Historical Society*, 40 (1990): 121–51, and Skinner, *Liberty before Liberalism* (Cambridge: Cambridge University Press, 1998). I should like to make it clear at the outset that, of these three, only Pettit claims Astell is republican, a claim Pocock and Skinner would deny. Pocock's case for republicanism is in any event different, tracing the lineaments of transatlantic thought that did produce a republic: the American republic. For Pettit and Skinner, however, republicanism, as freedom from domination, is a moral project. (Hence, the attempt to enlist Astell.) For my critique of that moral project, see Springborg 1987, 1989a, 1989b, 1990, 1991, 1993 and 2001.
3. See Upham's 'A Parallel Case for Richardson's *Clarissa*', *Modern Language Notes*, 103–5. It is notable, however, that standard works on Richardson, including the authoritative biography by T. C. Duncan Eaves and Ben D. Kimpel, *Samuel Richardson, A Biography* (Oxford: Clarendon, 1971), and Tom Keymer, Howard Erskine-Hill and John Richetti, *Richardson's 'Clarissa' and the*

Eighteenth Century Reader (Cambridge: Cambridge University Press, 1992), do not even include Astell in the index.

4. Alfred, Lord Tennyson, *Poetical Works of Alfred, Lord Tennyson* (London: Eyre and Spottiswoode, 1905), 167, 176, and noted in 'A Refuge from Men: The Idea of a Protestant Nunnery', *Past and Present*, 117 (1987): 107–30, esp. 107.

5. Bridget Hill, *The First English Feminist: 'Reflections Upon Marriage' and Other Writings by Mary Astell* (Aldershot, Hants: Gower Publishing, 1986).

6. For the nineteenth-century reception of Astell see Carl D. Bulbring, *Mary Astell: An Advocate of Women's Rights Two Hundred Years Ago* (London: 1891); Katherine S. Pattinson, 'Mary Astell', *Pall Mall Magazine* (1892); and Harriet McIlquham, 'Mary Astell: A Seventeenth Century Women's Advocate', *Westminister Review*, 149 (1898).

7. For the information on Mary Hays I am grateful to Sarah Hutton.

8. Florence M. Smith, *Mary Astell* (New York: Columbia University Press, 1916), and Ruth Perry's carefully researched *The Celebrated Mary Astell* (Chicago: University of Chicago Press, 1986). Perry includes a number of useful appendices comprising Astell's poems, letters, the book collection of Ann of Coventry, for instance, Astell's friend, and the inventory of the estate of her father, Peter Astell.

9. Bridget Hill, *The First English Feminist* (Aldershot, Hants: Gower Publishing, 1986), and Moira Ferguson, *First Feminists: British Women Writers 1578–1799* (Bloomington: Indiana University Press, 1985).

10. Patricia Springborg, ed., *Mary Astell (1666–1731): Political Writings* (Cambridge: Cambridge University Press, 1996); *Mary Astell, A Serious Proposal to the Ladies* (London: Pickering & Chatto, 1997); and *Mary Astell's A Serious Proposal to the Ladies, Parts I* (1694) and *II* (1697) (Peterborough, Ontario: Broadview Press, 2002).

11. For earlier essays see J. E. Norton, 'Some Uncollected Authors XXVII; Mary Astell, 1666–1731', *The Book Collector*, 10, 1 (1961): 58–60; Joan K. Kinnaird, 'Mary Astell and the Conservative Contribution to English Feminism', *Journal of British Studies*, 19 (1979): 53–79; Regina James, 'Mary, Mary, Quite Contrary, Or, Mary Astell and Mary Wollstonecraft Compared', *Studies in Eighteenth Century Culture*, 5 (1976): 121–39; Ruth Perry's two fine articles, 'Mary Astell's Response to the Enlightenment', *Women in History*, 9 (1984): 13–40 and 'Radical Doubt and the Liberation of Women', *Eighteenth Century Studies*, 18, 4 (1985): 472–93; Bridget Hill, 'A Refuge from Men: The Idea of a Protestant Nunnery', *Past and Present*, 117 (1987): 107–30; Patricia Ward Scaltsas, 'Women as Ends – Women as Means in the Enlightenment', in A. J. Arnaud and E. Kingdom, eds., *Women's Rights and the Rights of Man* (Aberdeen: Aberdeen University Press, 1990), 138–48; John McCrystal, 'An Inadvertent Feminist: Mary Astell (1666–1731),' M.A. thesis, Department of Political Studies, Auckland University, New Zealand, 1992, and his 'A Lady's Calling: Mary Astell's Notion of Women', *Political Theory Newsletter*, 4 (1992): 156–70.

12. Anonymous reader's report.

13. See E. Derek Taylor's excellent essay 'Mary Astell's Ironic Final Assault on John Locke's Theory of Thinking Matter', *Journal of the History of Ideas*, 62

(2001): 505–22; and Sarah Ellenzweig, 'The Love of God and the Radical Enlightenment: Mary Astell's Brush with Spinoza', *Journal of the History of Ideas*, 64, 3 (2003): 379–87.

14. John Pocock and Quentin Skinner have identified both 'anachronism' (the attribution to authors of concepts not available to them) and 'prolepsis' (the anticipation of arguments that could only be the outcome, rather than the presupposition, of the process in question) as two persistent errors of historicism, understood in the Popperian sense as reading the past back from the present. Perhaps my notion of reverse anachronism comes closest to the latter. See Quentin Skinner, *Visions of Politics*, 1 (Cambridge: Cambridge University Press, 2002), 73, 88, and his earlier 'Reply to my Critics' in James Tully, ed., *Meaning and Context* (Princeton, N.J.: Princeton University Press, 1988), 231–88.

15. I have been privileged to review a proposal by Melinda Zook for an essay entitled 'Religious Conformity and the Problem of Dissent in the Works of Aphra Behn and Mary Astell' in a proposed volume, *Mary Astell: Reason, Gender, Faith*, edited by William Kolbrener and Michelle Michelson. Zook's project is to examine the idiom of Behn's lampoons of the dissenters in her plays, *Sir Patient Fancy* (1678), *the City Heiress* (1682) and *The Roundheads* (1681), an idiom very similar to that invoked by Astell in *Moderation Truly Stated*. Astell undoubtedly knew of Behn, who had dedicated her *History of the Nun* (1689) to Hortense Mancini, the Countess of Mazarine, to whom Astell had dedicated *Reflections upon Marriage*.

16. For recent essays on Astell's women contemporaries in the public sphere see Hilda L. Smith's edited volume, *Women Writers and the Early Modern British Political Tradition* (Cambridge: Cambridge University Press, 1998), particularly her Introduction, 'Women, Intellect and Politics: Their Intersection in the Seventeenth Century', 1–14, and her essay 'Women as Sextons and Electors: King's Bench and Precedents for Women's Citizenship' in the same volume, 324–43; Lois Schwoerer's excellent essay 'Women's Public Political Voice in England: 1640–1740', 56–74; Susan Staves's 'Investments, Votes and "Bribes": Women as Shareholders in the Chartered National Companies', 259–78; and Barbara J. Todd's ' "To Be Some Body": Married Women and *The Hardships of the English Laws*', 343–62.

17. For a succinct formulation of this argument see Eileen O'Neill, 'Women Cartesians, "Feminine Philosophy", and Historical Exclusion', in Susan Bordo, ed., *Feminist Interpretations of Descartes* (University Park: Pennsylvania State University Press, 1999), 232–57, discussed later.

18. Thrasymachus, who rushes onto the stage as a rowdy democrat, is the most serious interlocutor Socrates faces in the Preliminaries, *Republic* 336b–54c. His challenge structures Plato's subsequent argument in the dialogue, forcing him to make good his claims that politics is a human endeavour that appeals to knowledge, and that politics is appropriately governed by the principle of meritocracy rather than rule of the strongest – or a majority.

19. For the political uses of the terms 'hard' and 'soft', see, for instance, former U.S. Assistant Secretary of State, and Sultan of Oman Professor of International Relations and Dean of the John F. Kennedy School of Government at

Harvard University, Joseph S. Nye, Jr.'s recent book, *Soft Power: The Means to Success in World Politics* (New York: Public Affairs, 2004), where soft means the velvet glove rather than the mailed fist. For analogous language see Ben Barber's *Strong Democracy* (Berkeley: University of California Press, 1984), which means, I suppose, that democrats are not wimps and can stand up to tyrants.

20. On the myth of the state see the percipient earlier critiques of Ernst Cassirer (1874–1945) and Friederich Meinecke (1862–1954), both of whom were profoundly affected by the experience of Nazi Germany. Cassirer, who was Jewish and fled to Sweden, was the author of the important work of the title, *The Myth of the State*, published posthumously in 1946, while Meinecke, a Berlin professor, in his early works on Prussia, treated the state both as the repository of power and as the privileged bearer of cultural values, and only in *Idee der Staatsraïson in der neueren Geschichte* (1924; tr. as *Machiavellism*, 1957) exposed the myth of the state or Machiavellian *étatism* as the irresponsible exercise of power, reflecting in *Die deutsche Katastrophe* (1946; tr. as *The German Catastrophe*, 1950) on the rise of National Socialism and German guilt.

21. See Springborg, 'Politics, Primordialism and Orientalism', *American Political Science Review*, 80, 1 (1986): 185–211; 'The Contractual State: Reflections on Orientalism and Despotism', *History of Political Thought*, 8, 3 (1987): 395–433; and *Western Republicanism and the Oriental Prince*.

22. Carl Schmitt, *The Leviathan in the State Theory of Thomas Hobbes* (1938, tr. George Schwab (Westport, Conn.: Greenwood Press, 1996). On Hobbes's use of the aphorism '*homo homini lupus*', see Gianni Paganini, 'Hobbes, Gassendi e la psicologia del meccanicismo', in Arrigo Pacchi, *Hobbes Oggi*, Actes du Colloque de Milan, 18–21 May 1988 (Milano: Franco Angeli Editore, 1990), 351–445, esp. 438, a discovery made simultaneously by Olivier Bloch in his 'Gassendi et la théorie politique de Hobbes', in Yves Charles Zarka and Jean Bernhardt, eds., *Thomas Hobbes, Philosophie première, théorie de la science et politique*, Actes du Colloque de Paris (Paris: Vrin, 1990), 345. See also the seminal piece by François Tricaud, ' "Homo homini Deus", "Homo homini Lupus": Recherche des Sources des deux formules de Hobbes', in R. Koselleck, and R. Schnur, eds., *Hobbes-Forschungen* (Berlin: Duncker & Humblot, 1969), 61–70. On Hobbes and Schmitt, see Horst Bredekamp, 'From Walter Benjamin to Carl Schmitt, via Thomas Hobbes', *Critical Inquiry*, 25 (1999): 247–66, and *Thomas Hobbes visuelle Strategien* (Berlin: Akademie-Verlag, 1999).

23. Sigmund Freud (1856–1939) introduced the idea of narcissism of minor differences to help explain externalization, coining the phrase and describing it as 'the basis of feelings of strangeness and hostility'.

24. See, for instance, Stephen Greenblatt, *Renaissance Self-Fashioning, from More to Shakespeare* (Chicago: University of Chicago Press, 1980); Richard Helgerson, *Forms of Nationhood: The Elizabethan Writing of England* (Chicago: University of Chicago Press, 1992); and Peter Holbrook and David Bevington, eds., *The Politics of the Stuart Court Masque* (Cambridge: Cambridge University Press, 1998), a few items from a now large and sophisticated literature on nation-building in early modern England.

25. On the role of women as political pamphleteers, see especially Catherine Gallagher, *Nobody's Story: The Vanishing Acts of Women Writers in the Market Place, 1670–1820* (Berkeley: University of California Press, 1994); and Cristina Malcolmson and Mihoko Suzuki, eds., *Debating Gender in Early Modern England* (New York: Palgrave, 2002). For women dramatists see Derek Hughes, ed., *Eighteenth-Century Women Playwrights*, 6 vols. (London: Pickering & Chatto, 2001), which comprises plays by Delariviere Manley, Eliza Haywood, Mary Pix, Catherine Trotter, Susanna Centlivre, Elizabeth Griffith, Hannah Cowley and Elizabeth Inchbald, including Delariviere Manley: *The Lost Lover* and *The Royal Mischief*; Catherine Trotter Cockburn: *Love at a Loss* and *The Revolution of Sweden* (vol. 2); and Susan Centlivre, *The Basset-Table*, *The Busie Body*, and *The Wonder! A Woman Keeps a Secret*; and *A Bold Stroke for a Wife* (vol. 3).

26. E. Derek Taylor's otherwise excellent essay 'Mary Astell's Ironic Assault on John Locke's Theory of Thinking Matter', 505, opens by declaring: 'Mary Astell . . . has lurked for years at the edges of that infinitely contentious category "feminism," but she is only now beginning to receive her rightful inheritance as a theological and philosophical thinker, probably the title she would most have preferred.'

27. See Carole Pateman's excellent Conclusion to Hilda L. Smith's edited volume, *Women Writers and the Early Modern British Political Tradition*, 'Women's Writing, Women's Standing: Theory and Politics in the Early Modern Period', 363–82, esp. 374, where she addresses two widely used anthologies, Linda Nicholson, ed., *Feminism/Postmodernism* (New York: Routledge, 1990) and Judith Butler and Joan Scott, eds., *Feminists Theorize the Political* (New York: Routledge, 1992), as well as Anna Yeatman's 'Voice and Representation in the Politics of Difference', in Sneja Gunew and Anna Yeatman, eds., *Feminism and the Politics of Difference* (Boulder, Colo.: Westview Press, 1993), 238.

28. See the large literature on women and work, women and development, including the following publications of the International Labour Office (ILO), Geneva: J. Siltanen, J. Jarman and R. M. Blackburn, *Gender Inequality in the Labour Market: Occupational Concentration and Segregation: A Manual on Methodology* (1995); *Rural Women in Micro-Enterprise Development: A Training Manual and Programme for Extension Workers* (1996); Richard Anker, *Gender and Jobs – Sex Segregation of Occupations in the World* (1998); Helinä Melkas and Richard Anker, *Gender Equality and Occupational Segregation in Nordic Labour Markets* (1998); L. Lean Lim, ed., *The Sex Sector: The Economic and Social Bases of Prostitution in Southeast Asia* (1998); Linda Wirth, *Breaking through the Glass Ceiling: Women in Management* (2001); Shauna Olney, Elizabeth Goodson, Kathini Maloba-Caines and Faith O'Neil, eds., *Gender Equality: A Guide to Collective Bargaining* (2002); *Ethiopian Women Entrepreneurs: Going for Growth* (2003); Nabeel A. Goheer, *Women Entrepreneurs in Pakistan: How to Improve Their Bargaining Power* (2003); *Zambian Women Entrepreneurs: Going for Growth* (2003); Ingeborg Heide, *Gender Roles and Sex Equality: European Solutions to Social Security Disputes* (2004).

29. See Rachel J. Weil, 'The Politics of Legitimacy: Women and the Warming Pan Scandal', in Lois G. Schwoerer, ed., *The Revolution of 1688–1689* (Cambridge: Cambridge University Press, 1992), 65–82.

30. Weil, 'The Politics of Legitimacy', 75, citing Aphra Behn, *A Congratulatory Poem to Her Most Sacred Majesty* (London, 1688), and Elizabeth Cellier, *To Dr. – An Answer to his Queries* (London, 1688).

31. See Jacqueline Broad's excellent study, *Women Philosophers of the Seventeenth Century* (Cambridge: Cambridge University Press, 2002).

32. See Rahel Weil, *Political Passions: Gender, the Family and Political Argument in England, 1680–1714* (Manchester: Manchester University Press, 1999), 231. See also Melinda S. Zook, 'Review of Rachel Weil, *Political Passions: Gender, the Family and Political Argument in England, 1680–1714*', *The American Historical Review*, 106, 2 (2001): 641–2.

33. Richard Allestree (1619–81), author of *The Ladies Calling* (1673), Part 2, §3, 'Of Wives', a work extensively cited by Astell in *A Serious Proposal, Part II*.

34. For a critical account of the *Begriffsgeschichte* of Reinhart Koselleck and its convergence with the contextualism of the Cambridge School, see my essay 'What Can We Say about History? Reinhart Koselleck and *Begriffsgeschichte*', in Jussi Kurunmäki and Kari Palonen, eds., *Zeit, Geschichte und Politik: zum achtzigsten Geburtstag von Reinhart Koselleck* (Jyväskylä, Finland: University of Jyväskylä Press, 2003), 55–84; and the recent excellent collection *Begriffsgeschichte, Diskursgeschichte, Metapherngeschichte*, ed. Hans Erich Böeker, Göttinger Gespräche zur Geschichtswissenschaft, Band 14 (Göttingen: Wallstein Verlag, 2002).

35. K. M. Squadrito, 'Mary Astell's Critique of Locke's View of Thinking Matter', *Journal of the History of Philosophy*, 25 (1987): 433–40; Eileen O'Neill, 'Astell, Mary (1666–1731)', in E. Craig, ed., *Routledge Encyclopedia of Philosophy* (London: Routledge, 1998), 1, 527–30; and the numerous excellent essays by Sarah Hutton published in the 1990s on Cambridge Platonism, Anne Conway and Margaret Cavendish.

36. K. M. Squadrito, 'Mary Astell's Critique of Locke's View of Thinking Matter', *Journal of the History of Philosophy*, 25 (1987): 433–40.

37. Taylor's 'Mary Astell's Ironic Assault on John Locke's Theory of Thinking Matter'.

38. Ellenzweig, 'The Love of God and the Radical Enlightenment'.

39. See Eileen O'Neill, 'Astell, Mary (1666–1731)', in Craig, *Routledge Encyclopedia of Philosophy*, 1, 527–3. See also Jacqueline Broad's chapter on Astell in *Women Philosophers of the Seventeenth Century*, 90–113, which misses, however, the point of Astell's wavering between Malebranchean occasionalism and a Lockean solution to the Cartesian mind–body problem in terms of 'a sensible congruity' between them, addressed by E. Derek Taylor and Sarah Ellenzweig.

40. On Astell and Cartesianism see O'Neill, 'Women Cartesians, "Feminine Philosophy"'; Margaret Atherton, 'Feminist Critiques of Cartesianism' in *Encyclopedia of Feminist Theories*, vol. 8 (London: Routledge, 2000), 556–9; and Atherton, 'Cartesian Reason and Gendered Reason', in Louise M. Antony and Charlotte Witt, eds., *A Mind of One's Own: Feminist Essays on Reason and Objectivity* (Boulder, Colo.: Westview Press, 1992), 21–33.

41. In clarifying this point, I am grateful for Sarah Hutton's comment. For a percipient account of the republican Macaulay see J. G. A. Pocock, 'Catharine Macaulay: Patriot Historian', in Hilda L. Smith, ed., *Women Writers and the*

Early Modern British Political Tradition (Cambridge: Cambridge University Press, 1998), 243–58.

42. Astell, *A Serious Proposal, Part I*, ed. Springborg (2002), 81.

43. On Descartes' doctrine of the beast-machine, see O'Neill, 'Women Cartesians', 234ff.

44. Judith Drake, *An Essay in Defence of the Female Sex* (London: 1696, Wing A4058), excerpted as Appendix A to Astell, *A Serious Proposal, Parts I and II*, ed. Springborg (2002), 244.

45. The opening lines of the Introduction to Hobbes' *Leviathan* introduce the beast-machine, conjuring up images of Leviathan itself as a great danking beast, to present the state as a human artifice, a work of engineering: *Art* goes yet further, limiting that great Leviathan called a 'Commonwealth' or 'State' (in Latin *Civitas*), which is but an artificial man, though of greater stature and strength than the natural, for whose protection and defence it was intended; and in which the *sovereignty* is an artificial soul, as giving life and motion to the whole body; the *magistrates* and other *officers* of judicature and execution, artificial *joints*; *reward* and *punishment*...are the *nerves*....

Nature (the art whereby God hath made and governs the world) is by the *art* of man, as in many other things, so in this also imitated, that it can make an artificial animal. For seeing life is but a motion of limbs, the beginning whereof is in some principal part within, why may we not say that all *automata* (engines that move themselves by springs and wheels as doth a watch) have an artificial life? For what is the *heart*, but a *spring*; and the *nerves*, but so many *strings*; and the *joints*, but so many *wheels*, giving motion to the whole body, such as was intended by the artificer?

46. Drake, *Essay*, 246.

47. *Ibid.*, 247.

48. On the 'shackled runner' argument see Nathan Glazer, *Affirmative Discrimination* (New York: Basic Books, 1975), 45; Tom Beauchamp, 'The Justification of Reverse Discrimination', in William T. Blackstone and Robert D. Heslep, eds., *Social Justice and Preferential Treatment* (Athens: University of Georgia Press, 1977), 34–110; Thomas Sowell, *Civil Rights: Rhetoric or Reality?* (New York: Quill Paperbacks, 1984), 38; and Thomas Nagel, 'A Defense of Affirmative Action', reprinted in Tom L. Beauchamp and Norman E. Bowie, eds., *Ethical Theory and Business*, 3rd edn. (Englewood Cliffs, N.J.: Prentice-Hall, 1988), 346.

49. Drake, *Essay*, 247–8.

50. Hobbes in *Leviathan*, Chapter 26 (1651 edn., 102–3), ed. Richard Tuck (Cambridge: Cambridge University Press, 1991), 139–40, insisted that women in the state of nature had dominion over their children, in part to deny Filmer's claim that patriarchalism originated in nature. See Teresa Brennan and Carole Pateman, '"Mere Auxilliaries to the Commonwealth": Women and the Origins of Liberalism', *Political Studies* 27, 2 (1979), 183–200, and Jane S. Jaquette, 'Contract and Coercion: Power and Gender in *Leviathan*', in Smith, *Women Writers and the Early Modern British Political Tradition*, 200–19.

51. On Rousseau on *bourgeois* and *citoyen* in a Marxist context, see the enormously influential lectures of Andre Kojève, *Introduction to the Reading of Hegel: Lectures on the Phenomenology of Spirit* (1947; assembled by Raymond Queneau; ed.

Allan Bloom; tr. James H. Nichols, Jr. [Ithaca, N.Y.: Cornell University Press, 1969]), delivered in the 1930s but published in English only in *Rousseau and Marx*. For Marxist feminist applications of these arguments, see particularly Catherine MacKinnon, *Toward a Feminist Theory of the State* (Cambridge, Mass.: Harvard University Press, 1989); and Nancy Hartsock, *Money, Sex and Power: Towards a Feminist Materialism* (Boston: Northeastern University Press, 1985).

52. Charles Davenant (1656–1714), author of *Political and Commercial Works*, was the probable source for Astell's knowledge about slavery. About 1700, Davenant noted that every individual, white or black, in the West Indies was seven times more profitable than an individual at home in England.

53. Astell's analysis of the commercial republic in her long disquisition on Charles Davenant, the political economist, that prefaces *Moderation Truly Stated* has yet to be analyzed for its specific economic content.

54. Marie de Gournay (1565–1645), protégée and literary executor of Montaigne, wrote numerous works, including one short novel, Latin translations, poems, essays on the French language and translation, education, morality, education and critical analysis of contemporary writers. Like Astell, de Gournay was never married and depended on her income from writing. For recent appraisals of her work, see the entry on Gournay in Katharina M. Wilson and Frank J. Warnke, eds., *Women Writers of the Seventeenth Century* (Athens: University of Georgia Press, 1989).

55. Astell complained to Norris in Letter VII of the *Letters*, 149, on the subject of Malebranche, that 'she wish[ed] [she] could read that ingenious Author in his own language, or that he spake [hers]'.

56. Anna Maria van Schurman (1607–78), scholar, artist, author and theologian, was Dutch but born in Germany. See Eileen O'Neill's entry in the *Routledge Encyclopedia of Philosophy* 8, 556–9, along with her biographical and bibliographical sketches of thirteen women philosophers, in Michael Ayers and Daniel Garber, eds., *Cambridge History of Seventeenth-Century Philosophy* (Cambridge: Cambridge University Press, 1998), II, 1399, 1410–11, 1412–13, 1415, 1423–4, 1431–2, 1444–5, 1449, 1460–1, 1461–2, 1462–3, 1464, 1467.

57. *Reflections upon Marriage*, xiii/21.

58. See Wilson and Warnke, *Women Writers of the Seventeenth Century*, xiii, 167, citing evidence from Anna Maria van Schurman's collected writings published in 1638.

59. See Broad, *Women Philosophers of the Seventeenth Century*, 66, who cites Leibniz's letter of 1697 to Thomas Burnet of Kemnay, noting the similarity between his views and those of the late 'Countess of Conway'. See Gottfried Wilhelm Liebniz, *Die Philosophischen Schriften von Gottfried Wilhelm Liebniz*, ed. C. I. Gerhardt (Berlin: Georg Olms Hildesheim, 1960), 3, 216. On Conway and Leibniz see Carolyn Merchant, 'The Vitalism of Anne Conway': Its Impact on Leibniz's Concept of the Monad', *Journal of the History of* Philosophy, 17, 3 (1979): 255–69; Sarah Hutton, 'Anne Conway, Margaret Cavendish and Seventeenth-Century Scientific Thought', in Lynette Hunter and Sarah Hutton, eds., *Women, Science and Medicine 1500–1700* (Stroud: Sutton: 1997), 218–34; and Stephen Clucas, 'The Duchess and the Viscountess: Negotiations between Mechanism and Vitalism in the Natural Philosopher

of Margaret Covendish and Anne Conway', *In-Between: Essays and Studies in Literary Criticism*, 9, 1(2000), 125–360.

60. More to Conway [undated], 1665, in Marjorie Hope Nicolson, ed., *The Conway Letters*, 237 (Oxford: Oxford University Press, 1992), cited by Broad, *Women Philosophers of the Seventeenth Century*, 66.

61. Broad, *Women Philosophers of the Seventeenth Century*, 66–8, and Hutton comment.

62. See Susan James's useful Introduction to Margaret Cavendish, Duchess of Newcastle, *Political Writings* (Cambridge: Cambridge University Press, 2003), x, ff.

63. See Astell's references to Dacier in *A Serious Proposal*, ed. Springborg (2002), 53, 83 and notes.

64. *A Serious Proposal*, ed. Springborg (2002), 53, 83 and notes.

65. Astell adds de Scudéry to the list of serious French women thinkers in the 1701 edition of *A Serious Proposal*, 51; see Springborg (2002), 83 and note.

66. *A Serious Proposal*, ed. Springborg (2002), 83.

67. See Joan Kelly, 'Early Feminist Theory and the Querelle des Femmes, 1400–1789', in *Women, History and Theory: The Essays of Joan Kelly* (Chicago: University of Chicago Press, 1984), 65–109. I am also indebted for the following account to Andrew Lister's *History of Political Thought*, 25 (2004), 44–72. 'Marriage and Misogyny: The Place of Mary Astell in the History of Political Thought'.

68. See F. Nussbaum, *The Brink of All We Hate: English Satires on Women, 1660–1750* (Lexington: University of Kentucky Press, 1984), 26, 34. Nussbaum reproduces a facsimile of the 1690 edition along with a list of responses in her *Satires on Women*, Augustan Reprint Publication 180 (1976).

69. Edward Ward's *The Pleasures of a Single Life* was published, pirated and republished in 1701 (three times), 1702, 1705, 1708, 1709 (four times), 1710, 1720, 1730, 1747, 1760, 1765, 1770 and 1772. See *Eighteenth-Century British Erotica I*, ed. Alexander Pettit and Patrick Spedding (London: Pickering & Chatto, 2002), Volume 1 of which is devoted to the reception of Ward's scurrilous sative.

70. Astell, *Reflections upon Marriage*, ed. Springborg, 36.

71. *Ibid.*

72. *Ibid.*

73. *Ibid.*, 37–8.

74. *Ibid.*

75. *Ibid.*, 5.

76. *Ibid.*, 79.

77. *Ibid.*, 58–9.

78. See my remarks concluding the last chapter of this book on the myth of the state, in particular the liberal-democratic state characterized by the public–private, civil society and the state distinctions.

79. See Janet Todd's recent critical edition of Behn's complete works and Irwin Primer's interlinear edition of Behn's translations of La Rochefoucuald's *Maximes, Seneca Unmasqued* (New York: AMS Press, 2001).

80. See Derek Hughes, *The Theatre of Aphra Behn* (New York: Palgrave, 2001), 193.

81. *Ibid.*, 147, cited in Mark Fulk, 'Recent Trends in Research on Seventeenth-Century Women Writers', *Eighteenth Century Studies*, 36, 4 (2004): 593–603, esp. 597.

82. See, for instance, the excellent essay by Elaine Beilin that situates Elizabeth Cary's *The Tragedie of Miriam* historiographically, the essay by Naomi J. Miller on Mary Wroth's *The Countess of Montgomery's Urania* and Anita Pacheco's essay on Aphra Behn's *The Rover, Part I*, collected in Anita Pacheco, ed., *A Companion to Early Modern Women Writing* (Oxford: Blackwell, 2002), and discussed in Mark Fulk, 'Recent Trends in Research on Seventeenth-Century Women Writers', 595–6.

83. Ellenzweig, 'The Love of God and the Radical Enlightenment', 383.

84. *Ibid.*, 382.

85. Jonathan Israel, *Radical Enlightenment: Philosophy and the Making of Modernity 1650–1750* (Oxford: Clarendon Press, 2001). See my critique of Israel's thesis in Springborg, 'The Enlightenment of Thomas Hobbes', Review Essay on Noel Malcolm, *Aspects of Hobbes'*, *British Journal for the History of Philosophy*, 12, 3 (2004): 513–34.

86. For an indication of probable print runs for pamphlets in this period, see Mark Goldie, 'The Revolution of 1689 and the Structure of Political Argument', *Bulletin of Research in the Humanities*, 83 (1980): 473–564.

87. O'Neill, 'Women Cartesians, "Feminine Philosophy", and Historical Exclusion', 233. This argument is developed at greater length by O'Neill in 'Disappearing Ink: Early Modern Women Philosophers and Their Fate in History', in Janet Kourany, ed., *Philosophy in a Feminist Voice* (Princeton, N.J.: Princeton University Press, 1998), 17–62, and was to some extent foreshadowed by Genevieve Lloyd in *The Man of Reason: 'Male' and 'Female' in Western Philosophy* (London: Routledge, 1984).

88. O'Neill, 'Women Cartesians, "Feminine Philosophy", and Historical Exclusion', 251–2.

89. Cited in *ibid.*, 249, and Londa Schiebinger, *The Mind Has No Sex! Women in the Origins of Modern Science* (Cambridge, Mass.: Harvard University Press, 1989), 138.

90. O'Neill, 'Women Cartesians, "Feminine Philosophy", and Historical Exclusion', 251, citing Jenny d'Hericourt, *A Woman's Philosophy of Woman; or Woman Affranchised* (New York: Carleton, 1864), 73.

91. O'Neill, 'Women Cartesians', "Feminine Philosophy", and Historical Exclusion', 250–1.

92. *Ibid.*, 251, citing Rousseau's *Lettre à Monsieur d'Alembertsure les spectacles* of 1758, ed. L. Brunel (Paris: Hachette, 1896); and Kant's *Beobachten über das Gefühl des Schönen und Erhabenen* (Königsberg: Johan Jakob Kanter, 1764), both noted in Schiebinger, *The Mind Has No Sex!*, 156 and 146, respectively.

93. Thomas Kuhn, *The Structure of Scientific Revolutions* (Chicago: University of Chicago Press, 1962).

94. On the 'unfinished project of modernity', see Michel Foucault's *Power/Knowledge* (New York: Pantheon, 1980); the Foucault–Habermas exchange in Jürgen Habermas, *The Philosophical Discourse of Modernity* (Cambridge, Mass.: MIT Press, 1987); and Björn Wittrock, 'Early Modernities: Varieties and Transitions', *Daedelus*, 127, 3 (1998): 19–40.

Chapter 1

1. See Lois G. Schwoerer's excellent account of the Glorious Revolution and its constitutional importance in *The Declaration of Rights, 1689* (Baltimore: The Johns Hopkins University Press, 1981).

2. On Hobbes's mechanical psychology, see Gianni Paganini, 'Hobbes, Gassendi e la psicologia del meccanicismo', in Arrigo Pacchi, *Hobbes Oggi*, Actes du Colloque de Milan, 18–21 May 1988 (Milan: Franco Angeli Editore, 1990), 351–2. For the response of Anne Conway and Margaret Cavendish to Hobbesian mechanism, see Stephen Clucas, 'The Duchess and Viscountess: Negotiations between Mechanism and Vitalism in the Natural Philosophies of Margaret Cavendish and Anne Conway', in *In-Between: Essays and Studies in Literary Criticism*, 9, 1 (2000): 125–36.

3. On the general milieu of religious scepticism of the period and Hobbes's role in it, see David Berman, 'Deism, Immortality, and the Art of Theological Lying', in J. Leo Lemay, ed., *Deism, Masonry and the Enlightenment* (Newark: University of Delaware Press, 1987), 61–78; Berman, 'Disclaimers as Offence Mechanisms in Charles Blount and John Toland', in M. Hunter and D. Wootton, eds., *Atheism from the Reformation to the Enlightenment* (Oxford: Clarendon Press, 1992), 255–72; Edwin Curley, 'Calvin and Hobbes, or Hobbes as an Orthodox Christian', *Journal of the History of Philosophy*, 34 (1996): 257–71; and Curley, 'Reply to Professor Martinich', *Journal of the History of Philosophy*, 34 (1996): 285–7.

4. The Lady Catherine Jones (1672–1740), to whom Astell refers was the daughter of Richard Jones, third Viscount and first Earl of Ranelagh. She was prominent in court circles and entertained George I at Ranelagh Gardens in 1715. According to the *British Biographical Archive*, Catherine Boyle (d. 1691) married Arthur Jones, Viscount of Ranelagh, becoming Lady Catherine Jones, Countess of Ranelagh. These must have been Lady Catherine's parents, about whom little is known. Lady Catherine Jones, Mary Astell's patron, was the dedicatee of the correspondence between John Norris and Astell, the *Letters Concerning the Love of God* (1695) and the addressee of Astell's *The Christian Religion as Proffes'd by a Daughter of the Church* (1705). See Bridget Hill's introduction to *The First English Feminist: 'Reflections upon Marriage' and Other Writings by Mary Astell* (Aldershot, Hants: Gower, 1986).

5. See Appendices C and D to Perry's biography, *The Celebrated Mary Astell* (Chicago: University of Chicago Press, 1986), 335–454.

6. See David Cressy, 'Literacy in Seventeenth-Century England: More Evidence', *Journal of Interdisciplinary History*, 8 (1977): 141–50, and *Literacy and Social Order: Reading the Writing in Tudor and Stuart England* (Cambridge: Cambridge University Press, 1980).

7. See Jacqueline Broad, *Women Philosophers of the Seventeenth Century* (Cambridge: Cambridge University Press, 2002), 11.

8. See George Ballard, *Memoirs of Several Ladies of Great Britain Who have been Celebrated for their Writings or Skill in the Learned Languages, Arts and Sciences* (1752), ed. Ruth Perry (Detroit: Wayne State University Press, 1985).

9. See John Nicols, ed., *The Epistolary Correspondence . . . of the Right Reverend Francis Atterbury*, 1, 19–20, cited in Perry, *The Celebrated Mary Astell*, 219–20.

10. Letter dated 4 January 1746, Stowe MSS 753:61–2, cited by Perry in *The Celebrated Mary Astell*, 219.

11. See Richard Ackworth, *The Philosophy of John Norris of Bemerton* (New York: Olms, 1979), and E. Derek Taylor, 'Mary Astell's Ironic Assault on John Locke', *Journal of the History of Ideas*, 62 (2001): 507–9. I accept Taylor's criticism that in my essay 'Astell, Masham and Locke: Religion and Politics', in Hilda L. Smith, ed., *Women Writers and the Early Modern British Political Tradition* (Cambridge: Cambridge University Press, 1998), 105–25, I tended to underestimate the importance of Norris as a philosopher and critic of Locke, an omission I have sought here to remedy.

12. Taylor, 'Mary Astell's Ironic Assault on John Locke', 508.

13. *The Life and Errors of John Dunton* (1705; reprinted New York: Garland, 1974); 'To the Impartial Readers', cited in Taylor, 'Mary Astell's Ironic Assault on John Locke', 508. Dunton was not an impartial source, however. As the printer of Malebranche and the promoter of his ideas in England, he was also a promoter of Norris. See Sarah Ellenzweig, 'The Love of God and the Radical Enlightenment': Mary Astell's Brush with Spinoza', *Journal of the History of Ideas*, 64, 3 (2003): 386.

14. For an account of this strange chapter in Norris–Locke relations, see Charlotte Johnston, 'Locke's Examination of Malebranche and John Norris', *Journal of the History of Ideas*, 19 (1958): 551–8, and Taylor 'Mary Astell's Ironic Assault on John Locke', 521.

15. Astell in *A Serious Proposal*, Part 1, 1694 edn., 85–6, recommends that English-women should improve themselves with the 'study of Philosophy (as I hear the *French Ladies* do) *Des Cartes, Malebranche* and others'. In *A Serious Proposal, Part II*, she draws heavily on Descartes, citing '*Les Principes del la Philosofie de M. Des Cartes*, Pt. I. §45', at some length on 134 (1697 edn.), declaring on 250–1; 'But this being already accounted for by *Des Cartes* [*Les Passions de l'Ame*] and *Dr. More*, in his excellent *Account of Vertue*, I cannot pretend to add any thing to what they have so well Discours'd'.

16. 'Mr. *Locke's* Supposition that it is possible for Matter to Think, consider'd' comprises §§259–71 of Astell's *The Christian Religion*.... (1705 edn., 250–63), the first two parts of which (§§1–105, 1–95) are devoted to establishing 'What it is that a late Book concerning the *Reasonableness of Christianity*, etc., pretends to drive at.' For modern commentary see the articles by Kathleen M. Squadrito, 'Mary Astell's Critique of Locke's View of Thinking Matter', *Journal of the History of Philosophy*, 25 (1987): 433–40, and Patricia Ward Scaltsas, 'Women as Ends – Women as Means in the Enlightenment', in A. J. Arnaud and E. Kingdom, eds., *Women's Rights and the Rights of Man* (Aberdeen: Aberdeen University Press, 1990), 138–48.

17. See, for instance, her sarcastic remark in *An Impartial Enquiry*, 40/177: 'Only let me recommend to all such Thinkers, Mr. *Lock's* Chapter *of the Association of Ideas*; they need not be afraid to read it, for that ingenious Author is on the right side'. Astell makes reference to, Chapter 33, of Locke's *Essay Concerning Human Understanding*, 'On the Association of Ideas', and frequently references the *Essay* both in *A Serious Proposal, Part II*, and in *The Christian Religion* (esp. §§259–71, 1705 edn., 250–63). Among those who underestimate

the severity of Astell's critique of Locke, see for instance Squadrito, 'Mary Astell's Critique of Locke's View of Thinking Matter', 435, who actually credits Astell with 'an attempted reconciliation of the views of Norris and Locke' in those very sections of *The Christian Religion* that are most trenchantly anti-Locke.

18. The second edition of 1722 appeared under the title *an Enquiry after Wit, wherein the Trifling Arguing and Impious Raillery of the Late Earl of Shaftesbury in his letter concerning Enthusiasm and other Profane Writers are fully answered and justly exposed.*

19. Philip Pettit, *Republicanism: A Theory of Freedom and Government* (Oxford: Clarendon Press, 1997).

20. Allestree, *The Ladies Calling*, part 2, §3, 'Of Wives'.

21. In the Short Title Catalogue, Drake's work (Wing A4058) is also listed as Astell's. For these items in Locke's library, see John Harrison and Peter Laslett, *The Library of John Locke*, 2nd edn. (Oxford: Clarendon Press, 1971), items 1104, 1105 and 1914.

22. Mary Astell, *Reflections upon Marriage, To which is added a Preface in Answer to Some Objections*, 3rd edn. (London: Printed for R. Wilkin, at the King's Head in St. Paul's Church Yard), Preface, ii–iii.

23. See the Appendix.

24. On the role of seditious libel in eighteenth-century politics, see Philip A. Hamburger, 'Revolution and Judicial Review: Chief Justice Holt's Opinion in *City of London v. Wood*', *Columbia Law Review*, 94, 7 (1994): 2091–153.

25. I am indebted to Schwoerer's account in *The Declaration of Rights*, 32–4, and to J. R. Jones, 'Shaftesbury's "Worthy Men": A Whig View of the Parliament of 1679', *Bulletin of the Institute of Historical Research*, 30 (1957): 232–41, where these terms are explained.

26. Schwoerer's Appendix 3 to her *Declaration of Rights*, 302–5, lists the Rights Committees in the House of Commons, indicating Shaftesbury's ratings.

27. Schwoerer, *Declaration of Rights*, 34.

28. *Ibid.*, 32–3.

29. See J. G. A. Pocock, 'Catharine Macaulay: Patriot Historian', in Smith, *Women Writers and the Early Modern British Political Tradition*, 244–5.

30. For recent Hobbes scholarship see Quentin Skinner, *Reason and Rhetoric in the Philosophy of Thomas Hobbes* (Cambridge: Cambridge University Press, 1996); and the important essays written over three decades, now collected in Skinner, *Visions of Politics*, 3, *Hobbes and Civil Science* (Cambridge: Cambridge University Press, 2002). See J. G. A. Pocock's pathbreaking essay on Hobbes's theology, 'Time, History and Eschatology in the Thought of Thomas Hobbes', in *Politics, Language and Time: Essays on Political Thought* (London: Methuen 1972), 148–201; and Pocock, 'Thomas Hobbes: Atheist or Enthusiast? His Place in a Restoration Debate,' *History of Political Thought*, 11, 4 (1990): 737–49. See also Johan Sommerville, *Thomas Hobbes: Political Ideas in Historical Context* (London: Macmillan, 1992); Gabriella Slomp, *Thomas Hobbes and the Political Philosophy of Glory* (London: Macmillan, 2000); Patricia Springborg, 'Thomas Hobbes on Religion', in Tom Sorell, ed., *Cambridge Companion to Hobbes* (Cambridge: Cambridge University Press, 1996), 346–80; Noel

Malcolm, *Aspects of Hobbes* (Oxford: Clarendon Press, 2002), esp. 'Hobbes, Ezra and the Bible: The History of a Subversive Idea', 383–431, and 'Hobbes and the European Republic of Letters', 457–545. See the review essay by Patricia Springborg, 'The Enlightenment of Thomas Hobbes, Review of Noel Malcolm, *Aspects of Hobbes*', *British Journal for the History of Philosophy*, 12, 3 (2004): 513–34.

31. But see, for instance, Astell, *Reflections upon Marriage*, 45/56, discussed later, where Astell quite clearly targets Hobbes's *Leviathan*.

32. On Hobbes's possible reaction to the Cambridge Platonists and the foundation of the Chairs of Greek at Oxford and Cambridge, see Sarah Hutton, 'Plato and the Tudor Academies', in Francis Ames-Lewis, ed., *Sir Thomas Gresham and Gresham College: Studies in the Intellectual History of London in the Sixteenth and Seventeenth Centuries* (London: Ashgate, 1999), 106–24. See also Hutton, 'Thomas Jackson, Oxford Platonist, and William Twisse, Aristotelian', *Journal of the History of Ideas* 39 (1978): 635–52.

33. See Bernard Williams's excellent essay on Descartes in *The Encyclopedia of Philosophy* (London: Collier Macmillan, 1967), vol. 5, 344–54, esp. 344–5. Chandoux, both a philosopher and a chemist, about whom little is now known, was executed in 1631 as a counterfeiter (Pierre Larousse, *Grand Dictionnaire encyclopédique Larousse* [Paris: Librairie Larousse, c. 1982]).

34. For Hobbes on toleration, see Alan Ryan, 'Hobbes, Toleration and the Inner Life', in David Miller and Larry Siedentop, eds., *The Nature of Political Theory* (Oxford: Clarendon Press, 1983).

35. Astell, *An Impartial Enquiry*, 1704, 41/178.

36. See Laslett's Introduction to the 1988 edition of the *Two Treatises*, 75.

37. On Astell and Locke, see the essays by Patricia Springborg: 'Mary Astell (1666–1731), Critic of Locke', *American Political Science Review*, 89, 3 (1995): 621–33; 'Astell, Masham and Locke', in Smith, *Women Writers and the Early Modern British Political Tradition*, 105–25; 'Mary Astell and John Locke', in Steven Zwicker, ed., *The Cambridge Companion to English Literature, 1650 to 1750* (Cambridge: Cambridge University Press, 1998), 276–306; 'Mary Astell (1666–1731), Critic of the Marriage Contract/Social Contract Analogue', in Anita Pacheco, ed., *A Companion to Early Modern Women Writing* (Oxford: Blackwell, 2002), 216–28.

38. See Shaftesbury's contemptuous remarks in 'Advice to an Author', part 3, §1. Anthony Ashley Cooper, third Earl of Shaftesbury. 'Soliloquy: Or, Advice to an Author'. *Standard Edition. Complete Works, Selected Letters and Posthumous Writings*, ed. Gerd Hemmerich/Wolfram Benda (Stuttgart, Bad Cannstatt: Frommann-Holzboog, [1723], 1981), vol. 1.1, 34–301.

39. Arnauld, *Quatrième Objections* (1641). See Harry M. Bracken, in *Encyclopedia of Philosophy* (London: Collier Macmillan, 1967), vol. 1, 165–7, esp. 165.

40. Sources for the following overview of currents in the Restoration church include Justin Champion, *The Pillars of Priestcraft Shaken* (Cambridge: Cambridge University Press, 1992); John Spurr, ' "Latitudinarianism" and the Restoration Church', *The Historical Journal*, 31, 1 (1988): 61–82; Spurr, ' "Rational Religion" in Restoration England', *Journal of the History of Ideas*,

49, 4 (1988): 563–85; and Spurr, 'The Church of England, Comprehension and the Toleration Act of 1689', *English Historical Review*, 104, 413 (1989): 927–46. For the contest between Cambridge Platonism and Arminianism see the excellent Ph.D. dissertation by William Craig Diamond, 'Public Identity in Restoration England: From Prophetic to Economic', Johns Hopkins University (Ann Arbor, Mich.: University Microfilms, 1982).

41. Diamond, 'Public Identity', 17–18.

42. I owe this observation, as well as substantial revisions to my view of Astell's relation to Cambridge Platonism, to Sarah Hutton one of the readers for Cambridge University Press.

43. Charles J. McCracken, *Malebranche and British Philosophy* (Oxford: Clarendon Press, 1983), 115.

44. Taylor, 'Mary Astell's Ironic Assault on Locke', 509ff.; and Ellenzweig, 'The Love of God and the Radical Enlightenment', 390ff.

45. See John Muirhead, *The Platonic Tradition in Anglo-Saxon Philosophy* (New York: Macmillan, 1931), 64–5, quoting from the Cudworth MSS at the British Museum, vol. 4, 106. Cudworth proposed as a 'psychological hypothesis':

> there must be in the soul one common focus or centre . . . in which all is recollected and knit together, something that is conscious of all congruities, both higher and lower, of all the cogitations, powers, and faculties of the soul. . . . Now this is the whole soul redoubled on to itself, which both comprehends itself and, holding itself as it were in its own hands, turns itself this way and that way . . . this is the . . . (autoekastos), that which is properly called 'I myself in every man'.

46. John Smith, 'Of Prophecy', in *Select Discourses* (London, 1660; New York: Scholars Facsimiles and Reprints, 1979, 170, spoke of access to revealed truth:

> the souls of men are as capable of conversing with it, though it does not naturally arise out of the fecundity of their own Understanding, as they are with any Sensible and External Objects. And as our Sensations carry the motions of Material things to our Understandings which were before unacquainted with them, so there is some Analogical way whereby the knowledge of Divine Truth may also be revealed to us.

47. Smith, 'A Discourse Concerning the True Way of attaining to Divine Knowledge', in *Select Discourses*, 2:

> indeed without such an internal sensating Faculty as this is we should never know when our souls are in conjunction with the Deity or be able to relish the ineffable sweetness of True Happiness.

48. *Ibid.*, 3.

49. *Ibid.*, 2–3.

> As the eye cannot behold the Sun . . . unless it be Sunlike, and hath the form and resemblance of the Sun drawn in it; so neither can the Soul of man behold God . . . unless it be Godlike, hath God formed in it, and made partaker of the Divine Nature.

50. Smith, 'The Excellency and Nobleness of True Religion', in *Select Discourses*, 407.

51. Smith, 'Of Prophecy', *Select Discourses*, 222.

52. For Hobbes on memory, his sensationalist psychology and historiography, see Patricia Springborg, 'Leviathan, Mythic History and National Historiography', in David Harris Sacks and Donald Kelley, eds., *The Historical Imagination in Early Modern Britain* (Cambridge: Cambridge University Press/Woodrow Wilson Press, 1997), 267–97; and Springborg, 'Hobbes and Historiography: Why the Future, He Says, Does Not Exist', in G. A. J. Rogers and Tom Sorell, eds., *Hobbes and History* (London: Routledge, 2000), 44–72.

53. Smith, 'Of Prophecy', *Select Discourses*, 222 (cited by Diamond, 'Public Identity', 36).

54. *Ibid.*, 105–6.

55. See, for instance, John Spurr in ' "Latitudinarianism" and the Restoration Church', 76–7, citing Joseph Glanvil in *Some Discourses, Sermons and Remains* (London, 1681), 406–7, who put it nicely:

> Faith, their airy Faith, that prescinds from moral goodness is all. All is believing, receiving, trusting, relying; which are great duties, part of Faith, but this, as justifying implies more, *viz.* an entire obedience to the Gospel.

56. John Standish, *A Sermon Preached before the King...September 26, 1675* (London, 1676), 24–5 (cited by Diamond, 'Public Identity', 86), who characterizes the Latitudinarians as

> false Apostles and deceitful workers [who] would supplant Christian religion with Natural Theologie; and turn the Grace of God into a wanton notion of Morality, who impiously deny both our Lord and his Holy Spirit; who make reason, reason, reason, their only Trinity.

57. See Spurr, ' "Latitudinarianism" and the Restoration Church', 81.

58. South, *Sermons*, 6 vols. (London, 1692), vol. II, 147, 157–8; c.v. Anon., *A Free and Impartial Inquiry* (London, 1763), 5, cited by Spurr, ' "Latitudinariamism" and the Restoration Church', 80.

59. Simon Patrick, *Works*, 9 vols. (Oxford, 1859), vol. 9, 425–6; Fowler, *Principles*, 223, 228–30, 239–43, 175; John Tillotson, *Sermons*, ed. Ralph Barker, 6 vols. (London, 1695–1704), vol. 6, 412; George Bull, *Harmonia Apostolica* (1670: Oxford 1844 edn.), cited by Spurr, ' "Latitudinarianism" and the Restoration Church', 82.

60. Cited by Diamond, 'Public Identity', 144–7.

61. *Ibid.*, 150–1.

62. John Norris, *Cursory Reflections upon a Book Called, An Essay Concerning Humane Understanding....* appended to *Christian Blessedness, or Discourses upon the Beatitudes of our Lord and Saviour Jesus Christ* (London: For S. Manship, 1690 [Wing 1246]).

63. Locke, *Works*, 1823 edn., 10, 248.

64. See Maurice Cranston, *John Locke: A Biography* (New York: Macmillan, 1957), 478, noted in Ellenzweig, 'The Love of God and the Radical Enlightenment', 393.

65. Norris may deliberately echo the title of Gilbert Burnet's apologetic for William III, Burnet's most Whiggish and therefore most detested work, *An Enquiry into the Measures of Submission to the Supream Authority: And of the Grounds upon which it may be Lawful or necessary for Subjects, to defend their Religion,*

Lives and Liberties, in *Six Papers by Gilbert Burnet, D. D.* (London, 1689; Folger Library, B5913).

66. Norris, *Cursory Reflections,* 30–1.
67. Locke, 'Remarks', in *Works,* 1823 edn., 10, 247.
68. *Ibid.,* 248.
69. *Ibid.,* 248–9.
70. *Ibid.,* 249.
71. *Ibid.*
72. *Ibid.,* 250.
73. Willis Doney, 'Malebranche, Nicholas (1638–1715), in *Encyclopedia of Philosophy* (New York: Collier Macmillan, 1967), 5, 140–4, esp. 141.
74. Locke, 'Remarks', in *Works,* 1823 edn, 10, 250.
75. This section of Locke's essay was subjected to scrutiny in Astell's refutation of Locke on thinking matter in *The Christian Religion* (1705), §263 and §264, 251–3.
76. Locke, 'Remarks', in *Works,* 1823 edn., 10, 250–1.
77. *Ibid.,* 252.
78. See Ellenzweig, 'The Love of God and the Radical Enlightenment', 384ff., on pantheism as an heretical smear.
79. Locke, 'Remarks', in *Works,* 1823 edn., 10, 250–1.
80. *Ibid.*
81. *Ibid.*
82. *Ibid.,* 253.
83. *Ibid.*
84. *Ibid.,* 254.
85. *Ibid.,* 255.
86. *Ibid.*
87. *Ibid.*
88. *Ibid.,* 256
89. *Ibid.*:

> This therefore may be a sufficient excuse of the ignorance I have owned of what our ideas are, any farther than as they are perceptions we experiment in ourselves; and the dull unphilosophical way I have taken of examining their production, only so far as experience and observation lead me; wherein my dim sight went not beyond sensation and reflection.

90. John Norris, *Reason and Religion; or, the Grounds and Measures of Devotion, considered from the Nature of God, and the Nature of Man. In several Contemplations. With Exercise of Devotion applied to every Contemplation,* Parts I and II (London: Printed for Samuel Manship, 1689 [Wing 1265]), Part II, Contempl. II, §29, 204.
91. Locke, 'Remarks', in *Works,* 1823 edn., 10, 256.
92. *Ibid.,* 256–7.
93. *Ibid.,* 257.
94. Norris, *Reason and Religion,* Part II, Contempl. II., §30, 206.
95. Locke, 'Remarks', in *Works,* 1823 edn., 10, 257.
96. Smith, *Select Discourses.*

97. Locke, *Correspondence*, 2. Letter 684, cited by Sarah Hutton in 'Damaris Cudworth, Lady Masham: Between Platonism and Enlightenment', *British Journal for the History of Philosophy*, 1, 1 (1993): 29–54, esp. 43. On Masham's influence on Locke's philosophy more generally, see Sheryl O'Donnell, '"My Idea in Your Mind": John Locke and Damaris Cudworth Masham', in Ruth Perry and Martine Brownley, eds., *Mothering the Mind* (New York: Homes & Meier, 1984), 26–46.

98. Locke, *Essay*, I.i.I., cited by Hutton, in 'Damaris Cudworth, Lady Masham', 44, n. 62.

99. *The Correspondence of John Locke*, ed. E. S. De Beer, 8 vols. (Oxford: Clarendon Press, 1976), 2, Letter 684, cited by Hutton, 'Damaris Cudworth, Lady Masham', 48.

100. Hutton, 'Damaris Cudworth, Lady Masham'.

101. Locke, *Correspondence*, 3, Letter 1040, cited by Hutton, 'Damaris Cudworth, Lady Masham', 48.

102. Norris, *Practical Discourses, on Some Divine Subjects*, 3rd edn. (London: Printed for Samuel Manship, 1694 [Wing 1259]), 34, cited by Jacqueline Broad, 'Mary Astell', in *Women Philosophers of the Seventeenth Century* (Cambridge: Cambridge University Press, 2002), 100, to whom I am indebted for the following analysis of Astell's response to Malebranchean occasionalism.

103. Norris, *Practical Discourses*, 3, 55, cited by Broad, 'Mary Astell', 100.

104. Norris to Astell, 13 November 1693, in Astell and Norris, *Letters Concerning the Love of God* (London: Printed for Samuel Manship, 1695 [Wing 1254]), 62, cited by Broad, 'Mary Astell', 101.

105. Astell to Norris, 21 September 1693, *ibid.*, 5, cited by Broad, 'Mary Astell', 103.

106. Norris to Astell, 13 October 1693, *ibid.*, 17, cited by Broad, 'Mary Astell', 103.

107. Astell to Norris, 14 August 1694, *ibid.*, 278, cited by Broad, 'Mary Astell', 104.

108. Astell to Norris, 14 August 1694, *ibid.*, 280–2, cited by Broad, 'Mary Astell', 105.

109. Astell–Norris *Letters*, 289, cited by Taylor in 'Mary Astell's Ironic Assault on John Locke', 512–13.

110. *Ibid.*, 513.

111. *Ibid.*, 512.

112. Astell, *A Serious Proposal*, Part II, 165, cited by Broad, 'Mary Astell', 109.

113. Astell, *The Christian Religion* (London: Printed by S. H. for R. Wilkin at the King's Head in St. Paul's Church-yard, 1705 [Folger Library 216595]), 51, cited by Broad, *ibid.*, 109.

114. Astell, *The Christian Religion*, 244.

115. Astell–Norris *Letters*, 295–301, cited by Taylor in 'Mary Astell's Ironic Assault on John Locke', 512.

116. *Ibid.*, 289, cited by Taylor, *ibid.*

117. Perry, *The Celebrated Mary Astell*, 79, citing Locke, 'Remarks upon Some of Mr Norris' Books' (written in 1693 but published in 1704), in *The Works of John Locke*, 10 vols. (London, 1812), 10, 249.

118. Taylor, 'Mary Astell's Ironic Assault on John Locke', 512.
119. *Ibid.*, 514. I accept Taylor's criticism that I have perhaps been too ready to read *A Serious Proposal, Part II*, as a full-scale attack on Locke when there is still some ambivalence on Astell's part; witness her apparently laudatory reference to Locke's *Essay*, where she notes (139): 'But this is not a place to say all that this Subject [i.e. the proper use of particles in speech and writing] deserves; they who wou'd have much in a little, may consult an Ingenious Author who has touch'd upon't [**Lock* of Hum. Und. B.3, Ch. 7]'.
120. Taylor, 'Mary Astell's Ironic Assault on John Locke's Theory of Thinking Matter', 514.
121. *Ibid.*, 516. Taylor finds my evidence for the view that Astell knew full well Masham to be the author unconvincing, and I am prepared to concede the point.
122. Ellenzweig, 'The Love of God and the Radical Enlightenment', 385, citing Astell, 'to Mr. Norris', Letter III, *Letters* 45.
123. *Ibid.*, 385.
124. Leibniz to Arnauld, 4/14 January 1688, in *G. W. Leibniz, Philosophical Texts*, tr. Richard Francks and R. S. Woodhouse (Oxford: Oxford University Press, 1998), 135–6. Cited in Ellenzweig, 'The Love of God and the Radical Enlightenment', 385.
125. Richard Burthogge, *An Essay upon Reason* (London, 1694), 109, 116, 118, cited in Ellenzweig, 'The Love of God and the Radical Enlightenment', 386.
126. Ellenzweig, 'The Love of God and the Radical Enlightenment', 386.
127. Sarah Hutton, who is sceptical of Ellenzweig's thesis, has pointed this out to me in precisely these terms.
128. Gerard Winstanley, *The Law of Freedom* (1648), quoted in Stuart Brown, ' "Theological Politics" and the Reception of Spinoza in the early English Enlightenment', *Studia Spinozana*, 9 (1994), 182, and noted by Ellenzweig, 'The Love of God and the Radical Enlightenment', 382.
129. Warburton, *The Divine Legation of Moses Demonstrated* (1738), 2 vols. (London, 1837), 1, 517, 506, cited in Ellenzweig, 'The Love of God and the Radical Enlightenment', 382.
130. Ellenzweig, 'The Love of God and Radical Enlightenment', 392, citing Locke to Molyneux, 26 April 1695, Locke, *Correspondence*, 5, 352–3. Ellenzweig notes that 'over the course of his career Locke was charged with a wide array of religious and political heterodoxies, ranging from deism and So-cinianism [*sic*], to materialism, republicanism and even Spinozism'.
131. Locke, *An Examination of Malebranche's Opinion of Seeing All Things in God*, in Locke, *Works*, 10 vols. (London, 1963), 9, 222, cited in Ellenzweig, 'The Love of God and the Radical Enlightenment', 392.
132. Locke, *Examination, ed. cit.*, 242 and 254, cited in Ellenzweig, *ibid.*
133. Locke, *Remarks upon Some of Mr. Norris's Books* in Locke, *Works*, 242 and 254, cited in Ellenzweig, *ibid.*
134. Dr. Robert South to Locke, 6 December 1699, Locke, *Correspondence*, 6, 753, cited in Ellenzweig, *ibid.*

135. Locke, *The Reasonableness of Christianity*, ed. John C. Higgins-Biddle (Oxford: Clarendon Press, 1999), cited in Ellenzweig, 'The Love of God and the Radical Enlightenment', 387.
136. Masham, *Discourse Concerning the Love of God* (London: Printed for Awnsham and John Churchill, 1696), 71–2.
137. See Nicolas Malebranche, *De la Recherche de la Verité, ou l'on traitte de la nature de l'esprit de l'homme, & de l'usage qu'il en doit faire pour éviter l'erreur dans les sciences*, 4th revised and enlarged edn. (Paris: André Pralard, 1678 [Folger Library B 1893.R.3.1678.Cage]).
138. See the 1700 translation by Thomas Taylor, *Father Malebranche his treatise concerning the search after truth . . .*, 2nd corrected edn. (London: Printed by W. Bowyer, for Thomas Bennet, and T. Leigh and D. Midwinter [Folger Library, M318]), which Astell may well have used. Discussing the greater excitability of women, Taylor, 64, accurately translates Malebranche, 1678 edn., 105–6.
139. Astell, Letters *Concerning the Love of God*, Letter IX, St. Philip and St. James, 1694; 1695 edn., 212.
140. Letter VII, 1695 edn., 128.
141. Letter XI, 21 June 1694; 1695 edn., 272–3:

> The vulgar and Men of carnal Appetites partly out of Ignorance, and partly to lighten as they fancy their own Crimes, being too prone to reflect that Dash of secular Interest, that time-serving or over-great Solicitude for the World, or perhaps their too great Opinion of themselves, or Censoriousness on others, which zealous Pretenders to Piety are sometimes apt to slip into, even on that unblemished Beauty, whose Livery they wear, which I am sure gives no Allowance to such unsuitable Mixtures, however her Votaries happen to admit them.

142. Letter XI, 21 June 1694; 1695 edn., 268–9.
143. Letter XI, 21 June 1694; 1695 edn., 271.
144. Letter IX, St. Philip and St. James, 1694; 1695 edn., 203.
145. *Ibid.*
146. Letter IX, St. Philip and St. James, 1694; 1695 edn., 203–4.
147. Letter IX, St. Philip and St. James, 1694; 1695 edn., 207.
148. Letter XI, 21 June 1694; 1695 edn., 261–2.
149. See Perry, *The Celebrated Mary Astell*, 324.
150. *Ibid.*, 488, n. 8.
151. See Mary Evelyn's Letter to Ralph Bohun, her son, 7 April 1695, in the British Library, London, the 'Evelyn Papers' (uncatalogued), quoted by Jacqueline Broad, 'Mary Astell', 92–3.
152. See James G. Buickerood's unpublished essay, 'What Is It with Damaris, Lady Masham? The Historiography of One Early Modern Woman Philosopher', which notes, 12, not only that both 'John Norris in his reply to *A Discourse* (1698) and Mary Astell in her *A Serious Proposal, Part II* (1697) and *The Christian Religion* (1705) at least affect to believe that it was Locke's work, but that Abel Boyer, in The *History of the Reign of Queen Anner, Digested into Annals Year the Third* (London: A Roper, 1705), attributed [Masham's] *Occasional Thoughts* to Locke in his 1705 death notice of that philosopher.

Moreover, Masham's second book was reissued in the mid-eighteenth century as *Thoughts on a Christian Life* by John Locke Esq. (London: T. Walter, 1747). Buickerood notes other eighteenth-century misattributions of *Occasional Thoughts* to Locke, citing E. S. de Beer, 'Bishop Law's List of Books Attributed to Locke', *The Locke Newsletter*, 7 (1976): 47–54.

153. See *Discourse* 20, where Masham cites from 165 of the *Letters*, as well as other references to '*Letters Philosophical and Divine*'. I am indebted to Taylor, 'Mary Astell's Ironic Assault on John Locke', 516 n., for his careful observation that 'the title Masham uses mirrors the half-title inserted just before the actual letters (i.e., after the preface) and is also printed as the running title of the Astell–Norris *Letters*'.

154. Taylor gives one, that to which I have already referred (*Discourse* 20, citing from 165 of the *Letters*). See Hutton, 'Damaris Cudworth, Lady Masham', 29–54, and Taylor, 'Mary Astell's Ironic Assault on John Locke', 516, n., citing Springborg, 'Astell, Masham and Locke', 114–15 n. 34.

155. See Buickerood, 'What Is It with Damaris, Lady Masham?'.

156. Masham, *Discourse*, 8, citing Norris, *Practical Discourses*, vol. 3, 12–13, as noted in 'What Is It with Damaris, Lady Masham?', 14.

157. Masham, *Discourse*, sig A3r–v, cited in 'What Is It with Damaris, Lady Masham?', 13.

158. *Ibid.*, sig A2v.

159. *Ibid.*, 2.

160. Masham, *Discourse*, 6, quoting Stillingfleet, *A Discourse Concerning the Idolatry Practised in the Church of Rome* (London: Henry Mortlock, 1671), 335.

161. *Ibid.*, 6–7.

162. Buickerood, 'What Is It with Damaris, Lady Masham?', 34 n., notes that Masham in the *Discourse* quotes from Norris's *Practical Discourses* at sig. A3v, 8 (twice), 9, 11, 12, 19–20, 35, 36, 37, 37–8, 38, 81–2, 84–5, 87, 89, 90, 91, 92, 94, 114, 115, 116 and 119; that she cites Malebranche at 71, 72–3, 74, 74–5, 75–6, 103–4, 107, 108, 120–1, 122 and 125; and the Astell–Norris letters are quoted at 15, 20 and 121.

163. Buickerood, 'What Is It with Damaris, Lady Masham?', 15, citing Baker, *Sancta Sophia, Or Directions for the Prayer of Contemplation* (Douay: Ian Patle and Thomas Fievet, 1657).

164. Buickerood, 'What Is It with Damaris, Lady Masham?', 15.

165. *Ibid.*

166. *Ibid.*

167. *Ibid.*, 17, citing Masham, *Discourse*, 78.

168. *Ibid.*, 17.

169. Masham, *Discourse*, 6, quoting Stillingfleet, *A Discourse Concerning the Idolatry Practised in the Church of Rome*, 335.

170. Buickerood, 'What Is It with Damaris, Lady Masham?', 16ff., where the author makes a number of spirited allegations against me and Ruth Perry for concluding, on too little evidence, that Masham had a dispute with Astell.

171. Buickerood, 'What Is It with Damaris, Lady Masham?', 31 n., notes that Catharine Trotter Cockburn's correspondence on Masham, with whom she

was acquainted, makes no mention of Masham responding to Astell, citing *The Works of Mrs Catharine Cockburn*, ed. Thomas Birch (London: J and Knapton, 1751), 2, 185, 189–90, 182, 190, 191, 195, 202, 204, 207.

172. Masham, *Discourse*, 121.

173. *Ibid.*, 120.

174. *Ibid.*, 122.

175. *Ibid.*

176. *Ibid.*

177. *Ibid.*

178. See Locke, *Correspondence*, 4, Letters 1546, 1564, 1575 and 1606, cited by Hutton, 'Damaris Cudworth, Lady Masham', 35 n. 23.

179. Masham, *Discourse*, 8.

180. *Ibid.*, 9.

181. *Ibid.*

182. Astell, *Letters Concerning the Love of God*, 4–7.

183. Masham, *Discourse*, 9.

184. *Ibid.*, 12–13.

185. *Ibid.*, 18–19:

> Love being only a Name given to that Disposition, or Act of the Mind we find in our selves towards any thing we are pleas'd with; And so far as it is simply Love consists barely in That; and cannot be distinguish'd into different Acts of wishing well, and desiring; which are othere different Acts of the Mind consequential to Love, according to the difference of the Object.

186. *Ibid.*, 24–5.

187. *Ibid.*, 26.

188. *Ibid.*, 27.

189. *Ibid.*, 28.

190. *Ibid.*, 29.

191. *Ibid.*

192. *Ibid.*, 30.

193. *Ibid.*

194. *Ibid.*, 31.

195. Locke, *Essay*, bk. 2, ch. 26, §1.

196. Masham, *Discourse*, 31–2.

197. Locke, 'Remarks', in *Works*, 1823 edn., 10, 249.

198. Masham, *Discourse*, 32.

199. *Ibid.*, 33.

200. *Ibid.*, 33–4:

> We are moreover told, That the whole of our Duty, and Happiness, consists in making God the sole Object of our Desires; *The least spark of which sacred Fire cannot light upon the Creatures, without so far defrauding him:* And that the Reason of this Duty is, because *the Creatures are not the efficient Causes of our Sensations.* If this be so, this seems also to lay an Imputation upon the Wisdom and the Goodness of God, who has laid the foundation of our Duty in a Reason which he has concealed from us. For this great Cause why we should love him alone, (*viz. because the Creataures are not the efficient Causes of our Sensations*) is so hidden from us by all the Art, and Contrivance, observable in Nature, that if it were purposely design'd to be conceal'd, and we purposely intended

to be misled, it could not be more so. For in Effect till this last Age, it has not been discover'd; Or at least very sparingly; And even still (as it seems) only Heads cast in *Metaphysical Moulds* are capable of it.

201. *Ibid.*, 38–9.
202. *Ibid.*, 55–6.
203. *Ibid.*, 57.
204. *Ibid.*, 57–8.
205. *Ibid.*, 58.
206. See the chapters on Nicole and Arnauld in Patricia Springborg, *The Problem of Human Needs and the Critique of Civilization* (London: Allen & Unwin, 1981).
207. Masham, *Discourse*, 60.
208. *Ibid.*, 62, 64.
209. *Ibid.*, 65.
210. *Ibid.*, 65–6. The passage, an important one, reads in full:

> Let it be true, that the Creatures have receiv'd no efficiency from God to excite pleasing Sensations in us, and are but the occasional Causes of those we feel: Yet does a Child in the Cradle know this? Or is this apparent so soon as it is that the Fire pleases us when we are Cold? or meat when we are Hungry? No, nor is it at any time a self-evident Truth. We must know many other Truths before we come to know this; which is a Proposition containing many complex Ideas in it; and which we are not capable of framing, till we have been long acquainted with pleasing Sensations. In the mean while, it is certain, that till we can make this Discovery, we shall necessarily Love that which appears to us to be the Cause of our Pleasure.

211. *Ibid.*
212. Astell, Letter IX, St. Philip and St. James, 1694, 209–10.
213. Masham, *Discourse*, 68.
214. *Ibid.*, 72–6.
215. *Ibid.*, 74–5.
216. *Ibid.*, 76–7.
217. *Ibid.*, 87.
218. *Ibid.*, 88.
219. *Ibid.*, 89.
220. *Ibid.*, 90–1.
221. *Ibid.*, 102.
222. *Ibid.*, 82–3.
223. *Ibid.*
224. *Ibid.*, 120–1.
225. *Ibid.*, 123.
226. Astell, *The Christian Religion*, 296.
227. Masham, *Discourse*, 110.

Chapter 2

1. *A Serious Proposal* (London: Printed for R. Wilkin, 1694 [Folger Library, 145912], 145/102). Richard Allestree's proposals, even more pointedly, were directed to 'Women of Quality that converse among those who call themselves the *Wits* of the *Age*'. Allestree lamented that women 'are excluded

out of the Scheme of Education . . . as below the regard of Persons of Quality' (*The Ladies Calling* [Oxford: Printed at the Theater, 1673], 1705 edn., part 1, §5, 106, and part 2, §2, 219).

2. E. Derek Taylor, in 'Mary Astell's Ironic Assault on John Locke', *Journal of the History of Ideas*, 62 (2001), 516ff., sees no reason to doubt that Astell took Masham's *Discourse* to be the work of Locke and uses the Locke/Masham designation to refer to its author, a practice I have refrained from adopting.

3. These works are reprinted in Foster Watson, *Vives and the Renascence Education of Women* (London: Edward Arnold, 1912). See Paula L. Barbour's Introduction to the Augustan Reprint edition, v–vi.

4. *The Catechism of Thomas Becon*, ed. Rev. John Ayre (Cambridge: Parker Society, 1844), 376–7, cited in Bridget Hill, 'A Refuge from Men: The Idea of a Protestant Nunnery', *Past and Present*, 117 (1987), 110.

5. George Hickes, *Sermons on Several Subjects*, 2 vols. (London, 1713), I, 397, cited by Hill, 'A Refuge from Men', 114.

6. Hickes's translation of Fénélon's *L'Education des Filles* was published as *Instructions for the Education of a Daughter*.

7. See Hickes's letter to Dr. Charlett of 9 December 1704 commending her intolerance of nonconformity or occasional conformity. See George Ballard, *Memoirs of Several Ladies of Great Britain Who Have Been Celebrated for Their Writings or Skill in the Learned Languages, Arts and Sciences*, ed. Ruth Perry (Detroit: Wayne State University Press, 1985).

8. The founder of the Saint Cyr school, Françoise d'Aubigné, Marquise de Maintenon, the nature of its charter and relations with Fénelon are the subjects of Carolyn Lougee's *Les Paradis des Femmes: Women, Salons, and Social Stratification in Seventeenth-Century France* (Princeton, N.J.: Princeton University Press, 1976), part 4, 'Saint-Cyr: The Counterinstitution'.

9. See Eileen O'Neill, 'Anna Maria van Schurman', in *Routledge Encyclopedia of Philosophy* (London: Routledge, 1998), vol. 8, 556–9.

10. See Bathsua Makin's *An Essay to Revive the Antient Education of Gentlewomen, in Religion, Manners, Arts & Tongues, with An Answer to the Objections against this Way of Education*, sig. A2 (London: Printed by J. D. to be sold by the Parkhurst at the Bible and Crown at the lower end of Cheapside, 1673 (Los Angeles, Calif.: Augustan Reprint Society, 1980), echoed in *A Serious Proposal* (1694), 78–9 / 79–80.

11. Astell, *A Serious Proposal*, 1694, 13/55. See Makin, *Antient Education of Gentlewomen*, sig. A2ᵛ. See Paula L. Barbour's Introduction to the Augustan Reprint edn. iii–xi.

12. *Makin, op cit.*, 4.

13. On Swift see the excellent work of Ann Cline Kelly, *Swift and the English Language* (Philadelphia: University of Pennsylvania Press, 1988); and Kelly, *Jonathan Swift and Popular Culture: Myth, Media and the Man* (New York: Palgrave, Macmillan, 2002). On Swift's contribution to the Battle of the Books, see Joseph M. Levine, *The Battle of the Books: History and Literature in the Augustan Age* (Ithaca, N.Y.: Cornell University Press, 1991).

14. George Wheler, *The Protestant Nunnery* (London, 1698), cited in Hill, 'A Refuge from Men', 115.

15. See Gilbert Burnet's biography, *History of His Own Time*, 2 vols., published posthumously by his sons, Gilbert and Thomas (London: 1724–34), II, 653.

16. Daniel Defoe, *An Essay upon Projects* (1697) in *The Earlier Life and Chief Earlier Works of Daniel Defoe*, 145–6, cited in Hill, 'A Refuge from Men', 118.

17. See Astell's Foreword to the second edition of *Bart'lemy Fair*, 1722, A2a. See also *Tatler*, 63, 1–3 September, 1709. Perry, in *The Celebrated Mary Astell* (229–30, 516 n. 81), and Hill, in 'A Refuge from Men' (118, nn. 47 and 48), ascribe authorship of the *Tatler* pieces to Swift, but the revised *Tatler* does not, and Astell clearly believes them to be the work of Steele.

18. *The Works of the Celebrated Mrs. Centlivre*, 3 vols. (London, 1761), 1, 210, 218, cited in Hill, 'A Refuge from Men', 120. Susanna Centlivre, a gentlewoman whose family, which fled to Ireland at the Restoration, may have disliked Astell's politics, *Basset Table* having been written after the publication of Astell's royalist political pamphlets of 1704. Twice widowed, Centlivre was a friend of Richard Steele, and in 1706 she married Queen Anne's chief cook, Joseph Centlivre (*Encyclopaedia Britannica*, 11th edn. [London: Encyclopaedia Britannica Co., 1911], 5, 674).

19. Alfred, Lord Tennyson, *Poetical Works of Alfred, Lord Tennyson* (London: Eyre and Spottiswoode, 1905), 167, 176, cited by Hill, 'A Refuge from Men', 107.

20. *The Letters and Works of Lady Mary Wortley Montagu*, 5 vols. ed. Lord Wharncliffe (London, 1837), 4, 184, letter to the Countess of Bute, 20 October 1752, cited by Hill, 'A Refuge from Men', 120. Mary Wortley Montagu, wife of the English ambassador to Constantinople, Edward Montagu, and cousin of Charles Montagu, Lord Halifax, First Lord of the Treasury in George I's ministry, in *Letters from the East* (published in an unauthenticated edition, supposed to have been prepared by John Cleland, in 1763), related journeys she made alone in 1639 to Russia and the Orient. Astell's preface was written in 1724, but the *Letters* were not published until 1763.

21. *The Works of Samuel Richardson*, 19 vols. (London: William Miller, bookseller and stationer, 1811), 16, 155–6, cited by Hill, 'A Refuge from Men', 121. See also the authoritative modern edition of Richardson's *History of Sir Charles Grandison*, 3 vols., ed. Jocelyn Harris (Oxford: Clarendon Press, 1986), 2, 255–6 and notes.

22. But she did it more than once. See her letter of 19 May 1756 to Lady Bute, where she remarks that 'Books are so far from giving Instruction, they fill the Head with a set of wrong Notions from whence spring the Tribes of Clarissas, Harriets, etc.' (*The Complete Letters of Lady Mary Wortley Montagu*, 3, 40, cited by Carol Houlihan Flynn, *Samuel Richardson: A Man of Letters* (Princeton, N.J.: Princeton University Press, 1982), 59.

23. Sara Chapone, mid-eighteenth-century bluestocking, advised George Ballard to read the Astell–Norris correspondence, for instance. See letter to George Ballard dated 12 March 1742, Ballard MSS 43:132, cited by Perry, *Celebrated Mary Astell*, 488 n. 8.

24. Judith Drake, *An Essay In Defence of the Female Sex* (London: Printed for A. Roper and E. Wilkinson at the Black Boy and R. Clavel at the Peacock, in Fleetstreet [Folger Library, A4058a]), 247–8.

25. *Ibid.*, 1–2.

26. *Mary Astell's A Serious Proposal to the Ladies* (1694), ed. Patricia Springborg (London: Pickering & Chatto, 1997).
27. Drake, *Essay*, 3.
28. Swift, *Bickerstaff Papers and Pamphlets on the Church*, ed. Henry Davis (Oxford: Blackwell, 1957), editor's introduction, xxix–xxx.
29. Wotton, 'Of Ancient and Modern Eloquence and Poetry', in *Reflections upon Ancient and Modern Learning* (London, 1694), 20ff. (1697 edn., 35), cited in Levine, *The Battle of the Books*, 36.
30. Levine, *The Battle of the Books*, 41.
31. Drake, *Essay*, 4–5.
32. Levine, *The Battle of the Books*, 409.
33. Drake, *Essay*, 4–5.
34. See Wotton, *Reflections upon Ancient and Modern Learning*, 2nd edn., (London, 1696), 414.
35. Drake, *Essay*, 4–5.
36. Wotton, *Reflections upon Ancient and Modern Learning*, 2nd edn.,
37. Drake, *Essay*, 11–12.
38. *Ibid.*, 12.
39. *Ibid.*, 18.
40. *Ibid.*, 13.
41. *Ibid.*, 13–14.
42. The clearest account of progress based on the reciprocal development of needs and the means of satisfaction is in Rousseau's *Second Discourse*, which owes an acknowledged debt both to Hobbes's theory of social contract and to Locke's labour theory of value in his *Second Treatise*. See Patricia Springborg, *The Problem of Human Needs and the Critique of Civilization* (London: Allen and Unwin, 1981), chapter 3, 'Rousseau on Natural and Artificial Needs'.
43. Drake *Essay*, 15–16.
44. *Ibid.*, 16.
45. *Ibid.*, 24.
46. *Ibid.*, 24–5.
47. *Ibid.*, 27–8.
48. *Ibid.*, 28.
49. *Ibid.*
50. Jansenism was a philosophical movement named after its founder, Cornelius Jansen (1585–1638). Basically, Jansen argued that without special grace from God it is impossible to perform his commandments, and that the operation of grace is irresistible. This spiritual determinism and theological pessimism was expressed in the general rigor of the movement, the unifying characteristic of which was antagonism to the Jesuits. See *the Oxford Dictionary of the Christian Church*, 3rd ed., ed. E. A. Livingstone and F. L. Cross (Oxford: Oxford University Press, 1997).
51. See the *Encyclopaedia Britannica*, vol. 12, 130.
52. *A Serious Proposal to the Ladies, Part II* (London: Printed for Richard Wilkin at the King's Head in St. Paul's Church-yard, 1697), 277/228.
53. *Ibid.*, 278/229.

54. Astell, *Letters Concerning the Love of God, between the Author of the Proposal to the Ladies and Mr. John Norris* (London: Printed for Samuel Manship, 1695 [Wing 1254]), 1–2.

55. Chapter 8 of Antoine Arnauld's *Logic, or the Art of Thinking* (London, 1693 [Wing A3724]) is entitled, 'Of the Clearness and Distinctness of Ideas'.

56. Locke's first letter to Edward Stillingfleet (*The Works of John Locke* [London: Printed for Thomas Tegg, W. Sharpe and Son, *et al.*, 1823], 4, 1–96) is dated January 7, 1696/7; his second (*Works*, 1823 edn., 4, 97–184), is dated June 29, 1697; and his third (*Works*, 1823 edn., 4, 191–498), is dated May 4, 1698.

57. In *Moderation truly Stated* (London: Printed by J. L. for R. Wilkin at the King's Head in St. Paul's Church-yard, 1704 [Folger Library, BX5202.A8.Cage]), 53–6off.

58. Astell, *The Christian Religion* (London: Printed by S. H. for R. Wilkin at the King's Head in St. Paul's Church-yard, 1705 [Folger Library, 216595]), §87, 82.

59. *Ibid.*, §1, 2.

60. See Justin Champion *The Pillars of Priestcraft Shaken: The Church of England and Its Enemies, 1660–1730* (Cambridge: Cambridge University Press, 1992), 111.

61. Astell, *The Christian Religion*, §29, 22.

62. Astell, *ibid.*, noted by Taylor in 'Mary Astell's Ironic Final Assault on Locke', 515 n.

63. In *Moderation Truly Stated*, 53–6off.

64. See Maurice Cranston, *John Locke: A Biography* (New York: Macmillan, 1957), 430–1; and Sheryl O'Donnell, 'Mr. Locke and the Ladies: The Indelible Words on the *Tablula Rasa*', *Studies in Eighteenth-Century Culture*, 8 (1979): 151–64, esp. 154.

65. Masham, *A Discourse Concerning the Love of God* (London: Printed for Awnsham and John Churchill, 1696), 120.

66. See James G. Buickerood, 'What Is It with Damaris, Lady Masham?, The Historiography of One Early Modern Woman Philosopher', unpublished essay, citing Masham's *Discourse*, 78.

67. *A Serious Proposal, Part II*, 118/166. In *The Christian Religion*, §88, 83, Astell returns to the question, however, as seeming to vindicate Malebranche again.

68. See E. J. F. and D. B., 'George Berkeley and *The Ladies Library*', *Berkeley Newsletter* (Dublin), 4 (December 1980), 5–13.

69. *Ibid.*, 6. It is noteworthy that *The Ladies Library* (vol. 3, §§285–334, of 'Religion') also reproduces Pierre Nicole's *Moral Essays*, 2, Pt. 2, 'The True Idea's [*sic*] of Things', in the 1677–80 English translation (See Greg Hollingshead, 'Sources for the *Ladies' Library*', *Berkeley Newsletter*, 1989–90, 2, who incorrectly cites Pierre Nicole as the translator, rather than co-author, of the 1677–80 English edition).

70. G. A. Aitken, in 'Steele's "Ladies' Library"', *The Athenaeum*, 2958 (5 July, 1884), 16–17, earlier attributed to Astell sections excerpted from *A Serious Proposal, Part I* (1690 edn.), in *The Ladies Library*, 1, 438–524. Hollingshead in, 'Sources for the *Ladies' Library*', 1–9, esp., 1, attributes some 17,000 words of Astell's *A Serious Proposal, Part II* [1697 edn., 68–189/144–97 = ch. 3, §§1–5, except for the last three paragraphs], comprising §§7–96 of the section on

'Ignorance' of *The Ladies Library*, 2. Astell's work appears alongside *The Ladies Calling* (*LL* 1, 32–48, 240–58; 2.38–57, 87–106, 184–205, 347–75, 377–85; 3.22–53, 292–303, 332–42). Fénelon's *Education of a Daughter* (*LL* 2, 270–346), was also included, as well as Locke's *Some Thoughts Concerning Education* (see E. J. F. and D. B., 'George Berkeley and *The Ladies Library*', 6).

71. Astell, *Bart'lemy Fair* (1722), Preface, A2a.

72. Descartes made a radical separation between the mental and material realms in his famous mind–body distinction.

73. François Poullain de la Barre (1647–1723) applied Cartesian principles to the question of female inequality, demonstrating by rational argument that customary arguments for male superiority were nothing more than unfounded prejudice. He published three books anonymously on this topic in the 1670s, including, *De l'education des Dames pour la conduite de l'esprit dans les sciences et dans les moeurs* (Paris: Jean Du Puis, 1674), advocating a programme of enlightened female education not dissimilar to Astell's, and *De l'excellence des hommes, contre l'egalité des sexes* (Paris: Jean Du Puis, 1675), a curious rhetorical rebuttal to his own arguments – a rebuttal that he promptly countered, thus strengthening his original position.

74. Jacqueline Broad, in *Women Philosophers of the Seventeenth Century* (Cambridge: Cambridge University Press, 2002), notes 'striking similarities both in the language and content' between Astell's arguments and those of Poullain de la Barre. See also Siep Stuurman, 'Social Cartesianism: François Poullain de la Barre and the Origins of the Enlightenment', *Journal of the History of Ideas*, 58 (1997): 617–40; and Stuurman, 'From Feminism to Biblical Criticism: The Theological Trajectory of François Poullain de la Barre', *Eighteenth-Century Studies*, 33, 3 (2000): 367–82.

75. Astell, Preface to *Reflections upon Marriage*, 3rd edn. (London: Printed for R. Wilkin at the King's Head, St. Paul's Church-yard, 1706), xi/18–19.

76. Astell, *A Serious Proposal, Part II*, 129/170.

77. *Ibid.*

78. Astell, *A Serious Proposal, Part II*, 273–4/120.

79. *Ibid.*, 41–2/133–4.

80. *Ibid.*, 43/134.

81. *Ibid.*, 43–4/134–5.

82. Locke is believed to have undertaken the translation at the instruction of his patron, Anthony Ashley Cooper (1621–83), first Earl of Shaftesbury. Although Harry M. Bracken claims in the *Encyclopedia of Philosophy* (London: Macmillan, 1967), vol. 5, 502 that Locke's translations were not published until the nineteenth century, the translations of the 1680s by 'A Gentleman of Quality', the pseudonym used elsewhere by Locke and/or Shaftesbury, bear his stamp.

83. *A Serious Proposal, Part II*, 50/137.

84. *Ibid.*, 47/136.

85. *Ibid.*, 54/139.

86. *Mr. Locke's Letter to the Bishop of Worcester*, in *The Works of John Locke*, 12th ed., 1823/1963, IV, 1–96.

87. *Essay Concerning Human Understanding*, bk. 2, ch. 23, §2, 1689, edn, 157–8.

88. Reported by Locke, *ibid.*, 3–4.
89. See Mark Goldie, 'The Theory of Religious Intolerance in Restoration Eng-land', in O. Grell, J. I. Israel and N. Tyacke, eds., *From Persecution to Toleration* (Oxford: Oxford University Press, 1991), 333, 342.
90. *Ibid.*, 46–7.
91. *Ibid.*, 8–9.
92. *Mr. Locke's Letter to the Bishop of Worcester*, 1823 edn., 8, quoting his *Essay Concerning Human Understanding*, bk. 2, ch. 23, §§1–3; bk. 2, ch. 13, §19. It is noteworthy that the casuists Locke quotes are the Calvinists Sanderson and Bugersdicius, and not Aquinas or the scholastics.
93. *Mr. Locke's Letter to the Bishop of Worcester*, 6.
94. *Ibid.*, 6.
95. *Ibid.*, 11.
96. *Ibid.*, 18–19.
97. *Ibid.*, 10, 19.
98. *Ibid.*, 23–4.
99. *ibid.*, 10.
100. *Ibid.*, 20–1.
101. *Ibid.*, 30; cf. Astell's refutation in *A Serious Proposal, Part II*, ch. 3, 72–3/147–8 and 134–8/172–3. From comparison of two or more clearly conceived ideas arises a judgement framed as a proposition. Distinctness involves clearness but not vice versa, she argues.
102. *Mr. Locke's Letter to the Bishop of Worcester*, 36, citing the *Essay Concerning Human Understanding*, bk. 4, ch. 10, §5.
103. *Ibid.*, 32, 39.
104. *Ibid.*, 40.
105. *Ibid.*, 50–3, 55.
106. *Ibid.*, 59.
107. *Ibid.*, 59–60.
108. *A Serious Proposal, Part II*, 91–2/155.
109. *Ibid.*, 74/148.
110. *Mr. Locke's Letter to the Bishop of Worcester*, 10.
111. *A Serious Proposal, Part II*, 71/146, §1.
112. *Ibid.*, 124–5/168–9.
113. *Ibid.*, 72/147.
114. *Ibid.*, 138/174.
115. In fact the phraseology is directed at Masham, who in *Discourse Concerning the Love of God*, 121, had convicted the Platonists' project of denying human sociability, making 'it impossible to live in the daily Commerce and Conver-sation of the World, and love God as we ought to do'.
116. *A Serious Proposal, Part II*, 74/148. See *ibid.*, 235–6/212, Astell's Platonist paean to the Divinity that continues the metaphor of veiled light:

> Let then these little things be drawn aside, these Clouds that hide the most adorable Face of GOD from us, these Mud-walls that enclose our Earthly Tabernacle and will not suffer us to be pierc'd with the Beams of his Glory, and wounded, not to Death but Life, with the Arrows of his Love and Beauty. In him we find that infinite Good which alone can satisfie us, and which is not to be found elsewhere. Somewhat in which we

lose our selves with Wonder, Love and Pleasure! Somewhat too inefiable to be nam'd, too Charming, too Delightful not to be eternally desir'd! And were we not sunk into Sense, and buried alive in a crowd of Material Beings, it might seem impossible to think of any thing but Him. For whether we consider the Infinite Perfection of his Nature, or the Interest we have in, and our entire dependance on him. Whether we consider him as Maker and Governor of all things, as filling all places, intimately acquainted with all Events, as Righteous in all his ways, and holy in all his works. Whether we contemplate his Almighty Power; or what seems more suitable to our Faculties and Condition, the Spotless Purity of his Nature, which guided by Infallable Wisdom always Chuses what Best.

117. *Ibid.*, 121–2/167.
118. *Ibid.*, 83/152.
119. *Ibid.*, 115/164.
120. *Ibid.*, 78–9/150.
121. *Ibid.*, 132/171.
122. Locke, the *Reasonableness of Christianity*, in *The Works of John Locke* (1695), 279.
123. *A Serious Proposal, Part II*, 202–3/200.
124. *The Christian Religion*, 402–3. Note that by the use of italics as usual Astell deliberately indicates quotation from Locke.
125. *A Serious Proposal II*, 203/200.
126. *Ibid.*, 87/153.
127. *Ibid.*, 89/154.
128. *Ibid.*, 87–8/153.
129. *Ibid.*, 77/149: 'Moral Certainty is a Species of Knowlege whose Proofs are of a compounded Nature, in part resembling those which belong to Science, and partly those of Faith.'
130. *Ibid.*, 134–5/172–3, following Chapter 8 of Antoine Arnauld's *Art of Thinking*, entitled 'Of the Clearness and Distinctness of Ideas'.
131. *Ibid.*, 124–5/168–9.
132. *Ibid.* See Locke's first letter to Stillingfleet, 1823 edn., 52–3, where he contests Descartes' notion of clear and distinct ideas with reference to his claims in *An Essay Concerning Human Understanding*, bk. 4, ch. 10, §7.
133. Astell, *A Serious Proposal, Part II.*, 134–5/172, citing *Les Principes de la Philosophy of M. Des Cartes*, Part 1, §45.
134. *Ibid.*, 134/172. Astell appears to understand by 'distinctness' the power to individuate:

The First and Principal thing therefore to be observed in all the Operations of the Mind is, That we determine nothing about those things of which we have not a Clear Idea, and as distinct as the Nature of the Subject will permit, for we cannot properly be said to Know any thing which does not Clearly and Evidently appear to us. Whatever we see Distinctly we likewise see Clearly, Distinction always including Clearness, tho this does not necessarily include that, there being many Objects Clear to the view of the Mind, which yet can't be said to be Distinct.

135. *Ibid.*, 135/173.
136. *Ibid.*

137. The syllogism is a classical form of logical proof that involves the deduction of a conclusion (third term) from a principle (first term), applied to circumstances (second term). It was made famous by Aristotle.

138. *Logic, or The Art of Thinking*, part 3, chs. 2–15, 221–89.

139. *A Serious Proposal, Part II*, 160–1/183.

140. *Ibid.*, 161/183.

141. *The Christian Religion*, §§257–9, 247–50.

142. *Ibid.*, §259, 249–50.

143. *Ibid.*, §§261, 262, 250–2.

144. Astell, *A Serious Proposal, Part II*, 135/173.

145. *The Christian Religion*, §263, 253.

146. *Ibid.*, §259, 1705, 230.

147. *Ibid.*, Astell takes the triangle as a case in point:

> *whatever Excellency, not contain'd in its essence, be superadded to* a Triangle *it does not destroy the essence of* a Triangle *if it leaves it* a Figure bounded by three Right Lines; *for whereever that is there is the essence of* a Triangle

148. *Ibid.*, §264, 1705, 255. Astell cites Locke's Third Letter to Stillingfleet, 402, as acknowledged in a marginal note.

149. Astell's note reads '*Ibid.*, 405.'

150. Astell inserts '405'.

151. Astell inserts '400'.

152. See especially Taylor, 'Mary Astell's Ironic Assault on John Locke's Theory of Thinking Matter'.

Chapter 3

1. See *Reflections upon Marriage* (London: Printed for R. Wilkin at the King's Head, St. Paul's Church-yard, 1706), 29, 32, 38–41, 92–5. The corresponding pages in Patricia Springborg, *Mary Astell (1666–1731), Political Writings* (Cambridge: Cambridge University Press, 1996), are 27/46, 31/48, 36–41/51–4, 87–92/76–80) Henceforth citations will be to the 1706/1996 editions given in this format.

2. Charles Leslie, Supplement, 4–7, to his *The New Association, Part II* (London, 1703).

3. Carole Pateman, *The Sexual Contract* (Cambridge: Polity Press, 1988).

4. Hobbes, *Leviathan*, ed. Richard Tuck (Cambridge: Cambridge University Press, 1991), 139–40.

5. See Patricia Springborg, '*Leviathan*, the Christian Commonwealth Incorporated', *Political Studies*, 24, 2 (1976): 171–83 (reprinted in John Dunn and Ian Harris, eds., *Great Political Thinkers* [Cheltenham: Elgar, 1997], 2, 199–211), which briefly reviews the concept and Hobbes's use of it.

6. See Otto F. von Gierke, *Political Theories of the Middle Ages*, tr. F. W. Maitland (Cambridge: Cambridge University Press, 1900), and *Natural Law and the Theory of Society 1500–1800*, tr. E. Barker (Cambridge: Cambridge University Press, 1934).

7. See Gordon Schochet's authoritative *Patriarchalism in Political Thought* (Oxford: Blackwell, 1975).

8. See Richard Tuck, *Natural Rights Theories, Their Origin and Development* (Cambridge: Cambridge University Press, 1981), 17.

9. See R. W. K. Hinton, 'Husbands, Fathers and Conquerors', two parts, *Political Studies*, 15, 3 (1967): 291–300 and 16, 1 (1968): 55–67; Mary Lyndon Shanley, 'Marriage Contract and Social Contract in Seventeenth Century English Political Thought', *Western Political Quarterly*, 32 (1979): 79–91; Pateman, *The Sexual Contract*, and Pateman, 'God Hath Ordained to Man a Helper: Hobbes, Patriarchy and Conjugal Right', *British Journal of Political Science*, 19 (1989): 445–64.

10. Pateman, *The Sexual Contract*.

11. For the social and legal ramifications of the marriage contract from antiquity, see H. J. Wolff, 'Marriage Law and Family Organization', *Traditio*, 2 (1944): 43–95; and Margaret Sommerville's exhaustive examination of medieval and early modern writings on marriage, *Sex and Subjection: Attitudes to Women in Early-Modern Society* (London: Matthew Arnold, 1995).

12. Keith Thomas, 'Women and the Civil War Sects', *Past and Present*, 13 (1958): 42–62.

13. Duns Scotus, XI. 2. 816, cited in Sommerville, *Sex and Subjection*, ch. 2, 10.

14. On corporation in medieval and early modern jurisprudence see the now classic studies by Otto von Gierke, *Political Theories of the Middle Ages*, ed. F. W. Maitland (Cambridge: Cambridge University Press, 1900) and *Natural Law and the Theory of Society*, ed. Ernest Barker (Cambridge: Cambridge University Press, 1934).

15. See the celebrated study by Ernst Kantorowicz, *The King's Two Bodies: A Study in Medieval Political Theology* (Princeton, N.J.: Princeton University Press, 1957).

16. See *ibid.* and Patricia Springborg's investigation of the roots of this doctrine in Egyptian animism in *Royal Persons: Patriarchal Monarchy and the Feminine Principle* (London: Unwin Hyman, 1990).

17. See Frederick W. Maitland, 'The King as Corporation' and 'Moral Personality and Legal Personality', in his *Selected Essays*, ed. H. D. Hazeltine, G. Lapsley and H. Winfield (Cambridge: Cambridge University Press, 1936).

18. Kantorowicz, *The King's Two Bodies*, 228.

19. Cardinal Pole, *Ad Enricum VIII... pro ecclesiasticae unitatis defensione*, cited by Kantorowicz, *The King's Two Bodies*, 229.

20. Kantorowicz, *The King's Two Bodies*, 215–21.

21. *Ibid.*, 223.

22. *Ibid.*

23. *Ibid.*, 217.

24. Thomas Smith in *De Republica Anglorum* (Cambridge: Cambridge University Press, 1906), book 1, cited by Hinton, 'Husbands, Fathers and Conquerors', (1967), 293.

25. G. W. F. Hegel, *Philosophy of Right*, tr. T. M. Knox (Oxford: Clarendon Press, 1957), §238.

26. See Schochet, *Patriarchalism in Political Thought*.

27. See Paolo Rossi, *The Dark Abyss of Time: The History of the Earth and the History of Nations from Hooke to Vico*, tr. Lydia G. Cochrane (Chicago: University of Chicago Press, 1979); John Gascoigne, ' "The Wisdom of the Egyptians" and the Secularisation of History in the Age of Newton', and Garry W. Trompf, 'On Newtonian History', in Stephen Gaukroger, ed., *The Uses of Antiquity* (Dordrecht: Kluwer Academic, 1991), 213–49 and 171–212, respectively.

28. Sir Robert Filmer (c. 1595–1653), a political writer born in Kent, was educated at Trinity College, Cambridge, and knighted by Charles I. As a strong royalist he suffered much during the Civil War, his house was plundered several times, and he himself was imprisoned in Leeds Castle in Kent in 1644. His major work, *Patriarcha or The Natural Power of Kings Asserted*, which argued that the notion of the divine right of kings was merely a modern manifestation of the biblical notion of the right of inheritance, as reflected in the Old Testament, although written earlier, was not published until 1680 (*DNB* and *Who's Who in the History of Philosophy*).

29. Schochet, *Patriarchalism in Political Thought*.

30. *Ibid.* See J. G. A. Pocock's classic study, *The Ancient Constitution and the Feudal Law* (Cambridge: Cambridge University Press, 1957, 1970), and the discussion by Johann Sommerville in 'History and Theory: The Norman Conquest in Early Stuart Political Thought', *Political Studies*, 34 (1986): 249–61 and in his *Politics and Ideology in England 1603–40* (London: Routledge, 1986).

31. See Sommerville, 'History and Theory: The Norman Conquest', 258–9.

32. Johann Sommerville, Introduction to his edition of *Sir Robert Filmer, Patriarcha and Other Writings* (Cambridge: Cambridge University Press, 1991), xi.

33. Sommerville, 'History and Theory: The Norman Conquest', 260.

34. Mary Astell, *An Impartial Enquiry into the Causes of Rebellion and Civil War* (London: Printed by E. for R. Wilkin at the King's Head in St. Paul's Churchyard [Folger Library, BV 4253.KY.C75.Cage]), 34/170.

35. Hinton, 'Husbands, Fathers and Conquerors', parts 1 and 2.

36. Hobbes, *Leviathan*, 139–40.

37. Hobbes, *Elements of the Laws*, in W. Molesworth, ed., *The English Works* (London: Bohn, 1839–45), 4, 207.

38. Hobbes, *Leviathan*, 117.

39. See Patricia Springborg, '*Leviathan* and the Problem of Ecclesiastical Authority', *Political Theory*, 3, 3 (1975): 289–303 (reprinted in Dunn and Harris, *Great Political Thinkers*, 2, 144–59); and Springborg, '*Leviathan*, the Christian Commonwealth Incorporated', *Political Studies*, 24, 2 (1976): 171–83 (reprinted in Dunn and Harris, *Great Political Thinkers*, 2, 199–211).

40. See Pateman, 'God Hath Ordained to Man a Helper.'

41. See Wolff's excellent account in 'Marriage, Law and Family Organization', 43–95.

42. Moses Finley, 'Marriage, Sale and Gift in the Homeric World', *Revue Internationale des Droits de l'Antiquité*, 3rd series, 2 (1955): 167–94.

43. Hegel, *Philosophy of Right*, tr. T. Knox (Oxford: Clarendon Press, 1952), §§159, 159A.

44. Hobbes, *Leviathan*, 135.

45. John Locke, *Two Treatises of Government*, ed. Peter Laslett (Cambridge: Cambridge University Press, 1988), bk. 2, §119, 347–8.
46. Astell, Preface to *Reflections upon Marriage*, x/16.
47. Mary Astell, *Moderation truly Stated: or A Review of a Late Pamphlet, Entitul'd, Moderation a Vertue.... With a Prefatory Discourse to Dr. D'Avenant, Concerning His Late Essays on Peace and War* (London: Printed by J. L. for Richard Wilkin at the King's-Head, in St. Paul's Church-yard, 1704 [Folger Library, BX5202.A8.Cage]), 80, citing Milton's *Eikonoklastes in Answer to a Book Intitl'ed Eikon Basilike* (London: Printed by Matthew Simmons, 1649), 237.
48. Ruth Perry, *The Celebrated Mary Astell: An Early English Feminist* (Chicago: University of Chicago Press, 1986).
49. The 1706 preface was amplified and printed as an appendix to later editions.
50. Astell, Preface to the 1706 edition of *Reflections upon Marriage*, v/10–11.
51. *Ibid.*, xi/18–19.
52. Thomas, 'Women and the Civil War Sects', 50.
53. Filmer, 'The Anarchy of a Limited of Mixed Monarchy' (1648), in Johann Sommerville, ed., *Patriarcha and Other Writings* (Cambridge: Cambridge University Press, 1991), 142.
54. *Ibid.*
55. John Nalson, *The True Liberty and Dominion of Conscience*, 2nd edn. (London, 1678), 13, cited in Thomas, 'Women and the Civil War Sects', 54.
56. Astell, *Reflections upon Marriage*, xxii/29.
57. *Ibid.*, ix–x/15–16.
58. *Ibid.*, i/7.
59. *Ibid.*, 53–4/60.
60. *Ibid.*, 82/76.
61. *Ibid.*, 56/62.
62. Independents belonged to congregations that believed they had local autonomy independent of any external authority. The term 'independency' prevailed in England in the seventeenth century but was not favoured in New England, where the term for the same movement was 'Congregationalism' (*Oxford English Dictionary*, 1989, vol. 7, 848).
63. Mary Astell, *An Impartial Enquiry*, 9–10/141–2.
64. Henry Sacheverell, *The Political Union. A Discourse Shewing the Dependence of Government on Religion.... *(Oxford: Printed by Leonard Lichfield for George West and Henry Clements, 1702 [Folger Library, BV 629.S2.P6.Cage]), cited by Mark Goldie, 'Tory Political Thought, 1689–1714', Ph.D. dissertation, University of Cambridge, 1978.
65. Astell, *Some Reflections upon Marriage* (London: Printed for John Nutt, 1700 [Folger Library, 181431, Wing A4067]), 140, 143.
66. *Ibid.*, 31/48–9.
67. *Ibid.*, 44/55.
68. *Ibid.*, 47/57.
69. Astell, *Reflections upon Marriage*, 45/56.
70. Hobbes, *Leviathan*, 1651, bk. 1, ch. 15.
71. Astell, *Reflections upon Marriage*, 46/56.
72. *Ibid.*, 37/52.

73. *Ibid.*, 32–3/49–50.
74. *Ibid.*, ii/8.
75. *Ibid.*, 31/48.
76. *Ibid*, 27/46–7.
77. Milton, *Eikonoklastas*, 237.
78. Milton, *Of Reformation, Milton's Prose Works (MPW)* 1.781, cited in David Norbrook, *Writing the English Republic 1627–1660: Poetry, Rhetoric and Politics 1627–1660* (Cambridge: Cambridge University Press, 1998), 112.
79. Milton, *Of Reformation, MPW* 1, 791, cited in *ibid.*
80. *Ibid.*, 1. 544, cited in *ibid.*
81. Milton, *Second Defense, MPW* 1. 625, cited in *ibid.*, 115.
82. Milton, *Political Writings*, ed. Martin Dzelzainis (Cambridge: Cambridge University Press, 1991), 1, cited in Quentin Skinner, *Liberty before Liberalism* (Cambridge: Cambridge University Press, 1998), 19.
83. Astell, *Reflections upon Marriage*, 31/48, 27/46–7.
84. *Ibid.*, xiii/21.
85. This is a basic contention of Mark Goldie in 'Tory Political Thought 1689–1714'.
86. Astell, *Reflections upon Marriage*, x/17.
87. Rousseau, *Second Discourse, On the Origins of Inequality, in Jean-Jacques Rousseau, The First and Second Discourses*, ed. Roger D. Masters (New York: St. Martins Press, 1964), Second Part, 141ff.; and Karl Marx, *Economic and Philosophic Manuscripts of 1844*, Third Manuscript, 'The Power of Money', *Marx-Engels Collected Works* (London: Lawrence and Wishart, 1975), 3, 324.
88. Rousseau, 'A Discourse on Political Economy', in *The Social Contract and Discourses* (London: J. M. Dent, 1952), 235–6: 'it follows that *public* economy, which is my subject, has been rightly distinguished from *private* economy, and that, the State having nothing in common with the family except the obligations which their heads lie under of making both of them happy, the same rules of conduct cannot apply to both'. Rousseau's articulation of the private and public spheres is one of the most succinct.
89. Astell, *Reflections upon Marriage*, 12–87/38–77.
90. *Ibid.*, 54/61.
91. *Ibid.*, 55–6/61.
92. *Ibid.*, 87–8/77.
93. *Ibid.*, 89/78.
94. *Ibid.*, iv/10.
95. *Ibid.*, v/10.
96. *Ibid.*, Patricia Springborg, *Mary Astell (1666–1731), Political Writings* (Cambridge: Cambridge University Press, 1996), 8–10 and notes.
97. *Ibid.*
98. *Ibid.*, xxiii–xxiv/29.
99. *Ibid.*, xxiv/29.
100. *Ibid.*, x/16.
101. *Ibid.*, xi/18–19.
102. *Ibid.*, xxv–vi/31.
103. Astell, *The Christian Religion . . . .* (London: Printed by S. H. for R. Wilkin at the King's Head in St. Paul's Church-yard, 1705 [Folger Library, 216595]),

262, 263, etc., citing the *Two Treatises*, '*Mr* Lock's *Third Letter to the Bishop of Worcester*, 409', and his *Essay* throughout. Until the death of William III, Locke's patron, Astell showed customary reluctance to name Locke, and even in 1704 she frequently attacked his arguments through surrogates.

Chapter 4

1. See Quentin Skinner, 'Conquest and Consent: Thomas Hobbes and the Engagement Controversy', in G. E. Aylmer, ed., *The Interregnum: The Quest for Settlement 1646–1660* (London: Macmillan, 1972) 85; and Mark Goldie, 'Tory Political Thought 1689–1714', Ph.D. dissertation, University of Cambridge, 1978.
2. Its first mention in print was *The Secret History of the Calves' Head Club*, by Edward Ward (1667–1731), reprinted in the *Harleian Miscellany*. Astell refers to its irreverent revels in *An Impartial Enquiry into the Causes of Rebellion and Civil War* (London: Printed by E. for R. Wilkin at the King's Head in St. Paul's Church-yard, 1704 [Folger Library, BV 4253.K4.C75.Cage]), 16/146 (*Encyclopaedia Britannica*, 1910 edn.).
3. *An Impartial Enquiry* (1704), 16/146.
4. See Anon., *A Philosophick Essay Concerning Ideas, According to Dr. Sherlock's Principles (1705)*, ed. James G. Buickerood (New York: AMS Press, 1996).
5. Goldie, 'Tory Political Thought 1689–1714', 64.
6. See Jonathan Scott, 'Radicalism and Restoration: The Shape of the Stuart Experience', *Historical Journal*, 31, 2 (1988): 453–67, esp. 460–1.
7. See the prefatory advertisement to White Kennett, *A Compassionate Enquiry into the Causes of the Civil War. In a Sermon Preached in the Church of St. Botolph Aldgate, On 31 January, 1704. the Day of the Fast of the Martyrdom of King Charles the First* (London: Printed for A. and J. Churchil in Pater-Noster Row, 1704).
8. See Kennett, *A Compassionate Enquiry into the Causes of the Civil War*, 19.
9. *Ibid.*, 16.
10. See Johann Sommerville, 'From Suarez to Filmer: A Reappraisal', *Historical Journal*, 25 (1982): 525–40, and *Politics and Ideology in England 1603–40* (London: Routledge, 1986). *Ibid.*, 16.
11. Astell, *An Impartial Enquiry*, 26ff./157ff.
12. Goldie, 'Tory Political Thought 1689–1714', 51.
13. White Kennett, *The Witchcraft of the Present Rebellion* (1715), 5, cited by Goldie, 'Tory Political Thought 1689–1714', 325.
14. Mark Goldie, 'The Revolution of 1689 and the Structure of Political Argument', *Bulletin of Research in the Humanities*, 83 (1980): 473–564, esp. 499.
15. Skinner, 'Conquest and Consent'; and Jonathan Scott, 'Radicalism and Restoration: The Shape of the Stuart Experience', *The Historical Journal*, 31, 2 (1988): 453–67.
16. Goldie, 'Tory Political Thought 1689–1714', 79.
17. Mary Astell, *A Fair Way with the Dissenters and their Patrons* (London: Printed for E. by R. Wilkin at the King's Head in St. Paul's Church-yard, 1704 [Folger Library, BX5202.A7,Cage]), 214.

18. J. G. A. Pocock, *The Ancient Constitution and the Feudal Law* (Cambridge: Cambridge University Press, 1957; 2nd edn. 1987), 233ff.
19. *Ibid.*, 38.
20. Preface to the third edition of *Reflections upon Marriage* (London: Printed for R. Wilkin at the King's Head in St. Paul's Church-yard, 1706), iv/9–10.
21. See Goldie, 'The Revolution of 1689 and the Structure of Political Argument', 508–9.
22. See Patricia Springborg, 'Thomas Hobbes and Cardinal Bellarmine: *Leviathan* and the Ghost of the Roman Empire', *History of Political Thought*, 16, 4 (1995): 503–31.
23. 'Let every person render obedience to the governing authorities; for there is no authority except from God, and those in authority are divinely constituted.' *The Holy Bible* (Nashville, Tenn.: Giddeons International, 1986), 843.
24. Goldie, 'Tory Political Thought 1689–1714', 100. See especially Johann Sommerville's perceptive treatment of Hobbes and Bellarmine in *Thomas Hobbes: Political Ideas in Historical Context* (London: Macmillan, 1992), 113–19, which complements his overview of papalist theory and Anglican responses in his *Politics and Ideology in England, 1603–40* (London: Routledge, 1986), 189–203. On the perceived convergence of Presbyterianism and popery on the power to depose kings, see Sommerville's 'From Suarez to Filmer: a Reappraisal', *Historical Journal*, 25 (1982): 525–40 and the Introduction to his edition of Sir Robert Filmer's *Patriarcha and Other Writings* (Cambridge: Cambridge University Press 1991), esp. xv, xxi–iv. On the medieval roots of consent theory see Francis Oakley, 'Legitimation by Consent: The Question of the Medieval Roots', *Viator*, 14 (1983): 303–35, and Oakley's *Omnipotence, Covenants, and Order* (Ithaca, N.Y.: Cornell University Press, 1984), esp. 48–91.
25. See Peter Laslett's Introduction to his edition of Locke's *Two Treatises of Government* (Cambridge: Cambridge University Press, 1988), 62–5.
26. See Mark Goldie, 'The Revolution of 1689 and the Structure of Political Argument', *Bulletin of Research in the Humanities*, 83 (1980): 473–564, esp. 476.
27. Goldie, 'Tory Political Thought 1689–1714', 167. See the brilliant article on the legal ramifications of the Kentish petitioners' claims by Philip A. Hamburger, 'Revolution and Judicial Review: Chief Justice Holt's Opinion in *City of London v. Wood*', *Columbia Law Review*, 94, 7 (1994): 2091–153.
28. Goldie, 'Tory Political Thought 1689–1714', 168.
29. See John Pocock, *The Ancient Constitution and the Feudal Law*, 436–48; Goldie, 'Tory Political Thought 1689–1714', 168.
30. See the remarks of the eighteenth-century commentator George Ballard, in his *Memoirs of Several Ladies of Great Britain Who have been Celebrated for their Writings or Skill in the Learned Languages, Arts and Sciences* (1752), cited by Ruth Perry, *The Celebrated Mary Astell: An Early English Feminist* (Chicago: University of Chicago Press, 1986).
31. Goldie, 'Tory Political Thought 1689–1714', 169, 173.
32. Davenant, *Essays upon Peace and Home and War Abroad 1704*, in *Works*, ed. Sir C. Whitworth (London, 1771), printed for R. Horsefield, T. Becket and P. A. DeHondt, and T. Cadell and T. Evans, IV, §§1 and 13.

33. Astell, *An Impartial Enquiry*, 34/170–1.
34. *Ibid.*, 7/139.
35. *Ibid.*, 5/138.
36. *Ibid.*, 8/139–40.
37. *Ibid.*, 22/152.
38. *Ibid.*, 9/141.
39. *Ibid.*, 8/148.
40. *Ibid.*, 48/185.
41. *Ibid.*, 32/169.
42. *Ibid.*, 29/162.
43. See Bodleian MSS Locke e.18, reprinted in James Farr and Clayton Roberts, 'John Locke on the Glorious Revolution: A Rediscovered Document', *The Historical Journal*, 28 (1985): 385–98, esp. 395–8. Clarke was a member of Parliament with whom Locke had earlier corresponded.
44. See Charles Leslie, *The Divine Rights of the British Nation and Constitution Vindicated... against Mr. Hoadly's Considerations* (London, 1710 [Folger Library, 181–316q]).
45. Martyn Thompson, 'Significant Silences in Locke's *Two Treatises of Government*: Constitutional History, Contract and Law', *The Historical Journal*, 31 (1987): 275–94, esp. 291–2.
46. Lois G. Schwoerer, 'Locke, Lockean Ideas and the Glorious Revolution', *Journal of the History of Ideas*, 51, 4 (1990): 531–48, esp. 540–1.
47. See Richard Tuck's 'Review of Michael Mendle, *Dangerous Positions: Mixed Government, the Estates of the Realm, and the Answer to the XIX Propositions* (University of Alabama Press, 1985)', *Journal of Modern History*, 59, 3 (1987): 570–2.
48. Goldie, 'Tory Political Thought 1689–1714', 64.
49. Keith Thomas, 'Women and the Civil War Sects', *Past and Present*, 13 (1958), 55.
50. Clarendon, *Life*, I (London, 1827), 358–9, cited by Thomas, *ibid.*, 57.
51. See Johann Sommerville, ed., Introduction to *Sir Robert Filmer, 'Patriarcha' and Other Writings*. See also Gordon Schochet, *Patriarchalism in Political Thought* (Oxford: Blackwell, 1975).
52. Aristotle, *Politics*, ed. H. Rackham, Loeb Classical Library edition (London: Heinemann, 1932), bk. 1, §2, 1252a 9–15, 3.

   Those then who think that the natures of the statesman [*politikon*], the royal ruler [*basilikon*], the head of an estate [*oikonomikon*] and the master of a family [*despotikon*] are the same, are mistaken (they imagine that the difference between these various forms of authority is between greater and smaller numbers, not a difference in kind – that is, that the ruler over a few people is a master, over more the head of an estate, over more still a statesman or royal ruler, as if there were no difference between a large household and a small city....

53. Filmer, *Patriarcha*, ed. Sommerville, 3. Astell in *An Impartial Enquiry* 24–8/154–62 undertook to supply chapter and verse, drawing on Henry Foulis, *The History of Romish Treasons* ....(London: Printed for Thomas Basset, Richard Chisevell, Christopher Wilkinson and Thomas Dring, 1681 [Folger Library,

F1641]), bk. 2, ch. 3, 75 ff., who had analyzed the specific indebtedness of Presbyterian advocates of popular sovereignty to the scholastics and Jesuits, a claim that Astell repeated, to target Locke and the Whigs.

54. See William Nicholls (1664–1712), *The Duty of Inferiors towards Their Superiors, in Five Practical Discourses* (London: Printed for E. Evets, at the Green Dragon, T. Bennet at the Half-Moon, in St. Paul's Church-yard, 1701 [Folger Library, 178–610q]), 'Discourse IV, The Duty of Wives to Their Husbands', which Astell attacks in the opening pages of the Preface to the 1706 edition of *Reflections upon Marriage.*

55. *DNB* and British Biographical Archive.

56. Astell, *An Impartial Enquiry*, 16/146: 'Since a Dr. *Binks*, a Mr. *Sherlock*, a Bishop of St. *Asaph*, and some few more, take occasion to Preach upon this Day such antiquated Truths as might have past upon the Nation in the Reign of K. *Charles* II. or in *Monmouth's* Rebellion'

57. Locke to Molyneux, 22 February 1697, *The Correspondence of John Locke*, ed. E. S. de Beer, 8 vols. (Oxford: Clarendon Press, 1976–89), 6, 2202, cited in the introduction by James Buickerood to his edition of *A Philosophick Essay Concerning Ideas According to Dr. Sherlock's Principles* (1705) (New York: AMS Press, 1996), iii.

58. South to Locke, 18 July 1704, *The Correspondence of John Locke*, 8, 3591, cited by Buickerood, in his Introduction to (Anon.), *A Philosophick Essay*, vi.

59. Astell, *An Impartial Enquiry*, 34/170–1.

60. William Sherlock, *A Vindication of the Case of Allegiance*, 1691, 11, cited by Goldie, 'Tory Political Thought 1689–1714', 93.

61. Sherlock, *The Case of Allegiance Due to Sovereign Powers*, 1691, 2, cited by Goldie, *loc. cit.*

62. Sherlock, *ibid.*, 21, 14, 45, 42, cited by Goldie, *ibid.*, 94.

63. The epithet refers to the way in which their positions evoked the Engagement Controversy of 1649–52.

64. Sherlock, *The Case of Allegiance Due to Sovereign Powers*, 1691, 15, cited by Goldie, 'Tory Political Thought 1689–1714', 95.

65. Locke's manuscript on Sherlock is reproduced as Appendix A to Goldie, *ibid.*, 330–45.

66. Patrich Riley, 'An Unpublished Manuscript of Leibniz on the Allegiance Due to Sovereign Powers', *Journal of the History of Philosophy*, 11 (1973): 319–36, cited by Goldie, *ibid.*, 103.

67. Oxford: The Bodleian Library, Locke MSS c.28, fo. 91v, cited by Goldie, *op. cit.*

68. Bodl. Locke MSS c.28, fo. 96r, cited by Goldie, *ibid.*, 104.

69. Sherlock, *Vindication of the Case*, 18, 13, cited by Goldie, *ibid.*, 104.

70. John Locke, *Two Treatises of Government*, ed. Peter Laslett (Cambridge: Cambridge University Press, 1988), bk. 2, §23, 284.

71. Astell, *An Impartial Enquiry*, 34/170.

72. *Ibid.*

73. *Ibid.*, 292.

74. See Mark Goldie, 'John Locke's Circle and James II', *The Historical Journal*, 35, 3 (1992): 557–86.

75. Locke, *Two Treatises*, bk. 2, §198, 398.
76. *Ibid.*, bk. 2, §122, 349.
77. Bodleian MSS Locke e 18, fo. 5, reprinted in Farr and Roberts, 'John Locke on the Glorious Revolution: A Rediscovered Document [Bodleian MSS Locke e. 18, fo. 4V]', *The Historical Journal*, 28 (1985), 395–8.
78. *Ibid.*
79. See Quentin Skinner, 'Conquest and Consent: Thomas Hobbes and the Engagement Controversy', in G. E. Aylmen, ed., *The Interregnum: The Quest for Settlement 1646–1660* (London: Macmillan, 1972); and Goldie, 'Tory *Political Thought, 1688–1714*', 98.

Chapter 5

1. From around 1718, he took less interest in political matters but continued to write on many diverse topics. He published over 250 works including *Robinson Crusoe*.
2. As Hobbes, in *Leviathan*, ed. Richard Tuck (Cambridge: Cambridge University Press, 1991), bk. 1, ch. 15, formulated the problem: 'The Lawes of Nature oblige *in foro interno*; that is to say, they bind to a desire they should take place: but *in foro externo*; that is, to the putting them in act, not alwayes'.
3. See Gordon Schochet, in his excellent essay 'John Locke and Religious Toleration', in Lois G. Schwoerer, ed., *The Revolution of 1688–1689, Changing Perspectives* (Cambridge: Cambridge University Press, 1992), 150–1, to whom I am indebted for this account, has emphasized. Schochet distances himself from Richard Tuck's account in *Natural Rights Theories, the Origin and Development* (Cambridge: Cambridge University Press, 1979). See also Brian Tierney, 'Tuck on Rights: Some Medieval Problems', *History of Political Thought*, 4 (1983): 429–41, and Tierney, 'Origins of Natural Rights Language', *History of Political Thought*, 3 (1982): 615–46.
4. As Schochet, in 'John Locke and Religious Toleration', 147–64, esp. 149.
5. Schochet, 'John Locke and Religious Toleration', 154.
6. *Ibid.*, 152, citing Andrew Marvell's *An Account of the Growth of Popery and Arbitrary Government in England* ['printed in Amsterdam'] (London, 1678).
7. *Ibid.*, 156.
8. *Ibid.*, 157–8. See also Carolyn E. Edie, 'Revolution and the Rule of Law: The End of the Dispensing Power, 1689', *Eighteenth-Century Studies*, 10 (1977): 434–50; and Lois G. Schwoerer, *The Declaration of Rights, 1689* (Baltimore: Johns Hopkins University Press, 1981), 59–64.
9. Schochet, 'John Locke and Religious Toleration', 157, citing James II, 'His Majesty's Gracious Declaration to All His Loving Subjects for Liberty of Conscience', reprinted in *English Historical Documents*, ed. A. Browning (London: Eyre & Spottiswoode, 1953–), vol. 8 (1660–1714), doc. 146, 395–6.
10. Schochet, 'John Locke and Religious Toleration', 150, citing John Locke, 'Second Tract on Government', in *Two Tracts on Government (1660–61)*, ed. and tr. Philip Abrams (Cambridge: Cambridge University Press, 1967), 238–9. Abrams notes parallel arguments in Robert Sanderson, *De Obligatione Conscientiae, Praelectiones Decem* (London, 1660), bk. 6, §iv and v, and in

Jeremy Taylor, *The Liberty of Prophesying, Ductor Dubitantium* (London, 1648), bk. 3, §i.

11. Schochet, 'John Locke and Religious Toleration', 150, citing John Locke, 'An Essay Concerning Toleracon 1667', Bodleian MSS Locke c. 28, fols. 21– 32, es fol. 22r. A modernized and corrected version of this manuscript was published by Carlo A Viano in *John Locke, Scritti Editi e Inediti Sulla Tolleranzo* (Turin: Taylor Torino, 1961), 81–105; see esp. 86.

12. Schochet, 'John Locke and Religious Toleration', 147, citing Locke, *Epistola de Tolerantia* (Gouda, 1689; written c. 1685), tr. J. W. Gough in Locke *Epistola de Tolerantia/A Letter on Toleration*, ed. J. W. Gough and Raymond Klibansky (Oxford: Oxford University Press, 1968), 59.

13. Locke, *Epistola de Tolerantia*, 71, 85–7, cited in Schochet, 'John Locke and Religious Toleration', 148.

14. As Schochet, 'John Locke and Religious Toleration', 152 n., points out, our best evidence for the dating of Locke's *Letter on Toleration* is, in fact, a letter from van Limborch to Damaris Masham, dated 24 March 1704/5, noting that Locke 'wrote the famous letter concerning toleration to me' in the winter of 1685 while he was in Holland hiding from British agents.

15. Schochet, 'John Locke and Religious Toleration', 159 n., notes that manuscripts dealing with the politics of dissent are to be found among Locke's papers in the Bodleian and the British Public Record Office from 1667, 1671/2, 1679 and 1681–2, as well as being the topic of bk. 4 of the *Essay Concerning Human Understanding*.

16. Defoe, *More Short-Ways, with the Dissenters* (London, 1704 [Library of Congress, BX5202.D36]), 21.

17. Astell, *The Shortest Way*, 7, referring to Defoe, *The Shortest Way with the Dissenters: Or Proposals for the Establishment of the Church* (London, 1702 [Folger Library, 134–622 q]), 8.

18. Defoe's reference on 21 of *More Short-Ways*, which Astell cites, is clearly to the High Flyers, Charles Leslie and Henry Sacheverell.

19. See Astell's postscript to *A Fair Way with the Dissenters and their Patrons* (London: Printed for E. by R. Wilkin at the King's Head in St. Paul's Church-yard, 1704 [Folger Library, BX5202.A7.Cage]), 24–7/114–21.

20. *Ibid.*

21. Leslie, *The New Association of those Called Moderate Church-Men*, 3rd corrected edn. (London, 1702 [Folger Library, 151–330 q]), 10.

22. Defoe, *More Short-Ways*, 8.

23. *Ibid.*, 21.

24. *Ibid.*, 18.

25. Defoe, *More Short-Ways*, 13.

26. *Ibid.*, 1.

27. *Ibid.*, 4.

28. *Ibid.*, 2.

29. Sacheverell, *The Nature and Mischief of Prejudice and Partiality Stated in a Sermon Preach'd at St. Mary's in Oxford at the Assizes held there*, 2nd edn., London: 1708 [Folger Library, 152422]), 14.

30. Defoe, *More Short-Ways*, 2.

31. Astell, *An Impartial Inquiry into the Causes of Rebellion and Civil War* (London: Printed by E. for R. Wilkin at the King's Head in St. Paul's Church-yard, 1704 [Folger Library, BV 4253.K4.C75.Cage]), 29/163.

32. Defoe, *More Short-Ways,* 7ff. and 3, respectively.

33. Sacheverell, *The Nature and Mischief of Prejudice,* 24. Defoe, in *More Short-Ways,* argued that Sacheverell had 'Preach'd and Printed too, that the Dissenters were a Brood of Traytors, and the Spawn of the Rebels, and not fit to live?' intimating the same punishment for them as was meeted out to the Huguenots on the St. Bartholomew's Day massacre, 24 August 1576.

34. Sacheverell, *The Nature and Mischief of Prejudice,* 9–15.

35. *Ibid.,* 1, reads:

> Astell in *A Fair Way with the Dissenters,* like Sacheverell, and like the anonymous author of *An Essay upon Government* of 1705, applies the epithets 'base', 'licentious', 'mercenary' and 'ignorant' to Defoe in particular.

36. Sacheverell, *The Nature and Mischief of Prejudice,* 1.

37. Defoe, *More Short-Ways,* 10.

38. Defoe, *The Shortest Way,* 5, 12–13.

39. Defoe's *More Short-Ways,* 8, quotes them in turn as 'the very first Lines' of Sacheverell's sermon under discussion. Astell works carefully through the 14 points in *The Shortest Way with the Dissenters,* 16–20/107–10.

40. Defoe, *More Short-Ways,* 15.

41. Sacheverell, *The Nature and Mischief of Prejudice,* 9, 13.

42. *Ibid.,* 14.

43. Defoe, *More Short-Ways,* 4.

44. *Ibid.,* 5–6, where Defoe owned to being a pupil of '*Charles Morton* of *Newington Green*'.

45. Wesley, *A Letter from a Country Divine to his Friend in London, Concerning the Education of Dissenters in Their Private Academies . . . ,* 2nd edn. (London: Printed for R. Clavel and Knaplock, 1704 [Folger Library, PR3763.W6.L3.Cage]).

46. Defoe, *More Short-Ways,* 5–6.

47. *Ibid.,* 14.

48. *Ibid.,* 5.

49. *Ibid.,* 24. Defoe is also referring to *The Dissenters' Sayings Published in Their Own Words* (1681), the work of Roger L'Estrange (1616–1704), in his capacity of first Surveyor of the Imprimery, a position he used to draw up a list of seditious pamphlets and propositions for the king. See Lois G. Schwoerer, 'The Right to Resist: Whig Resistance Theory, 1688 to 1694', in Nicholas Phillipson and Quentin Skinner, eds. *Political Discourse in Early Modern Britain* (Cambridge: Cambridge University Press, 1993), 232–52, esp. 235. It is worth noting that Defoe begins *The Shortest Way* (1) with 'a story in his [L'Estrange's] Collection of Fables, of the Cock and the Horses'.

50. *Moderation Truly Stated* (London: Printed by J. L. for Richard Wilkin at the King's Head in St. Paul's Church-yard, 1704 [Folger Library, BX5202.A8.Cage]), 24; for the dating see Bridget Hill, *The First English Feminist* (Aldershot, Hants: Gower, 1986), 214 n. 2.

51. See Richard Ashcraft, *Revolutionary Politics and Locke's Two Treatises of Government* (Princeton, N.J.: Princeton University Press, 1986), 482–4, 500–1; and Lois G. Schwoerer, 'Locke, Lockean Ideas and the Glorious Revolution', *Journal of the History of Ideas*, 51, 4 (1990), 545.
52. See Defoe, *More Short-Ways*, 2, 9–10.
53. Astell, *A Fair Way with the Dissenters*, 16/108.
54. Mary Astell's observation, 'If all Men are born free, how is it that all Women are born slaves?' (*Reflections upon Marriage*, 3rd edn. [London: Printed for R. Wilkin at the King's Head in St. Paul's Church-yard, 1706]), xi/18), could as well refer to Burnet as to Locke. On Burnet, see especially Bruce Lenman, 'The Poverty of Political Theory in the Scottish Revolution of 1688–89', in Schwoerer, *The Revolution of 1688–1689*, 246–7.
55. Defoe, *More Short-Ways*, 8.
56. *Ibid.*, 10, presumably the same he referred to a page earlier as 'the Reverend Bishop of *Salisbury*'s Speech in the House of Lords. (See Astell, *A Fair Way with the Dissenters*, 16 and note.) Defoe is referring to the various Test Acts directed at Roman Catholics and later nonconformists, in particular, that of Elizabeth I of 1563, imposing the oath of allegiance and abjuration of the power of Rome on all office-holders but peers; and that of Charles II of 1673, which extended the provisions of the Corporation Act of 1661 to include all office-holders without exception, and which included a declaration against transubstantiation.
57. Defoe, *More Short-Ways*, 14.
58. Astell, *A Fair Way with the Dissenters*, 17/108–9.
59. Defoe, *More Short-Ways*, 15.
60. On 5 July, 1641 the Commons had abolished the courts of High Commission and Star Chamber.
61. The Ulster insurrection of October 1641 was to provoke Cromwell's notorious occupation of Ireland.
62. Defoe, *More Short-Ways*, 15.
63. See Edward Hyde, first Earl of Clarendon (1609–74), *The History of the Rebellion and Civil Wars in England, begun in the Year 1641. With the precedent Passages, and Actions, that contributed thereunto, and the happy end, and Conclusion thereof by the King's blessed Restoration, and Return upon the 29th of May, in the Year 1660* (Oxford: Printed at the Theater [Folger Library, DA.400.C6.1702.Cage]), 1, 52.
64. *Ibid.*, 1, 71, cited by Astell, *Moderation Truly Stated*, 8.
65. *Ibid.*, 1, 166, cited by Astell, *op. cit.*
66. *Ibid.*, 1, 205–6, cited by Astell, *op. cit.*
67. James Owen, *Moderation a Vertue* (London: Printed for A. Baldwin in Warwick-lane [Folger Library, 134–622 q], 1703), 36–49.
68. *Ibid.*, 36.
69. *Ibid.*, Preface, ii.
70. Sacheverell, *The Nature and Mischief of Prejudice*, 15.
71. Defoe, *More Short-Ways*, 10.
72. *Ibid.*, 3.

73. Astell, *Reflections upon Marriage* (1706), xxvi/31.
74. Astell, Postscript to *A Fair Way with the Dissenters*, 24.
75. Owen, *Moderation Still a Virtue* (London: Printed for J. Taylor, at the Ship, in St. Paul's Church-yard, 1704 [Folger Library, 166828]); see iii, 3–4, 32, 59, 60, 67–96.
76. Astell, Postscript to *A Fair Way with the Dissenters*, 24.
77. Owen, *Moderation Still a Virtue*, 3.
78. *Ibid.*, Preface, ii.
79. *Ibid.*, 21.
80. Astell, *Moderation Truly Stated*, 53–60ff.
81. Astell's source for the claims documented in *Moderation Truly Stated*, at the pages cited here and following, is overwhelmingly Clarendon's *History of the Rebellion*.
82. See Owen, *Moderation Still a Virtue*, 2–3, italicized in the original), quoted by Astell in *Moderation Truly Stated*, 36.
83. Astell, *op. cit.*
84. *Ibid.*, 62–79.
85. Astell refers to the comparison of conflicting views among Independents in *Moderation Truly Stated*, at 51, 52 and 80, which she documents with quotations from Edward's *Gangraena*, 87 and *Gangraena* Pt. 2, 1646, 240; the Preface to Coleman-Street's *Conclave Visited* (1648); an *Extract of the Act*, Dec. 26, 1644 [establishing A Committee of Both Kingdoms]; [Peter] Sterry's *England's Deliverance* (1651), 7; [John] Saltmarsh's *[The Smoke in the Temple...] Answer to [Master] Ley*, 1646, 7; [John Goodwin's] *Some Modest and Humble Queries*, 1646, 7; [John] Bastwick's *Postscript to Burton*; [John Price's] *Pulpit Incendiary*, 1648, 45; Pryn [William Prynne] cited by [John] Goodwin, *Innocency and Truth [Triumphing Together]*, 1633 [1645] and Milton's *Eikonoklastes* (1649), 237.
86. Astell, *Moderation Truly Stated*, 66–7.
87. *Ibid.*, 80.
88. See Owen, *Moderation Still a Virtue*, 2, and ch. 4, 24–7, of his *Moderation a Virtue*.
89. Astell, *Moderation Truly Stated*, 80.
90. *Ibid.*, 70.
91. *Ibid.*, 63.
92. Astell references in a marginal note 'Sir Henry Vane's *Speech at a Common Hall*, Oct. 27, 1643'.
93. Owen, *Moderation Still a Virtue*, 82.

Chapter 6

1. See the following works by Martyn Thompson: 'The Reception of Locke's *Two Treatises of Government*, 1690–1705', *Political Studies*, 24 (1976): 184–91; 'The Idea of Conquest in Controversies over the 1688 Revolution', *Journal of the History of Ideas*, 38 (1977), 33–46; and 'Revolution and Influence: A Reply to Nelson on Locke's *Two Treatises of Government*', *Political Studies*, 28 (1980): 100–8. See also the fine essays by Mark Goldie: 'The Roots of

True Whiggism, 1688–1694', *History of Political Thought*, 1 (1980): 195–236; 'The Revolution of 1689 and the Structure of Political Argument', *Bulletin of Research in the Humanities*, 83 (1980): 473–564; 'Danby, the Bishops and the Whigs' in T. Harris, Paul Seaward and M. A. Goldie, eds., *The Politics of Religion in Restoration England* (Oxford Blackwell, 1990); 'The Theory of Religious Intolerance in Restoration England', in O. Grell, J. I. Israel and N. Tyacke, eds., *From Persecution to Toleration* (Oxford: Oxford University Press, 1991); 'John Locke's Circle and James II', *The Historical Journal*, 35, 3 (1992): 557–86; and 'Priestcraft and the Birth of Whiggism' in Nicholas Phillipson and Quentin Skinner, eds., *Political Discourse in Early Modern Britain* (Cambridge: Cambridge University Press, 1993), 209–31.

2. Peter Laslett, Introduction to *John Locke: Two Treatises of Government* (Cambridge: Cambridge University Press, 1988).

3. Goldie, 'Tory Political Thought 1689–1714', Ph.D. dissertation, University of Cambridge, 1978.

4. *Ibid.*, 76.

5. *Ibid.*, 230–1.

6. Richard Ashcraft, *Revolutionary Politics and Locke's Two Treatises of Government* (Princeton, N.J.: Princeton University Press, 1986), 579.

7. Lois G. Schwoerer, 'Locke, Lockean Ideas and the Glorious Revolution', *Journal of the History of Ideas*, 51, 4 (1990), 533.

8. Goldie, 'The Revolution of 1689 and the Structure of Political Argument', 508–9.

9. Schwoerer, 'Locke, Lockean Ideas and the Glorious Revolution', 533.

10. The position of Thompson, 'The Reception of Locke's *Two Treatises of Government*, 1690–1705'.

11. In 1689 Locke was first named as the author of the *Two Treatises*, an identification repeated several times in this period, which makes the long delay before it was properly examined as a work by Locke all the more curious.

12. Astell, *An Impartial Enquiry into the Causes of Rebellion and Civil War* (London: Printed by E. for R. Wilkin at the King's Head in St. Paul's Church-yard, 1704 [Folger Library, BV 4253.K4.C75.Cage]), 41/178.

13. There is no conclusive evidence for this, but see the speculations of Maurice Cranston, *John Locke, a Biography* (New York: Macmillan, 1957), 325; see also Schwoerer, 'Locke, Lockean Ideas and the Glorious Revolution', 543.

14. James Farr and Clayton Roberts, 'John Locke on the Glorious Revolution: A Rediscovered Document [Bodleian MSS Locke e. 18, fo. 4V]', *The Historical Journal*, 28 (1985), 391; Schwoerer, 'Locke, Lockean Ideas and the Glorious Revolution', 546.

15. Jeffrey M. Nelson, 'Unlocking Locke's Legacy: A Comment', *Political Studies*, 26, 1 (1978): 101–8, esp. 105, citing Thompson, 'The Reception of Locke's *Two Treatises*', 187.

16. See Lois G. Schwoerer, 'Propaganda in the Revolution of 1688–9', *American Historical Review*, 82 (1977): 843–74, esp. 851–3.

17. See Johann P. Sommerville, ed., Introduction to *Sir Robert Filmer, 'Patriarcha' and Other Writings* (Cambridge: Cambridge University Press, 1991), xi.

18. Ashcraft, *Revolutionary Politics*, 187.

19. Gordon Schochet, *Patriarchalism in Political Thought* (Oxford: Blackwell, 1975).
20. Thompson, 'Significant Silences in Locke's *Two Treatises of Government:* Constitutional History, Contract and Law', *The Historical Journal,* 31 (1987), 280–2.
21. Note that Thompson, in 'Revolution and Influence: A Reply to Nelson on Locke's *Two Treatises of Government*', revises his 1976 position in light of Nelson's critique.
22. Schwoerer, 'Locke, Lockean Ideas and the Glorious Revolution', 532–5.
23. Nelson, 'Unlocking Locke's Legacy', 106–7.
24. Thompson, 'Significant Silences in Locke's *Two Treatises*'.
25. Schwoerer, 'Locke, Lockean Ideas, and the Glorious Revolution', 540–3. The Letter to Clarke of 1689 predates Locke's Minute to Edward Clarke of 1690; see Farr and Roberts, 'John Locke on the Glorious Revolution', 397, and Goldie 'The Theory of Religious Intolerance'.
26. Thompson, 'Significant Silences in Locke's Two Treatises', 290–1.
27. Astell, *An Impartial Enquiry*, 8/140, 14/145, 30/163, etc.
28. Tutchin, *Observator,* 7–10 April 1703. See Nicholas Phillipson, 'Politeness and Politics in the Reigns of Anne and the Early Hanoverians', in J. G. A. Pocock, Gordon J. Schochet and Lois G. Schwoerer, eds., *The Varieties of British Political Thought, 1500–1800* (Washington, D.C.: Folger Institute, 1993), 211–45, es218.
29. Tutchin, *Observator,* 14–18 September 1706, cited by Nicholas Phillipson, 'Politeness and Politics in the Reigns of Anne and the Early Hanoverians', 218.
30. Ballard Ms 41:133, cited by Florence M. Smith, *Mary Astell* (New York: Columbia University Press, 1916), 113, and Ruth Perry *The Celebrated Mary Astell: An Early English Feminist* (Chicago: University of Chicago Press, 1986).
31. Smith, *Mary Astell,* 113, who supplies no evidence.
32. See Locke's manuscript on Sherlock, reproduced as Appendix A to Goldie, 'Tory *Political Thought 1689–1714*', 330–45; Farr and Roberts, 'John Locke on the Glorious Revolution', 385–98.
33. Astell, *Moderation Truly Stated* (London: Printed by J. L. for Richard Wilkin at the King's Head in St. Paul's Church-yard, 1704 [Folger Library, BX5202.A8.Cage]), 10–11.
34. *Ibid.*, 12.
35. Astell, *An Impartial Enquiry*, 40/176–7.
36. J. R. Jones, *Charles* II: Royal Politician (London: Allen & Unwin, 1987), 152–5.
37. In *The Works of John Locke* (London: Printed for Thomas Tegg, W. Sharpe and Son, *et al.*, 1823), 2, 148–57.
38. See Phillipson, 'Politeness and Politics in the Reigns of Anne and the Early Hanoverians', 211–45.
39. *A Fair Way with the Dissenters and Their Patrons* (London: Printed for E. by R. Wilkin at the King's Head in St. Paul's Church-yard, 1704 [Folger Library, BX5202.A7.Cage]), 2–3/88–90.
40. Astell, *An Impartial Enquiry,* 29/163.

41. *An Essay upon Government* (1705), 59–60.
42. Goldie, 'Tory Political Thought 1689–1714', 48–9.
43. Astell, *The Christian Religion* (London: Printed by S. H. for R. Wilkin at the King's Head in St. Paul's Church-yard, 1705 [Folger Library, 216595]), §139, 133; §§312, 305–6.
44. *An Impartial Enquiry*, 10/141, 12/143, 17/147, 19/149, 31/168, 54/189.
45. *Ibid.*, 10/141.
46. Locke, *Two Treatises*, 404–5.
47. *Ibid.*, §209, 404–5, editor's note.
48. Astell, *Reflections upon Marriage*, 3rd edn. (London: Printed for R. Wilkin at the King's Head in St. Paul's Church-yard, 1706), Preface, x/16.
49. Locke, *Two Treatises*, 347–8.
50. *Ibid.*, bk. 2, §§176, 182, 186, 202, 207.
51. *An Impartial Enquiry*, 54/189.
52. Astell, *Moderation Truly Stated* (1704 edn.), 80.
53. *An Impartial Enquiry*, 54/189.
54. Pocock, *The Ancient Constitution and the Feudal Law* (Cambridge: Cambridge University Press, 1957), 53–4, 148–50.
55. Locke, *Two Treatises*, bk. 2, §176, 385.
56. Hobbes, *Leviathan*, ed. Richard Tuck (Cambridge: Cambridge University Press, 1991), ch. 10, 67.
57. *Ibid.*, ch. 14, 98
58. Locke, *Two Treatises*, bk. 2, §202, 401.
59. *Ibid.*, 387, editor's note 15.
60. *Ibid.*, 390.
61. *Ibid.*, 393.
62. *Ibid.*
63. *Ibid.*, 403.
64. *Ibid.*, 403–4.
65. *The Second Treatise*, ch. 16, 'Of conquest' (1988, 384). See Laslett's note on §175 as belonging to 'the early stages of composition' and 'probably written in 1681 or 1682', although arguably inserted in 1689.
66. Preface to *Reflections upon Marriage* (1706 edn.), x/17.
67. See Locke, *Two Treatises*, §209, 404–5, editor's note.
68. See Martyn Thompson, 'Revolution and Influence: A Reply to Nelson on Locke's *Two Treatises of Government*'.
69. Charles Leslie, 'A Supplement', dated 25 March 1703, entitled 'With a short Account of the *Original of Government*. Compared with the *Schemes of the Republicans* and *Whigs*' to *The New Association. Part II. With farther Improvements. . . . an Answer to some* Objections *in the Pretended* D. Foe's *Explication in 'the Reflections upon the Shortest Way. . . .'* (London and Westminister, 1703 [Folger Library, BX.9180.L3.Cage]), 6–7.
70. Preface to *Reflections upon Marriage* (1706 edn.), x–xi.
71. Locke, *Two Treatises*, bk. 1, ch. 1, §2, 142.
72. See Thomas, 'Women and the Civil War Sects', *Past and Present*, 13 (1958), 50.
73. Astell, *A Fair Way with the Dissenters*, 16/108.

74. Gilbert Burnet, *An Enquiry into the Measures of Submission to the Supream Authority: And of the Grounds upon which it may be Lawful or necessary for Subjects, to defend their Religion, Lives and Liberties*. In *Six Papers by Gilbert Burnet, D. D.* (Edinburgh, 1689 [Folger Library, B5913]), 53.

75. Astell, Preface to *Reflections upon Marriage* (1706 edn.), xi/18–19.

76. *Two Treatises*, 284.

77. *Ibid.*, 367.

78. *The Christian Religion* (1705 edn.), §139, 133, already cited on p. 145.

79. Locke, *Two Treatises*, Bk 2, §23, 1988 edn, 284.

80. Astell, *Moderation Truly Stated* (1704), 105.

81. *Ibid.*, 93.

82. *Ibid.*

83. Astell, *The Christian Religion*, 82

84. *Ibid.*, §157, 154.

85. *Ibid.*, §140, 135.

86. *Ibid.*, 120, 179, 181, 217, 232, 335, 383, respectively.

87. *Ibid.*, 383.

88. *Ibid.*, §147, 143.

89. Charles Leslie, *The New Association, Part I* (London, 1702 [Folger Library, 151–330q]; *Part II* (London and Westminster, 1703 [Folger Library, BX.9180.L3.Cage]).

90. Astell, *A Fair Way with the Dissenters*, 15.

91. See Thompson, 'The Reception of Locke's *Two Treatises*', esp. 187, 189.

92. Charles Leslie, *Considerations of Importance to Ireland* (1698), 3, cited by Thompson, 'The Reception of Locke's *Two Treatises*', esp. 187, 189.

93. See Perry, *The Celebrated Mary Astell*, 172–3.

Chapter 7

1. For the fate of natural rights theories in this period see J. G. A. Pocock, *The Ancient Constitution and the Feudal Law* (Cambridge: Cambridge University Press, 1957; 2nd edn. 1987); and Mark Goldie, 'Tory Political Thought 1689–1714', Ph.D. dissertation, University of Cambridge, 1978.

2. Astell, *An Impartial Enquiry into the Causes of Rebellion and Civil War* (London: Printed by E. for R. Wilkin at the King's Head in St. Paul's Church-yard, 1704 [Folger Library, BV4253.K4.C75.Cage]), 48/184. Astell cites Henry Foulis, *The History of the Wicked Plots and Conspiracies of Our Pretended Saints. . . .*, 2nd edn. (Oxford: Printed by Henry Hall for Ric. Davis, 1674 [Folger Library, F1643]), 204, 205:

   The Blood of many thousand Christians, shed in these Wars and before, crieth aloud against Presbytery, as the People only guilty of the first occasion of Quarrel (*Ibid.*, 105.). Of whom *Grotius* says, 'That he looks upon them as factious, turbulent, and Rebellious Spirits'.

3. This is emphasized in Johann Sommerville, 'History and Theory: The Norman Conquest in Early Stuart Political Thought', *Political Studies*, 34 (1986): 249–61.

4. See the essays in A. J. Arnaud and E. Kingdom, eds., *Women's Rights and the Rights of Man* (Aberdeen: Aberdeen University Press, 1986); and Stephanie Palmer, 'Feminism and the Promise of Human Rights: Possibilities and Paradoxes', in Susan James and Stephanie Parker, eds., *Visible Women: Essays on Feminist Legal Theory and Political Philosophy* (Oxford: Hart, 2002), 91–116.

5. Drake, *An Essay In Defence of the Female Sex* (London: Printed for A. Roger and E. Wilkinson at the Black Boy and R. Clavel at the Peacock, in Fleet Street, 1696 [Folger Library, A4058a]), 13–14.

6. Carole Pateman, 'Conclusion: Women's Writing, Women's Standing: Theory and Politics in the Early Modern Period', in Hilda L. Smith, ed., *Women Writers and the Early Modern British Political Tradition* (Cambridge: Cambridge University Press, 1998), 370, citing Pateman, 'The Rights of Man and Early Feminism', *Swiss Yearbook of Political Science*, and Pateman, 'Democracy, Freedom and Special Rights', in David Boucher and Paul Kelly, eds., *Taking Justice Seriously: Perspectives in the Problem of Social Justice* (London: Routledge, 1997).

7. See J. G. A. Pocock, *The Machiavellian Moment: Florentine Political Thought and the Atlantic Republican Tradition* (Princeton, N.J.: Princeton University Press, 1975); Quentin Skinner, *Liberty before Liberalism* (Cambridge: Cambridge University Press, 1998); and Philip Pettit, *Republicanism: A Theory of Freedom and Government* (Oxford: Clarendon Press, 1997). As already stated, of these three early Pettit claims that Ostell is republican, a claim that flies in the face of the facts.

8. Skinner, *Liberty before Liberalism*.

9. Pettit, *Republicanism*, 31–4.

10. James Harrrington, *The Commonwealth of Oceana and a System of Politics*, ed. J. G. A. Pocock (Cambridge, Cambridge University Press, 1992), 269, cited by Pettit, *Republicanism*, 32.

11. *Cato's Letters*, 6th edn., ed. John Trenchard and Thomas Gordon (New York: Da Capo, 1971), ii, 249–50, cited by Pettit, *Republicanism*, 33.

12. Pettit, *Republicanism*, 139.

13. See Richard Tuck, *Natural Rights Theories, Their Origin and Development*, (Cambridge: Cambridge University Press, 1981).

14. See Springborg, *Western Republicanism and the Oriental Prince* (Cambridge: Polity Press; Austin: Texas University Press, 1992), ch. 1, 'Aristotle on Greeks and Barbarians, Freedom and Slavery'.

15. Machiavelli, *The Complete Works and Others*, tr. Allan Gilbert, 3 vols. (Durham, N.C.: Duke University Press, 1965), 33, cited by Pettit, *Republicanism*, 32, who does not give the volume number.

16. See Tuck, *Natural Rights Theories, the Origin and Development* (Cambridge: Cambridge University Press, 1979); and Michael J. Lacey and Knud Haakonssen, 'From Natural Law to the Rights of Man', in Lacey and Haakonssen, *A Culture of Rights: The Bill of Rights in Philosophy, Politics and Law – 1791–1991* (Washington, D.C.: Woodrow Wilson Center and Cambridge University Press, 1989), 1–59.

17. Skinner, in *Liberty before Liberalism*, 55 n. acknowledges: 'although there are political writers (for example, John Locke) who espouse the theory of liberty I am discussing without being republicans in the strict sense of opposing the

institution of monarchy, it remains the case that all avowed republicans in the period I am discussing espouse the theory of liberty I am describing and use it to undergird their repudiation of monarchy.' At the same time, Skinner admits, 54, 'many of the writers I am considering actively prefer a system of mixed government in which there is a monarchical element together with an aristocratic senate and a democratic assembly to represent the citizens as a whole', in other words, a system barely distinguishable from constitutional monarchy.

18. See Leonard Krieger, *The German Idea of Freedom* (Boston: Beacon Press, 1957), and on a comparison between the absolutists, Hobbes, Grotius and Pufendorf, and the liberal theory of freedom of Rousseau and his successors, see Krieger, *The Politics of Discretion: Pufendorf and the Acceptance of Natural Law* (Chicago: University of Chicago Press, 1965).

19. See, however, Arnaud and Kingdom, *Women's Rights and the Rights of Man*, and the very considerable literature on Mary Wollstonecraft's *A Vindication of the Rights of Men* (1790) and *A Vindication of the Rights of Woman* (1792), ed. Sylvana Tomeselli (Cambridge: Cambridge University Press, 1995).

20. Mark Goldie makes this point in 'Tory Political Thought 1689–1714'. See the famous treatment of Herbert Butterfield, *The Whig Interpretation of History* (New York: Norton, 1930), and, more recently, Annabel Patterson, *Nobody's Perfect: A New Whig Interpretation of History* (New Haven, Conn.: Yale University Press, 2002).

21. John Locke, *The Two Treatises of Government*, ed. Peter Laslett (Cambridge: Cambridge University Press, 1988), 284. I make the case, in fact, that Astell was the first systematic critic of Locke's entire corpus, and in particular of the *Two Treatises of Government*, in 'Mary Astell (1666–1731), Critic of Locke', *American Political Science Review*, 89 (1995): 621–33.

22. Tuck, *Natural Rights Theories*, 17.

23. 'Iure naturali omnes liberi nascuntur', *Digest*, 1.1.14, cited in Tuck, *Natural Rights Theories*, 18.

24. 'Ex hoc iure gentium introducta bella, dicretae gentes, regna condita, dominia distincta, agris termini positi, aedificia collocata, commercium…' *Digest* 1.1.5, cited in Tuck, *Natural Rights Theories*, 18, but I have amended the paraphrase somewhat.

25. The connection is implied, it might be argued, in studies of Locke as a natural rights theorist. See, for instance, Tuck, *Natural Rights Theories*, and J. Lacey and Haakonssen, 'From Natural Law to the Rights of Man'.

26. On Hobbes's ecclesiology and knowledge of patristics, see Patricia Springborg, 'Thomas Hobbes on Religion', in Tom Sorell, ed., *Cambridge Companion to Hobbes* (Cambridge: Cambridge University Press, 1996), 346–80, and Springborg, 'Hobbes's Theory of Civil Religion', in Gianni Paganini and Edoardo Tortarolo, eds., *Pluralismo e religione civile, una prospettiva storica e filosofica* (Milano: Bruno Mondadori, 2004), 59–94. See also Patricia Springborg's Introduction to Thomas Hobbes's Historia Ecclesiastica: A Critical Edition, ed. Patricia Springborg with Patricia Stablein.

27. See in the case of Hobbes, for instance, the brief discussion in Maurice Goldsmith's essay, 'Hobbes on Law', in the *Cambridge Companion to Hobbes*

(Cambridge: Cambridge University Press, 1996), 287–9 of Hobbes's reliance in the *Dialogue between a Philosopher and a Student of the Common Laws*, on Christopher St. German's *Dialogues betwixt a Doctour of Divinitie and a Student in the Lawes of England* of 1523. St. German tried to fit the laws of England into the civil law mold, using *ius naturale, ius gentium* distinctions borrowed from Jean Gerson, who was reliant on Aquinas, in turn. Robinson A. Grover, in 'The Legal Origins of Thomas Hobbes's Doctrine of Contract', *Journal of the History of Philosophy* 18 (1980): 177–94, argues that Hobbes knew and used St. German's *Doctor and Student*, as it was known, when formulating his theories of Natural law and contract as early as *The Elements of Law*, as Goldsmith, 'Hobbes on Law', 302, n. 58.

28. Aristotle, *Politics*, ed. H. Rackham (London: Heinemann [Loeb Classical Library], 1932), bk. 1, §2, 1252a 9–15, 3.

29. *Ibid.*

30. *Behemoth, or The Long Parliament*, ed. Ferdinand Tönnies (London, 1889; facsimile edn. ed. Stephen Holmes, Chicago: University of Chicago Press, 1990), 39.

A. Why may not men be taught their duty, that is, the science of just and unjust, as divers other sciences have been taught, from true principles, and evident demonstration; and much more easily than any of those preachers and democratical gentlemen could teach rebellion and treason?

See Springborg, 'Behemoth and Hobbes's "*Science of Just and Unjust*"', *Filozofski vestnik*, special issue on Hobbes's *Behemoth*, ed. Tomaz Mastnak, 14, 2 (2003): 267–89.

31. Aristotle, *Politics*, bk. 1, §2, 1252a 9–15, 3.

32. Astell, *The Christian Religion* (London: Printed by S. M. for R. Wilkin at the King's Head in St. Paul's Church-yard, 1705 [Folger Library, 216595]), 288.

33. See *Nicomachean Ethics*, ed. H. Rackham (London: Heinemann [Loeb Classical Library], 1926), 1109b, 30–2, where Aristotle distinguishes between voluntary actions, which are either praised or blamed, and involuntary actions, which 'are condoned, and sometimes even pitied'.

34. Locke, *Essay Concerning Human Understanding*, in *The Works of John Locke* (London: Printed for Thomas Tegg, W. Sharpe and Son, *et al.*, 1823), bk. 2, ch. 21. It is true that Locke's use of the term 'determination', which Astell uses to refer to determination by the passions, or a species of determinism, and which Locke uses to refer to the outcome of deliberation, might serve to obscure the similarity of their arguments. But in fact, as a perusal of the relevant sections of Aristotle's *Nicomachean Ethics*, bk. 3 on voluntary and involuntary conduct, will show, Locke's position on freedom is quite standardly Aristotelian, as is hers.

35. See Skinner's own work on the Glossators, Post-Glossators and Roman humanism in *Foundations of Political Thought* (Cambridge: Cambridge University Press, 1978), 1, is one of the most authoritative commentators on both the Glossators and Post-Glossators, and on Roman humanism. I am also mindful that Skinner is not a small man and welcomes constructive critique.

36. On Hobbes and Valla, see the excellent essays by Gianni Paganini, 'Thomas Hobbes e Lorenzo Valla. Critica umansitica e filosofia moderna', *Rinscimento, Rivista dell' Instituto Nazionale di Studi sul Rinascimento*, 2nd series, 39 (1999): 515–68 and 'Hobbes, Valla e i problemi filosofici della teologia umanisitica: la riforma "dilettica" della Trinità', in L. Simonutti, ed., *Dal necessario al possibile. Determinismo e libertà nel pensiero anglo-olandese del XVII secolo* (Milan: Franco Angeli, 2001), 11–45, translated as 'Hobbes, Valla and the Trinity' in the *British Journal for the History of Philosophy* 11, 2 (2003): 183–218.

37. On classical modeling see Tony Grafton and Lise Jardine, '"Studied for Action": How Gabriel Harvey Read His Livy', *Past and Present*, 129 (1990): 30–78); James R. Jacob and Timothy Raylor, 'Opera and Obedience: Thomas Hobbes and *A Proposition for the Advancement of Morality* by Sir William Davenant', *The Seventeenth Century*, 6 (1991): 241–9; and Patricia Springborg, 'Classical Translation and Political Surrogacy: English Renaissance Classical Translations and Imitations as Politically Coded Texts', *Finnish Yearbook of Political Thought*, 5 (2001): 11–33.

38. See the exemplary essay by Reinhart Koselleck, '*Historia Magistra Vitae*: The Dissolution of the Topos into the Perspective of a Modernized Historical Process', reprinted in Koselleck, *Futures Past: On the Semantics of Historical Time*, tr. Keith Tribe (Cambridge, Mass.: MIT Press, 1985), 21–38, and the excellent chapter on Hobbes by Koselleck in *Kritik und Krise. Eine Studie zur Pathogenesis der bürgerlichen Welt* (Munich: Karl Albert Verlag, 1959), published in English as *Critique and Crisis: Enlightenment and the Pathogenesis of Modern Society* (Cambridge, Mass.: MIT Press, 1988). Koselleck's treatment of the topos in '*Historia Magistra Vitae*' is treated in my essay 'What Can We Say about History? Reinhart Koselleck and *Begriffsgeschichte*', in Jussi Kurunmäki and Kari Palonen, eds., *Zeit, Geschichte und Politik: zum achtzigsten Geburtstag von Reinhart Kostelleck* (Jyväskylä, Finland: Jyväskylä University Press, 2003).

39. For a brief notice of the parallels between Hobbes and Machiavelli see Springborg, 'Review Article: The View from the "Divell's Mountain"; Review of Quentin Skinner, *Reason and Rhetoric in the Philosophy of Hobbes*', *History of Political Thought*, 17, 4 (Winter 1996): 615–22.

40. Springborg, 'Republicanism, Freedom from Domination and the Cambridge Contextual Historians', *Political Studies*, 49, 5 (2001): 851–76; Mark Goldie's proposal to treat Astell's ' "Machiavellian" Toryism' or ' "Roman" Toryism' in his essay 'Mary Astell and Tory Polemic' in the proposed volume, *Mary Astell: Reason, Gender, Faith*, for which I was a publisher's reader, raises the same query.

41. The Twelve Tables (c. 450 B.C.) were written by the Decemviri Consulari Imperio Legibus Scribundis (the ten Consuls) and primarily concerned substantive judicial rights, promoted public prosecution of crimes, and instituted a system whereby injured parties could seek just compensation in civil disputes. Plebeians were protected from the legal abuses of the ruling patricians, especially in the enforcement of debts. Serious punishments were levied for theft, and the law gave male heads of families enormous

social power. Originally ten laws were drafted, but two statutes were added later prohibiting marriage between the classes and affirming the binding nature of customary law, indicative of the fact that the laws were designed to conserve the *status quo* between the social orders.

42. Skinner, *Liberty before Liberalism*, 39, citing Justinian's *Digest*, 1.5.3., ed. Theodor Mommsen and Paul Krueger, translation ed. Alan Watson (Philadelphia: University of Pennsylvania Press, 1985), 1, 15: 'Summa itaque de iure personarum divisio haec est, quod omnes homines aut liberi sunt aut servi'. Skinner notes that the different status of slave and free persons is also the subject of Book 40 of the *Digest* on manumission.

43. See *Digest*, 1.5.4, 1, 15: 'Servitus est…qua quis dominio alieno contra naturam subicitur'. This explains how it is that Book 1 of the *Digest* can claim that slaves are persons but Book 41, on ownership, can, like Aristotle, refer to them as living tools. See Skinner, *Liberty before Liberalism*, 40, citing Peter Garnsey, *Ideas of Slavery from Aristotle to Augustine* (Cambridge: Cambridge University Press, 1996).

44. See Hobbes, *Leviathan*, ed. Richard Tuck (Cambridge: Cambridge University Press, 1991), ch. 26, 102–3, 139–40, where he insisted that women in the state of nature had dominion over their children, and Drake's assertion in her *Essay* (Springborg, 2002 edn., 247), discussed earlier, that women and men 'in the Infancy of the World were…Equals and Partners in Dominion'.

45. Once again it is a question of *Begriffsgeschichte* and the fine nuances of terminology in circulation at the time. See Skinner, *Liberty before Liberalism*, 41, citing *Digest* 2.9.2, vol. 1, 52; 9.4.33, vol. 1, 303; 11.1.16, vol. 1, 339; 48.10.14, vol. 4, 825.

46. Skinner, *Liberty before Liberalism*, 42, citing *Digest* 11.3.14, vol. 1., 344; 18.1.81, vol. 2, 526; 26.7.57, vol. 2, 772; 34.1.15, vol. 3, 145; 46.1.47, vol. 4, 693; 48.15.1, vol. 4, 834.

47. Skinner, *Liberty before Liberalism*, 77–81.

48. See Sallust, *Bellum Catalinae* 6.7, 'regium imperium, quod initio conservandae libertatis atque augendae rei publicae fuerat, in superbiam dominationemque se convortit', in *Sallust*, tr. J. C. Rolfe (London: Heinemann [Loeb Classical Library], 1931), 12; and Machiavelli, *Discorsi*, bk. 2, on *grandezza*, cited in Skinner, *Liberty before Liberalism*, 61–2.

49. Sallust, *Bellum Catalinae* 11.4, 18–20, cited in Skinner, *Liberty before Liberalism*, 65.

50. Harrington, *The Commonwealth of Oceana*, 44, cited in Skinner, *Liberty before Liberalism*, 65.

51. Skinner, *Liberty before Liberalism*, 46, citing Livy 35.32.11, on *libertas* as the quality 'quae suis stat viribus, non ex alieno arbitrio pendet'. See Livy, *Books XXXV–XXXVII*, tr. Evan T. Sage (London, 1935), 94.

52. Skinner, *Liberty before Liberalism*, 65 n., citing Blair Worden, 'English Republicanism', in J. H. Burns and Mark Goldie, eds., *Cambridge History of Political Thought 1450–1700* (Cambridge: Cambridge University Press, 1991), 467–8, notes that later English republicans in the neo-Roman tradition, such as Robert Molesworth and John Trenchard, took this observation to heart,

explicitly denouncing imperial conquest and the pursuit of military glory. See the fine essays on English republicanism by Blair Worden; 'Marchamont Nedham and the Beginnings of English Republicanism, 1649–1666'; 'James Harrington and *The Commonwealth of Oceana*, 1656'; and 'Republicanism and the Restoration, 1660–1683' in David Wootton, ed., *Republicanism, Liberty, and Commercial Society 1649–1776* (Stanford, Calif.: Stanford University Press, 1994), 45–81, 82–110 and 139–93, respectively; and his essay, 'Milton and Marchamont Nedham', in David Armitage and Armand Himy, eds., *Milton and Republicanism* (Cambridge: Cambridge University Press, 1995), 156–80.

53. Marchamont Nedham, *The Excellency of a Free State*, ed. Richard Baron (London, 1767), xxvi, cited in Skinner, *Liberty before Liberalism*, 63–4. Nedham was a popularizer rather than a scholar. His justification for his defense of the Protectorate under Oliver Cromwell in *The Case of the Commonwealth of England, Stated* (1650), ed. Philip A. Knachel (Charlottesville: University Press of Virginia, 1969), reveals the main positions of the Cromwellian regime. In *The Excellency of a Free State* (1656), ed. Richard Baron (London: A. Millar and T. Cadell, 1767), he uses the term 'compact', but without citing Hobbes, to designate an agreement between the people that creates a society, not an agreement between a ruler and the people, as contemplated in the covenant model, advanced by Johannes Althusius in *Politica* (see the abridged translation of Atthusias's *Politics Methodically Set Forth and Illustrated with Sacred and Profane Examples*, ed. Frederick S. Carney [Indianapolis: Liberty Fund, 1995]), and Samuel Rutherford in *Lex, Rex* (Edinburgh: Robert Ogle and Oliver & Boyd, 1644), evidence that the term 'social contract' or 'compact' was already in the air during this period.

54. Milton, *The Readie and Easie Way to establish a Free Commonwealth*, in *The Complete Prose Works of John Milton*, ed. Robert W. Ayers, revised edn. (New Haven, Conn.: Yale University Press, 1980), 7, 407, 409, 422, 448–9, cited in Skinner, *Liberty before Liberalism*, 38.

55. Milton, *Eikonoklastes*, in *The Complete Prose Works of Johh Milton*, ed. Robert W. Ayers, revised edn. (New Haven, Conn.: Yale University Press, 1962), 3, 462, cited in Skinner, *Liberty before Liberalism*, 49.

56. *Ibid.*, 454, cited in Skinner, *Liberty before Liberalism*, 73.

57. Astell, *Reflections upon Marriage*, 31/48, 27/46–7.

58. Harrington, *Oceana*, 8, 20, cited in Skinner, *Liberty before Liberalism*, 75.

59. Algernon Sidney, *Discourses concerning Government*, Thomas G. West (Indianaopolis: Bobbs-Merrill, 1990), ch. 1, 85, 17, cited in Skinner, *Liberty before Liberalism*, 72.

60. Nedham, *The Excellency of a Free State*, xv, 23, cited in Skinner, *Liberty before Liberalism*, 30.

61. Nedham, *The Excellency of a Free State*, 38, cited in Skinner, *Liberty before Liberalism*, 31.

62. Thomas Hobbes, *Behemoth or the Long Parliament*, ed. Ferdinand Tönnies, introd. M. M. Goldsmith, 2nd edn. (New York: Barnes and Noble, 1969), cited in Skinner, *Liberty before Liberalism*, 60.

63. Hobbes, *Leviathan*, 149, cited in Skinner, *Liberty before Liberalism*, 85.
64. See, for instance, Michel Foucault, *Discipline and Punish: The Birth of the Prison*, tr. Alan Sheridan (New York: Vintage, 1977), and the innumerable works on the way in which repressive social relations are reproduced in the workplace to discipline labour. See also the important essays on the legal condition of modern women in the collection edited by Susan James and Stephanie Parker, *Visible Women: Essays on Feminist Legal Theory and Political Philosophy* (Oxford: Hart, 2002), esp. Ngaire Naffine, 'Can Women Be Legal Persons'; Stephanie Palmer, 'Feminism and the Promise of Human Rights: Possibilities and Paradoxes'; and Nicola Lacey, 'Violence, Ethics and Law: Feminist Reflections on a Familiar Dilemma'.
65. I owe this insight to Zhiyuan Cui in discussions at the Wissenschaftskolleg zu Berlin, 12–16 January 2004, for which I truly thank him and the Kolleg. Cui in his writings, as both a theoretician and an activist, promotes republicanism in the school of Pocock and Skinner as 'a third way', or three-term solution, by means of which China might be able to avoid democracy as privatization, which seems to be the ineluctable conclusion of the civil society–state dichtomy.
66. Skinner, *Liberty before Liberalism*, 36 ff; Pettit, *Republicanism*, 22, 31–2.
67. Locke, *Second Treatise*, 4.23, 284.
68. *Ibid.*, 284 n.
69. Drake, *Essay*, excerpted in Springborg (2002) 247.
70. *Ibid.*, 247–8.
71. *Ibid.*, 22.
72. *Ibid.*, 248
73. *Ibid.*, 249.
74. Gordon Schochet in *Patriarchalism in Political Thought* (Oxford: Blackwell, 1975) gives a brilliant analysis of the Filmerian genetic fallacy.
75. For discussions of Wollstonecraft on slavery, see Virginia Sapiro, *A Vindication of Political Virtue: The Political Theory of Mary Wollstonecraft* (Chicago: University of Chicago Press, 1992); Moira Ferguson, 'Mary Wollstonecraft and the Problematic of Slavery', in Maria J. Falco, ed., *Feminist Interpretations of Mary Wollstonecraft* (University Park: Pennsylvania State University Press, 1996), 125–49; Saba Bahar, *Mary Wollstonecraft's Social and Aesthetic Philosophy: An Eve to Please Me* (Basingstoke: Palgrave, 2002); and Lena Halldenius's unpublished paper, 'The Primacy of Right: On the Triad of Liberty, Equality and Virtue in Wollstonecraft's Political Thought', delivered at the Swedish Collegium for Advanced Study in the Social Sciences, Uppsala (2003), and to be published in the *British Journal of the History of Philosophy* (forthcoming) to which I am indebted for this short account.
76. Halldenius, 'Liberty, Equality and Virtue in Wollstonecraft's Political Thought', 4.
77. Halldenius, citing Sapiro, *A Vindication of Political Virtue*, 118.
78. Halldenius, citing Wollstonecraft, *A Vindication of the Rights of Woman*, 119.
79. Rousseau, *The Social Contract* (1751), ch. 1, in *The Social Contract and Discourses* (London: J. M. Dent, 1952), 3.

80. Throughout his works Rousseau expresses his indebtedness to Hobbes and Locke on property and social contract, and to Grotius and Pufendorf on natural law and natural right.
81. See Thomas Cole, *Democritus and the Sources of Greek Anthropology* (Cleveland: Case Western Reserve University Press, 1967).
82. For a fuller account of this anthropology, see Patricia Springborg, *The Problem of Human Needs and the Critique of Civilization* (London: George Allen & Unwin, 1981).
83. J. Gilmore in *Argument from Roman Law* (Philadelphia: University of Pennsylvania Press, 1944), 8, speaking of the period from the twelfth to the sixteenth century, remarks:

    Finally there was the complete reception of the Roman law in Germany, a development which was the logical extreme of the process which was elsewhere a matter of degree, with the minimum represented by England. During this time there are instances in which courts applied law which was neither immemorial custom nor the decree of a sovereign power but which rested on the decision of an Italian jurisconsult, commenting a text of Justinian.

84. See Scott Davidson, *Human Rights* (Buckingham and Philadelphia, Open University Press, 1995); *The Human Rights Reader*, ed. Micheline R. Ishay (London: Routledge, 1997); *Debating Human Rights: Critical Essays from the United States and Asia*, ed. Peter Van Ness (London: Routledge, 1999).
85. Leonard Krieger, *The German Idea of Freedom: History of a Political Tradition from the Reformation to 1871* (Chicago: University of Chicago Press, 1957).
86. This is a characteristically Marxist feminist argument, made on the analogue of Marx's argument in *On the Jewish Question*, that the idealization of the state, as a mythical celestial realm in which citizens sublimate their desire for freedom, legitimates the rank growth of economic forces in the private sphere, where real exploitation takes place. It is nowhere better expounded than in the works of Catherine MacKinnon, and particularly her *Toward a Feminist Theory of the State* (Cambridge, Mass.: Harvard University Press, 1989).
87. Hegel, *Philosophy of Right*, tr. T. M. Knox (Oxford: Clarendon Press, 1952), §33, 35.
88. *Ibid.*, §§41–56, esp. §46, 42.
89. *Ibid.*, §33, 35, §62, 50–1.
90. *Ibid.*, 116.
91. *Ibid.*, Remark to §175, 118.
92. Astell, *Reflections Upon Marriage*; Karl Marx, 'On the Jewish Question', in *Marx-Engels Collected Works* (London: Lawrence and Wishart, 1975), 3, 146–74.
93. For the classic explication of these different legal discourses, see J. G. A. Pocock, *The Ancient Constitution and the Feudal Law* (Cambridge: Cambridge University Press, 1957; 2nd edn., 1987). Astell's works are peppered with satirical references to the free rights of Englishmen. See in particular her

discussion, in the context of 'that ingenious Author . . . Mr *Lock*', and her attack on those 'who seek to destroy the Government in Church and State, and to set up a Model of their own Invention, aggreable to their own private Interests and Designs, under the specious Pretences of the Peoples Rights and Liberties.' Astell, *An Impartial Enquiry*, 40–1/177–9.

94. Catharine Macaulay is a notable exception.

95. Oakeshott's works covered a trajectory from his early neo-Hegelian *Experience and Its Modes* (Cambridge: Cambridge University Press [1933] 1985); the influential Introduction to his edition of Hobbes's *Leviathan* (Oxford: Blackwell, 1946); through his seminal *Rationalism in Politics and Other Essays* (London: Macmillan, 1960; reprinted Indianapolis: Liberty Fund, 1991); to *On Human Conduct* (Oxford: Oxford University Press, 1975); and *On History and Other Essays* (Oxford: Basil Blackwell, 1983; reprinted Indianapolis: Liberty Fund, 2002). I must acknowledge a great personal debt to Michael Oakeshott, who, when I was a young student researching a master's thesis on Thomas Hobbes in the British Museum, saw me several times and gave me invaluable advice. Even greater is my debt to John Pocock, Quentin Skinner and Leszek Kolakowski, who have been characteristically generous with their time and assistance over many years.

96. Marx developed a powerful critique of the modern liberal-democratic state and the separation of civil society and the state in his critical review of Bruno Bauer's *Die Jugendfrage* for the *Deutsch Französicher Jahrbücher* of 1844. The terms of the dichotomy had been first coined by Rousseau in his Second Discourse, *On the Causes of Social Inequality* – as an elaboration of the distinctiveness of the terms '*bourgeois*' and '*citoyen*' – and was taken up by Hegel in his *Philosophy of Right*. In his 'Preface to a Critique of Hegel's Philosophy of Right', Marx's second contribution to the *Deutsch Französicher Jahrbücher* of 1844, he further develops the notion of myth of the state as a secular religion that projects hopes for amelioration in the present into a utopian otherworldly realm in which all the distinctions in terms of rights, property, wealth and social standing that characterize individuals in civil society are masked by the promise of freedom and equality before the law and made explicit in documents like the French Declaration of the Rights of Man and Citizen of 1689 and the American Bill of Rights.

97. On Marxism as a religion see Leszek Kolakowski's magisterial work, *Main Currents of Marxism, Its Origin Growth and Dissolution*, 3 vols., tr. 1978, (Oxford: Clarendon Press), in conjunction with his superb books on religion: *Religion: If There Is No God: On God, the Devil, Sin, and Other Worries of the So-Called Philosophy of Religion* (Oxford: Oxford University Press, 1982); *God Owes Us Nothing: A Brief Remark on Pascal's Religion and on the Spirit of Jansenism* (Chicago: University of Chicago Press, 1998); and *Metaphysical Horror*, tr. Agnieszka Kolakowska (Chicago: University of Chicago Press, 2001).

98. Hegemonic stability theory is a fertile subfield of international relations theory. See the seminal works of Charles P. Kindleberger, *The World in Depression: 1929–1939* (Berkeley: University of California Press, 1973); Robert Keohane, *After Hegemony: Cooperation and Discord in the World Political Economy* (Princeton, N.J.: Princeton University Press, 1984); and Robert

Gilpin, *The Political Economy of International Relations* (Princeton, N.J.: Princeton University Press, 1987).

99. See Patricia Springborg, *Western Republicanism and the Oriental Prince*, Part II, on Roman appropriation of the freedom of the Greeks as a legitimation of imperialism. For a specific account of the Roman 'democratization' of Egypt, see Alan K. Bowman, *The Town Councils of Roman Egypt* (Toronto: University of Toronto Press, 1971).

100. I use the term 'world of small things' in the sense in which it is used by Simone de Beauvoir to denote the intimate life or the world of the private. See Simone de Beauvoir, *The Second Sex* (1949) tr. H. M. Parshley (New York: Vintage, 1989).

101. Edward Said develops this theme with specific reference to Jane Austen in *Culture and Imperialism* (New York: Alfred A. Knopf, 1993).

102. I use the term 'life-world' in the way that it is used by phenomenologists, and in particular by Alfred Schutz in *Structures of the Life-World* (*Strukturen der Lebenswelt*) with Thomas Luckmann, tr. Richard M. Zaner and H. Tristram Engelhardt (Evanston, Ill.: Northwestern University Press, 1973).

103. Chapter IVA of Hegel's *Phenomenology of Spirit*, 'Independence and Dependence of Self-Consciousness: Lordship and Bondage', is more familiarly known as the master–slave dialectic, according to which it is only the slave, who furnishes the master's necessities of life, who can properly conceive of freedom, which is taken for granted by the master, an intuition to which the slave owes her eventual emancipation. See the standard English translation, *The Phenomenology of Mind*, tr. J. B. Baillie (Oxford: Clarendon Press, 1910, revised 1931), and Alexandre Kojève's *Introduction to the Reading of Hegel*, which made the master–slave dialectic the focus of Hegel's work.

104. In *Reflections upon Marriage*, 55–6/61, Astell gives a particularly witty disquisition upon just this theme in a mocking series of rhetorical questions:

> But how can a Woman scruple intire Subjection, how can she forbear to admire the worth and excellency of the Superior Sex, if she at all considers it? Have not all the great Actions that have been perform'd in the World been done by Men? Have not they founded Empires and overturn'd them? Do not they make Laws and continually repeal and amend them? Their vast Minds lay Kingdoms wast, no bounds or measures can be prescrib'd to their Desires. War and Peace depend on them, they form Cabals and have the Wisdom and Courage to get over all the Rubs which may lie in the way of their desired Grandeur. What is it they cannot do? They make Worlds and ruine them, form Systems of universal nature and dispute eternally about them; their Pen gives worth to the most trifling Controversie; nor can a fray be inconsiderable if they have drawn their Swords in't. All that the wise Man pronounces is an Oracle, and every Word the Witty speaks a Jest. It is a Woman's Happiness to hear, admire and praise them, especially if a little Ill-nature keeps them at any time from bestowing due Applauses on each other! And if she aspires no further, she is thought to be in her proper Sphere of Action, she is as wise and as good as can be expected from her!

105. Malcolm, 'Hobbes and the European Republic of Letters', in *Aspects of Hobbes* (Oxford: Clarendon Press, 2002), 539–44. See my review of Malcolm's excellent book, 'The Enlightenment of Thomas Hobbes: Review Essay on

Noel Malcolm's *Aspects of Hobbes'*, *British Journal for the History of Philosophy*, 12, 3 (2004): 513-34.

106. *Moderation Truly Stated* (1704) is, ironically, Astell's shrillest work, perhaps the reason it is scarcely looked at in the secondary literature. Reminiscent of Locke's *First Treatise* against Filmer or Marx's *German Ideology*, it is written in a polemical tone that jars so long after the controversy has passed.

Select Bibliography

Primary Texts

Allestree, Richard. 1673. *The Ladies Calling*. Oxford: Printed at the Theater.

Ames, Richard. 1691. *The Folly of Love*. London: Printed for A. Turner. Reprinted 1701.

Anon. 1700. *A Satire against Marriage*. British Library, 1346 m. 44.

Anon. 1704. *A Ladies Religion: In a Letter to the Honourable My Lady Howard. The Second Edition. To which is added, A Second Letter to the same Lady, concerning the Import of Fear in Religion*, 'by a Divine of the Church of England'. London: Printed for A. and J. Churchill at the Black-Swan in Paternoster Row. Folger Library, 144781 (Wing 159).

Anon. 1705a. *An Essay upon Government: Wherein the Republican Schemes Reviv'd by Mr. Locke Are Fairly Commder'd and Refuted*. Reprinted in Mark Goldie, ed., *The Perception of Locke's Politics: From the 1690s to the 1830s*. London: Pickering & Chatto, 1999, 6 vols.

Anon. 1705b. *A Philosophick Essay Concerning Ideas, According to Dr. Sherlock's Principles (1705)*, ed. James G. Buickerood. New York: AMS Press, 1996.

Aristotle. 1926. *Nicomachean Ethics*, ed. H. Rackham. London: Heinemann (Loeb).

Aristotle. 1932. *Politics*, ed. H. Rackham. London: Heinemann (Loeb).

Arnauld, Antoine [and Pierre Nicole, 1662]. *Logic, or the Art of Thinking*. London: 1693 (Wing A3724).

Arnauld, Antoine. [1683] 1990. *On True and False Ideas*, tr. with an Introduction by Stephen Gaukroger. New York: St. Martin's Press.

Astell, Mary. 1689. *A Collection of Poems Humbly Presented and Dedicated to the Most Reverend Father in God William [Sancroft] by Divine Providence Lord Archbishop of Canterbury etc.*, Rawlinson MSS poet. 154:50. Oxford: The Bodleian Library. Excerpted in Bridget Hill, *The First English Feminist: 'Reflections upon Marriage' and Other Writings by Mary Astell*. Aldershot, Hants: Gower/Maurice Temple Smith, 1986, 183–4. Published in full as 'Appendix D' to Ruth Perry's *The Celebrated Mary Astell: An Early English Feminist*. Chicago: University of Chicago Press, 1986, 400–54.

Astell, Mary. 1694. *A Serious Proposal to the Ladies for the Advancement of Their True and Greatest Interest.* London: Printed for R. Wilkin (Folger Library, 140765 [Wing A4063]). Reprinted in Patricia Springborg, *Mary Astell's A Serious Proposal to the Ladies* (1694). Diplomatic edition with commentary and introduction. London: Pickering & Chatto, 1997.

Astell, Mary. 1695a. *Letters Concerning the Love of God, between the Author of the Proposal to the Ladies and Mr. John Norris.* Published by J. Norris, Rector of Bemerton nr. Sarum. London: Printed for Samuel Manship (Wing 1254).

Astell, Mary. 1695b. *A Serious Proposal to the Ladies for the Advancement of Their True and Greatest Interest.* London: Printed for R. Wilkin (Folger Library, 145912). 2nd edn. corrected; 4th edn. 1701, London: Printed by J. R. for R. Wilkin (Folger Library, PR3316.A655.S3.Cage).

Astell, Mary. 1697a. *A Serious Proposal to the Ladies, Part II, Wherein a Method is Offer'd for the Improvement of Their Minds.* London: Printed for Richard Wilkin at the King's Head in St. Paul's Church-yard.

Astell, Mary. 1697b. *A Serious Proposal to the Ladies for the Advancement of Their True and Greatest Interest, Parts I and II.* London: Printed for T. W. and R. Wilkin at the King's Head in St. Paul's Church-yard. Part II has a separate title page, 'A Serious Proposal . . .' (entered in Wing as C40654). Reprinted in Patricia Springborg, *Mary Astell's A Serious Proposal to the Ladies* (1694). Diplomatic edition with commentary and introduction. London: Pickering & Chatto, 1997; and in Springborg, *Mary Astell's A Serious Proposal to the Ladies, Parts I (1694) and II (1697).* Diplomatic edition with commentary, introduction and appendices. Peterborough, Ontario: Broadview Press, 2002.

Astell, Mary. 1700. *Some Reflections upon Marriage, Occasion'd by the Duke & Dutchess of Mazarine's Case . . .* , 2nd edn. London: Printed for John Nutt (Folger Library, 181431 [Wing A4067]).

Astell, Mary. 1701. *A Serious Proposal to the Ladies for the Advancement of Their True and Greatest Interest,* 4th edn. London: Printed by J. R. for R. Wilkin (Folger Library, PR3316.A655.S3.Cage).

Astell, Mary. 1704a. *A Fair Way with the Dissenters and Their Patrons.* London: Printed for E. by R. Wilkin at the King's Head in St. Paul's Church-yard (Folger Library, BX5202.A7.Cage). Reprinted in Patricia Springborg, *Mary Astell (1666–1731), Political Writings.* Cambridge: Cambridge University Press, 1996.

Astell, Mary. 1704b. *An Impartial Enquiry into the Causes of Rebellion and Civil War in this Kingdom in an Examination of Dr. Kennett's Sermon, Jan. 31, 1703/4 and Vindication of the Royal Martyr.* London: Printed by E. for R. Wilkin at the King's Head in St. Paul's Church-yard (Folger Library, BV 4253.K4.C75.Cage). Reprinted in Patricia Springborg, *Mary Astell (1666–1731), Political Writings.*

Astell, Mary. 1704c. *Moderation Truly Stated: or a Review of a Late Pamphlet, Entitul'd Moderation a Virtue, or, The Occasional Conformist Justified from the Imputation of Hypocrisy. . . . With a Prefatory Discourse to Dr. D'Avenant, Concerning His Late Essays on Peace and War.* London: Printed by J. L. for Richard Wilkin at the King's Head in St. Paul's Church-yard (Folger Library, BX5202.A8.Cage).

Astell, Mary. 1705. *The Christian Religion as Profess'd by a Daughter of the Church of England in a Letter to the Right Honourable T. L., C. I.* London: Printed by S. H. for R. Wilkin at the King's Head in St. Paul's Church-yard (Folger Library, 216595).

Astell, Mary, 1706. *Reflections upon Marriage, to Which Is Added a Preface in Answer to Some Objections*, 3rd edn. London: Printed for R. Wilkin at the King's Head in St. Paul's Church-yard. Reprinted in Patricia Springborg, *Mary Astell (1666–1731), Political Writings*.

Astell, Mary. 1709. *Bart'lemy Fair, or an Enquiry after Wit* in Which Due Respect Is Had to a Letter Concerning Enthusiasm. To my Lord XXX by Mr. Wotton [pseud.]. London (Folger Library, BR112.A7.Cage). The 1722 edition appeared under the title *an Enquiry after Wit*, wherein the Trifling Arguing and Impious Raillery of the Late Earl of Shaftesbury in his letter concerning Enthusiasm and other Profane Writers are fully answered and justly exposed.

Astell, Mary, 1730. *Reflections upon Marriage, to Which Is Added a Preface in Answer to Some Objections*, 4th edn. London: Printed for R. Wilkin at the King's Head in St Paul's Church-yard.

Ballard, George. [1752] 1985. *Memoirs of Several Ladies of Great Britain Who Have Been Celebrated for Their Writings or Skill in the Learned Languages, Arts and Sciences*, ed. Ruth Perry. Detroit: Wayne State University Press.

Baxter, Richard. 1653. *Christian Concord.* London (Folger Library, B1218).

Baxter, Richard. 1659. *Five Disputations of Church-Government, and Worship . . .*, London: Printed by R. W. for Nevil Simmons, Bookseller in Kederminster . . . and by Thomas Johnson at the Golden Key in St. Paul's Church-yard (Folger Library, B1267).

Behn, Aphra. 1688. *A Congratulatory Poem to Her Most Sacred Majesty.* London.

Behn, Aphra. 1994. *The Complete Works of Aphra Behn*, ed. Janet Todd, 5 vols. Columbus: Ohio State University Press.

Browne, Thomas. 1977. *Religio Medici* in *The Major Works of Sir Thomas Browne*, ed. C. A. Patrides. Harmondsworth: Penguin.

Burnet, Bishop Gilbert. 1704. *The Bishop of Salisbury's Speech in the House of Lords, upon the Bill against Occasional Conformity.* (Folger Library, BX5203.5.B8). London.

Burnet, Gilbert. 1685. *Some Letters Containing an Account of What Seemed Most Remarkable in Switzerland, Italy, etc.* London.

Burnet, Gilbert. 1688. *An Enquiry into the Measures of Submission to the Supream Authority: And of the Grounds upon Which It May Be Lawful or necessary for Subjects, to Defend their Religion, Lives and Liberties.* In *Six Papers by Gilbert Burnet, D. D.* Edinburgh (n.d.), reprinted and distributed in Holland, 1688, and London, 1689 (Folger Library, B5913).

Burnet, Gilbert. 1689. *Enquiry into the Present State of Affairs.* Printed for John Starky and Ric. Chiswell (Wing B2883 revised to Wing B5811). London.

Burnet, Gilbert. 1724–34. *History of His Own Time*, 2 vols. London.

Burthogge, Richard. 1694. *An Essay upon Reason.* London.

Cavendish, Margaret, Duchess of Newcastle. 1999. *The Convent of Pleasure and Other Plays*, ed. Anne Shaver. Baltimore: Johns Hopkins University Press.

Cavendish, Margaret, Duchess of Newcastle. 2001. *Observations upon Experimental Philosophy*, ed. Eileen O'Neill. Cambridge: Cambridge University Press.

Cavendish, Margaret, Duchess of Newcastle. 2003. *Political Writings*, ed. Susan James. Cambridge: Cambridge University Press.

Cawdrey, Daniel. 1657. *Independencie a Great Schism: Proved against Dr. (John—RB) Owen, His Apology in his Tract of Schism.* London: By J. S for John Right (Wing C1630).

Cellier, Elizabeth. [1688]. *To Dr. – An Answer to His Queries.* London.

Centlivre, S. 1760. 'Basset Table', in *Works.* London: Printed for J. Knapton *et al.* (Folger Library, PR 3339.C6.1760.Cage).

Church of England. [1604] 1675. *A Collection of Articles Injunctions, Canons, Orders, Ordinances and Constitutions Ecclesiastical. . . .* London: Printed for Robert Pawlet in Chancery Lane (Folger Library, S4825).

Church of England. 1687. *Certain Sermons or Homilies Appointed to be Read in Churches in the Time of Queen Elizabeth of Famous Memory: And Now Reprinted for the Use of Private Families.* London: Printed for George Wells at the Sun, Abel Swall at the Unicorn, in St. Paul's Church-yard, and George Pawlett at the Bible in Chancery-Lane (Folger Library, 158869).

Cockburn, Catharine Trotter. 1751. *The Works of Mrs Catharine Cockburn*, ed. Thomas Birch. London: J. and Knapton.

Conway, Anne [1692] 1982. *The Principles of the Most Ancient and Modern Philosophy*, ed. Peter Lopston. The Hague: Martinus Nijhoff.

Conway, Anne. [1642–84] 1992. *The Conway Letters: The Correspondence of Anne, Viscountess Conway, Henry More and Their Friends, 1642–1684*, ed. Marjorie Hope Nicholson. Oxford: Oxford University Press.

Cowper, William. 1979–86. *Letters and Prose Writings of William Cowper*, ed. James King and Charles Ryskamp, 5 vols. Oxford: Clarendon Press.

Cudworth, Ralph. 1678. *The True Intellectual System of the Universe.* London.

Defoe, Daniel. 1697. 'An Academy for Women', in *An Essay upon Projects.* London: Printed by R. R. for Theo. Cockerill at the Corner of Warwick-Lane, near Paternoster Row (Folger Library, 145226).

Defoe, Daniel. 1698. *An Enquiry into the Occasional Conformity of Dissenters.* London (Folger Library, 142677).

Defoe, Daniel. 1700/1701. *The True Born Englishman. A Satyr. . . .* London (Folger Library, D849).

Defoe, Daniel. 1701. *The Legion Memorial.* Reprinted 1702 with *The Memorial, alias Legion, answered. . . .* London (Folger Library, PR3404.L32.M3.Cage)

Defoe, Daniel. 1702a. *The Legionites Plot.* London: Printed for E. Mallett (Folger Library, 193–504q).

Defoe, Daniel. 1702b. *A New Test of the Church of England's Loyalty.* London (Folger Library, BV5135.D42.Cage).

Defoe, Daniel. 1702c. *The Shortest Way with the Dissenters: Or Proposals for the Establishment of the Church.* London (Folger Library, 134–622q).

Defoe, Daniel. 1704a. *The Legions Humble Address to the Lords.* London (Folger Library, PR3404.L3.Cage).

Defoe, Daniel. 1704b. *More Short-Ways with the Dissenters.* London (Library of Congress, BX5202.D36).

Defoe, Daniel. 1704c. *A New Test of the Church of England's Honesty.* London (Folger Library, PR3404.N5.Cage).

Defoe, Daniel. 1706. *Jure Divino. A Satyr in Twelve Books.* London (Folger Library, 232560).

Dennis, John. 1702. *The Danger of Priestcraft to Religion and Government: with Some Politick Reasons for Toleration. Occasion'd by a Discourse of Mr. Sacheverel's intitul'd, The Political Union, etc.* . . . London (Folger Library, BV.D4.D3. Cage).

Descartes, René. 1628–9. *Regulae ad Directionem Ingenii.* Paris.

Descartes, René. 1991. *The Philosophical Writings of Descartes*, tr. John Cottingham, Robert Stoothoff, Dugald Murdoch and Antony Kenny. Cambridge: Cambridge University Press.

Descartes, René. 1992, *The Cambridge Companion to Descartes*, ed. John Cottingham. Cambridge: Cambridge University Press.

Drake. Judith. 1696. *An Essay In Defence of the Female Sex.* London: Printed for A. Roper and E. Wilkinson at the Black Boy and R. Clavel at the Peacock, in Fleetstreet (Folger Library, A4058a).

Dunton, John. [1705] 1974. *The Life and Errors of John Dunton.* Reprinted New York: Garland Publishing.

Edwards, Thomas. 1644. *Antapologia, or a full Answer to the Apologeticall Narration of Mr. Goodwin, Mr. Nye, Mr. Sympson, Mr Burroughes, Mr Bridge, Members of the Assembly of Divines.* London (Folger Library, 143243).

Edwards, Thomas. 1646a. *Gangraena; or a Catalogue and Discovery of many Errours, Heresies, Blasphemies, and pernicious Practices of the Sectaries of this Time, Vented and Acted in England in These Four Last Years.* . . . London: Printed for Ralph Smith (Folger Library, E228).

Edwards, Thomas. 1646b. *The Second Part of Gangraena; or a Fresh and Further Discovery of the Errours . . . of the Sectaries of this Time.* . . . London: Printed by T. E. and E. M. for Ralph Smith (Folger Library, E235 Bd. w. E228).

Edwards, Thomas. 1646c. *The Third Part of Gangraena, or A New and Higher Discovery of the Errours . . . of the Sectaries of These Times.* . . . London: Printed by T. E. and E. M. for Ralph Smith (Folger Library, E237 Bd. w. E228).

Ficino, Marsilio [1561] 1959. *Opera Omnia*, 2 vols. Basle. Reprinted Turin.

Filmer, Sir Robert. 1987. 'In Praise of the Vertuous Wife', in Margaret J. M. Ezell, *The Patriarch's Wife: Literary Evidence and the History of the Family.* Appendix I, 169–90. Chapel Hill: University of North Carolina Press.

Filmer, Robert [1680] 1991. *Patriarcha and Other Writings*, ed. Johann Sommerville. Cambridge: Cambridge University Press.

Foulis, Henry. 1674. *The History of the Wicked Plots and Conspiracies of Our Pretended Saints.* . . . , 2nd edn. Oxford: Printed by Henry Hall for Ric. Davis (Folger Library, F1643).

Foulis, Henry. 1681. *The History of the Romish Treasons and Usurpations.* . . . London: Printed for Thomas Basset, Richard Chiswell, Christopher Wilkinson and Thomas Dring (Folger Library, F1641).

Gould, Robert. 1682. *Love Given O're: Or, A Satyr against the Pride, Lust and Inconstancy etc. of Women.* See Felicity Nussbaum's facsimile edition, published together with a list of responses in her *Satires on Women*, Augustan Reprint Publication 180, 1976.

Grotius, Hugo. 1641. *Appendix ad interpretationem Locorum Novi Testamenti quae De Antichristo agunt aut agere putantur.* . . . Amsterdam: Cornelius Blaev (Folger Library, BT.985.G7.1641).

Harrington, James. [1656] 1992. *The Commonwealth of Oceana*, ed. J. G. A. Pocock. Cambridge: Cambridge University Press.

Hericourt, Jenny d'. 1864. *A Woman's Philosophy of Woman; or Woman Affranchised*. New York: Carleton.

Hickes, George. 1713. *Instructions for the Education of a Daughter*. London. Hickes's translation of Fénélon's *L'Education des Filles*, 3rd edn. London (Folger Library, 168205).

Hickes, George. 1713. *Sermons on Several Subjects*. 2 vols. London.

Hoadly, Benjamin. 1710. *The Original and Institution of Civil Government, discuss'd*. London (Folger Library, 148–325q).

Hobbes, Thomas. [1681] 1971. *Dialogue between a Philosopher and a Student of the Common Laws of England*, ed. Joseph Cropsey. Chicago, University of Chicago Press.

Hobbes, Thomas. [1679] (1889), 1990. *Behemoth, or The Long Parliament*, ed. Ferdinand Tönnies. London, 1889, facsimile edn., ed. Stephen Holmes. Chicago: University of Chicago Press, 1990.

Hobbes, Thomas. [1651] 1991. *Leviathan*, ed. Richard Tuck. Cambridge: Cambridge University Press.

Hooper, George. 1704. 'A Sermon preach'd before the Lords Spiritual and Temporal in Parliament Assembled, in the Abbey-Church of Westminister, on Monday, 31 Jan. 1703/4, the Fast-Day for the Martyrdom of King Charles the 1st. By George Lord Bishop of St. Asaph. London: Printed by J. Leake for Walter Kettilby at the Bishop's Head in St. Paul's Church-Yard, 1704 (Folger Library, BV 4253, H 88, S 6, Cage).

Howe, John. 1701. *Some Consideration of a Preface to an Enquiry Concerning the Occasional Conformity of Dissenters, etc.* London (Folger Library, 134–622q).

Hyde, Edward, First Earl of Clarendon. 1702. *The History of the Rebellion and Civil Wars in England, begun in the Year 1641. With the precedent Passages, and Actions, that contributed thereunto, and the happy end, and Conclusion thereof by the King's blessed Restoration, and Return upon the 29th of May, in the Year 1660*. Oxford: Printed at the Theater (Folger Library, DA.400.C6.1702.Cage).

Justinian. 1985. *The Digest of Justinian*, ed. Theodor Mommsen and Paul Krueger, tr. Alan Watson, 4 vols. Philadelphia: University of Pennsylvania Press.

Kant, Immanuel. 1764. *Beobachten über das Gefühl des Schönen und Erhabenen*. Königsberg: Johan Jakob Kanter.

Kennett, White. 1704. *A Compassionate Enquiry into the Causes of the Civil War. In a Sermon Preached in the Church of St. Botolph Aldgate, On 31 January 1704. the Day of the Fast of the Martyrdom of King Charles the First*. London: Printed for A. and J. Churchil in Pater-Noster Row.

Leibniz, Gottfried W. 1998. *Philosophical Texts*, tr. Richard Francks and R. S. Woodhouse. Oxford: Oxford University Press.

Leslie, Charles. 1695. *The Charge of Socinianism against Dr. Tillotson Considered*. Edinburgh (Folger Library, 134270).

Leslie, Charles. 1699. *A Short and Easie Method with the Deists . . . To Which Is Added a Second Part to the Jews*, 2nd edn. London (Folger Library, 152881).

Leslie, Charles. 1702. *The New Association of those Called Moderate-Church-man, with the Modern-Whigs and Fanaticks to Under-mine and Blow-up the present*

Church and Government. . . . , 3rd corrected edn. London (Folger Library, 151–330q).

Leslie, Charles. 1703a. *A Case of Present Concern: in a Letter to a Member of the House of Commons.* London (Folger Library, 148–428q).

Leslie, Charles. 1703b. *The New Association. Part II. With farther Improvements.* . . . *An Answer to Some Objections in the Pretended D. Foe's Explication in 'the Reflections upon the Shortest Way'.* . . . with 'A Supplement', dated March 25, 1703, entitled 'With a short Account of the *Original of Government.* Compared with the *Schemes* of the *Republicans* and *Whigs*' to *The New Association. Part II. With farther Improvements.* . . . *An Answer to some* Objections *in the Pretended* D. Foe's *Explication in 'the Reflections upon the Shortest Way.* . . . ' London and Westminster (Folger Library, BX.9180.L3.Cage).

Leslie, Charles. 1703c. *Reflections upon Some Scandalous and Malicious Pamphlets, viz. I The Shortest Way with the Dissenters.* . . . London (Folger Library, PR 3404.S585.1703.R4.Cage).

Leslie, Charles. 1704a. *The Bishop of Salisbury's Proper Defence from a Speech Cry'd about the Streets in His Name, and Said to Have Been Spoken by Him in the House of Lords, upon the Bill against Occasional Conformity.* London and Westminster (Folger Library, BX 5203.5.B8.L25.Cage).

Leslie, Charles. 1704b. *A Vindication of the Royal Martyr King Charles I.: from the Irish Massacre in . . . 1641, cast upon him in the Life of Richard Baxter . . . and since the Abridgment by E. Calamy.* London (Folger Library, 191–961q).

Leslie, Charles. 1704c. *The Wolf Stript of his Shepherd's Cloathing. In Answer to a Late Celebrated Book Intituled Moderation a Vertue.* London (Folger Library, 134–622q).

Leslie, Charles. 1704–5. *Cassandra. (But I Hope not) Telling what will come of it. In Answer to the Occasional Letter. Num. I. Wherein The New-Associations, etc., Are Considered.* Printed and sold by the Booksellers of London and Westminster (Folger Library, DA.490.L29.Cage).

Leslie, Charles. 1707. *The Second Part of the Wolf Stript of his Shepherds Cloathing.* London (Folger Library, 199284).

Leslie, Charles. 1708. *A View of the Times Their Principles and Practices in the First Volume of the Rehearsals.* London (Folger Library, 147241).

Leslie, Charles. 1709. *Best of All.* . . . *Wherein Mr. Hoadly's Second Part of his Measures of Submission . . . is fully Answer'd.* London (Folger Library, BV 629.H6.L4.Cage).

Leslie, Charles. 1710. *The Divine Rights of the British Nation and Constitution Vindicated.* . . . *against Mr. Hoadly's Considerations.* London (Folger Library, 181–316q).

Livius, Titus Quinctus. 1935. *Livy Books XXXV–XXXVII,* tr. Evan T. Sage. London: Heinemann (Loeb).

Locke, John. [1660–1] 1967. *Two Tracts on Government (1660–61),* ed. Philip Abrams. Cambridge: Cambridge University Press.

Locke, John. [1667] 1961. 'An Essay Concerning Toleracon 1667', Bodleian MSS. Locke c. 28, fols. 21–32. Reprinted with corrections by Carlo A Viano in *John Locke, Scritti Editi e Inediti Sulla Tolleranzo.* Turin: Taylor Torino, 81–105.

Locke, John. [1689] 1968. *Epistola de Tolerantia* (Gouda, 1689; written c. 1685), tr. J. W. Gough in Locke, *Epistola de Tolerantia/A Letter on Toleration,* ed. J. W. Gough and Raymond Klibansky. Oxford: Oxford University Press.

Locke, John. [1689] 1823. *Essay Concerning Human Understanding*. In *The Works of John Locke*, London: Printed for Thomas Tegg, W. Sharpe and son, *et al.*, vols. 1–4.

Locke, John. [1690a] 1988. *John Locke's Two Treatises of Government*, ed. Peter Laslett. Cambridge: Cambridge University Press.

Locke, John. [1690b] 1985. Minute to Edward Clarke, Bodleian MS Locke e 18, fol. 4v. Published in James Farr and Clayton Roberts, 'John Locke on the Glorious Revolution: A Rediscovered Document'. *The Historical Journal*, 28, 385–98.

Locke, John. [1693] 1823. 'Remarks Upon Some of Mr. Norris' Books, wherein he asserts Malebranche's Opinion of seeing all Things in God'. In *The Works of John Locke*. London: Printed for Thomas Tegg, W. Sharpe and son, *et al.*, vol. 9, 247–59.

Locke, John. [1695a] 1823. *The Reasonableness of Christianity, as Delivered in the Scriptures*. In *The Works of John Locke*. London: Printed for Thomas Tegg, W. Sharpe and son, *et al.*, vol. 7, 1–158.

Locke, John. [1695b] 1999. *The Reasonableness of Christianity*, ed. John C. Higgins-Biddle. Oxford: Clarendon Press.

Locke, John. [1695c] 1989. *Some Thoughts Concerning Education* (begun as a collection of letters between Locke and Edward Clarke, 1684–91. Third edition. London: Printed for A. and J. Churchill at the Black Swan, 1695. Ed. John Yeoton (Oxford: Oxford University Press, 1989).

Locke, John. 1963. *An Examination of Malebranche's Opinion of Seeing all Things in God*. In Locke, *Works*, 10. vols. London: Aelan Scientia.

Locke, John. 1976. *The Correspondence of John Locke*, ed. E. S. De Beer, 8 vols. Oxford: Clarendon Press.

Makin, Bathusa. *An Essay to Review the Antient Education of Gentlewomen, in Religion, Manners, Arts & Tongues, with An Answer to the Objections against This Way of Education*. London: Printed by J. D. to be sold by Tho. Pankhunsf at the Bible and Crown at the lower end of Cheapside. Reprinted Los Angeles, Calif.: Auguston Reprint Society, 1980.

Malebranche, Nicolas. 1678. *De la Recherche de la Verité, ou l'on traitte de la nature de l'esprit de l'homme, & de l'usage qu'il en doit faire pour éviter l'erreur dans les sciences*, 4th revised and enlarged edn. Paris: André Pralard (Folger Library, B1893.R.3.1678.Cage).

Malebranche, Nicolas. 1694, 1695. *Malebranche's search after truth: or a treatise of the nature of the humane mind*, vol. 1, London: Printed for J. Dunton and S. Manship (Wing M315, Folger Library, 147104); vol. 2, London: Printed for S. Manship (Wing M316, Folger Library, 147103).

Malebranche, Nicolas. 1700. *Father Malebranche his treatise concerning the search after truth. The whole work complete. . . .*, tr. T. Taylor. 2nd corrected edn. London: Printed by W. Bowyer, for Thomas Bennet, and T. Leigh and D. Midwinter (Folger Library, Wing M318).

Mancini, Hortense, Duchess of Mazarine. n.d. *Memoires de Madame la Duchesse de Mazarin*. Cologne: Chez Perre du Marteau, Libraire Renommé (Folger Library, DC.130.M28.A3).

Mancini, Hortense, Duchess of Mazarine. 1676. *The Memoires of the Dutchess Mazarine. Written in French by her Own Hand, and Done into English by Porter, Esq;*

Together with the Reasons of her Coming into England. Likewise, A Letter containing a True Character of her Person and Conversation. London: Printed . . . by Silliam Cademan, at the Popes-Head in the New-Exchange, and the Middle-Exchange in the Strande (Folger Library, S355).

Mancini, Hortense, Duchess of Mazarine. 1713. *Memoirs of the Dutchess of Mazarine.* Written in her name by The Abbott of St. Réal, with a Letter Containing a True Character of Her Person and Conversation . . . n.d. or publisher (Folger Library, 187040).

Marvell, Andrew. 1678. *An Account of the Growth of Popery and Arbitrary Government in England.* London ['printed in Amsterdam'].

Marx, Karl. 1975. *Economic and Philosophic Manuscripts of 1844*, Third Manuscript, 'The Power of Money', *Marx–Engels Collected Works*, vol. 3. London: Lawrence and Wishart.

Masham, Damaris. 1696. *A Discourse Concerning the Love of God.* London: Printed for Awnsham and John Churchill.

Masham, Damaris. 1705. *Occasional Thoughts in Reference to a Vertuous or Christian Life.* London: Printed for A. and J. Churchill.

Milton, John. 1649. *Eikonoklastes in Answer to a Book Initl'd Eikon Basilike, The Portrature of His Sacred Majesty in His Solitudes and Sufferings.* London: Printed by Matthew Simmons, next dore to the gilded Lyon in the Aldergate Street.

Milton, John. [1660] 1980. *The Readie and Easie Way to Establish a Free Commonwealth, and the Excellence Thereof Compar'd with the Inconveniences and Dangers of Readmitting Kingship in This Nation.* London: Printed by T. N. for Livervell Chapman at the Crown in Popes-Head Alley. Reprinted in *The Complete Prose Works of John Milton*, 7th ed. Robert W Ayers, rev. edn. New Haven, Conn.: Yale University Press, 407–63.

Milton, John. 1991. *Political Writings*, ed. Martin Dzelzainis. Cambridge: Cambridge University Press.

Mirandola, Giovanni Pico della. 1965. 'On the Dignity of Man'. In *On the Dignity of Man and other Works*, tr. Charles Glen Wallace *et al.* Indianapolis: Bobbs-Merrill.

More, Henry. 1653. *An Antidote against Atheisme, or An Appeal to the Natural Faculties of the Minde of Man, Whether There Be Not a God.* London.

More, Henry. 1671. *Enchiridion metaphysicum sive, de rebus incorporeia succincta & luculenta dissertatio.* London.

Nedham, Marchamont. 1767. *The Excellency of a Free State*, ed. Richard Baron. London.

Nicholls, William. 1701. *The Duty of Inferiours Towards Their Superiours, in Five Practical Discourses.* London: Printed for E. Evets, at the Green Dragon, and T. Bennet at the Half-Moon, in St. Paul's Church-yard (Folger Library, 178–610q).

Norris, John. 1689. *Reason and Religion; or, the Grounds and Measures of Devotion, Considered from the Nature of God, and the Nature of Man. In several Contemplations. With Exercises of Devotion Applied to Every Contemplation. Parts I and II.* London: Printed for Samuel Manship (Wing 1265).

Norris, John. 1690a. *Cursory Reflections upon a Book Called 'An Essay Concerning Humane Understanding'* . . . appended to *Christian Blessedness, or Discourses upon the Beatitudes of our Lord and Saviour Jesus Christ.* London: Printed for S. Manship (Wing 1246).

Norris, John. 1690b. *Reflections upon the Conduct of Human Life with Reference to the Study of Learning and Knowledge: in a Letter to the Excellent Lady, the Lady Masham.* London: Printed for S. Manship (Wing N1267).

Norris, John. 1691a. *The Charge of Schism Continued.* London: Printed for Samuel Manship (Wing 1254).

Norris, John. 1691b. *Practical Discourses on Some Divine Subjects.* First edition. London: Printed for Samuel Manship (Wing 1257); reprinted 1692 (Wing 1258), 1693 (twice, Wing 1261, Wing 1263), 1694 (Wing 1259), 1698 (thrice, Wing 1264, 1264a, 1264b).

Norris, John. 1695. *Letters Concerning the Love of God between the Author of the Proposal to the Ladies and Mr. John Norris,* 1st edn. 1695. London: Printed for Samuel Manship (Wing 1254); 2nd edn. 1705, Corrected by the author and with some few things added; 4th edn., 1730.

Norris, John. 1701, 1704. *Essay towards the Theory of an Ideal and Intelligible World,* 2 vols. London.

Norris, John. 1717. *A Collection of Miscellanies.* London.

Owen, James. 1703. *Moderation a Vertue: or, The Occasional Conformist Justify'd from the Imputation of Hypocrisy. . . .* London: Printed for A. Baldwin, in Warwick-lane (Folger Library, 134–622q).

Owen, James. 1704. *Moderation Still a Virtue: in Answer to Several Bitter Pamphlets: especially Two, Entituled Occasional Conformity a Most Unjustifiable Practice,* and *The Wolf Stripp'd of His Shepherd's Cloathing.* London: Printed for J. Taylor, at the Ship, in St. Paul's Church-yard (Folger Library, 166828).

Owen, John. 1651. *The Advantage of the Kingdome of Christ in the Shaking of the Kingdoms of the World: . . . in a sermon preached to the Parliament,* October 24. Oxford: Printed by Leon. Lichfield for Tho. Robinson (Folger Library, 133795, Wing 711).

Plato. 1969. *Republic,* tr. Paul Shorey. London: Heinemann (Loeb Classical Library edn.).

Pufendorf, Samuel. 1672. *De Iure Naturae et Gentium Libri Octo.* London: Scanorum.

Rainolds, John. 1637. *An Excellent Oration of the Late Famously Learned John Rainolds, DD . . . very useful for all such as affect the Studies of Logick and Philosophie and admire profane learning,* ed. John Leycester. Oxford.

Rousseau, J.-J. [1751] 1964. *Second Discourse, On the Origins of Inequality.* In *The First and Second Discourses,* ed. Roger D Masters. New York: St. Martin's Press.

Roussseau. J.-J. [1758] 1896. *Lettre á Monsieur d'Alembert sure les spectacles,* ed. L. Brunel. Paris: Hachette.

Rousseau, J.-J. 1952. 'A Discourse on Political Economy'. In *The Social Contract and Discourses.* London: J. M. Dent.

Sacheverell, Henry. 1702. *The Political Union. A Discourse Shewing the Dependence of Government on Religion. . . .* Oxford: Printed by Leonard Lichfield for George West and Henry Clements (Folger Library, BV 629.S2.P6.Cage).

Sacheverell, Henry. 1702. *A Sermon Preach'd before the University of Oxford on the Tenth Day of June 1702. Being the Fast Appointed for the Imploring a Blessing on Her Majesty and Allies Engag'd in the Present War against France and Spain.* Printed for Geo. West, and Henry Clements, at the Theatre in Oxford (Folger Library, 188–048q).

Sacheverell, Henry. 1708. *The Nature and Mischief of Prejudice and Partiality Stated in a Sermon Preach'd at St. Mary's in Oxford at the Assizes held there, March 9, 1703/4*, 2nd edn. (Folger Library, 152422).

Sacheverell, Henry. 1710. *The Doctrine of Passive Obedience and Nonresistance, as Established in the Church of England.* . . . London (Folger Library, JC.328.D7.Cage).

Scargill, Daniel. 1669. *The Recantation of Daniel Scargill Publickly made before the University of Cambridge in Greas St. Maries, July 25, 1669*. London: A. Maxwel.

Sidney, Algernon. 1698. *Discourses concerning Government*. London: Printed for the Booksellers of London and Westminster.

St. Evremont. 1698. *Plaidoyez de Mr. Herard Pour Monsieur le Duc de Mazarin contre Madame la Duchesse de Mazarin son Epouse; Et Le Factum pour Madame la Duchesse de Mazarin contre Monsieur le Duc de Mazarin son Mari par Mr. de St. Evremont* (Folger Library, DC.130.M39.E7.1698, 'Suivant la Copie de Paris').

Stillingfleet, Edward. 1671. *A Discourse Concerning the Idolatry Practised in the Church of Rome*. London: Henry Mortlock.

Swift, Jonathan. 1957. *Bickerstaff Papers and Pamphlets on the Church*, ed. Herbert Davis. Oxford: Blackwell.

Taylor, Jeremy. 1648. *The Liberty of Prophesying, Ductor Dubitantium*. London.

Twisse, William. 1631. *Discovery of Doctor Jackson's Vanity*. Amsterdam.

Vives, Juan Luis. 1555. *De prima philosophia*. In *Opera*, 2 vols. Basle: N. Episcopius and I. Parcus.

Warburton, William. 1737–41. *The Divine Legation of Moses Demonstrated*. 2 vols. London.

Ward, Edward. 1701. *The Pleasures of a Single Life, or the Miseries of Matrimony: Occasionally writ upon the many divorces lately granted by Parliament*. British Library, 11631 f. 26. See *Eighteenth-Century British Erotica I*, ed. Alexander Pettit and Patrich Spedding. London: Pickering & Chatto, 2002.

Wesley, Samuel. 1704. *A Letter from a Country Divine to His Friend in London: Concerning the Education of Dissenters in Their Private Academies.* . . . London: Printed for R. Clavel and Knaplock, 1702 [written in 1693] 2nd ed. (PR3763.W6.L3 Cage).

Whiston, William. 1696. *A New Theory of the Earth, from Its Original, to the Consummation of All Things.* . . .

White, Thomas. 1655. *The Grounds of Obedience and Government*. London: Printed by J. Flesher, for Lawrence Chapman (Folger Library, 143990).

Winstanley, Gerard. 1648. *The Law of Freedom*. London.

Wollstonecraft, Mary. [1790, 1792] 1995. *A Vindication of the Rights of Men, A Vindication of the Rights of Woman*, ed. Sylvana Tomeselli. Cambridge: Cambridge University Press.

Wollstonecraft, Mary [1798] 1989. *The Wrongs of Woman, or Maria*, in *The Works of Mary Wollstonecraft*, vol. 1, ed. J. Todd and M. Butler. London: William Pickering.

Secondary Texts

Ackworth, Richard. 1979. *The Philosophy of John Norris of Bemerton*. New York: Olms.

Aitken, G. A. 1884. 'Steele's "Ladies' Library"', *The Athenaeum*, no. 2958, 16–17.

Anderson, Paul Bunyan. 1936. 'Mistress Delariviere Manley's Biography', *Modern Philology*, 33 (3), 261–78.

Armitage, David, Armand Himy and Quentin Skinner, eds. 1995. *Milton and Republicanism*. Cambridge: Cambridge University Press.

Arnaud, A. J. and E. Kingdom, eds. 1986. *Women's Rights and the Rights of Man*. Aberdeen: Aberdeen University Press.

Ashcraft, Richard. 1986. *Revolutionary Politics and Locke's Two Treatises of Government*. Princeton, N.J.: Princeton University Press.

Ashcraft, Richard. 1992a. 'The Radical Dimensions of Locke's Political Thought: A Dialogic Essay on Some Problems of Interpretation', *History of Political Thought*, 13 (4), 703–72.

Ashcraft, Richard. 1992b. 'Simple Objections and Complex Reality: Theorizing Political Radicalism in Seventeenth-Century England', *Political Studies*, 40, 99–117.

Atherton, Margaret. 1992. 'Cartesian Reason and Gendered Reason', in L. Antony and C. Witt, eds., *A Mind of One's Own: Feminist Essays in On Reason and Objectivity*. Boulder, Colo.: Westview Press, 19–34.

Atherton, Margaret. 2000. 'Feminist Critiques of Cartesianism', *Encyclopedia of Feminist Theories*. London: Routledge.

Ayers, Michael. 1991 *Locke* (2 vols. 1: *Epistemology*. 2: *Ontology*). London: Routledge.

Backschneider, Paula, Felicity Nussbaum and Philip B. Anderson, eds. 1977. *An Annotated Bibliography of Twentieth-Century Critical Studies of Women and Literature 1660–1800*. Garland Reference Library of the Humanities, 64. New York: Garland.

Backschneider, Paula R. 1989. *Daniel Defoe: His Life*. Baltimore: The Johns Hopkins University Press.

Backschneider, Paula R. and John J. Richetti, eds. 1996. *Popular Fiction by Women 1660–1730: An Anthology*. Oxford: Clarendon Press.

Bahar, Saba. 2002. *Mary Wollstonecraft's Social and Aesthetic Philosophy: An Eve to Please Me*. Basingstoke: Palgrave.

Ball, Jerry. 1996. 'The Despised Version: Hobbes's Translations of Homer', *Restoration*, 20 (1), 1–16.

Battigelli, Anna. 1998. *Margaret Cavendish and the Exiles of the Mind*. Lexington: University of Kentucky Press.

Beal, Peter. 1987. *Index of English Literary Manuscripts*, vol. 2, Part 1. London and New York: Mansell Publishing.

Beauchamp, Tom. 1977. 'The Justification of Reverse Discrimination', in William T. Blackstone and Robert D. Heslep, eds. *Social Justice and Preferential Treatment*. Athens: University of Georgia Press, 34–110.

Bennett, G. V. 1975. *The Tory Crisis in Church and State 1688–1730: The Career of Francis Atterbury, Bishop of Rochester*. Oxford: Oxford University Press.

Berman, David. 1987. 'Deism, Immortality, and the Art of Theological Lying', in J. Leo Lemay, ed., *Deism, Masonry and the Enlightenment*. Newark: University of Delaware Press, 61–78.

Berman, David. 1992. 'Disclaimers as Offence Mechanisms in Charles Blount and John Toland', in M. Hunter and D. Wootton, eds., *Atheism from the Reformation to the Enlightenment*. Oxford: Clarendon Press, 255–72.

Bingham, Edwin R. 1947. 'The Political Apprenticeship of Benjamin Hoadly', *Church History*, 16, 154–65.

Blanchard, Rae. 1929. 'Richard Steele and the Status of Women', *Studies in Philology*, 26 (3), 325–55.

Bloch, Olivier. 1990. 'Gassendi et la théorie politique de Hobbes', in Yves Charles Zarka and Jean Bernhardt, eds., *Thomas Hobbes, Philosophie première, théorie de la science et politique*, Actes du Colloque de Paris. Paris: Vrin, 339–46.

Böeker, Hans Erich, ed. 2002. *Begriffsgeschichte, Diskursgeschichte, Metapherngeschichte*, Göttinger Gespräche zur Geschichtswissenschaft, Band 14. Göttingen: Wallstein Verlag.

Bredekamp, Horst. 1999. 'From Walter Benjamin to Carl Schmitt, via Thomas Hobbes', *Critical Inquiry*, 25, 247–66.

Brennan, Teresa and Carole Pateman. 1979. '"Mere Auxilliaries to the Commonwealth": Women and the Origins of Liberalism', *Political Studies*, 27 (2), 183–200.

Broad, Jacqueline. 2002. *Women Philosophers of the Seventeenth Century*. Cambridge: Cambridge University Press.

Brown, Alison. 1986. 'Platonism in Fifteenth Century Florence and Its Contribution to Early Modern Political Thought', *Journal of Modern History*, 58, 383–413.

Brown, Irene Q. 1982. 'Domesticity, Feminism, and Friendship: Female Aristocratic Culture and Marriage in England, 1660–1760', *Journal of Family History*, 7, 406–24.

Brown, Stuart. 1994. '"Theological Politics" and the Reception of Spinoza in the Early English Enlightenment', *Studia Spinozana*, 9, 181–200.

Buickerood, James G. 'What Is It with Damaris, Lady Masham? The Historiography of One Early Modern Woman Philosopher', unpublished essay.

Bulbring, Carl D. 1891. *Mary Astell: An Advocate of Women's Rights Two Hundred Years Ago*. London.

Butler, Judith and Joan Scott, eds. 1992. *Feminists Theorize the Political*. New York: Routledge.

Butler, Melissa. 1978. 'Early Liberal Roots of Feminism: John Locke and the Attack on Patriarchy', *American Political Science Review*, 72 (1), 135–50.

Butterfield, Herbert. 1930. *The Whig Interpretation of History*. New York: Norton.

Champion, J. A. I. 1992. *The Pillars of Priestcraft Shaken: The Church of England and Its Enemies, 1660–1730*. Cambridge: Cambridge University Press.

Clucas, Stephen. 1994. 'The Atomism of the Cavendish Circle: A Reappraisal', *The Seventeenth Century*, 9 (2), 247–73.

Clucas, Stephen. 2000. 'The Duchess and Viscountess: Negotiations between Mechanism and Vitalism in the Natural Philosophies of Margaret Cavendish and Anne Conway', *In-Between: Essays and Studies in Literary Criticism*, 9 (1), 125–36.

Cole, Thomas. 1967. *Democritus and the Sources of Greek Anthropology*. Cleveland: Case Western Reserve University Press.

Cottingham, John. 1986. *Descartes*. Oxford: Blackwell.

Cottingham, John. 1993. *A Descartes Dictionary*. Oxford: Blackwell.

Cranston, Maurice. 1957. *John Locke, a Biography*. New York: Macmillan.

Cressy, David. 1977. 'Literacy in Seventeenth-Century England: More Evidence', *Journal of Interdisciplinary History*, 8, 141–50.

Cressy, David. 1980. *Literacy and Social Order: Reading the Writing in Tudor and Stuart England*. Cambridge: Cambridge University Press.

Curley, Edwin. 1978. *Descartes against the Sceptics*. Oxford: Blackwell.

Curley, Edwin. 1996. 'Calvin and Hobbes, or Hobbes as an Orthodox Christian', *Journal of the History of Philosophy*, 34, 257–71.

Curley, Edwin. 1996. 'Reply to Professor Martinich', *Journal of the History of Philosophy*, 34, 285–7.

Davidson, Scott. 1995. *Human Rights*. Buckingham and Philadelphia: Open University Press.

Diamond, Craig Wm. 1982. 'Public Identity in Restoration England'. Ph.D. dissertation, Johns Hopkins University Press, Baltimore.

Dictionary of British and American Writers 1660–1800. Web version, ed. Janet Todd.

Dictionary of National Biography. Oxford: Oxford University Press, 1995.

Dunne, John. 1984. *Locke*. Oxford: Clarendon Press.

Edie, Carolyn E. 1977. 'Revolution and the Rule of Law: The End of the Dispensing Power, 1689', *Eighteenth Century Studies*, 10, 434–50.

Ellenzweig, Sarah. 2003. 'The Love of God and the Radical Enlightenment: Mary Astell's Brush with Spinoza', *Journal of the History of Ideas*, 64 (3), 379–87.

Encyclopaedia Britannica, 11th edn. 1910–11. London.

Encyclopedia of Feminist Theories. 2000. London: Routledge.

Encyclopedia of Philosophy. 1967. 8 vols. London: Macmillan.

Estcourt, Edgar E. and J. O. Payne. 1885. *The Catholic Non-jurors of 1715*. New York: Catholic Publication Society.

European Authors 1000–1900. Ed. H. W. Wilson, Wilson Web Data Base.

Ezell, Margaret J. M. 1987. *The Patriarch's Wife: Literary Evidence and the History of the Family*. Chapel Hill: University of North Carolina Press.

Farr, James and Clayton Roberts. 1985. 'John Locke on the Glorious Revolution: A Rediscovered Document [Bodleian MS Locke e. 18, fo. 4v]'. *The Historical Journal*, 28, 385–98.

F. E. J. and D. B. 1980. 'George Berkeley and *The Ladies Library*', Berkeley Newsletter (Dublin), 4 (December), 5–13.

Ferguson, Moira. 1985. *First Feminists: British Women Writers 1578–1799*. Bloomington: Indiana University Press.

Ferguson, Moira. 1996. 'Mary Wollstonecraft and the Problematic of Slavery', in Maria J. Falco, ed., *Feminist Interpretations of Mary Wollstonecraft*. University Park: Pennsylvania State University Press, 125–49.

Foucault, Michel. 1966, 1994. *Les Mots et les Choses, Archéologie des sciences humaines*. Paris: Gallimard. Translated as *The Order of Things: An Archaeology of Human Sciences*. London: Routledge.

Foucault, Michel. 1977. *Discipline and Punish: The Birth of the Prison*, tr. Alan Sheridan. New York: Vintage.

Foucault, Michel, 1981. *Power/Knowledge*. New York: Pantheon.

Frankel, Lois. 1987. 'Anne Finch, Viscountess Conway', in M. E. Waithe, ed., *History of Women Philosophers*. Dordrecht: Kluwer, 3, 41–58.

Frankel, Lois. 1993. 'The Value of Harmony', in Steven Nadler, ed., *Causation in Early Modern Philosophy: Cartesianism, Occasionalism, and Pre-Established Harmony.* University Park: Pennsylvania State University Press, 197–216.

Friedman, Jeffrey. 1988. 'Locke as Politician', *Critical Review*, 2, 64–101.

Fulk, Mark. 2004. 'Recent Trends in Research on Seventeenth-Century Women Writers', *Eighteenth Century Studies*, 36 (4), 593–603, esp. 597.

Gallagher, Catherine. 1988. 'Embracing the Absolute: The Politics of the Female Subject in Seventeenth-Century England', *Genders*, 1, 24–39.

Gallagher, Catherine. 1994. *Nobody's Story: The Vanishing Acts of Women Writers in the Market Place, 1670–1820.* Berkeley: University of California Press.

Gardiner, Samuel Rawson, ed. 1906. *The Constitutional Documents of the Puritan Revolution, 1625–1660*, 3rd edn. Oxford: Clarendon Press.

Garnsey, Peter. 1996. *Ideas of Slavery from Aristotle to Augustine.* Cambridge: Cambridge University Press.

Gascoigne, John. 1991. '"The Wisdom of the Egyptians" and the Secularisation of History in the Age of Newton', in Stephen Gaukroger, ed., *The Uses of Antiquity.* Dordrecht: Kluwer, 213–49.

Gatens, Moira. 1991. *Feminism and Philosophy: Perspectives on Difference and Equality.* Cambridge: Polity Press.

Gatens, Moira. 1998. *Feminist Ethics.* Ashgate, Dartmouth: Aldershot.

Gatens, Moira and Genevieve Lloyd. 1999. *Collective Imaginings: Spinoza Past and Present.* London: Routledge.

Gatens, Moira and Alison McKinnon. 1998. *Gender and Institutions: Welfare, Work and Citizenship.* Melbourne: Cambridge University Press.

Gaukroger, Stephen. 1997. *Descartes: An Intellectual Biography.* Oxford: Oxford University Press.

George, Margaret. 1973. 'From "Goodwife" to "Mistress": The Transformation of the Female in Bourgeois Culture', *Science and Society*, 37, 152–77.

Gierke, Otto F. von. 1900. *Political Theories of the Middle Ages*, tr. F. W. Maitland. Cambridge: Cambridge University Press.

Gierke, Otto F. von. 1934. *Natural Law and the Theory of Society 1500–1800*, tr. E. Barker. Cambridge: Cambridge University Press.

Gilmore, J. 1944. *Argument from Roman Law.* Philadelphia: University of Pennsylvania Press.

Glazer, Nathan. 1975. *Affirmative Discrimination.* New York: Basic Books.

Goldie, Mark. 1978. 'Tory Political Thought 1689–1714', Ph.D. dissertation, University of Cambridge.

Goldie, Mark. 1980a. 'The Revolution of 1689 and the Structure of Political Argument', *Bulletin of Research in the Humanities*, 83, 473–564.

Goldie, Mark. 1980b. 'The Roots of True Whiggism, 1688–1694', *History of Political Thought*, 1, 195–236.

Goldie, Mark. 1987. 'The Huguenot Experience and the Problem of Toleration in Restoration England', in C. E. J. Caldicott, H. Gough and J. Pittion, eds., *The Huguenots and Ireland.* London: Huguenot Society, 185–8.

Goldie, Mark. 1990. 'Danby, the Bishops and the Whigs', in T. Harris, Paul Seaward and M. A. Goldie, eds., *The Politics of Religion in Restoration England.* Oxford: Blackwell.

Goldie, Mark. 1991. 'The Theory of Religious Intolerance in Restoration England', in O. Grell, J. I. Israel and N. Tyacke, eds., *From Persecution to Toleration*. Oxford: Oxford University Press, 331–68.

Goldie, Mark. 1992. 'John Locke's Circle and James II', *The Historical Journal*, 35 (3), 557–86.

Goldie, Mark. 1993. 'Priestcraft and the Birth of Whiggism', in Nicholas Phillipson and Quentin Skinner, eds., *Political Discourse in Early Modern Britain*. Cambridge: Cambridge University Press, 209–31.

Goldie, Mark, ed. 1999. *The Receptory of Locke's Works from the 1690s to the 1830s*. London: Pickering & Chatto (6 vols.)

Goldsmith, Maurice. 1996. 'Hobbes on Law', in the *Cambridge Companion to Hobbes*, ed. Tom Sorell. Cambridge: Cambridge University Press, 287–9.

Grafton, Tony and Lise Jardine. 1990. '"Studied for Action": How Gabriel Harvey Read His Livy', *Past and Present*, 129, 30–78.

Greenblatt, Stephen. 1980. *Renaissance Self-Fashioning, from More to Shakespeare*. Chicago: University of Chicago Press.

Grover, Robinson A. 1980. 'The Legal Origins of Thomas Hobbes's Doctrine of Contract', *Journal of the History of Philosophy*, 18, 177–94.

Habermas, Jürgen. 1987. *The Philosophical Discourse of Modernity*. Cambridge, Mass.: MIT Press.

Halldenius, Lena. 2003. 'The Primacy of Right: On the Triad of Liberty, Equality and Virtue in Wollstonecraft's Political Thought', unpublished paper, Swedish Collegium for Advanced Study in the Social Sciences, Uppsala, Sweden, to be published in the *British Journal for the History of Philosophy* (forthcoming).

Hamilton, J. 1978. 'Hobbes's Study in the Hardwick Hall Library', *Journal of the History of Philosophy*, 16, 445–53.

Hankins, James. 1990. *Plato and the Italian Renaissance*, 2 vols. Leiden: Brill.

Harrison, John and Peter Laslett. 1971. *The Library of John Locke*, 2nd edn. Oxford: Clarendon Press.

Hartmann, Van C. 1998. 'Tory Feminism in Mary Astell's *Bart'lemy Fair*', *The Journal of Narrative Technique*, 28 (3), 243–65.

Hartsock, Nancy. 1985. *Money, Sex and Power: Towards a Feminist Materialism*. Boston: Northeastern University Press.

Helgerson, Richard. 1992. *Forms of Nationhood: The Elizabethan Writing of England*. Chicago: University of Chicago Press.

Higgins, Patricia. 1973. 'The Reactions of Women, with Special Reference to Women Petitioners', in Brian Manning, ed., *Politics, Religion and the English Civil War*. New York: St. Martin's Press, 178–222.

Hill, Brian W. 1998. *Robert Harley: Speaker, Secretary of State and Premier*. New Haven, Conn.: Yale University Press.

Hill, Bridget. 1986. *The First English Feminist: 'Reflections upon Marriage' and Other Writings by Mary Astell*. Aldershot, Hants: Gower Publishing.

Hill, Bridget. 1987. 'A Refuge from Men: The Idea of a Protestant Nunnery', *Past and Present*, 117, 107–30.

Hinton, R. W. K. 1967, 1968. 'Husbands, Fathers and Conquerors', 2 parts, *Political Studies*, 15 (3), 291–300; 16 (1), 55–67.

Hintz, Carrie. 1996. 'But One Opinion: Fear of Dissent in Cavendish's New Blazing World', *Utopian Studies*, 7 (1), 25–37.

Holbrook, Peter and David Bevington, eds. 1998. *The Politics of the Stuart Court Masque*. Cambridge: Cambridge University Press.

Hollingshead, Greg. 1989–90. 'Sources for the *Ladies' Library*', *Berkeley Newsletter*, 11, 1–9.

Hughes, Derek. 2001. *The Theatre of Aphra Behn*. New York: Palgrave.

Hughes, Derek, ed. 2001. *Eighteenth-Century Women Playwrights*, 6 vols. London: Pickering & Chatto.

Hughes, John Jay. 1977. 'The Missing "Last Words" of Gilbert Burnet in July 1687', *Historical Journal*, 20, 221–7.

Hutton, Sarah. 1978. 'Thomas Jackson, Oxford Platonist, and William Twisse, Aristotelian', *Journal of the History of Ideas*, 39, 635–52.

Hutton, Sarah, ed. 1990. *Henry More, 1614–1687. Tercentenary Studies*. Dordrecht: Kluwer.

Hutton, Sarah. 1993. 'Damaris Cudworth, Lady Masham: Between Platonism and Enlightenment', *British Journal for the History of Philosophy*, 1 (1), 29–54.

Hutton, Sarah. 1995. 'Anne Conway Critique d'Henry More: L'Esprit de la Matiere', *Archives de Philosophie*, 58 (3), 371–84.

Hutton, Sarah. 1997a. 'Anne Conway, Margaret Cavendish and Seventeenth-Century Scientific Thought', in Lynette Hunter and Sarah Hutton, eds., *Women, Science and Medicine 1500–1700*. Stroud: Sutton, 218–34.

Hutton, Sarah. 1997b. 'Cudworth, Boethius and the Scale of Nature', in G. A. J. Rogers, ed., *The Cambridge Platonists in Philosophical Context*. Dordrecht: Kluwer, 93–100.

Hutton, Sarah. 1997c. 'In Dialogue with Thomas Hobbes: Margaret Cavendish's Natural Philosophy', *Women's Writing*, 4 (3), 421–32.

Hutton, Sarah. 1998a. 'Cockburn, Catharine (1679–1749), in E. Craig, ed., *Routledge Encyclopedia of Philosophy*. London: Routledge, 11, 386–7.

Hutton, Sarah. 1998b. 'Conway, Anne (c. 1630–79)', in E. Craig, ed., *Routledge Encyclopedia of Philosophy*. London: Routledge, 11, 669–71.

Hutton, Sarah. 1999. 'Plato and the Tudor Academies', in Francis Ames-Lewis, ed., *Sir Thomas Gresham and Gresham College: Studies in the Intellectual History of London in the Sixteenth and Seventeenth Centuries*. London: Ashgate, 106–24.

Hutton, Sarah. 2003. 'Margaret Cavendish and Henry More', in Stephen Clucas, ed., *A Princely Brave Woman: Essays on Margaret Cavendish, Duchess of Newcastle*. London: Ashgate, 185–98.

Ishay, Micheline R., ed. 1997. *The Human Rights Reader*. London: Routledge.

Israel, Jonathan. 2001. *Radical Enlightenment: Philosophy and the Making of Modernity 1650–1750*. Oxford: Clarendon Press.

Jacob, James R. and Timothy Raylor. 1991. 'Opera and Obedience: Thomas Hobbes and *A Proposition for the Advancement of Morality* by Sir William Davenant', *The Seventeenth Century*, 6, 241–9.

Jaquette, Jane S. 1998. 'Contract and Coercion: Power and Gender in *Leviathan*', in Hilda L. Smith, ed., *Women Writers and the Early Modern British Political Tradition*. Cambridge: Cambridge University Press, 200–19.

James, Regina. 1976. 'Mary, Mary, Quite Contrary, or, Mary Astell and Mary Wollstonecraft Compared', *Studies in Eighteenth-Century Culture*, 5, 121–39.

James, Susan. 1999. 'The Innovations of Margaret Cavendish', *British Journal for the History of Philosophy*, 7 (2), 219–44.

James, Susan and Stephanie Parker, eds. 2002. *Visible Women: Essays on Feminist Legal Theory and Political Philosophy*. Oxford: Hart.

Johnston, Charlotte. 1958. 'Locke's Examination of Malebranche and John Norris', *Journal of the History of Ideas*, 19, 551–8.

Jolley, Nicholas. 1975. 'Leibniz on Hobbes, Locke's *Two Treatises* and Sherlock's *Case of Allegiance*', *Historical Journal*, 18, 21–35.

Jones, J. R. 1957. 'Shaftesbury's "Worthy Men": A Whig View of the Parliament of 1679', *Bulletin of the Institute of Historical Research*, 30, 232–41.

Jones, J. R. 1987. *Charles II: Royal Politician*. London: Allen & Unwin.

Kantorowicz, Ernst H. 1957. *The King's Two Bodies: A Study in Medieval Political Theology*. Princeton, N.J.: Princeton University Press.

Kelly, Ann Cline. 1988. *Swift and the English Language*. Philadelphia: University of Pennsylvania Press.

Kelly, Ann Cline. 2002a. *Catherine Trotter: An Early Modern Writer in the Vanguard of Feminism*. Hampshire and Burlington, Va.: Ashgate.

Kelly, Ann Cline. 2002b. *Jonathan Swift and Popular Culture: Myth, Media and the Man*. New York: Palgrave.

Kelly, Joan. 1984. 'Early Feminist Theory and the Querelle des Femmes, 1400–1789', in *Women, History and Theory: The Essays of Joan Kelly*. Chicago: University of Chicago Press, 65–109.

Kenyon, J. 1977. *Revolution Principles: The Politics of Party 1689–1720*. Cambridge: Cambridge University Press.

Kinnaird, Joan K. 1979. 'Mary Astell and the Conservative Contribution to English Feminism', *Journal of British Studies*, 19, 53–79.

Klein, Lawrence E. 1993. 'Shaftesbury, Politeness and the Politics of Religion', in Nicholas Phillipson and Quentin Skinner, eds., *Political Discourse in Early Modern Britain*. Cambridge: Cambridge University Press, 283–301.

Koselleck, Reinhart. 1959. *Kritik und Krise. Eine Studie zur Pathogenesis der bürgerlichen Welt*. Munich: Karl Albert Verlag. Published in English as *Critique and Crisis: Enlightenment and the Pathogenesis of Modern Society*. Cambridge, Mass.: MIT Press, 1988.

Koselleck, Reinhart. 1985. '*Historia Magistra Vitae*: The Dissolution of the Topos into the Perspective of a Modernized Historical Process', reprinted in Koselleck, *Futures Past: On the Semantics of Historical Time*, tr. Keith Tribe. Cambridge, Mass.: MIT Press, 21–38.

Krieger, Leonard. 1957. *The German Idea of Freedom*. Boston: Beacon Press.

Krieger, Leonard. 1965. *The Politics of Discretion: Pufendorf and the Acceptance of Natural Law*. Chicago: University of Chicago Press.

Kristeller, Oscar. 1943. *The Philosophy of Marsilio Ficino*, tr. Virginia Conant. Reprinted Gloucester, Mass.: Peter Smith, 1964.

Kuhn, Thomas. 1962. *The Structure of Scientific Revolutions*. Chicago: University of Chicago Press.

Lacey, Michael J. and Knud Haakonssen. 1998. 'From Natural Law to the Rights of Man', in Lacey and Haakonssen, eds., *A Culture of Rights: The Bill of Rights in Philosophy, Politics and Law – 1791–1991*. Washington, D.C.: Woodrow Wilson Center and Cambridge University Press, 1–59.

Lacey, Nicola. 2002. 'Violence, Ethics and Law: Feminist Reflections on a Familiar Dilemma', in Susan James and Stephanie Parker, *Visible Women: Essays on Feminist Legal Theory and Political Philosophy*. Oxford: Hart, 117–36.

Larousse, Pierre. 1969. *Grand Dictionnaire encyclopédique Larousse* en 11 vols. (10 vols. et un supplément de 1969). Paris: Dictionnaires, Encyclopédie, Larousse.

Laslett, Peter. 1988. Introduction to *John Locke's Two Treatises of Government*. Cambridge: Cambridge University Press.

Lenman, Bruce. 1992. 'The Poverty of Political Theory in the Scottish Revolution of 1688–9', in Lois G. Schwoerer, ed., *The Revolution of 1688–1689*. Cambridge: Cambridge University Press, 244–59.

Levine, Joseph M. 1991. *The Battle of the Books: History and Literature in the Augustan Age*. Ithaca, N.Y.: Cornell University Press.

Lister, Andrew. 2004. 'Marriage and Misogyny: The Place of Astell in the History of Political Thought,' *History of Political Thought*, 25, 44–72.

Lloyd, Genevieve. 1984. *The Man of Reason: 'Male' and 'Female' in Western Philosophy*. London: Routledge.

Lloyd, Genevieve. 1994. *Part of Nature: Self-knowledge in Spinoza's Ethics*. Ithaca, N.Y.: Cornell University Press.

Lloyd, Genevieve. 2001. *Spinoza: Critical Assessments*. London: Routledge.

Lloyd, Genevieve. 2002. *Feminism and History of Philosophy*. Oxford: Clarendon Press.

Lougee, Carolyn. 1976, *Les Paradis des Femmes: Women, Salons, and Social Stratification in Seventeenth-Century France*. Princeton, N.J.: Princeton University Press.

Mack, Phyllis. 1984. 'Women as Prophets during the English Civil War', in Margaret Jacob and James Jacob, eds., *The Origins of Anglo-American Radicalism*. London: George Allen & Unwin, 214–31.

MacKinnon, Catherine. 1989. *Toward a Feminist Theory of the State*. Cambridge, Mass.: Harvard University Press.

MacKinnon, Flora Isobel. 1910. 'The Philosophy of John Norris of Bemerton', *The Philosophical Monographs*, 1, (2).

Maitland, Frederick W. 1936. 'The King as Corporation' and 'Moral Personality and Legal Personality', in his *Selected Essays*, ed. H. D. Hazeltine, G. Lapsley and H. Winfield. Cambridge: Cambridge University Press.

Malcolm, Noel. 2002. *Aspects of Hobbes*. Oxford: Clarendon Press.

Malcolmson, Cristina and Mihoko Suzuki, eds. 2002. *Debating Gender in Early Modern England*. New York: Palgrave.

Marshall, John. 1992. 'John Locke and Latitudinarianism', in Richard Kroll, Richard Ashcraft and Perez Zagorin, eds., *Philosophy, Science and Religion in England, 1640–1700*. Cambridge: Cambridge University Press, 253–82.

Marshall, John. 1994. *John Locke: Resistance, Religion and Responsibility*. Cambridge: Cambridge University Press.

Martinich, A. 1992. *The Two Gods of Leviathan*. Cambridge: Cambridge University Press.

McCracken, Charles J. 1983. *Malebranche and British Philosophy*. Oxford: Clarendon Press.

McCrystal, John William. 1992. 'An Inadvertent Feminist: Mary Astell (1666–1731)'. M.A. thesis, Department of Political Studies, Auckland University, New Zealand.

McCrystal, John William. 1992. 'A Lady's Calling: Mary Astell's Notion of Women', *Political Theory Newsletter*, 4, 156–70.

McIlquham, Harriet. 1898. 'Mary Astell: A Seventeenth Century Women's Advocate', *Westminister Review*, 149.

McNally, David. 1989. 'Locke, Levellers and Liberty: Property and Democracy in the Thought of the First Whigs', *History of Political Thought*, 10, 17–40.

Mendle, Michael. 1985. *Dangerous Positions: Mixed Government, the Estates of the Realm, and the Answer to the XIX Propositions*. Tuscaloosa: University of Alabama Press.

Merchant, Carolyn. 1979. 'The Vitalism of Anne Conway: Its Impact on Leibniz's Concept of the Monad', *Journal of the History of Philosophy*, 17 (3), 255–69.

Miller, John. 1973. *Popery and Politics 1660–1688*. Cambridge: Cambridge University Press.

Monod, Paul Kléber. 1988. 'The Politics of Matrimony: Jacobitism and Marriage in Eighteenth-Century England', in Eveline Cruickshanks and Jeremy Black, eds., *The Jacobite Challenge*. Edinburgh: University of Edinburgh Press, 31–6.

Monod, Paul Kléber. 1989. *Jacobitism and the English People 1688–1788*. Cambridge: Cambridge University Press.

Myers, Mitzi. 1985. 'Domesticating Minerva: Bathusa Makin's "Curious" Argument for Women's Education', *Studies in Eighteenth-Century Culture*, 14, 173–92.

Naffine, Ngaire. 2002. 'Can Women Be Legal Persons', in Susan James and Stephanie Parker, eds., *Visible Women: Essays on Feminist Legal Theory and Political Philosophy*. Oxford: Hart, 69–90.

Nagel, Thomas. 1988. 'A Defense of Affirmative Action', reprinted in *Ethical Theory and Business*, 3rd edn., eds. Tom L. Beauchamp and Norman E. Bowie. Englewood Cliffs, N.J.: Prentice Hall.

Needham, Gwendolyn B. 1949. 'Mary de la Rivière Manley, Tory Defender', *Huntington Library Quarterly*, 12 (3), 253–88.

Nelson, Jeffrey M. 1978. 'Unlocking Locke's Legacy: A Comment', *Political Studies*, 26 (1), 101–8.

New Encyclopaedia Britannica. 2002. Online edition available at http://www.britannica.com.

Nicholson, Linda, ed. 1990. *Feminism/Postmodernism*. New York: Routledge.

Norbrook, David. 1998. *Writing the English Republic 1627–1660: Poetry, Rhetoric and Politics 1627–1660*. Cambridge: Cambridge University Press.

Norton, J. E. 1961. 'Some Uncollected Authors XXVII; Mary Astell, 1666–1731', *The Book Collector*, 10 (1), 58–60.

Nussbaum, Felicity. 1984. *The Brink of All We Hate: English Satires on Women, 1660–1750*. Lexington: University of Kentucky Press.

Oakley, Francis. 1983. 'Legitimation by Consent: The Question of the Medieval Roots', *Viator*, 14, 303–35.

Oakley, Francis. 1984. *Omnipotence, Covenants, and Order*. Ithaca, N.Y.: Cornell University Press, esp. 48–91

O'Donnell, Sheryl. 1978. 'Mr. Locke and the Ladies: The Indellible Words on the Tabula Rasa', *Studies in Eighteenth-Century Culture*, 8, 151–64.

O'Donnell, Sheryl. 1984. '"My Idea in Your Mind": John Locke and Damaris Cudworth Masham', in Ruth Perry and Martine Brownley, eds., *Mothering the Mind*. New York: Homes & Meier, 26–46.

O'Neill, Eileen. 1998a. 'Astell, Mary (1666–1731)', in E. Craig, ed., *Routledge Encyclopedia of Philosophy*. London: Routledge, vol. 1, 527–30.

O'Neill, Eileen. 1998b. 'Disappearing Ink: Early Modern Women Philosophers and Their Fate in History', in Janet Kourany, ed., *Philosophy in a Feminist Voice*. Princeton, N.J.: Princeton University Press, 17–62.

O'Neill, Eileen. 1999. 'Women Cartesians, "Feminine Philosophy", and Historical Exclusion', in S. Bordo, ed., *Feminist Interpretations of Descartes*. University Park: Pennsylvania State University Press, 232–57.

Pacheco, Anita, ed. 1998. *Early Women Writers 1600–1720*. New York: Longman.

Pacheco, Anita, ed. 2002. *A Companion to Early Modern Women Writing*, Oxford: Blackwell.

Paganini, Gianni. 1990. 'Hobbes, Gassendi e la psicologia del meccanicismo', in Arrigo Pacchi, ed., *Hobbes Oggi*, Actes du Colloque de Milan (May 18–21, 1988). Milan: Franco Angeli Editore, 351–445.

Paganini, Gianni. 1999. 'Thomas Hobbes e Lorenzo Valla. Critica umansitica e filosofia moderna', *Rinscimento, Rivista dell'Instituto Nazionale di Studi sul Rinascimento*, 2nd series, 39, 515–68.

Paganini, Gianni. 2001. 'Hobbes, Valla e i problemi filosofici della teologia umanisitica: la riforma "dilettica" della Trinità', in L. Simonutti, ed., *Dal necessario al possibile. Determinismo e libertà nel pensiero anglo-olandese del XVII secolo*. Milan: Franco Angeli, 11–45. Translated as 'Hobbes, Valla and the Trinity', *British Journal for the History of Philosophy*, 11 (2), 2003, 183–218.

Palmer, Stephanie. 2002. 'Feminism and the Promise of Human Rights: Possibilities and Paradoxes', in Susan James and Stephanie Parker, eds., *Visible Women: Essays on Feminist Legal Theory and Political Philosophy*. Oxford: Hart, 91–116.

Parker, Patricia. 1987. *Literary Fat Ladies: Gender, Rhetoric, Property*. London: Routledge.

Pateman, Carole. 1988. *The Sexual Contract*. Cambridge: Polity Press.

Pateman, Carole. 1989a. 'God Hath Ordained to Man a Helper: Hobbes, Patriarchy and Conjugal Right', *British Journal of Political Science*, 19, 445–64.

Pateman, Carole. 1989b. 'The Patriarchal Welfare State', in *The Disorder of Women*. Stanford, Calif.: Stanford University Press, 231–60.

Pateman, Carole. 1994. 'The Rights of Man and Early Feminism', in *Frauen und Politik*. Bern/Stuttgart/Vienna: Swiss Yearbook of Political Science, 19–31.

Pateman, Carole. 1995. 'Three Questions about Womanhood Suffrage', in Caroline Daley and Melanie Nolan, eds., *Suffrage and Beyond*. New York: New York University Press, 331–48.

Pateman, Carole. 1997. 'Democracy, Freedom and Special Rights', in David Boucher and Paul Kelly, eds., *Taking Justice Seriously: Perspectives in the Problem of Social Justice*. London: Routledge.

Pateman, Carole. 1998a. 'Democracy, Freedom and Special Rights: Social Justice: From Hume to Walzer', in David Boucher and Paul Kelly, eds., *Taking Justice Seriously: Perspectives in the Problem of Social Justice*. London: Routledge, 215–31.

Pateman, Carole. 1998b. 'Conclusion: Women's Writing, Women's Standing: Theory and Politics in the Early Modern Period', in Hilda L. Smith, ed., *Women Writers and the Early Modern British Political Tradition*. Cambridge: Cambridge University Press, 363–82.

Pateman, Carole. 2002. 'Self-Ownership and Property in the Person: Democratization and a Tale of Two Concepts', *The Journal of Political Philosophy*, 10 (1), 20–53.

Pateman, Carole., R. Goodin and R. Pateman. 1996. 'Simian Sovereignty', *Political Theory*, 25 (6), 821–49

Patterson, Annabel. 2002. *Nobody's Perfect: A New Whig Interpretation of History*. New Haven, Conn.: Yale University Press.

Pattinson, Katherine S. 1892. 'Mary Astell', *Pall Mall Magazine*.

Perry, Ruth. 1984. 'Mary Astell's Response to the Enlightenment', *Women in History*, 9, 13–40.

Perry, Ruth. 1985. 'Radical Doubt and the Liberation of Women', *Eighteenth-Century Studies*, 18 (4), 472–93

Perry, Ruth. 1986. *The Celebrated Mary Astell: An Early English Feminist*. Chicago: University of Chicago Press.

Pettit, Alexander and Patrick Spedding, eds. 2002. *Eighteenth-Century British Erotica I*. London: Pickering & Chatto.

Pettit, Philip. 1997. *Republicanism: A Theory of Freedom and Government*. Oxford: Clarendon Press.

Phillipson, Nicholas. 1993. 'Politeness and Politics in the Reigns of Anne and the Early Hanoverians', in J. G. A. Pocock, Gordon J. Schochet and Lois G. Schwoerer, eds., *The Varieties of British Political Thought, 1500–1800*. Washington, D.C.: Folger Institute, 211–45.

Pocock, J. G. A. 1957. *The Ancient Constitution and the Feudal Law*. Cambridge: Cambridge University Press. 2nd edn., 1987.

Pocock, J. G. A. 1972. 'Time, History and Eschatology in the Thought of Thomas Hobbes', in *Politics, Language and Time. Essays on Political Thought*. London: Methuen, 148–201.

Pocock, J. G. A. 1975. *The Machiavellian Moment: Florentine Political Thought and the Atlantic Republican Tradition*. Princeton, N.J.: Princeton University Press.

Pocock, J. G. A. 1990. 'Thomas Hobbes: Atheist or Enthusiast? His Place in a Restoration Debate,' *History of Political Thought*, 11 (4), 737–49.

Pocock, J. G. A. 1998. 'Catharine Macaulay: Patriot Historian', in Hilda L. Smith, ed., *Women Writers and the Early Modern British Political Tradition*. Cambridge: Cambridge University Press, 243–58.

Popkin, Richard H. 1990. 'The Spiritualistic Cosmologies of Henry More and Anne Conway', in Sarah Hutton, ed., *Henry More (1614–1678): Tercentenary Studies*. Dordrecht: Kluwer, 97–114.

Primer, Irwin. 2001. *Seneca Unmasqued: A Bilingual Edition of Aphra Behn's Translations of La Rochefoucauld's 'Maximes'*. New York: AMS Press.

Quintana, Ricardo. 1978. *Two Augustans: John Locke and Jonathan Swift*. Oxford: Oxford University Press.

Rogers, Katharine M. and William McCarthy, eds. 1987. *The Meridian Anthology of EarlyWomen Writers: British Literary Women from Aphra Behn to Maria Edgeworth, 1660–1800*. New York: Meridian–New American Library.

Rossi, Paolo. 1979. *The Dark Abyss of Time: The History of the Earth and the History of Nations from Hooke to Vico*, tr. Lydia G. Cochrane. Chicago: University of Chicago Press.

Routledge Encyclopedia of Philosophy. 1998. Ed. Edward Craig. London: Routledge.

Ryan, Alan. 1983. 'Hobbes, Toleration and the Inner Life', in David Miller and Larry Siedentop, eds., *The Nature of Political Theory*. Oxford: Clarendon Press.

Sapiro, Virginia. 1992. *A Vindication of Political Virtue: The Political Theory of Mary Wollstonecraft*. Chicago: University of Chicago Press.

Sarasohn, Lisa T. 1984. 'A Science Turned Upside Down: Feminism and the Natural Philosophy of Margaret Cavendish', *Huntington Library Quarterly*, 47, 299–307.

Sarasohn, Lisa. 1985. 'Motion and Morality: Pierre Gassendi, Thomas Hobbes and the Mechanical World View', *Journal of the History of Ideas*, 46, 363–80.

Scaltsas, Patricia Ward. 1990. 'Women as Ends – Women as Means in the Enlightenment', in A. J. Arnaud and E. Kingdom, eds., *Women's Rights and the Rights of Man*. Aberdeen: Aberdeen University Press, 138–48.

Schaffer, Simon. 1988. 'Wallification: Thomas Hobbes on School Divinity and Experimental Pneumatics', *Studies in History and Philosophy of Science*, 19, 275–98.

Schiebinger, Londa. 1987. 'Margaret Cavendish, Duchess of Newcastle', in M. E. Waithe, ed., *History of Women Philosophers*. Dordrecht: Kluwer, 3, 1–20.

Schiebinger, Londa. 1989. *The Mind Has No Sex! Women in the Origins of Modern Science*. Cambridge, Mass.: Harvard University Press.

Schmitt, Carl. [1938] 1996. *The Leviathan in the State Theory of Thomas Hobbes*, tr. George Schwab. Westport, Conn.: Greenwood Press.

Schneider, Herbert W. 1974. 'The Piety of Hobbes', in Ralph Ross, Herbert W. Schneider and Theodore Waldman, eds., *Thomas Hobbes in His Time*. Minneapolis: University of Minnesota Press.

Schochet, Gordon. 1975. *Patriarchalism in Political Thought*. Oxford: Blackwell.

Schochet, Gordon. 1992. 'John Locke and Religious Toleration', in Lois G. Schwoerer, ed., *The Revolution of 1688–1689, Changing Perspectives*. Cambridge: Cambridge University Press, 147–64.

Schwartz, Joel. 1985. 'Hobbes and the Two Kingdoms of God', *Polity*, 18 (1), 7–24.

Schwoerer, Lois G. 1977. 'Propaganda in the Revolution of 1688–89', *American Historical Review*, 82, 843–74.

Schwoerer, Lois G. 1981. *The Declaration of Rights, 1689*. Baltimore: The Johns Hopkins University Press.

Schwoerer, Lois G. 1990. 'Locke, Lockean Ideas and the Glorious Revolution', *Journal of the History of Ideas*, 51 (4), 531–48.

Schwoerer, Lois G., ed. 1992. *The Revolution of 1688–1689, Changing Perspectives*. Cambridge: Cambridge University Press.

Schwoerer, Lois G. 1993. 'The Right to Resist: Whig Resistance Theory, 1688 to 1694', in Nicholas Phillipson and Quentin Skinner, eds., *Political Discourse in Early Modern Britain*. Cambridge: Cambridge University Press, 232–52.

Schwoerer, Lois G. 1998. 'Women's Public Political Voice in England: 1640–1740', in Hilda L. Smith, ed., *Women Writers and the Early Modern British Political Tradition*. Cambridge: Cambridge University Press, 56–74.

Scott, Jonathan. 1988. 'Radicalism and Restoration: The Shape of the Stuart Experience', *The Historical Journal*, 31 (2), 453–67.

Shanley, Mary Lyndon. 1979. 'Marriage Contract and Social Contract in Seventeenth-Century English Political Thought', *Western Political Quarterly*, 32, 79–91.

Skinner, Quentin. 1972. 'Conquest and Consent: Thomas Hobbes and the Engagement Controversy', in G. E. Aylmer, ed., *The Interregnum: The Quest for Settlement 1646–1660*. London: Macmillan, 79–98.

Skinner, Quentin. 1974. 'The Principles and Practice of Opposition: The Case of Bolingbroke versus Walpole', in McKendrick, ed., *Historical Perspectives*. London: Europa, 93–128.

Skinner, Quentin. 1978. *Foundations of Modern Political Thought*, 2 vols. Cambridge: Cambridge University Press.

Skinner, Quentin. 1988. 'Reply to My Critics', in James Tully, ed., *Meaning and Context*. Princeton, N.J.: Princeton University Press, 231–88.

Skinner, Quentin. 1996. *Reason and Rhetoric in the Philosophy of Thomas Hobbes*. Cambridge: Cambridge University Press.

Skinner, Quentin. 1998. *Liberty before Liberalism*. Cambridge: Cambridge University Press.

Skinner, Quentin. 2002. *Visions of Politics*, vol. 3, *Hobbes and Civil Science*. Cambridge: Cambridge University Press.

Slomp, Gabriella. 2000. *Thomas Hobbes and the Political Philosophy of Glory*. London: Macmillan.

Smith, Florence M. 1916. *Mary Astell*. New York: Columbia University Press.

Smith, Hilda L. 1982. *Reason's Disciples*. Urbana: University of Illinois Press.

Smith, Hilda L. 1998a. Introduction, 'Women, Intellect and Politics: Their Intersection in the Seventeenth Century', in Smith, ed., *Women Writers and the Early Modern British Political Tradition*. Cambridge: Cambridge University Press, 1–14.

Smith, Hilda, L. 1998b. 'Women as Sextons and Electors: King's Bench and Precedents for Women's Citizenship', in *Women Writers and the Early Modern British Political Tradition*, 324–43.

Smith, Hilda L. and Susan Cardinale. 1990. *Women and the Literature of the Seventeenth Century: An Annotated Bibliography Based on Wing's Short-Title Catalogue*. New York: Greenwood Press.

Sommerville, Johann. 1982. 'From Suarez to Filmer: A Reappraisal', *Historical Journal*, 25, 525–40.

Sommerville, Johann. 1986a. 'History and Theory: The Norman Conquest in Early Stuart Political Thought', *Political Studies*, 34, 249–61.

Sommerville, Johann. 1986b. *Politics and Ideology in England 1603–40*. London: Routledge.

Sommerville, Johann, ed. 1991. Introduction to *Sir Robert Filmer, 'Patriarcha' and Other Writings*. Cambridge: Cambridge University Press.

Sommerville, Johann. 1992. *Thomas Hobbes: Political Ideas in Historical Context*. London: Macmillan.

Sommerville, Margaret R. 1995. *Sex and Subjection: Attitudes to Women in Early-Modern Society*. London: Arnold.

Sowell, Thomas. 1984. *Civil Rights: Rhetoric or Reality?* New York: Quill Paperbacks.

Springborg, Patricia. 1975. '*Leviathan* and the Problem of Ecclesiastical Authority', *Political Theory*, 3 (3), 289–303. Reprinted in John Dunn and Ian Harris, eds., *Great Political Thinkers*. Cheltenham: Elgar, 1997, 2, 144–59.

Springborg, Patricia. 1976. '*Leviathan*, the Christian Commonwealth Incorporated', *Political Studies*, 24 (2), 171–83. Reprinted in Dunn and Harris, eds., *Great Political Thinkers*, 2, 199–211.

Springborg, Patricia. 1981. *The Problem of Human Needs and the Critique of Civilization*. London: George Allen & Unwin.

Springborg, Patricia. 1986. 'Politics, Primordialism and Orientalism', *American Political Science Review*, 80 (1), 185–211.

Springborg, Patricia. 1987. 'The Contractual State: Reflections on Orientalism and Despotism', *History of Political Thought*, 8 (3), 395–433.

Springborg, Patricia. 1989a. 'Arendt, Republicanism and Patriarchalism', *History of Political Thought*, 10 (3), 499–523.

Springborg, Patricia. 1989b. 'Hannah Arendt and the Classical Republican Tradition', in Gisela T. Kaplan and Clive S. Kessler, eds., *Hannah Arendt: Thinking, Judging, Freedom*. Sydney: Allen & Unwin, 9–17.

Springborg, Patricia. 1990. *Royal Persons: Patriarchal Monarchy and the Feminine Principle*. London: Unwin Hyman.

Springborg, Patricia. 1992. *Western Republicanism and the Oriental Prince*. Cambridge: Polity Press; Austin: Texas University Press.

Springborg, Patricia. 1993. 'An Historical Note on Republicanism', in Wayne Hudson and David Carter, eds., *The Republicanism Debate*. Sydney: New South Wales University Press, 201–7.

Springborg, Patricia. 1994. 'Hobbes, Heresy and the *Historia Ecclesiastica*', *Journal of the History of Ideas*, 55 (4), 553–71. Reprinted in Dunn and Harris, eds., *Great Political Thinkers*, 3, 599–617.

Springborg, Patricia. 1995. 'Mary Astell (1666–1731), Critic of Locke', *American Political Science Review*, 89 (3), 621–33.

Springborg, Patricia. 1996a. *Mary Astell (1666–1731), Political Writings*. Critical edition of texts with commentary and introduction. Cambridge: Cambridge University Press. Chinese edition: China University of Political Science and Law Press/CUP, June 2003.

Springborg, Patricia. 1996b. 'Review Article: The View from the "Divell's Mountain"; Review of Quentin Skinner, *Reason and Rhetoric in the Philosophy of Hobbes*', *History of Political Thought*, 17 (4), 615–22.

Springborg, Patricia. 1996c. 'Thomas Hobbes on Religion', *Cambridge Companion to Hobbes*, ed. Tom Sorell. Cambridge: Cambridge University Press, 346–80.

Springborg, Patricia. 1997a. '*Leviathan*, Mythic History and National Historiography', in David Harris Sacks and Donald Kelley, eds., *The Historical Imagination in Early Modern Britain*. Cambridge: Cambridge University Press/Woodrow Wilson Press, 267–97.

Springborg, Patricia. 1997b. *Mary Astell's A Serious Proposal to the Ladies* (1694). Diplomatic edition with commentary and introduction. London: Pickering & Chatto.

Springborg, Patricia. 1998a. 'Astell, Masham and Locke: Religion and Politics', in Smith, ed., *Women Writers and the Early Modern British Political Tradition*, 105–25.

Springborg, Patricia. 1998b. 'Mary Astell and John Locke', in Steven Zwicker, ed., *The Cambridge Companion to English Literature, 1650 to 1750*. Cambridge: Cambridge University Press, 276–306.

Springborg, Patricia. 2000. 'Hobbes and Historiography: Why the Future, He Says, Does Not Exist', in G. A. J. Rogers and Tom Sorell, eds., *Hobbes and History*. London: Routledge, 44–72.

Springborg, Patricia. 2001a. 'Classical Translation and Political Surrogacy: English Renaissance Classical Translations and Imitations as Politically Coded Texts', *Finnish Yearbook of Political Thought*, 5, 11–33.

Springborg, Patricia. 2001b. 'Republicanism, Freedom from Domination and the Cambridge Contextual Historians', *Political Studies*, 49 (5), 851–76.

Springborg, Patricia. 2002a. 'Mary Astell (1666–1731), Critic of the Marriage Contract/Social Contract Analogue', in Anita Pacheco, ed., *A Companion to Early Modern Women Writing*. Oxford: Blackwell, 216–28.

Springborg, Patricia. 2002b. *Mary Astell's A Serious Proposal to the Ladies, Parts I (1694) and II (1697)*. Diplomatic edition with commentary, introduction, and appendices. Peterborough, Ontario: Broadview Press.

Springborg, Patricia. 2003a. '*Behemoth* and Hobbes's "Science of *Just* and *Unjust*"', *Filozofski vestnik*, special issue on Hobbes's *Behemoth*, ed. Tomaz Mastnak, 14 (2), 267–89.

Springborg, Patricia. 2003b. 'What Can We Say about History? Reinhart Koselleck and *Begriffsgeschichte*', in Jussi Kurunmäki and Kari Palonen, eds., *Zeit, Geschichte und Politik: zum achtzigsten Geburtstag von Reinhart Koselleck*. Jyväskylä, Finland: Jyväskylä University Press, 55–84.

Springborg, Patricia. 2004a. 'The Enlightenment of Thomas Hobbes', Review Essay on Noel Malcolm, *Aspects of Hobbes*', *British Journal for the History of Philosophy*, 12 (3), 513–34.

Springborg, Patricia. 2004b. 'Hobbes and Epicurean Religion', in Gianni Paganini and Edoardo Tortarolo, eds., *Der Garten und die Moderne: Epikureische Moral und Politik vom Humanismus bis zur Aufklarung*. Stuttgart: Rommann-Holzboog Verlag, 161–213.

Springborg, Patricia. 2004c. 'Hobbes's Theory of Civil Religion', in Gianni Paganini and Edoardo Tortarolo, eds., *Pluralismo e religione civile, Una Prospettiva storica e filosofica*. Milan: Bruno Mondadori, 59–94.

Spurr, John. 1988a. '"Latitudinarianism" and the Restoration Church', *The Historical Journal*, 31 (1), 61–82.

Spurr, John. 1988b. '"Rational Religion" in Restoration England', *Journal of the History of Ideas*, 494, 563–85.

Spurr, John. 1989. 'The Church of England, Comprehension and the Toleration Act of 1689', *English Historical Review*, 104, 927–46.

Squadrito, Kathleen. 1978. *John Locke*. Washington, D.C.: University Press of America.

Squadrito, Kathleen. 1987. 'Mary Astell's Critique of Locke's View of Thinking Matter', *Journal of the History of Philosophy*, 25, 433–40.

Squadrito, Kathleen. 1987. 'Mary Astell', in M. E. Waithe, ed., *A History of Women Philosophers*. Dordrecht: Kluwer, 3, 87–99.

Staves, Susan. 1998. 'Investments, Votes and "Bribes": Women as Shareholders in the Chartered National Companies', in Smith, ed., *Women Writers and the Early Modern British Political Tradition*, 259–78.

Stuurman, Sie. 1997. 'Social Cartesianism: François Poullain de la Barre and the Origins of the Enlightenment', *Journal of the History of Ideas*, 58, 617–40.

Stuurman, Sie. 2000. 'From Feminism to Biblical Criticism: The Theological Trajectory of François Poullain de la Barre', *Eighteenth-Century Studies*, 33 (3), 367–82.

Suzuki, Mihoko, ed. 2003. *Women and Gender in the Early Modern World*. Burlington Vt.: Ashgate.

Taylor, E. Derek. 2001. 'Mary Astell's Ironic Assault on John Locke's Theory of Thinking Matter'. *Journal of the History of Ideas*, 62, 505–22.

Thomas, Rev. D. R. 1874. *History of the Diocese of St. Asaph*. London: James Parker and Co.

Thomas, Keith. 1958. 'Women and the Civil War Sects', *Past and Present*, 13, 42–62.

Thompson, Martyn. 1976. 'The Reception of Locke's *Two Treatises of Government*, 1690–1705', *Political Studies*, 24, 184–91.

Thompson, Martyn. 1977. 'The Idea of Conquest in Controversies over the 1688 Revolution', *Journal of the History of Ideas*, 38, 33–46.

Thompson, Martyn. 1980. 'Revolution and Influence: A Reply to Nelson on Locke's *Two Treatises of Government*', *Political Studies*, 28, 100–8.

Thompson, Martyn. 1987. 'Significant Silences in Locke's *Two Treatises of Government*: Constitutional History, Contract and Law', *The Historical Journal*, 31, 275–94.

Tierney, Brian. 1982. 'Origins of Natural Rights Language', *History of Political Thought*, 3, 615–46.

Tierney, Brian. 1983. 'Tuck on Rights: Some Medieval Problems', *History of Political Thought*, 4, 429–41.

Todd, Barbara J. 1998. '"To Be Some Body": Married Women and *The Hardships of the English Laws*', in Smith, ed., *Women Writers and the Early Modern British Political Tradition*, 343–62.

Todd, Janet, ed. 1996. *Aphra Behn Studies*. New York: Cambridge University Press.

Todd, Janet, ed. 1999. *Aphra Behn*. Houndsmills, Basingstoke: Macmillan.

Travitsky, Betty S. and Patrick Cullen, eds. 1996–8. *The Early Modern Englishwoman: A Facsimile Library of Essential Works*. Brookfield, Vt.: Ashgate.

Tricaud, François. 1969. '"Homo homini Deus", "Homo homini Lupus": Recherche des Sources des deux formules de Hobbes', in R. Koselleck and R. Schnur, eds., *Hobbes-Forschungen*. Berlin: Duncker & Humblot, 61–70.

Trompf, Garry W. 1991. 'On Newtonian History', in Stephen Gaukroger, ed., *The Uses of Antiquity*. Dordrecht: Kluwer, 171–212.

Tuck, Richard. 1979. *Natural Rights Theories, the Origin and Development*. Cambridge: Cambridge University Press.

Tuck, Richard. 1987. 'Review of Michael Mendle, *Dangerous Positions: Mixed Government, the Estates of the Realm, and the Answer to the* XIX Propositions (University of Alabama Press, 1985)', *Journal of Modern History*, 59 (3), 570–2.

Tully, James. 1980. *A Discourse on Property: John Locke and His Adversaries.* Cambridge: Cambridge University Press.

Tully, James. 1993. 'Placing the *Two Treatises*', in Nicholas Phillipson and Quentin Skinner, eds., *Political Discourse in Early Modern Britain.* Cambridge: Cambridge University Press, 253–82.

Upham, A. H. 1913. 'English *Femmes Savantes* at the End of the Seventeenth Century', *Journal of English and Germanic Philology*, 12, 262–76.

Van Ness, Peter, ed. 1999. *Debating Human Rights: Critical Essays from the United States and Asia.* London: Routledge.

Vickery, Amanda. 1999. *The Gentleman's Daughter: Women's Lives in Georgian England.* New Haven, Conn.: Yale University Press.

Waithe, M. E., ed. 1987. *A History of Women Philosophers.* Dordrecht: Kluwer.

Wallace, John M. 1964. 'The Engagement Controversy 1649–1652: An Annotated List of Pamphlets', *Bulletin of the New York Public Library*, 68, 384–405.

Ward, Edward. 1701. *The Pleasures of a Single Life, or the Miseries of Matrimony: occasionally writ upon the many divorces lately granted by Parliament.* British Library, 11631 f. 26. (See Pettit and Spedding, 2002.)

Waswo, Richard. 1987. *Language and Meaning in the Renaissance.* Princeton, N.J.: Princeton University Press.

Weil, Rachel J. 1992. 'The Politics of Legitimacy: Women and the Warming Pan Scandal', in L. G. Schwoerer, ed., *The Revolution of 1688–1689.* Cambridge: Cambridge University Press, 65–82.

Weil, Rachel J. 1999. *Political Passions: Gender, the Family and Political Argument in England, 1680–1714.* Manchester: Manchester University Press.

Wilcox, Joel F. 1985. 'Ficino's Commentary on Plato's *Ion* and Chapman's Inspired Poet in the *Odyssey*', *Philological Quarterly*, 64, 195–209.

Wilson, Katharina M. and Frank J. Warnke, eds. 1989. *Women Writers of the Seventeenth Century.* Athens: University of Georgia Press.

Wittrock, Björn. 1998. 'Early Modernities: Varieties and Transitions', *Daedelus*, 127 (3), 19–40.

Wolff, H. J. 1944. 'Marriage Law and Family Organization', *Traditio*, 2, 43–95.

Wootton, David. 1989. 'John Locke: Socinian or Natural Law Theorist?', in James Crimmins, ed., *Religion, Secularization and Political Thought.* London: Routledge, 39–67.

Wootton, David. 1992. 'John Locke and Richard Ashcraft's *Revolutionary Politics*', *Political Studies*, 40, 79–98.

Wootton, David, ed. 1994. *Republicanism, Liberty, and Commercial Society 1649–1776.* Stanford, Calif.: Stanford University Press.

Worden, Blair. 1991. 'English Republicanism', in J. H. Burns and Mark Goldie, eds., *Cambridge History of Political Thought 1450–1700.* Cambridge: Cambridge University Press, 443–75.

Worden, Blair. 1994a. 'Marchamont Nedham and the Beginnings of English Republicanism, 1649–1656', in David Wootton, ed., *Republicanism, Liberty, and Commercial Society 1649–1776.* Stanford, Calif.: Stanford University Press, 45–81.

Worden, Blair. 1994b. 'James Harrington and *The Commonwealth of Oceana*, 1656', in Wootton, ed., *Republicanism, Liberty, and Commercial Society 1649–1776*, 82–110.

Worden, Blair. 1994c. 'Republicanism and the Restoration, 1660–1683', in Wootton, ed., *Republicanism, Liberty, and Commercial Society 1649–1776*, 139–93.

Worden, Blair. 1995. 'Milton and Marchamont Nedham', in David Armitage, Armand Himy and Quentin Skinner, eds., *Milton and Republicanism*. Cambridge: Cambridge University Press, 156–80.

Yeatman, Anna. 1993. 'Voice and Representation in the Politics of Difference', in Sneja Gunew and Anna Yeatman, eds., *Feminism and the Politics of Difference*. Boulder, Colo.: Westview Press, 228–45.

Yolton, Jean S. and John W. Yolton. 1985. *John Locke: A Reference Guide*. Boston: G. K. Hall.

Zook, Melinda S. 2001. 'Review of Rahel J. Weil, *Political Passions: Gender, The Family and Political Argument in England, 1680–1714* (Manchester: Manchester University Press, 1999)', *The American Historical Review*, 106, 2.

Zwicker, Steven N. 1993. *Lines of Authority: Politics and English Literary Culture, 1649–1689*. Ithaca, N.Y.: Cornell University Press.

Index

Starred items * indicate entries in the glossary and biographical notes, neither of which has been indexed.